Fusion

Integrated Reading and Writing

Third Edition

Includes the
MLA 9th Edition
& APA 7th Edition
Updates

Dave Kemper

Verne Meyer

John Van Rys
Redeemer University College

Pat Sebranek

 CENGAGE

Australia • Brazil • Canada • Mexico • Singapore • United Kingdom • United States

Fusion: Integrated Reading and Writing, Book 2, Third Edition with 2021 MLA and 2020 APA updates
Dave Kemper, Verne Meyer, John Van Rys, and Pat Sebranek

Product Team Manager: Laura Ross

Associate Product Manager: Nancy Tran

Associate Content Developer: Julie Bizzotto

Product Assistant: Jaime Manz

Associate Marketing Manager: Nathan Pires

Senior Content Project Manager: Margaret Park Bridges

Manufacturing Planner: Fola Orekoya

IP Analyst: Ann Hoffman

Senior IP Project Manager: Kathryn Kucharek

Art Director: Diana Graham

Compositor: Thoughtful Learning

Production & Managing Editor: Tim Kemper (Thoughtful Learning)

Designer: Mark Lalumondier (Thoughtful Learning)

Cover Image: sollia, 2017 / Used under license from Shutterstock.com

For product information and technology assistance, contact us at **Cengage Customer & Sales Support, 1-800-354-9706.**

For permission to use material from this text or product, submit all requests online at **www.cengage.com/permissions.** Further permissions questions can be emailed to **permissionrequest@cengage.com.**

Library of Congress Control Number: 2017949569

Student Edition: ISBN: 978-1-337-61518-1
Loose-leaf Edition: ISBN: 978-1-337-61520-4

Cengage
200 Pier 4 Boulevard
Boston, MA 02210
USA

Cengage is a leading provider of customized learning solutions with employees residing in nearly 40 different countries and sales in more than 125 countries around the world. Find your local representative at: **www.cengage.com.**

To learn more about Cengage platforms and services, register or access your online learning solution, or purchase materials for your course, visit **www.cengage.com**.

The content in this textbook for which Cengage holds the copyright has been updated to better fit MLA and APA guidelines for language that is inclusive and bias free. This updating could not be applied to content for which Cengage does not own the copyright, including excerpts from articles as well as student papers.

Printed at CLDPC, USA, 12-21

Brief Contents

Part 1: Reading and Writing for Success 1

1 The Reading-Writing Connection 3

2 Approaches to Reading and Writing 25

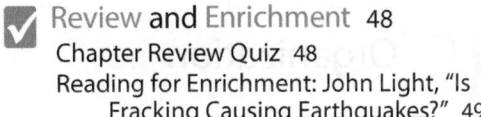

3 Critical Thinking and Viewing 55

Part 2: Reading and Writing Essays 83

4 Ideas 85

Part 3: Types of Reading and Writing 205

8 Reading and Writing Narrative Texts 207

9 Reading and Writing Expository Texts 231

10 Reading and Writing Arguments 257

Part 4: Research 283

11 Understanding Research 285

12 Research Report 301

Part 6: Word Workshops 367

Part 7: Punctuation and Mechanics Workshops 415

22 Capitalization 417

23 Commas 425

24 Quotation Marks and Italics 433

25 Other Punctuation 439

Part 8: Readings for Writers 447

 26 Anthology 449

Part 9: Appendices and Index 503

Preface

Developed to meet the needs of instructors teaching integrated reading and writing courses, *Fusion: Integrated Reading and Writing, Book 2* provides in-depth coverage of the reading and writing processes. Integrated reading and writing courses are challenging to teach because of the breadth of material to be covered. *Fusion* is designed to accelerate and support student progress by providing the integrated strategies, skills, and applications students need to be successful college readers and writers. As it guides students through the steps of reading and writing, *Fusion* teaches them to use the processes hand in hand. This structure helps students master the concepts of reading and generate thoughtful writing concurrently.

New Features of *Fusion: Integrated Reading and Writing, Book 2*

- **Practice Exercises.** The third edition features new and revised practice exercises to help students better apply learned skills. Parts 1 through 4 offer focused, integrated exercises; Parts 5 through 7 provide practical in-context grammar and proofreading activities.

- **Focus on Vocabulary.** While challenging words are defined, integrated vocabulary prompts in the "Reading for Enrichment" sections and Part 8 readings encourage students to practice defining words. Working in conjunction with Chapter 2's coverage of using a dictionary, context clues, and word parts, the new sections provide more contextualized vocabulary practice throughout the book.

- **Comprehension Checks.** Each reading selection in Part 8: "Readings for Writers" and the "Reading for Enrichment" sections in Chapters 1 through 10 now include an updated "Reflecting" section that contains comprehension and vocabulary questions that assess students' ability to understand and reflect on the readings.

- **Updated Readings.** The new edition offers topical, high-interest readings throughout the book. Part 8: "Readings for Writers" includes four new contemporary essays to help provoke thoughtful discussion and writing assignments. Many in-chapter readings have also been refreshed to include readings that exemplify the different rhetorical modes and cover current topics and themes.

- **Streamlined Design.** A new, clean design gives *Fusion* a fresh aesthetic that makes navigating the book simple and easy.

 ❝ I appreciate the many exercises within the chapters. Giving students opportunities to practice a new skill or concept is important, and *Fusion* provides these opportunities."

Elaine Bush, Albany State University

A More Integrated Approach to Reading and Writing

Fusion is structured to model the close relationship between reading and writing.

- **Parallel reading and writing strategies are introduced in Chapter 1: "The Reading-Writing Connection."** Students are introduced to the five shared features of reading and writing assignments: subject, type, role, audience, and purpose. Similarly, students learn how to apply the traits of writing to their reading and writing: ideas, organization, voice, word choice, sentence fluency, and conventions.

- **Chapter 2: "Approaches to Reading and Writing" sets the stage for the integrated reading and writing in *Fusion*.** Students are introduced to the reading and writing processes and important strategies such as annotating, note taking, and summarizing that they need to apply to their reading and writing projects.

- **Part 2: "Reading and Writing Essays" emphasizes the integration of reading and writing.** Chapters 4 through 7 introduce students to important traits common to reading and writing—ideas, organization, coherence, and voice—and offer strategies for reading these traits and applying them in writing.

- **Part 8: "Reading for Writers" offers an anthology of readings that foster critical thinking, comprehension, vocabulary, and writing opportunities.** Each reading includes comprehension and vocabulary questions that ensure students can identify key elements of the reading, such as the main idea, and continue to develop and strengthen their vocabulary skills. The readings also include critical thinking writing prompts and summarizing activities.

- **"Reading for Enrichment" sections reinforce reading, writing, and critical thinking strategies.** Chapters 1 through 10 contain a "Reading for Enrichment" section that includes a reading selection, pre- and post-reading activities, and writing prompts that challenge students to apply learned skills.

> ❝ *Fusion* does not allow students or instructors to separate reading and/from writing. It shows the relationship between the two and helps students understand how one impacts the other. For an undertaking that was quite intimidating (teaching reading and writing together), this text has certainly helped lessen the load and demonstrates how such a blended approach is possible.❞
>
> Dr. Jenny Billings, Rowan-Cabarrus Community College

Coverage of Key Reading and Writing Learning Objectives

Common Course Objectives	Where This Is Covered in *Fusion*
■ Critically read and respond to a variety of texts, demonstrating the ability to summarize, draw inferences, and analyze information.	See Chapter 2 for coverage of summary writing. In Chapter 3: "Critical Thinking and Viewing," students learn to consider basic thinking patterns, ask critical questions, and use analysis and evaluation strategies. In Chapter 4: "Ideas," drawing inferences is covered.
■ Identify audience and purpose, employ effective brainstorming strategies, gather relevant information, and integrate the ideas and words of other writers.	See Chapters 1 and 7, where identifying audience and purpose are discussed. In Chapter 4: "Ideas," various brainstorming strategies are covered. In Part 4: "Reading and Writing Research," students learn how to find, evaluate, and incorporate sources of information into their writing.
■ Generate ideas and gather information to craft effective thesis statements and supporting details; successfully recognize and write opening, middle, and closing paragraphs.	See Chapter 4: "Ideas" for instruction on finding and crafting main ideas and supporting details. Chapter 5: "Organization" reviews the three-part structure of essays, providing instruction on how to read and write beginning, middle, and closing paragraphs.
■ Understand and use appropriate vocabulary and transition words to develop clear and logical ideas in written work and demonstrate reading comprehension.	See Chapter 2: "Approaches to Reading and Writing" for detailed instruction on improving vocabulary skills. Chapter 6: "Coherence" teaches students to recognize transitions in reading and use them in their writing.
■ Select and apply the appropriate rhetorical strategies in both reading and writing.	See Part 3: "Types of Reading and Writing," where students learn how to apply strategies to read and write narratives, explanatory texts, and arguments.
■ Utilize revision strategies to ensure college-level work.	Part 3: "Types of Reading and Writing" features revising and editing instruction in context for narrative, expository, and argumentative writing. Part 5: "Sentence Workshops," Part 6: "Word Workshops," and Part 7: "Punctuation and Mechanics Workshops" provide additional grammar practice.
■ Read, comprehend, and respond to a wide variety of reading selections.	Part 8: "Readings for Writers" features selections demonstrating a variety of topics, voices, and patterns of organization. Each reading is accompanied by pre- and post-reading activities that emphasize reading and writing strategies.

Available Digital Resources

- *MindTap* **is a fully online, highly personalized learning experience built upon** *Fusion: Integrated Reading and Writing, Book 2*. *MindTap* combines student learning tools—an interactive ebook, instructive animations, additional readings, pre-built flashcards, practice activities, and assessments—into a singular Learning Path that guides students through their course. Instructors can personalize the experience by customizing respected Cengage content and learning tools with their own content. Engaging activities reinforce key concepts and provide students with the practice they need to build fundamental reading, writing, and grammar skills. *MindTap* can also be integrated with your school's learning management system.

  - **Teaches and promotes study skills in students.** The ebook includes highlighting and note-taking tools that allow students to annotate and engage with the content and a Study Hub app that lets students create their own study guides.

  - **Provides interactive exercises and activities to engage students.** Interactive activities and *Aplia* problem sets provide engaging exercises that challenge students and offer them a variety of ways to learn and connect with the content. Instant feedback reinforces key concepts and areas of improvement.

  - **Addresses students' busy lives.** Students can listen to chapters via the ReadSpeaker app while on the go and watch course videos in the small bursts of time that they have. The *MindTap* mobile app also allows students to digest and interact with course content to stay on top of all assignments and class activities. The *MindTap* app features the ebook, flashcards, practice quizzes, notifications, reminders, and more.

  - **Offers option to include** *Write Experience*. *Write Experience* encourages students to learn how to write well in order to communicate effectively and think critically. *Write Experience* provides students with additional writing practice without adding to an instructor's workload. Utilizing artificial intelligence to score student writing instantly and accurately, it provides students with detailed revision goals and feedback to help them constantly improve. *Write Experience* is powered by e-Write IntelliMetric Within—the gold standard for automated scoring of writing—used to score the Graduate Management Admissions Test (GMAT) analytical writing assessment. Visit http://www.cengage.com/training/wexp to learn more.

- *Aplia* **for** *Fusion*. Through diagnostic tests, succinct instruction, and engaging assignments, *Aplia* for *Fusion: Integrated Reading and Writing, Book 2* reinforces concepts and provides students with the practice they need to build fundamental reading, writing, and grammar skills.

  - Diagnostic tests provide an overall picture of a class's performance, allowing instructors to instantly see where students are succeeding and where they need additional help.

- Assignments include immediate and constructive feedback, reinforcing important ideas and motivating students to improve their reading and writing skills.
- Grades are automatically recorded in the *Aplia* grade book, keeping students accountable while minimizing time spent grading.
- The **Individualized Study Path (ISP).** An ISP course generates a personalized list of assignments for each student that is tailored to their specific strengths and weaknesses. ISP assignments are randomized, auto-graded problems that correspond to skills and concepts for a specific topic. Students get as much help and practice as they require on topics where they are weak. Conversely, if there are topics they understand well, no remediation is necessary and no additional assignments will be presented.

- **Instructor Companion Site.** This site includes helpful instructional materials.
  - **Instructor's Manual** contains detailed sample syllabi, including syllabi mapped to North Carolina and Texas state objectives, a variety of writing prompts to be used in class or as homework assignments, and a guide to teaching ESL learners using *Fusion*.
  - **Test Bank** includes chapter quizzes, a midterm exam, and a final exam.
  - **PowerPoint slides** include an overview of the key topics covered in each chapter.

Acknowledgments

Special thanks to all the reviewers who helped shape the third edition of *Fusion*:

Margie Askins, Blue Ridge Community College; Catherine Babbitt, Gateway Community College; Jenny Billings, Rowan-Cabarrus Community College; Michael Bloomingburg, Somerset Community College; Elaine Bush, Albany State University; Frances Camberlain, Gateway Community College; Maria Catalena, Blinn College; Karen Clark, Sandhills Community College; Janet Combs, Virginia Highlands Community College; Rebecca De La Rosa, Houston Community College; Shari De Licco, Navarro College; Virginia Dow, Liberty University; Victoria Efird, South Piedmont Community College; Cynthia Everson, Rowan-Cabarrus Community College; Danette Foster, Central Carolina Community College; Melody Fowler, Tarrant County College; Hattie Francis, Paul D. Camp Community College; Ruth Garrett, Hill College; Debra Gibes, Mott Community College; Diana Gibson, Tarleton State University; Julie Gunshenan, Surry Community College; Travis Holt, Liberty University; Jennifer Hurd, Blinn College; Johnnerlyn Johnson, Sandhills Community College; Stephanie Kinman, Georgia Northwestern Technical College; Desmond Lewis, Houston Community College; Bridgette McCann, Blinn College; Tiffany McDonald, Surry Community College; Shari Millikan, Navarro College; Shauna Moser, Rowan-Cabarrus Community College; Osariemen Osaghae, Texas Tech University; Tena Pair, Rowan-Cabarrus Community College; Diann Parker, Holmes Community College; Jen Parker, Sam Houston State University; Steven Preston, Darton State College and Albany State University; Erin Renfroe, Holmes Community College; Beth Reynolds, Wilkes Community College; Dana Richards, Rowan-Cabarrus Community College; Klaudie Stone, Sam Houston State University; Nathan Valle, Liberty University; Sangeeta Whig, Spartanburg Community College; Tina Willhoite, San Jacinto College; Justin Williams, Navarro College

Part 1:

Reading and Writing for Success

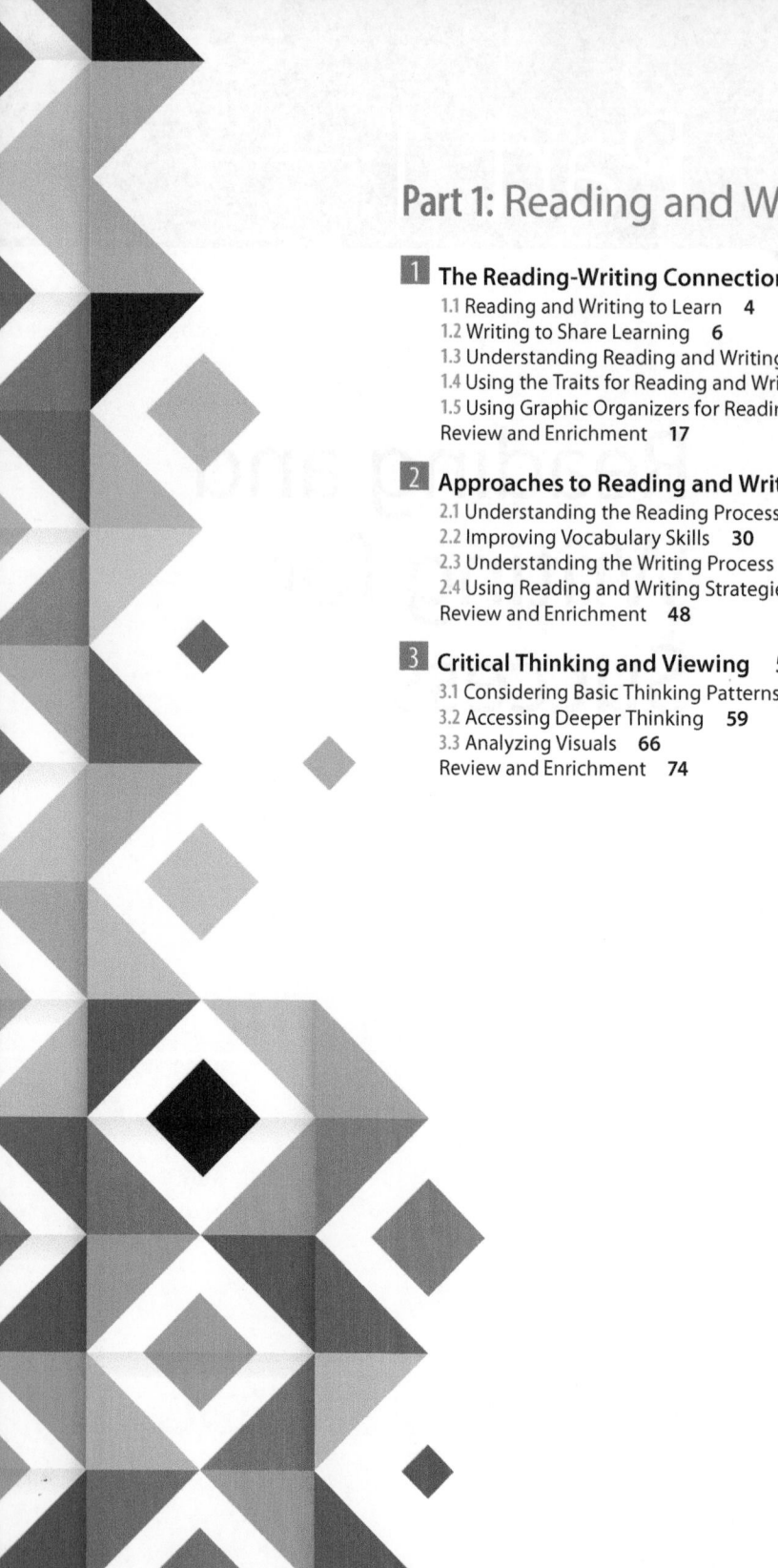

Part 1: Reading and Writing for Success

Tyler Olson, 2017 / Used under license from Shutterstock.com

The Reading-Writing Connection

If there is one profession that has always appreciated the special connection between reading and writing, it is that of the professional writer. "Read, read, read. Read everything," stated twentieth-century author William Faulkner. "There's nothing so exciting to me than to read books," states present-day novelist Toni Morrison. Writers know that reading helps them write and that their writing prompts them to read more.

As a student, you need to make your own special connection between reading and writing. You will be reading texts by experts in their fields. In order to make sense of this new information, to make it part of your own thinking, you will need to write about it. This chapter explores the reading-writing connection.

Chapter Outline

- Reading and Writing to Learn
- Writing to Share Learning
- Understanding Reading and Writing Assignments
- Using the Traits for Reading and Writing
- Using Graphic Organizers for Reading and Writing

1.1 Reading and Writing to Learn

For humans, making contact is an important aspect of communication. You make contact when you acknowledge someone with a smile, a handshake, or a hug. You make contact when you text someone or watch a favorite television show. The list could go on and on. But to be specific to reading and writing, consider these actions:

- By focusing on reading material, you make contact with the ideas and concepts developing on the page.
- By putting fingers to the keyboard (or pen to paper), you automatically make contact with your own ideas.

What's important for you to understand is the mutual relationship between reading and writing. As a student, you can expect to do a great deal of reading, which means you will come in contact with many new ideas. It's unlikely that everything you read will make sense to you right away. This is where writing can assist you. Writing allows you to respond to a text on a personal level—to make sense of it, to agree or disagree with it, to connect it with other texts—using your own thoughts and words.

Approaching Reading and Writing

Reading and writing work best when you think of them as learning tools. Reading assignments provide the important content; writing can help you engage with the content to learn from it. In fact, you can't effectively complete an academic reading assignment without employing some form of writing, even if that writing consists of nothing more than a list of ideas or a brief freewriting exercise. It's important to note that there are different reasons to write. When you write for yourself, you are writing to help yourself learn. When you write for an instructor, you are writing to show what you have learned.

Taking Class Notes

Keeping a class notebook or journal (either in print or digitally) is important if you are going to make writing a central part of your learning routine. Certainly you can take notes, but you can also use your notebook to explore your thoughts about your reading and about other aspects of your coursework by employing a variety of writing-to-learn strategies.

Writing-to-Learn Strategies

- **Note Taking** As you read, take notes to help you keep track of key ideas and details in the reading.
- **First Thoughts** Freely explore your first thoughts soon after you start reading. This writing gives you a point of reference for the rest of your reading and responding.

- **Status Check** Stop at various points of your reading to write about what you've read. These writings help you check your understanding of the text as it develops.

- **Listing** Freely list ideas about your reading. Listing can be useful as a quick review.

- **Written Dialogues** Write an imaginary conversation about your reading between two individuals. (You may be one of the speakers. The other speaker may be a character from the reading.) This strategy can help you connect to the reading.

- **Nutshelling** "Nutshell," or summarize, the importance of a reading in one sentence. Doing so clarifies your thinking about a text.

- **Pointed Questions** Ask and answer a series of *Why?* questions about the text.

- **Final Thoughts** Sum up your thoughts and feelings about the text. Consider what you have learned and what questions you still have about the topic.

Effective Academic Reading

Reading and learning go hand in hand. You read to learn about new concepts and ideas; you read to learn how to do something; and you read to understand the past, the present, and the future. To maximize how much you learn from your reading, follow these guidelines.

1. **Find a quiet place.** You'll need space to read and write without distractions.

2. **Gather your materials.** Have on hand a notebook or laptop, related handouts, an online connection, and a pen and/or highlighter if you are annotating the text.

3. **Divide the assignment into parts.** It's difficult to maintain the proper level of concentration over extended periods of time. Instead, try to read for 15-30 minutes at a time; then rest for a brief period. Use a timer to help you manage your reading.

4. **Approach your reading as a process.** Academic reading requires that you do a number of things—prereading, reading, rereading, reflecting—in a certain order.

5. **Use proven reading strategies.** For example, taking notes and annotating a text get you actively involved in your reading and help you learn.

6. **Identify the features of the reading.** For example, recognizing the intended audience and purpose will help you appreciate the text. Use the STRAP strategy to do this. (See Section 1.3.)

7. **Know what to look for.** In order to understand a reading, you need to identify the main idea or thesis of the text, plus the key points and details that support it.

8. **Summarize what you have learned.** Writing a summary helps you gauge your understanding of the reading. (See Section 2.4.)

9. **Note questions about the text.** Search for answers as soon as you can.

10. **Review the reading and your notes.** Doing this from time to time will help you internalize the information and connect it to new concepts you are studying.

1.2 Writing to Share Learning

Writing to learn is one function of writing; writing to share what you have learned is another important function. When you write to learn, you are your only audience. But when you write to share learning, your audience expands to include your instructor, your classmates, and others. When you develop assigned paragraphs, essays, and research papers, you are writing to share learning.

Understanding the Learning Connection

A direct link exists between clear thinking and developing strong writing. Writing to learn involves exploring and forming your thoughts, and writing to share involves clarifying and fine-tuning them.

All assigned writing projects begin with writing to learn as you read and collect your thoughts about the topic. Once you develop a first draft, your attention turns to making the writing clear, complete, and ready to share with others. Of course, writing to share learning demands more time and effort because it will be read and reviewed by your instructors and peers.

Reviewing the Range of Writing

The range of forms of writing is wide and varied, as you can see in Figure 1.1. Your college writing will likely cover the complete spectrum, with a focus on the more formal forms, such as essays and research papers.

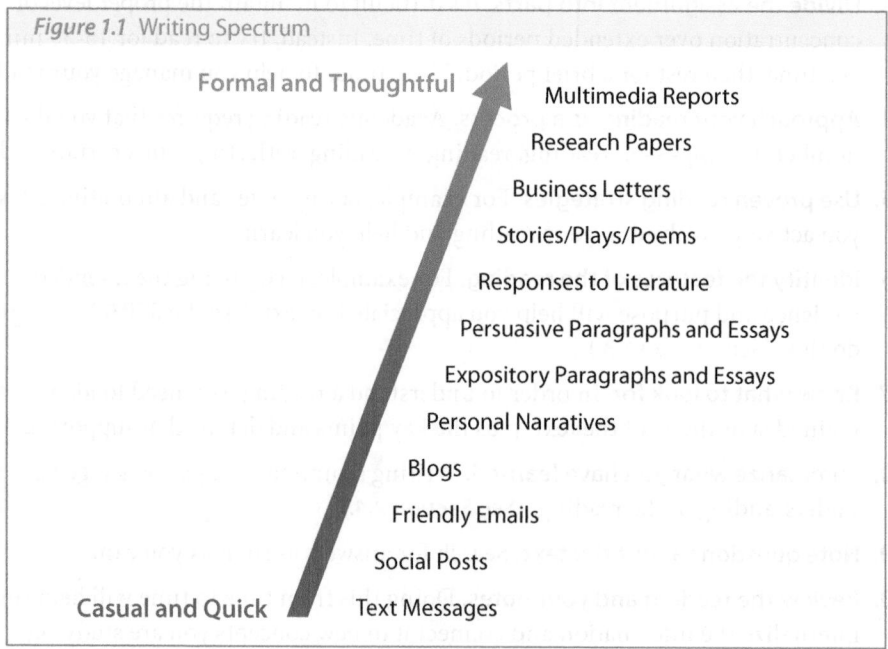

Figure 1.1 Writing Spectrum

Formal and Thoughtful

Multimedia Reports

Research Papers

Business Letters

Stories/Plays/Poems

Responses to Literature

Persuasive Paragraphs and Essays

Expository Paragraphs and Essays

Personal Narratives

Blogs

Friendly Emails

Social Posts

Casual and Quick   Text Messages

Effective Academic Writing

When your instructors give writing assignments, they will expect you to submit finished products that are clear, complete, and correct. Following these guidelines will help you meet their expectations.

1. **Find a quiet place to work.** Writing is essentially thinking on paper. You cannot think effectively if you are distracted. Quiet background music is okay if it helps you focus on your writing.

2. **Gather your materials.** Have on hand all of your notes from your reading, the assignment guidelines, related handouts, and whatever supplies you need to write.

3. **Identify the features of the assignment.** For example, knowing the purpose of the writing and the intended audience will help you develop your work. Use the STRAP strategy to do this. (See Section 1.3.)

4. **Understand the dynamics of the assignment.** Know what is expected of you: when the final copy is due and how the paper will be assessed.

5. **Approach your writing as a process.** Developing academic writing requires that you do a number of things—prewriting (planning), drafting, revising, editing—before the writing will be ready to share. Approaching your writing one step at a time helps you do your best work.

6. **Write from a position of strength.** Select writing topics that truly interest you and learn as much as you can about them. You'll find it much easier to develop a strong piece of writing if you have a lot of strong details to choose from.

7. **Keep time on your side.** Be sure to reserve enough time to develop your writing. The longer the piece of writing, the more time you must set aside. For important essays and reports, you may even want to set up a daily schedule of tasks to complete.

8. **Know the basics of writing.** Your writing should form a unified whole with strongly developed beginning, middle, and ending parts. And it should be built around a thoughtful thesis statement supported with plenty of details.

9. **Collaborate.** At different points during your writing, get feedback from your classmates, writing tutors, and/or instructor. Their insights and advice will help you keep on track and produce your best work.

10. **Learn from every writing experience.** Take note of strengths and weaknesses in each assignment you complete. Then, in future assignments, build on your strengths and address your weaknesses.

Jojie, 2017 / Used under license from Shutterstock.com

1.3 Understanding Reading and Writing Assignments

Being prepared is an important part of making good choices. For example, you would want to know the basics about a job or an internship before you applied for it. The same holds true for your college reading and writing assignments. Before you get started on your work, you should identify the main parts, including subject, purpose, audience, type (form), and the role of the writer. These two sample assignments will be used as examples for the discussion of each part:

Reading Assignment: Read Chapter 2 in your biology textbook. In this chapter, the authors trace nineteenth-century theories of evolution, leading up to Charles Darwin's groundbreaking discovery. Be prepared to explain each naturalist's theory.

Writing Assignment: In a posting on the class blog, reflect on the importance of a specific school-related experience. Consider who was involved, what happened, and why it was significant.

Using the STRAP Strategy

The first letters of the five parts of a reading or writing assignment can be arranged to spell STRAP. Thinking of this word will help you remember the five parts that you should identify. Here are the main parts for the sample reading assignment from the biology textbook using the STRAP strategy.

Subject:	Nineteenth-century theories of evolution
Type:	Biology textbook
Role:	Authors of a biology textbook
Audience:	Students
Purpose:	To inform readers about a landmark work leading up to Darwin's theory

Here are the main parts for the writing assignment for the class blog post.

Subject:	School-related experience
Type:	Class blog post
Role:	Student in the class
Audience:	Peers and instructor
Purpose:	To inform; to reflect upon the significance of the experience

Subject

The **subject** is the person, idea, event, or object being discussed or described. The terms *subject* and *topic* are often used interchangeably. Simply stated, you must identify the subject of your reading assignments. For writing assignments, you must understand what type of subject you are expected to write about. You can't begin either type of assignment without this information.

The subject for the sample reading assignment—nineteenth-century theories of evolution—is clearly identified. If that were not the case, you could identify the subject by skimming the title of the reading, the first few paragraphs, and, if needed, the first lines of other paragraphs. The subject for the sample writing assignment—a specific school-related experience—is clearly stated as well. If, for some reason, the subject of the writing is not clear to you, consult with your instructor before you get started.

Type

Type refers to the form of a reading selection or piece of writing to be produced. The primary type of informational readings will be textbook chapters, as is the case with the biology assignment. Textbook chapters are well organized and contain headings, subheadings, labels, glossaries, graphics, and summaries to make the information as accessible as possible. Other common forms of informational reading, such as essays, articles, and professional reports, may not be as accessible as textbook chapters because students are generally not their intended audience.

The typical types of academic writing include essays, reports, summaries, narratives, personal responses, and blog posts. Before you begin a writing project, be sure that you understand the key features of the form being assigned. For example, if your instructor assigns a blog posting, you will want to know the requirements for that type of writing.

Role

Role refers to what position the writer assumes. For textbook reading assignments, the authors assume the role of experts in their fields. Likewise, the authors of essays or articles in respected publications assume the role as individuals knowledgeable about their topics. The qualifications of authors are provided at the beginning or the end of textbooks and other respected publications. Writers in some fringe publications or questionable websites often try to assume positions of expertise but do not possess the qualifications to do so.

For academic writing assignments, you assume the role of a student producing essays and reports sharing what you have learned. To meet this expectation, you must approach your writing as a process requiring multiple drafts before it is ready to share. The same approach applies to any important informational writing that you produce in the workplace or community.

Audience

Audience, in this case, is the intended readership for written work that you read or write. For example, if the reading comes from a biology textbook, then, of course, biology students are the intended audience. Your instructors may also assign readings in which students may not be the primary audience—say, perhaps an article from a professional journal in which professionals in the field are the intended audience. With this information in mind, you would need to take extra care with your reading.

Since the sample writing assignment will be posted on a class blog, fellow students and the instructor are the intended audience. On the other hand, if you are writing in response to an exam prompt or you are developing an end-of-term research report, your instructor is the intended audience. Understanding the intended audience helps you shape your writing. When you are sharing a personal experience on a class blog, you may speak in a more relaxed style than you would when you are writing for an instructor or someone else in a position of authority.

Purpose

Purpose is the specific reason for the reading or writing. Generally, the reason for reading and writing assignments is either to inform, persuade, or share. The general purpose of a textbook, for example, is to inform the reader about a general subject. More specifically, however, the purpose may be to compare, analyze, evaluate, define, trace, or reflect upon.

In the reading assignment under discussion, the general purpose is to inform, but more specifically the reading is intended to trace the development of the different theories. For argumentative texts, the purpose is generally to persuade, but more specifically it may be to evaluate or review. For personal narratives and essays, the general purpose may be either to inform or to entertain, or perhaps a little bit of both, but more specifically to reflect or to analyze.

For the writing assignment under discussion, the general purpose is to inform, but more specifically, the writer must reflect upon (consider the importance) of the event. Usually, a key word in an assignment reveals the specific purpose of the writing: *Summarize* the article on vertical farming. *Explain* the results of your experiment. *Describe* your meeting with a career counselor.

Purpose Words

- **Analyze:** To examine the parts of a topic, noting any interrelationships
- **Argue:** To give reasons for or against something
- **Compare:** To point out the similarities and differences, perhaps with greater emphasis on similarities
- **Contrast:** To point out differences
- **Define:** To provide a concise or extended meaning of a topic
- **Describe:** To depict the appearance of a person, place, or thing; to give an account of; to convey an impression
- **Discuss:** To examine a topic from all sides

- **Evaluate:** To judge the value or condition of a topic in a thoughtful and careful way
- **Explain:** To make clear or easy to understand; show cause-effect relationships or a step-by-step process
- **Prove:** To give evidence to support a point
- **Review:** To re-examine the key characteristics or key points of a topic
- **Reflect:** To express carefully considered thoughts
- **Summarize:** To present the main points in a condensed, shortened form
- **Trace:** To present in sequence a series of steps or occurrences

Practice 1.1 Read the following sample assignments. Then, identify the main parts of the reading and writing assignments by answering the **STRAP** questions. Remember, these are sample assignments, not actual readings or writing tasks.

Assignment 1: Read the following selection from a textbook chapter entitled "Class and Stratification in the United States" by Diana Kendall, a professor of sociology. The selection discusses the influence that social ranking has on achievement in America.

1. What is the **s**ubject of the reading?
   a. The influence that social ranking has on achievement in America
   b. Ranking the most successful people in America
   c. The struggle of working-class Americans

2. What **t**ype of reading is it?
   a. A magazine article
   b. A personal narrative
   c. A selection from a textbook

3. What **r**ole does the writer assume?
   a. A reporter
   b. An expert professor
   c. An eyewitness

4. Who is the intended **a**udience?
   a. General readers
   b. Students
   c. Business people

5. What is the **p**urpose of the reading?
   a. To inform
   b. To persuade
   c. To entertain

Assignment 2: The ability to work in groups is important in school and in the workplace. Write an essay in which you work to convince the class that they should learn and practice the three or four group skills that you present.

6. What **s**ubject should you write about?
   a. Group skills to learn and practice
   b. Study skills to master
   c. Keys to success in the workplace

7. What **type** of writing should you develop?

  a. Report

  b. Essay

  c. Blog post

8. What **role** should you assume?

  a. Citizen

  b. Family member

  c. Student

9. Who is the intended **audience**?

  a. Family members

  b. Fellow students

  c. Employers

10. What is the **purpose** of this writing?

  a. To compare

  b. To persuade

  c. To entertain

1.4   Using the Traits for Reading and Writing

Using the traits of writing can help you gain a full understanding of reading assignments, and they can help you develop your own paragraphs and essays. The traits identify the key elements of written language, including ideas, organization, voice, word choice, sentence fluency, and conventions. If you're not sure what to look for in your reading assignments, follow the information on the left half of the charts. To help you know what to consider for writing assignments, follow the information on the right half of the charts.

Ideas

Informational texts are built upon a foundation of ideas. There is nothing more essential for you to remember.

When you read for ideas, you identify . . .	When you write for ideas, you develop . . .
■ the topic.	■ a thesis or focus.
■ the thesis (main idea).	■ your thoughts on the topic.
■ the key supporting details.	■ effective supporting details.

Organization

To create meaning, ideas need to be organized. Readers expect that a reading will follow a sensible pattern of organization.

When you read for organization, you identify . . .	When you write for organization, you develop . . .
▪ the beginning, middle, and ending parts. ▪ the organization of the supporting details.	▪ an effective beginning, middle, and ending. ▪ a logical presentation of supporting details.

Voice

A text also has voice, or tone, which refers to the special way the writer speaks to readers. Voice reflects on the writer's attitude about the topic and text.

When you read for voice, you identify . . .	When you write for voice, you develop . . .
▪ the level of the writer's interest in and knowledge about the topic.	▪ a voice that sounds interesting, honest, and knowledgeable.

Word Choice

Academic texts are characterized by specific terminology related to the subject. Personal texts are characterized by more informal, casual words.

When you read for word choice, you identify . . .	When you write for word choice, you develop . . .
▪ the quality of the words. (Are they interesting and clear?)	▪ words that are specific, clear, and fitting for the assignment.

Sentence Fluency

The sentences carry the ideas. In order to be effective, they must flow smoothly and clearly communicate the information.

When you read for sentence fluency, you identify . . .	When you write for sentence fluency, you develop . . .
▪ the effectiveness of the sentences. (Do they flow smoothly? Are they clear?)	▪ smooth-reading, clear, and accurate sentences.

Conventions

The conventions are the rules for grammar, usage, and mechanics that produce clear and correct texts.

When you read for conventions, you identify . . .	When you write for conventions, you develop . . .
■ to what degree the writing follows conventions (and why or why not).	■ paragraphs or essays that follow the conventions.

The Traits in Action

Here is how one student used the traits of writing to help her understand "Conversational Ballgames," a personal essay by Nancy Sakamoto that she had to read for an assignment.

Traits Analysis of "Conversational Ballgames"

Ideas

- **Topic:** Comparing Western-style conversations with Japanese conversations
- **Main idea (thesis):** The two conversation styles are very different.
- **Supporting details:** Western style conversations are like a tennis game, with a lot of back and forth. Japanese style conversations are like bowling, where everyone waits for a turn. There is little or no back and forth.

Organization

- **Beginning:** The writer, a Westerner, shares her experience with conversing in Japan. She realizes the styles are very different.
- **Middle:** She contrasts the two styles.
- **Ending:** She concludes that it is not easy to switch styles.
- **Organization of details:** Comparison/ contrast

Voice

- The writer speaks from personal experience.

Word Choice

- The words are easy to follow. The comparisons to tennis and bowling add interest.

Sentence Fluency

- The sentences flow smoothly and are easy to follow.

Conventions

- The writing follows the rules for grammar, usage, and mechanics.

1.5 Using Graphic Organizers for Reading and Writing

Graphic organizers help you map out your thinking for writing and reading assignments. You can, for example, use a Venn diagram or a T-chart to arrange your thoughts for a comparison essay assignment or to take notes about an essay you have just read. Other common graphics help you organize your thinking for problem-solution, cause-effect, and narrative writing and reading assignments. See **Figure 1.2** as well as other samples in the "Sample Graphic Organizers" section.

Charting a Reading Selection

A time line is a graphic organizer used to list the key actions in a reading selection that is organized chronologically (by time), such as a personal narrative or a historical account. A time line will not include many details or explanations. Here is a sample time line for an historical account from *The Path: A One-Mile Walk through the Universe* by Chet Raymo.

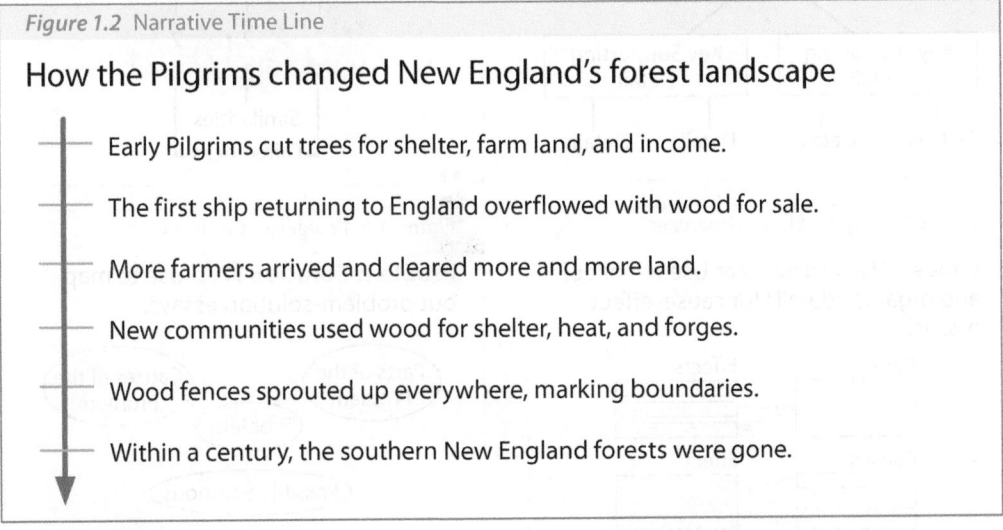

Figure 1.2 Narrative Time Line

How the Pilgrims changed New England's forest landscape

- Early Pilgrims cut trees for shelter, farm land, and income.
- The first ship returning to England overflowed with wood for sale.
- More farmers arrived and cleared more and more land.
- New communities used wood for shelter, heat, and forges.
- Wood fences sprouted up everywhere, marking boundaries.
- Within a century, the southern New England forests were gone.

Practice 1.2 ▸ Create a time line to list the main actions of an important school-related experience from your past.

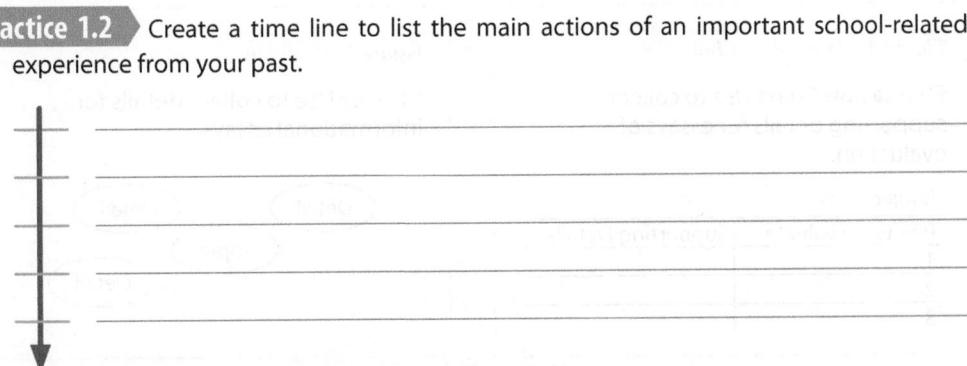

Sample Graphic Organizers

Figure 1.3 Time Line

Time Lines Use for personal narratives to list actions or events in the order they occurred.

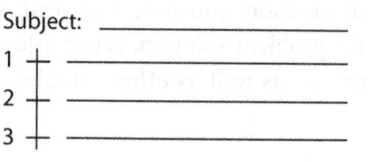

Subject: _____

1 _____
2 _____
3 _____

Figure 1.4 Process Diagram

Process Diagram Use to collect details for science-related writing, such as the steps in a process.

Topic: _____

Step 1 → Step 3
Step 2   Step 4

Figure 1.5 Line Diagram

Line Diagram Use to collect and organize details for informational essays.

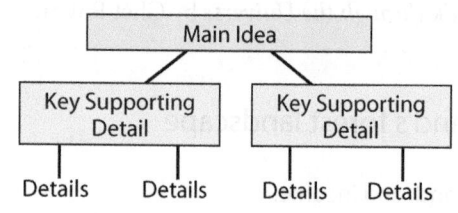

Main Idea

Key Supporting Detail   Key Supporting Detail

Details   Details   Details   Details

Figure 1.6 Venn Diagram

Venn Diagram Use to collect details to compare and contrast two topics.

Topic A   Topic B

1   1   1
2   2   2
3   3   3

Similarities
Differences

Figure 1.7 Cause-Effect Organizer

Cause-Effect Organizer Use to collect and organize details for cause-effect essays.

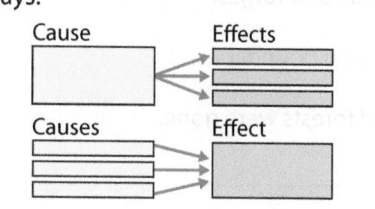

Cause   Effects

Causes   Effect

Figure 1.8 Problem-Solution Web

Problem-Solution Web Use to map out problem-solution essays.

Parts of the Problem   Causes of the Problem

Problem

Possible Solutions

Figure 1.9 Evaluation Chart

Evaluation Chart Use to collect supporting details for essays of evaluation.

Subject: _____

Points to Evaluate	Supporting Details
1	
2	
3	

Figure 1.10 Cluster

Cluster Use to collect details for informational essays.

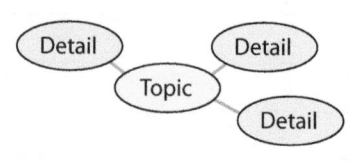

Detail   Detail

Topic

Detail

☑ Review and Enrichment

Chapter Review Quiz

Answer the questions about what you've learned in this chapter.

1. Why can reading and writing be considered learning tools?
   a. Reading and writing help you connect and interact with new ideas and concepts.
   b. Information in a reading assignment will be meaningless until you write about it.
   c. The only way to learn new information is to read and write about it.

2. What are pointed questions?
   a. Pointed questions are specific questions you ask someone about your reading.
   b. Pointed questions are a series of *why* questions that help you review a reading.
   c. Pointed questions summarize a reading text.

3. How is writing to learn different from writing to share learning?
   a. Writing to learn involves writing for yourself; writing to share learning involves writing to show your learning.
   b. Writing to learn focuses on clarity and completeness; writing to share learning focuses on freely exploring your ideas.
   c. Writing to learn is more important than writing to share learning.

4. What are two formal forms of writing?
   a. Text messages and blogs
   b. Emails and social posts
   c. Persuasive essays and research papers

5. What is the STRAP strategy?
   a. A strategy to help you check your writing before you share it
   b. A strategy for reviewing the five main parts of reading or writing assignments
   c. A strategy to help you remember the main parts of a textbook

6. What does each letter in STRAP stand for?
   a. Subject, type, role, audience, and purpose
   b. Source, tone, role, audience, and purpose
   c. Subject, topic, reason, audience, and purpose

7. Which writing trait focuses on the way a writer speaks to the reader?
   a. Ideas   b. Conventions   c. Voice

8. Which graphic organizer would you use to place events in the order they occurred?
   a. Time line   b. T-chart   c. Cluster

Reading for Enrichment

You will be reading a selection from *Becoming a Master Student* that provides directions for creating and using "to-do" lists to help you manage daily tasks. Use the guidelines for "Effective Academic Reading" to help you carry out your reading. (See Section 1.1.)

About the Author

Dave Ellis is an author, an educator, a workshop leader, and a lecturer. His book *Becoming a Master Student* is a best seller in its 16th edition, and it is used by students worldwide to help them succeed in school and beyond. He has coauthored other books on subjects such as human effectiveness and career planning.

Prereading

People in all walks of life establish processes to complete tasks. Chefs determine the best sequence to incorporate ingredients into their signature dishes; coaches break down fundamental skills into teachable steps; software developers provide step-by-step directions for downloading their newest products. List another example of a process established in a different profession. Then list a process that you have established for yourself.

Consider the Traits

As you read this selection, consider the **ideas**: What process is he explaining, and does he provide plenty of details? Also note the **organization**: Does the structure of ideas help you follow the process? Finally, note the author's **voice**: Does he sound interested in helping you, or is he simply presenting information?

On-the-job processes: _____

Personal processes: _____

Before you read, answer the STRAP questions to identify the main features of the assignment.

Subject:	What specific topic does the reading address?
Type:	What form (*essay, narrative, textbook selection*) does the reading take?
Role:	What position (*concerned individual, observer, participant, educator*) does the writer assume?
Audience:	Who is the intended audience?
Purpose:	What is the general goal of the reading (*to inform, to persuade, to share*)?

Reading and Rereading

As you read, make it your goal to (1) identify the topic, (2) confirm the purpose and audience, and (3) pay careful attention to the steps in the process. Consider taking notes to help you remember important points. Reread as needed to confirm your understanding of the text and to analyze its ideas and organization.

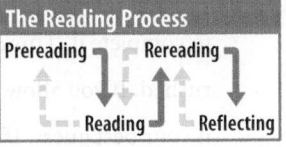

The ABC Daily To-Do List

One advantage of keeping a daily to-do list is that you don't have to remember what to do next. It's on the list. A typical day in the life of a student is full of separate, often unrelated tasks—reading, attending lectures, reviewing notes, working at a job, writing papers, researching special projects, running errands. It's easy to forget an important task on a busy day. When that task is written down, you don't have to rely on your memory.   1

The following steps present one method for creating and using to-do lists. This method involves ranking each item on your list according to three levels of importance—A, B, and C. Experiment with these steps, modify them as you see fit, and invent new techniques that work for you.   2

Step 1: Brainstorm tasks

To get started, list all of the tasks you want to get done tomorrow. Each task will become an item on a to-do list. Don't worry about putting the entries in order or scheduling them yet. Just list everything you want to accomplish on a sheet of paper or planning calendar or in a special notebook. You can also use 3x5 cards, writing one task on each card. Cards work well because you can slip them into your pocket or rearrange them, and you never have to copy to-do items from one list to another.   3

Step 2: Estimate time

For each task you wrote down in Step 1, estimate how long it will take you   4 to complete it. This can be tricky. If you allow too little time, you end up feeling rushed. If you allow too much time, you become less **productive**. For now, give it your best guess. If you are unsure, overestimate rather than underestimate how long it will take you for each task. Overestimating has two benefits: (1) It avoids a schedule that is too tight, missed deadlines, and the resulting feelings of frustration and failure; and (2) it allows time for the unexpected things that come up every day—the spontaneous to-dos. Now pull out your calendar or Time Monitor/Time Plan. You've probably scheduled some hours for activities such as classes or work. This leaves the unscheduled hours for tackling your to-do lists.

Add up the time needed to complete all your to-do items. Also add up the   5
number of unscheduled hours in your day. Then compare the two totals. The power of this step is that you can spot overload in advance. If you have eight hours' worth of to-do items but only four unscheduled hours, that's a potential problem. To solve it, proceed to Step 3.

Step 3: Rate each task by priority

To prevent over-scheduling, decide which to-do items are the most   6
important, given the time you have available. One suggestion for making this decision comes from the book *How to Get Control of Your Time and Your Life* by Alan Lakein: Simply label each task A, B, or C.

The A's on your list are those things that are the most critical. They include   7
assignments that are coming due or jobs that need to be done immediately. Also included are activities that lead directly to your short-term goals.

The B's on your list are important, but less so than the A's. B's might   8
someday become A's. For the present, these tasks are not as urgent as A's. They can be postponed, if necessary, for another day.

The C's do not require immediate attention. C priorities include activities   9
such as "shop for a new blender" and "research genealogy on the Internet." C's

are often small, easy jobs with no set time line. They, too, can be postponed.

Once you've labeled the items on your to-do list, schedule time for all of   10
the A's. The B's and C's can be done randomly during the day when you are in
between tasks and are not yet ready to start the next A.

Step 4: Cross off tasks

Keep your to-do list with you at all times. Cross off activities when you   11
finish them, and add new ones when you think of them. If you're using 3x5 note
cards, you can toss away or recycle the cards with completed items. Crossing off
tasks and releasing cards can be fun—a visible reward for your **diligence**. This
step fosters a sense of accomplishment.

When using the ABC priority method, you might experience an ailment   12
common to students: C fever. Symptoms include the uncontrollable urge to
drop the A task and begin crossing C's off your to-do list. If your history paper
is due tomorrow, you might feel compelled to vacuum the rug, call your third
cousin in Tulsa, and make a trip to the store for shoelaces. The reason C fever
is so common is that A tasks are usually more difficult or time-consuming to
achieve, with a higher risk of failure.

If you notice symptoms of C fever, ask yourself, "Does this job really need to   13
be done now? Do I really need to alphabetize my CD collection, or might I better
use this time to study for tomorrow's data-processing exam?" Use your to-do list
to keep yourself on task, working on your A's. But don't panic or berate yourself
when you realize that in the last six hours, you have completed eleven C's and
not a single A. Just calmly return to the A's.

Step 5: Evaluate

At the end of the day, evaluate your performance. Look for A priorities you   14
didn't complete. Look for items that repeatedly turn up as B's or C's on your list
and never seem to get done. Consider changing them to A's or dropping them

altogether. Similarly, you might consider changing an A that didn't get done to a B or C priority. When you're done evaluating, start on tomorrow's to-do list. Be willing to admit mistakes. You might at first rank some items as A's only to realize later that they are actually C's. And some of the C's that lurk at the bottom of your list day after day might really be A's. When you keep a daily to-do list, you can adjust these priorities before they become problems.

The ABC system is not the only way to rank items on your to-do list. Some people prefer the 80-20 system. This method is based on the idea that 80 percent of the value of any to-do list comes from only 20 percent of the tasks on that list. So on a to-do list of ten items, find the two that will contribute most to your life, and complete those tasks without fail.   *15*

Another option is to rank items as "yes," "no," or "maybe." Do all of the tasks marked "yes." Ignore those marked "no." And put all of the "maybes" on the shelf for later. You can come back to the "maybes" at a future point and rank them as "yes" or "no."   *16*

Or you can develop your own style for to-do lists. You might find that grouping items by categories such as "errands" or "reading assignments" works best. Be creative.   *17*

Keep in mind the power of planning a whole week or even two weeks in advance. Planning in this way can make it easier to put activities in context and see how your daily goals relate to your long-term goals. Weekly planning can also free you from feeling that you have to polish off your whole to-do list in one day. Instead, you can spread tasks out over the whole week.   *18*

In any case, make starting your own to-do list an A priority.   *19*

From Ellis, *Becoming a Master Student*, 13E. © 2011 Cengage Learning.

Reflecting

Answer the comprehension and vocabulary questions about the reading.

1. What is the subject of this selection?
   a. The process for creating and using to-do lists
   b. How to alphabetize a to-do list
   c. The value of keeping a journal

2. What graphic organizer works well to list the key points in an informational text?
   a. Process diagram
   b. Line diagram
   c. Venn diagram

3. Which best describes the character of the writer's voice?
   a. Knowledgeable but distant
   b. Knowledgeable and helpful
   c. Uncertain and questioning

4. Study how the word *productive* is used in the reading, and choose its definition.
   Productive (paragraph 4)
   a. Effective
   b. Careful
   c. Happy

5. Study how the word *diligence* is used in the reading, and choose its definition.
   Diligence (paragraph 11)
   a. Hard work
   b. Tardiness
   c. Overtime

Writing to Learn

Create a dialogue between you and another person (real or imagined) in which you discuss the reading selection. Consider what you learned, what questions remain unanswered, how the author's approach matches your own learning style, and so on. Keep the conversation going as long as you can. Set up your dialogue like this:

> **Your first name:** So what do you think of making to-do lists?
> **Other person's first name:** Well, . . .

Critical Thinking

- What assumption or belief has the writer made about the readers of his advice?
- How do you feel about turning tasks into processes?

Writing for Enrichment

What follows are possible writing activities to complete in response to the reading.

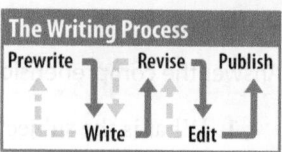

Prewriting

Choose one of the following writing ideas, or decide upon an idea of your own related to the reading.

1. In a personal blog post, illustrate whether or not you are a "process" person. Some people rely on directions and manuals, and others do not. (To **illustrate** means "to show with examples.")

2. Compare your process personality with that of a peer, workmate, or family member.

3. Explain in detail one of the on-the-job processes you identified in the Prereading section. Assume you are preparing your paper for someone new to the job. Consider using headings as is done in "The ABC Daily To-Do List."

4. Explain in detail one of the personal processes that you identified earlier in the Prereading section. Provide necessary background information and at least one example of the process in action.

5. Describe the most frustrating set of directions that you have ever tried to follow.

When planning . . .
- Complete the STRAP strategy for your writing.
- Gather plenty of details about your topic—including a complete listing of the steps in the process if you are responding to prompt 4 or 5.
- Establish a main idea (thesis) to serve as a focus for your writing. For example, a process may be very complicated, or your impulsiveness may lead you to dislike directions.
- Arrange your notes accordingly for writing.

When writing . . .
- Develop effective beginning, middle, and ending parts in your writing.
- Present your main idea in the beginning part.
- Support and explain the main idea in the middle part.
- Close your essay with final thoughts about your topic.

When revising and editing . . .
- Carefully review your first draft. Make sure that you have included enough detail to explain the process. Illustrate your experiences with directions.
- Ask at least one peer to review your writing as well.
- Improve the content as needed.
- Then edit your revised writing for smoothness and correctness.

somchai rakin, 2017 / Used under license from Shutterstock.com

2

Approaches to Reading and Writing

You can't expect to gain a full appreciation of a text with one quick read through it. Likewise, you can't expect to produce a quality piece of writing by producing one quick draft. Effective reading and writing are never the product of a single, quick step. You can't hurry either one. Instead, academic reading and writing are best approached as processes, each with a series of steps helping you carry out your task.

This chapter describes the steps in the reading and writing processes and shows you how the steps in each process work together. Along with the reading process, you will also learn about important vocabulary skills. Knowing *how* to approach reading and writing assignments effectively makes the actual work that much more satisfying and productive.

Chapter Outline

- Understanding the Reading Process
- Improving Vocabulary Skills
- Understanding the Writing Process
- Using Reading and Writing Strategies

2.1 Understanding the Reading Process

Reading an entertainment or fashion magazine can be easy because you are reading for enjoyment. Reading an academic text may feel entirely different because you are reading to gain information. To ensure that you read academic texts carefully, follow the steps in an effective process. By doing so, you will gain a full appreciation and understanding of a text.

The reading process helps you pace yourself and read actively. Active reading is close, thoughtful reading. It keeps you engaged with the text through annotating, note taking, and/ or summarizing, and it helps you understand the text's key parts.

Step	Activities
Prereading	First become familiar with the text and establish a starting point for reading.
Reading	Read the assignment once to get a basic understanding of the text. Use reading strategies such as annotating, outlining, and summarizing.
Rereading	Reread the text and analyze its parts as many times as needed until you have a clear understanding of the text's key topic and ideas.
Reflecting	Reflect on your reading experience: *How would you summarize the text? What have you learned? What questions do you have about the material? How has this reading changed or expanded what you know about the topic?*

Figure 2.1 presents the reading process in action. The arrows show how you may move back and forth between the steps. For example, after beginning your reading, you may refer back to something in your prereading.

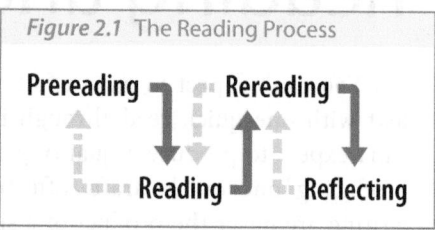

Figure 2.1 The Reading Process

Prereading

Prereading addresses what you should do *before* your actual reading. A cook reviews a recipe in order to have everything in place before starting; prereading serves a similar purpose. Here are the basic prereading tasks.

- **Review the title.** Many readers give the title very little thought. However, the title often identifies the topic of the reading and helps you understand the author's attitude or voice or tone.

- **Learn about the author.** Read the brief biography about the author if it is provided with the text. Otherwise, check online for information about the writer. This information may help you understand the author's approach.

- **Preview the text.** Read the first paragraph or two to get a general idea about the topic, the level of language used, and the writer's tone. Next, skim the text for headings, bold-faced words, and graphics. Then read the final paragraph or two to see how the text ends. Finally, use the STRAP strategy (see Section 1.3) to identify the main parts of the text.

- **Establish a starting point for reading.** Once you have done all of these things, write down your first thoughts about the text. Consider what you already know about the topic, what questions you have, and what you expect to learn.

- **Ask questions.** This will help you stay on task as you read. Base your questions on information that you've collected while previewing the text's title, objectives, headings, subheadings, first sentences in paragraphs, bold-faced terms, and visuals. Here are three possible prereading questions.

The learning objective "Explain when searches can be made without a warrant" can be turned into this question:	The heading "The Fourth Amendment" can be turned into this question:	The bold-faced term "probable cause" can be turned into this question:
When can searches be made without a warrant?	How does the Fourth Amendment protect the rights of the people?	What is meant by probable cause?

Reading

Reading a text requires your undivided attention. These are your goals during your first reading.

- **Confirm the key parts of the STRAP strategy,** especially the **purpose** and **audience.** Is the material intended to explain, describe, or persuade? And does it address general readers, college students, professionals, or some other audience?

- **Annotate the text.** Annotating involves making notes in the text (see Section 2.4). Use annotating to ask questions or highlight passages that you think are important or that you don't yet fully understand.

- **Identify the main idea or thesis** of the text. The main idea is the central aim or purpose of a text. It is the key idea that the author wants to emphasize.

- **Locate the evidence.** Look for the facts and details that support the main idea.

- **Consider the conclusion.** Review the closing thoughts of the writer.

Rereading

Rereading a text helps you to better understand its main points. These are your goals during your rereading.

- **Confirm your basic understanding of the text.** Are you still sure about the main idea and supporting details? If not, adjust your thinking as needed.

- **Study the development of the ideas.** Is the topic timely or important? Does the main idea seem reasonable? What types of support are provided—facts, statistics, or examples? Does the conclusion seem logical?

- **Check the voice and style of the writing.** Does the writer seem knowledgeable about the topic and interested in it? Are the ideas easy to follow?

- **Answer your annotations or side notes,** and make further annotations as needed.

Reflecting

Reflecting helps you fine-tune your thinking about the material. Writing about your reading is the best way to reflect on it. These are your goals during this step:

- **Summarize what you have learned.** What are the most important ideas in the text? (See Section 2.4.)

- **Explore your feelings about the reading.** Did the reading surprise you? Did it disappoint you? Did it answer your questions? How will you use what you learned? Does this new information change your thinking in any way? Explain.

- **Identify what questions you still have.** Then try to answer them.

Other Reading Processes

Two other reading processes—KWL and SQ3R—are variations on the prereading, reading, rereading, and reflecting process.

KWL

KWL stands for what I *know*, what I *want to know*, and what I *learned*. Identifying what you know (K) and want to know (W) occurs during prereading. Identifying what you learned (L) occurs after your reading, rereading, and reflecting.

1. Write the topic of your reading at the top of your paper. Then divide the paper into three columns and label them **K**, **W**, and **L**.
2. In the **K** column, identify what you already know.
3. In the **W** column, identify the questions you want answered.
4. In the **L** column, note what you have learned.

Figure 2.2 shows part of a KWL chart that one student completed while reading an online article explaining the Electoral College. Using the KWL strategy helped the student focus his reading efforts.

Figure 2.2 KWL Chart

Topic: Electoral College

K	W	L
Identify what you **KNOW**.	Identify what you **WANT** to know.	List what you **LEARNED**.
• Not the same as the popular vote • Based on the votes in each state • Necessary to win the Electoral College vote to become president	• Why do we have the Electoral College? • How does it work? • Do the results of this vote ever differ from the popular vote?	• Created as a compromise between electing the president in Congress and electing the president by popular vote • 538 electors based on Congressional representation in Washington • Electors cast their votes, based on the popular election in their state • Yes: Tilden/Hayes (1876) Harrison/Cleveland (1888), Gore/Bush (2000), and Clinton/Trump (2017)

SQ3R

SQ3R is a more thorough reading process than KWL. The letters SQ3R stand for *survey*, *question*, *read*, *recite*, and *review*.

Survey: When you survey, you skim the title, headings, graphics, and first and last paragraphs to get a general idea about the text.

Question: During this step, you ask questions that you hope the text will answer about the topic.

Read: While you do the reading, you take careful notes and reread challenging parts.

Recite: At the end of each page, section, or chapter, you should state out loud what you have learned. (This could involve answering the 5 W's and H—*who? what? when? where? why?* and *how?*) Reread as necessary.

Review: After reading, you study your notes, answer questions about the reading, and summarize the text.

2.2 Improving Vocabulary Skills

In the process of reading you may come across unfamiliar words. Academic readings, in particular, contain high-level words and technical terms related to specific fields of study. Instead of skimming these words, you can use a variety of tools to discover their meaning.

Using a Dictionary

The most basic way to understand a new word is to look up its meaning in a dictionary. Dictionaries are available in print and online formats, but you should make sure the one you choose is published by a reliable institution. Besides providing the spelling and definition of words, dictionaries include other features that can help you better understand the word and make it a permanent part of your memory (see Figure 2.3).

- **Pronunciation guides** break up words into parts and use symbols to explain how each part sounds. Accents show which syllables to stress. In addition, online dictionaries may include audio pronunciations.

- **Parts-of-speech abbreviations** tell how the word can be used in a sentence (*n.* for noun, *v.* for verb). Some words can be used as more than one part of speech.

- **Etymology** describes the history and language origins of a word.

- **Examples** show how the word is used in a sentence.

- **Inflected forms** show other forms of the word. For example, an inflected form of the word *spy* is *spies*, which is the plural form of the word.

Figure 2.3 Sample Dictionary Entry

Pronunciation guide ⟶ **augur** (AW-gur)

Definitions ⟶ *n.*　**1.** One of a group of ancient Roman religious officials who foretold events by observing and interpreting signs and omens.
　2. A seer or prophet; a soothsayer

Example ⟶ An *augur* predicted a bountiful harvest season.

Part of speech ⟶ *v.*　**1.** To foretell something or to predict the future
　2. To give a promise of

The closing of the community center seemed to *augur* the downturn of the neighborhood.

Etymology ⟶ ["Augur" comes from Latin and is related to the Latin verb "augēre," which means "to increase" and is the source of "augment," "auction," and "author."]

SPECIAL NOTE: Find a trustworthy print or online dictionary. Make sure you have access to it when you are completing a reading assignment.

Using Context

Another strategy for dealing with new words in your reading is to figure out what the words mean in context—or by looking for clues in the other words and ideas around them. In some cases, the **context clues** can be very easy to identify. In the following passage, the word "affiliates" is defined right after the word is mentioned (underlined).

> Broadcast networks can have as many *affiliates* as they want. Affiliates are stations that use network programming but are owned by companies other than the networks. No network, however, can have two affiliates in the same geographic broadcast area.

In other cases, you will need to study a text more carefully for context clues. In this passage, an antonym (opposite) suggested in the first part of a sentence (underlined) helps you understand the word "exemptions" in the second part.

> The French peasants slowly became aware of the contrasts between the taxes they had to bear and the *exemptions* enjoyed by the clergy and the nobility. When that discontent was later joined by the anger of the middle-class townspeople, the potential for revolution would exist.

Types of Context Clues

- **Cause-effect relationships**
  Since passengers not wearing seat belts are more likely to experience severe injuries during motor vehicle accidents, state officials made seat-belt use *mandatory*.

- **Definitions built into the text**
  Dr. Williams is an *anthropologist*, a person who scientifically studies the physical, social, and cultural development of humans.

- **Comparisons and contrasts**
  Lynn Dery lives in New York City, so she is used to a fast-paced lifestyle; Mandy Williams lives in the country, so she is used to a more *serene* lifestyle.

- **Words in a series**
  Spaghetti, lasagna, and *ziti* all have their own special shape.

- **Synonyms (words with the same meaning)**
  Hector's essay contains too many *banal*, overused phrases.

- **Antonyms (words with the opposite meaning)**
  Mrs. Wolfe still seemed strong and energetic after the storm, but Mr. Wolfe looked *haggard*.

- **The tone of the text**
  The street was filled with *bellicose* protesters who pushed and shoved their way through the crowd. The scene was no longer peaceful and calm, as the marchers promised it would be.

Understanding Word Parts

Roots, **prefixes**, and **suffixes** are different word parts. Many words in our language are made up of combinations of these parts. See Appendix E for a full list of word parts.

- **Roots** like *liber* (as in <u>liber</u>ate) or *rupt* (as in inter<u>rupt</u>) are the starting points for most words.
- **Prefixes** like *anti* (as in <u>anti</u>biotic) or *inter* (as in <u>inter</u>rupt) are word parts that come before roots to form new words.
- **Suffixes** like *dom* (as in boredom) or *ate* (as in liber<u>ate</u>) are word parts that come after roots to form new words.

Note the word *rearmament* in the following passage. You may already know the meaning of this word. If not, studying its parts can help you unlock its meaning.

> The huge road construction and public works programs [Hitler] began in 1934 absorbed a large portion of the pool of unemployed. With *rearmament*, the military was greatly enlarged, and munitions factories and their suppliers received government orders.

Word parts:

- *Re* is a prefix meaning "again."
- *Arm* is a root or base word meaning "equip or supply with weapons."
- The suffix *ment* basically means "act of."

Definition/explanation of *rearmament*:

- *Rearmament*, then, means "the act of arming again."

Practice 2.1 Answer the questions about key words in the following passage.

> The students were only in first grade, and Matos was **appalled** that they were already so **discouraged** about their futures, but he wasn't surprised. They were **undocumented immigrants**, brought to the United States by their parents.

1. Use a dictionary to define *appalled*.

   a. Thrilled

   b. Horrified

   c. Curious

2. Use word parts to define *discouraged*. (**Hint:** the prefix "dis" means *apart*; the root "cour" means *heart*; the suffix "age" means *state of*.)

   a. Losing heart or spirit

   b. Gaining heart or spirit

   c. Losing years or age

3. Use context clues from the passage to define *undocumented immigrants*.

   a. Hopeless citizens of the U.S.

   b. U.S. citizens without a social security number

   c. Noncitizens living in the U.S.

2.3 Understanding the Writing Process

When facing an extended writing assignment, a common question often comes to mind: How will I ever get this done? Even professional writers sometimes labor for the right answer. But have no fear. A writing project is much less challenging when you approach it as a process rather than as an end product.

You cannot change a flat tire with one simple action. It takes a number of steps to get the job done right. The same goes for writing. If you expect to complete a paper in one general attempt, you (and your instructor) will be disappointed in the results. On the other hand, if you follow the writing process, you'll complete the job in the right way—one step at a time.

Always use the writing process when you are writing to share learning and when you are writing certain personal forms. You don't need to use it when you are simply writing to learn, such as note taking and freewriting. Here's a quick overview of the process.

Step	Activities
Prewriting	Start the process by selecting a topic to write about; collecting details about it; and finding a focus or thesis to direct your writing.
Writing	Then write your first draft, using your prewriting plan as a general guide. Writing a first draft allows you to connect your thoughts about a topic.
Revising	Carefully review your first draft and have a classmate read it as well. Change any parts that need to be clearer, and add missing information.
Editing	Edit your revised writing by checking for style, grammar, punctuation, and spelling errors.
Publishing	During the final step, prepare your writing to share with your instructor, your peers, or another audience.

Like the reading process, there can be forward and backward movement between the steps in the writing process (see **Figure 2.4**). For example, after writing a first draft, you may decide to collect more details about your topic, which is actually a prewriting activity. When using the writing process, you need to understand the following points.

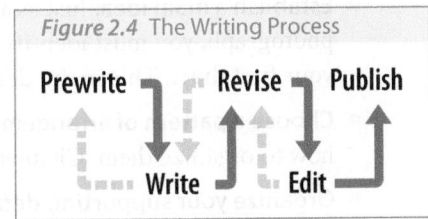

Figure 2.4 The Writing Process

- **All the steps require some type of writing.** Prewriting (planning), revising, and editing are as much writing activities as composing the first draft is.

- **It is unlikely that the process will work the same for any two writing assignments.** For one assignment, you may struggle with gathering details. For another, you may have trouble starting the first draft. For still another, you may move from step to step with little difficulty.

- **No two writers develop their writing in the same way.** Some writers need to talk about their writing early on, while others would rather keep their ideas to themselves. Some writers need to step away from their writing at times to let their thoughts develop. Other writers can't stop until they produce a first draft. Your own writing personality will develop as you gain more writing experience.

- **The writing process won't make you a better writer unless you make a sincere effort to use it.** You wouldn't expect to play the piano just by reading about it—you must follow the instructions and practice. The same holds true for writing.

TEST-TAKING NOTE: When you respond to a writing prompt on a test, use a shortened form of the writing process. Spend a few minutes gathering and organizing your ideas; then write your response. Afterward, read what you have produced and quickly revise and edit it.

Prewriting

Prewriting is the first step in the writing process. In many ways, it is the most important step because it involves all of the decisions and planning that come before writing a first draft. If you plan well, you will be well prepared to work through the rest of the process. These are the basic prewriting tasks.

- **Study the assignment.** Use the STRAP strategy (see Section 1.3) to help you identify the main parts of the assignment.

- **Identify a meaningful writing idea.** Pick a specific topic that meets the requirements of the assignment and that truly interests you. Otherwise, you will have a hard time writing about it.

- **Collect plenty of details.** Explore your thoughts and feelings about the topic. Then gather additional information through observations or interviews or by reading about the topic. Look for details in a variety of sources, such as books, websites, and academic journals.

- **Establish a main idea.** Just as a photographer focuses the subject before taking a photograph, you must identify a special part or feeling about the topic before writing your first draft. This main idea is usually expressed in a thesis statement.

- **Choose a pattern of arrangement.** Decide what supporting details to include and how to organize them. Chapter 5 discusses different patterns of organization.

- **Organize your supporting details.** With a pattern of arrangement in mind, you can organize your evidence in one of three basic ways:

  - **Make a quick list of main points and support.**
  - **Create a topic or sentence outline.** Draft a more formal arrangement of main points and subpoints.
  - **Fill in a graphic organizer.** Arrange the main points and details in a chart or diagram. See Section 1.5 for examples of graphic organizers.

Writing

Writing, or drafting, is the next step in the writing process. You have one important task during this step—to connect your thoughts and ideas about your topic in writing. Your first draft does not have to be perfectly worded; you just need something to work with. Here is a basic guide to drafting.

- **Strike while you're hot.** Write your first draft while your planning is still fresh in your mind.

- **Refer to your prewriting.** Use all of your planning and organizing as a basic writing guide. But also be open to new ideas as they come to mind.

- **Write as much as you can.** Keep writing until you get all of your ideas on paper or until you come to a natural stopping point. Concentrate on forming your ideas rather than on making everything correct.

- **Form a meaningful whole.** A meaningful whole for a paragraph means a topic sentence, multiple body sentences, and a closing sentence. For an essay, it means an opening paragraph (with a thesis statement), multiple middle paragraphs (with supporting details), and a closing paragraph.

Paragraph	Essay
Topic sentence ⟶	Opening paragraph (with thesis statement)
Body sentences ⟶	Middle paragraphs
Closing sentence ⟶	Closing paragraph

- **Pay special attention to each part.** All three parts—the opening, the middle, and the closing—play important roles in your writing. Give each part special attention.

  - The opening gets the reader's interest and states your thesis.
  - The middle supports your thesis with evidence (details).
  - The closing offers important final thoughts about the topic.

- **Look back to move forward.** Sometimes it helps to stop and reread what you have written to help you add new ideas.

- **Write naturally and honestly.** "Talk" to your readers, as if a group of classmates were gathered around you.

- **Remember, it's a draft.** A first draft is your first look at a developing writing idea. Don't worry about it being perfect. You will have plenty of opportunities to improve upon it later in the process.

Revising

Revising is the third step in the process. During this step, you shape and improve the ideas, organization, and voice in your first draft. You would never expect a musician to record a song after putting lyrics and music together for the first time. The same holds true with your writing. You still have a lot of work ahead of you. Here is a basic guide to revising.

- **Step away from your draft.** Your time away will help you see your first draft more clearly and with a fresh outlook.
- **Revisit the main parts of the assignment.** Does your writing meet the requirements for purpose, audience, and type of writing?
- **Read your draft many times.** Read it silently and out loud to get an overall impression of your work.
- **Have peers read it.** Their comments and questions will help you decide what changes to make.
- **Check your main idea.** Decide if it still works and if you have provided enough support for it.
- **Review each part.** Be sure that the opening sets the proper voice or tone for your writing, the middle part supports your thesis, and the closing provides worthy final thoughts about the topic.
- **Know your basic moves.** There are four basic ways to make changes—adding, cutting, rewriting, or reordering information. Each change or improvement that you make will bring you closer to a strong finished paper.

Add information to . . .
- make a main point more convincing.
- complete an explanation.
- improve the flow of your writing.

Cut information if it . . .
- doesn't support the thesis.
- seems repetitious.

Rewrite information if it . . .
- seems confusing or unclear.
- appears too complicated.
- lacks the proper voice.

Reorder information if it . . .
- seems out of order.
- would make more sense in another spot.

- **Follow a similar process for each remaining draft.** The best writing results from more than one revision.

Peer Revising

Sharing your writing with peers can help you gain valuable feedback as you develop your writing. Peer revision offers a fresh perspective on your writing, revealing strengths and weaknesses in your draft. To get the best feedback, writers and reviewers need to have a clear understanding of their roles and responsibilities.

Role of the Writer

The writer is responsible for creating an open environment that encourages reviewers to give honest feedback. Here are steps you should follow when sharing your writing for review.

- Introduce your writing and any requirements of the assignment.
- Describe your purpose and objectives for the writing.
- Share your concerns or areas of focus. For example, if you are concerned with the organization of the piece, ask the reviewer to pay special attention to it.
- Give the reviewer plenty of time to read and respond to your work.

Role of the Reviewer

The reviewer is responsible for giving honest and constructive feedback in a positive manner. If a writer asks you to review their work, be prepared to give clear, specific, and complete advice. You can do so by following the **OAQS Method: Observe, Appreciate, Question,** and **Suggest**.

1. **Observe** means to focus on what the writer's work is designed to do or say and judge how well the writing accomplishes its purpose. For example, you may say, "Your writing shows a clear cause-effect relationship between tropical deforestation and endangered species."

2. **Appreciate** means to highlight the strengths of the writing. This is meant to boost the writer's confidence and to show what is working well. You may say, "The evidence you've included is clear and convincing" or "I especially like . . ."

3. **Question** means to ask about what confuses you or what you still need to know. You might ask for more information or for clarification on a certain point. You may say, "You skimmed over the link between deforestation and increased river levels. Could you provide more information about that?"

4. **Suggest** ways to make possible changes. Keep your suggestions honest and courteous as well as specific. Don't say, "The ending was boring." Instead you may say, "Your beginning really pulled me in, and the middle explained the main idea strongly, but the ending felt a bit flat. Here are some ideas I have to help you bring the end of the essay all together."

Editing

Editing is the fourth step, when you check your writing for style and correctness. Editing becomes important *after* you have revised the content of your writing. Editing is like buffing out the smudges and scratches on a newly painted car. The buffing is important, but only after the main work—the actual painting—is complete. Here is a basic guide to editing.

- **Start with a clean copy.** Do your editing on a clean copy of your revised writing.
- **Check first for style.** Make sure that you have used the best words, such as specific nouns and verbs, and created smooth-reading sentences.

- **Then check for correctness.** Check for grammar, usage, punctuation, mechanics, and spelling.

- **For spelling, read from the last word to the first.** This strategy forces you to look at each word. A spell checker will not catch every error.

- **Circle punctuation.** This strategy will force you to look at each mark.

- **Refer to an editing checklist.** This will ensure that your editing will be complete and thorough.

> **Editing Checklist**
>
> ☐ Have I used specific nouns and verbs?
>
> ☐ Have I used more action verbs than "be" verbs (*is, are, was, were*)?
>
> ☐ Have I avoided improper shifts in sentences?
>
> ☐ Have I avoided fragments and run-ons?
>
> ☐ Do my subjects and verbs agree (*she speaks*, not *she speak*)?
>
> ☐ Have I used the right words (*their, there, they're*)?
>
> ☐ Have I capitalized first words and proper nouns and adjectives?
>
> ☐ Have I used commas after long introductory word groups and to separate items in a series?
>
> ☐ Have I used commas correctly in compound sentences?
>
> ☐ Have I used apostrophes correctly?

- **Get help.** Ask a trusted peer to check for errors.

Publishing

Publishing is the final step in the writing process. During this step, you prepare a final copy of your writing to share or submit. Follow these tips to publish your work:

- **Prepare a final copy.** Incorporate all of your editing changes.

- **Follow design requirements.** Format your final copy according to the requirements established by your instructor. Keep the design clear and uncluttered, and use easy-to-read black font.

- **Proofread the text.** Check your writing one last time for errors.

- **Submit your work.** Present a printed or electronic version of your writing to your instructor.

- **Save a copy for your writing portfolio.** A portfolio includes your finished pieces of writing.

2.4 Using Reading and Writing Strategies

Writing about your reading assignments is one of the best ways to understand them. The physical act of writing—recording one word after another—brings your thoughts into focus. So when you write about your reading, you are bringing the ideas in the text into focus.

It is no surprise then that three of most essential reading strategies involve writing: annotating, note taking, and summarizing. Each of these strategies builds upon the other, with annotating and note taking providing the support for writing a summary.

Annotating a Text

To **annotate** means "to add comments or make notes in a text." Annotating a text allows you to interact with the ideas from the reading. Here are some suggestions:

- Write questions in the margins.
- Underline, highlight, or bracket important points.
- Define new terms.
- Make connections to other parts.

SPECIAL NOTE: Annotate the material only if you own the text or if you are reading a photocopy.

Why is this so?

Democracy Does Not Always Allow for Quick Solutions

Democracy is government by the people through elected officials and representatives. Although constitutional democracies limit power and achieve stability by ensuring that changes happen gradually, the system also presents some serious challenges, especially in confronting environmental problems.

Main idea (thesis)

[Political institutions in most constitutional democracies are designed to allow gradual change that ensures economic and political stability.] In the United States, for example, rapid and destabilizing change is curbed by a system of checks and balances that distributes power among three branches of government—*legislative*, *executive*, and *judicial*—and among federal, state, and local governments.

Evidence

What are some other examples?

In passing laws, developing budgets, and formulating

Evidence

Find out
more about
these.

[regulations, elected and appointed government officials must deal with pressure from many competing special-interest groups.] Each of these groups advocates passing laws, providing subsidies or tax breaks, or establishing regulations favorable to its cause while attempting to weaken or repeal laws, subsidies, tax breaks, and regulations unfavorable to its position. Some special-interest groups such as corporations are profit-making organizations. Others are nongovernmental organizations (NGOs), most of which are nonprofit, such as labor unions and environmental organizations.

Drawbacks

The design for stability and gradual change in democracies is highly desirable. But several features of democratic governments hinder their ability to deal with environmental problems. For example, problems such as climate change and biodiversity loss are complex and difficult to understand. Such problems also have long-lasting effects, are interrelated, and require integrated, long-term solutions that emphasize prevention. But because local, state, and national elections are held as often as every two years, most politicians spend much of their time seeking re-election and tend to focus on short-term, isolated issues rather than on long-term, complex, and time-consuming problems.

First time the
writer directly
addresses
reader.

One of our greatest challenges is to place more emphasis on long-term thinking and policies and to educate political leaders and the public about the need for long-range thinking and actions. Another problem is that many political leaders, with hundreds of issues to deal with, have too little understanding of how the earth's natural systems work and how those systems support all life, economies, and societies. Again, there is an urgent need to educate politicians and voters about these vital matters.

Purpose—
to inform

Audience—
students

From Miller, Living in the Environment, 17E. © 2012 Cengage Learning.

Taking Effective Notes

Taking notes helps you to focus on reading material and understand it more fully. Notes change information you have read about to information that you are working with. Of course, taking effective notes makes summarizing texts and studying for exams much easier because note taking helps you highlight important information. When taking notes, follow these tips.

- Use your own words as much as possible.
- Record only key points and details rather than long passages.
- Consider **bold-faced** or *italicized* words, graphics, and captions as well as the main text.
- Use abbreviations and symbols to save time (vs., #, &, etc.).
- Decide on a system to organize or arrange your notes so they are easy to follow.

Using Two-Column Notes

To make your note taking more thoughtful, use a two-column system called the Cornell Method. One column (two-thirds of the page) is for your main notes, and the other column (one-third of the page) is for questions and key terms. Fill in this column after you're done with your main notes. To review your work, cover the main notes and answer the questions in the left column.

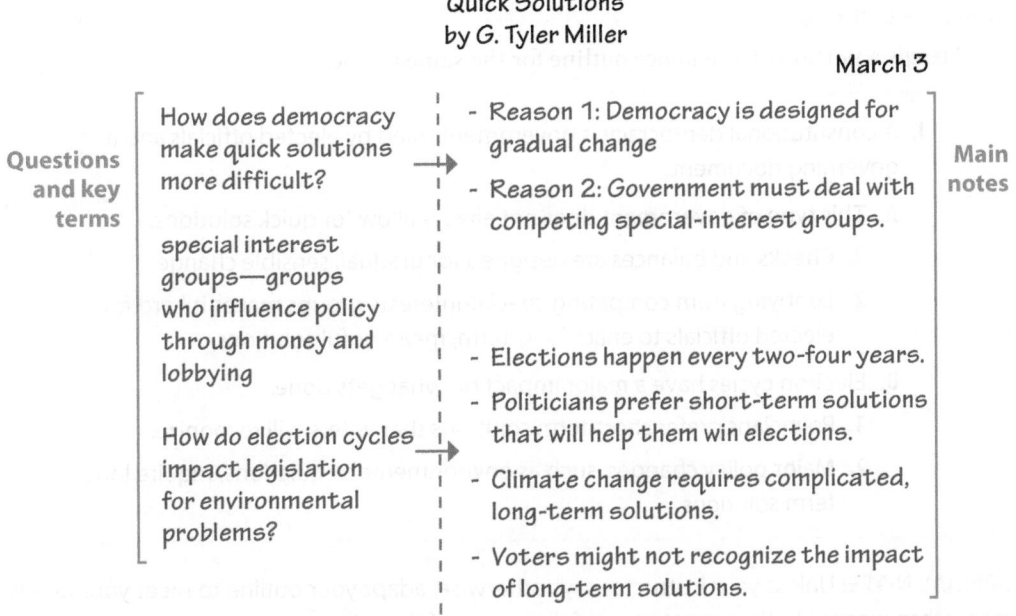

Democracy Does Not Always Allow for
Quick Solutions
by G. Tyler Miller

March 3

Questions and key terms

How does democracy make quick solutions more difficult?

special interest groups—groups who influence policy through money and lobbying

How do election cycles impact legislation for environmental problems?

Main notes

- Reason 1: Democracy is designed for gradual change
- Reason 2: Government must deal with competing special-interest groups.

- Elections happen every two-four years.
- Politicians prefer short-term solutions that will help them win elections.
- Climate change requires complicated, long-term solutions.
- Voters might not recognize the impact of long-term solutions.

SPECIAL NOTE: Save space at the bottom of the page to summarize the notes after class.

Using an Outline

An **outline** shows how ideas fit together. The ideas in a **topic outline** are expressed in words and phrases. The ideas in a **sentence outline** are expressed in sentences. In a traditional outline, each new division represents another level of detail. As is demonstrated, if you have a "I," you should have at least a "II." If you have an "A," you should at least have a "B," and so on.

Topic Outline

Here's the start of a topic outline for "Democracy Does Not Always Allow for Quick Solutions."

Text subject: Democracy and Change

    I. Constitutional democracies

        A. Designed for gradual change

            1. Checks and balances

            2. Lobbying

        B. Ruled by election cycles that encourage short-term solutions

    II. Environmental problems—climate change and biodiversity

        A. Complex problems

        B. Long-term solutions

Sentence Outline

Here is a portion of a sentence outline for the same article.

    I. A constitutional democracy is government ruled by elected officials and a governing document.

        A. This type of government does not always allow for quick solutions.

            1. Checks and balances are designed for gradual, sensible change.

            2. Lobbying from competing special-interests groups makes it hard for elected officials to enact long-term, meaningful solutions.

        B. Election cycles have a major impact on what gets done.

            1. Politicians prefer short-term solutions that voters will recognize.

            2. Major policy changes, such as environmental regulations, require long-term solutions.

SPECIAL NOTE: Unless your instructor says otherwise, adapt your outline to meet your needs rather than worry whether or not you've followed all of the rules.

Using Clusters or Webs

Clustering or webbing is a more graphic way to collect and organize the key points in a reading assignment. Begin a cluster with a nucleus word or idea—most often, the main idea in the reading. Then cluster key points and supporting details around the nucleus concept. Circle each point or detail and connect it to the closest related word. The end result should be a structure that graphically shows you all the important information in a reading selection at a glance.

The cluster in **Figure 2.5** presents the key facts and details in the essay "Democracy Does Not Allow for Quick Solutions." Study the cluster to see how it connects important information from the essay.

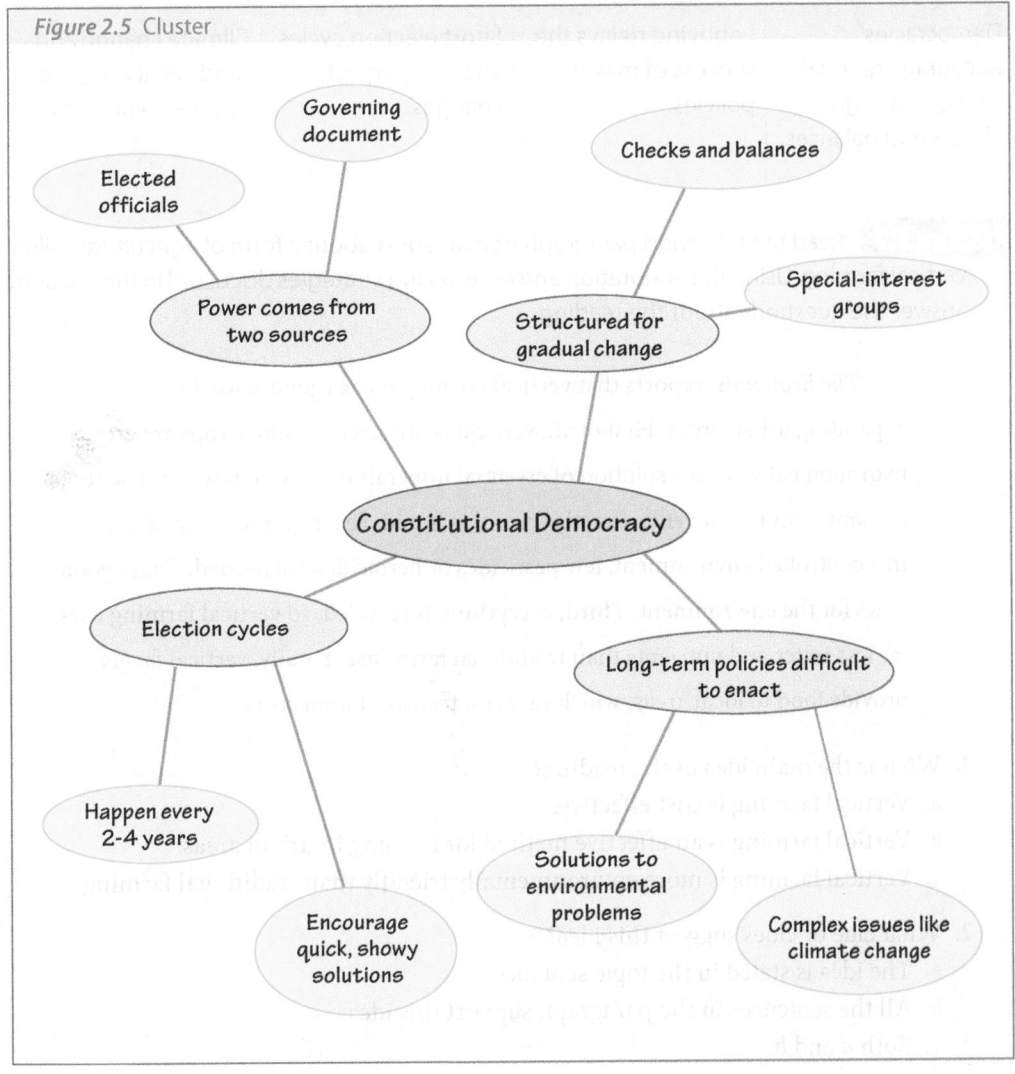

Figure 2.5 Cluster

Using a Table Diagram

Part of the challenge when reading an informative text is keeping track of the main idea and key supporting details. Filling in a table diagram works well for this purpose. In this graphic organizer, you identify the main idea, or thesis, of the reading at the top of the table and list the key supporting details underneath. You can refer back to this information as you write a summary of the text or study for a test.

Figure 2.6 shows a table diagram with the main idea and key supporting details from the essay "Democracy Does Not Allow for Quick Solutions."

Figure 2.6 Table Diagram

Constitutional democracies limit power and provide stability.			
Democracies encourage gradual change through checks and balances.	Lobbying delays the process of making policies.	Short election cycles encourage quick changes.	Climate change and biodiversity require long-term policies.

Practice 2.2 Read the following paragraph from a report about a form of agriculture called vertical farming. Using the annotation and note-taking strategies discussed in this section, answer the questions about the reading.

The Economist reports that vertical farming makes good sense in our expanding urban areas. First of all, vertical farms need no soil. Crops are grown hydroponically, or in a solution of essential minerals dissolved in water. The roots of plants absorb nutrients directly from this liquid. Second, since crops are grown in a controlled environment, few pesticides or herbicides are needed. That's good news for the environment. Third, everything is recycled, so vertical farming uses far less water and nutrients than traditional farms use. Finally, vertical farms provide food to local areas, which saves on transportation costs.

1. What is the main idea of the reading?
   a. Vertical farming is cost effective.
   b. Vertical farming is an effective method for farming in urban areas.
   c. Vertical farming is more environmentally friendly than traditional farming.

2. What clue or clues suggest this idea?
   a. The idea is stated in the topic sentence.
   b. All the sentences in the paragraph support this idea.
   c. Both *a* and *b*.

3. How many supporting details does the text include?
- a. 2
- b. 3
- c. 4

4. What clues suggest this number?
- a. Transition words introduce four key ideas (*first of all, second, third, finally*).
- b. The details of the paragraph are mostly about food and the environment.
- c. The paragraph includes three details about why vertical farms work.

Summarizing a Text

Summarizing a reading assignment is an especially effective form of writing to learn. It is the process of identifying and explaining the most important ideas in a text. Along with annotating and taking notes, summarizing is an excellent way of becoming actively involved in your reading.

When summarizing a text, you should present the main points in a clear, concise form using your own words as much as possible. Generally speaking, a summary should be about one-third as long as the original. Here are some other summarizing tips.

- Start by clearly stating the main idea of the text.
- Share only the essential supporting facts and details (names, dates, times, and places) in the next sentences.
- Present your ideas in a logical order.
- Tie all of your points together in a closing sentence.

This paragraph summarizes "Democracy Does Not Allow for Quick Solutions."

The opening identifies the main idea (underlined).

In "Democracy Does Not Allow for Quick Solutions," G. Tyler Miller explains that a constitutional democracy limits government power and provides stability, but can present challenges. To start, a constitutional

The middle describes essential supporting details.

democracy encourages gradual change through a series of checks and balances. A new policy must pass through each check and balance before going into effect. Elected and appointed officials must also deal with special-interest groups, who may lobby for competing policies. This system presents a drawback for environmental issues such as climate change because they are complex. Politicians are much more interested in

The closing sentence restates the thesis.

simpler issues, because they operate within short-term election cycles. The challenge for environmentalists is to educate politicians about complex issues so that they can deal with them properly.

Planning Your Summary

Most of your prewriting and planning will occur when you read and react to the text. During your planning . . .

- Annotate and take notes as needed.
- State the main idea or thesis of the text.
- Identify the key points that support the main idea. Remember that in academic texts each middle paragraph often addresses one key supporting point. This point is usually stated in the topic sentence.

Drafting Your Summary

A summary is usually one paragraph, starting with a topic sentence and following with supporting ideas. As you write your first draft . . .

- Use your own words as much as possible.
- Start with a topic sentence, naming the title, author, and topic of the text.
- Continue with the key points that explain the main idea. Focus on big ideas, rather than specific details.
- Arrange your ideas in the most logical order.
- Add a closing sentence if one seems necessary.

Revising and Editing Your Summary

Remember that your summary should address the essential information from the original text. As you review your first draft . . .

- Determine if it identifies the main idea of the text.
- Decide if you've limited yourself to key supporting details.
- Check if your summary reads smoothly and logically.
- Determine if you've used your own words, except for key ideas. For example, you may find it necessary to include a few exact ideas or specialized words from the original text. When this type of information is taken directly from the text, enclose it within quotation marks.

  Exact idea: The author describes himself as "soaring with a lightness I'd never known before" after the ceremony.

  Specialized word: One teacher recognized as a master teacher serves as a "standard-bearer" for all great teachers.

- Check your summary for proper usage and grammar.
- Fix any spelling, capitalization, and punctuation errors.

Forming Personal Responses

While summaries show how well you understood what you've read, personal responses reveal your personal thoughts and feelings about a reading. Personal responses help you think critically about what you've read—to agree with it, to question it, to make connections with it. This level of analysis is something college instructors will expect from you for almost everything you read.

Reserve part of your class notebook or create an online blog or document for personal responses. The length and form of your personal response doesn't matter so much as your level of thinking. Your goal is to make a thoughtful connection with the text. The following guidelines will help you do this:

- **Write freely and honestly** to make genuine connections with the text. Don't stop writing to worry about grammar, punctuation, or mechanics. These errors can be cleaned up before you share or submit your response.

- **Respond to ideas** that you like or agree with, information that confuses you, connections that you can make with other material, and ideas that seem significant.

- **Label and date your responses.** You can use these entries to prepare for exams or complete other assignments.

- **Share your discoveries.** Your entries can provide conversation starters in discussions with classmates.

- **Write several times for long texts,** perhaps once before you read, two or three times during the reading, and one time afterward.

Lu Mikhaylova, 2017 / Used under license from Shutterstock.com

Types of Personal Responses

Here are some specific ways to respond to a text:

Express	Share your feelings about the text.
Discuss	Write a fictional interview with the author in which you ask questions about the text and craft the author's possible answers.
Illustrate	Create graphics or draw pictures to help you figure out parts of the text.
Imitate	Continue the article or story line, trying to write like the author.
Reflect	Connect what you've read to your prior knowledge, beliefs, and experiences.

☑ Review and Enrichment

Chapter Review Quiz

Answer the questions about what you've learned in this chapter.

1. What are two things you should do during prereading?
   a. Review the title and preview the text.
   b. Ask questions and reflect on what you've read.
   c. Read the text and identify the key ideas.

2. What step in the reading process helps you clarify your thinking of a reading?
   a. Prereading
   b. Reading
   c. Reflecting

3. What type of context clue offers a word or phrase with the opposite meaning to an unfamiliar term?
   a. Synonym
   b. Antonym
   c. Definition

4. What word part is the starting point or base for most words?
   a. Suffix
   b. Prefix
   c. Root

5. Use the word parts to help you choose the correct definition.
   interrupt
   the prefix *inter* means "between"   the root *rupt* means "break"

   a. To cause a pause or break
   b. To set into action or motion
   c. To maintain

6. What are the steps in the writing process?
   a. Ideas, organization, voice, word choice, and sentence fluency
   b. Prewriting, writing, revising, editing, and publishing
   c. Survey, question, read, recite, and review

7. Which of these statements in *not* true about the writing process?
   a. All steps in the writing process require some type of writing.
   b. The process will work exactly the same for every writing assignment.
   c. No two writers develop their writing in the exact same way.

8. When is the best time to check your writing for style and correctness?
   a. During the development of the first draft
   b. After completing a draft of your writing
   c. After making improvements to the ideas, organization, and voice

9. What does annotating a text involve?
   a. Writing notes, comments, and questions in a text while reading
   b. Summarizing the information in a text
   c. Forming personal responses to a text

10. What is the main benefit of writing a personal response to a reading?
    a. It helps you follow all the steps in the writing process.
    b. It serves as an effective substitute for note taking.
    c. It helps you think critically about what you read.

Reading for Enrichment

In this section, you will read an online report by John Light about hydraulic fracturing (or "fracking"), the process of extracting natural gas from deep beneath the ground. This controversial practice has become common in states such as Oklahoma and Texas. Be sure to follow the steps in the reading process to help you gain a full understanding of the text. (See Section 2.1.)

About the Author

John Light is a reporter and digital producer for Moyers & Company. His work has appeared in *The Atlantic, Mother Jones, Salon,* and *Slate* and has been broadcast on Public Radio International. He is a graduate of the Columbia School of Journalism.

Prereading

Before you read, learn about the author, preview the text, and use the STRAP strategy to identify the main parts of the text.

Subject:	What specific topic does the reading address?
Type:	What form (*online report, personal essay, textbook chapter*) does the reading take?
Role:	What position (*journalist, engineer, professor*) does the writer assume?
Audience:	Who is the intended audience?
Purpose:	What is the general goal of the reading (*to inform, to persuade, to share*)?

Reading and Rereading

As you read, be sure to (1) consider the author's purpose and audience, (2) identify the main idea or thesis of the report, and (3) note the evidence that explains or supports the main idea. Consider annotating the text and/or taking notes as you read. Follow these annotating tips:

- Underline, bracket, or highlight important information. Comment on these ideas in the margin.
- Write questions in the margin.
- Circle words that you are unsure of. Then define them.

Reread as needed to examine important ideas more closely and to make sure you understand the key points in the text.

Is Fracking Causing Earthquakes?

In Texas, Oklahoma, Ohio, and other states, people who have rarely experienced earthquakes in the past are getting used to them as a fairly common phenomenon. This dramatic uptick in tremors is related to drilling for oil and natural gas, several reports find. And the growing popularity of **hydraulic** fracturing, or fracking, is in part to blame.   1

Between 1970 and 2000, there was an average of 20 earthquakes per year within the central and eastern United States. Between 2010 and 2013, there was an average of more than 100 earthquakes annually. A United States Geological Survey (USGS) released last month summarized research on man-made earthquakes conducted by one of the agency's **geophysicists**:   2

> USGS scientists have found that at some locations the increase in **seismicity** coincides with the injection of wastewater in deep disposal wells. Much of this wastewater is a byproduct of oil and gas production and is routinely disposed of by injection into wells specifically designed for this purpose.

So, the actual hydraulic fracturing process itself is not to blame in these   3 cases; instead, it's the injection of wastewater into deep wells that accompanies it.

Hydraulic fracturing produces a higher volume of wastewater than traditional drilling—as the name implies, drillers use millions of gallons of high-pressure water, sand, and chemicals to break apart rock and release gas trapped in pockets in the earth. The wastewater generated is often contaminated with salt or poisonous chemicals, and environmental regulations bar drilling companies from allowing it to mix with drinking water; oftentimes, the most economical way for these companies to dispose of it is to **sequester** it deep in the ground, below **aquifers**. Once there, it changes pressure underground and lubricates fault lines, with the potential effect of causing earthquakes.

4

In both Texas and Oklahoma, the number of earthquakes per year has increased ten-fold. And wells storing wastewater from fracking have also been linked to hundreds of earthquakes near Youngstown, Ohio.

5

Studies last year found that the largest quake ever recorded in Oklahoma—which was felt 800 miles away in Milwaukee, WI, damaged 14 homes, injured two people, and buckled a highway—could be linked to wastewater injection. Damage from the quake, which measured 5.6 on the Richter scale, "would be much worse if it were to happen in a more densely populated area," the USGS wrote.

6

And as quakes increase in frequency, residents of Oklahoma and Texas are taking notice. More noticeable than the shaking, for many, is the noise these quakes make: a loud boom, like artillery fire.

7

In the Netherlands, where the Groningen gas field lies, quakes have also become more frequent, increasing from about 20 each year before 2011 to an average of one per week. Shell and Exxon Mobile, active in the gas field, set aside $130 million to strengthen buildings as the quakes increased in **severity**.

8

But residents of the area worried that a 4-or-5 magnitude earthquake —the likelihood of which, experts warned, is increasing—would threaten the **integrity** of the country's dikes, which protect the low-lying northern Netherlands.

Last month, the country's government decided to scale back production of natural gas on the Groningen field, foregoing one billion euros a year by 2016, even as the country struggles to cope with the European Union's deficit reduction targets.

9

But similar reductions in the US are unlikely. The oil and gas industry employs hundreds of thousands of people in both Texas and Oklahoma, and natural gas has become widely popular among electric utilities for its low cost.

10

This article was originally published at BillMoyers.com on February 14, 2014. Reused with permission.

---

hydraulics
the science dealing with the mechanical properties of liquids such as water

seismicity
belonging to or related to earthquakes

sequester
to hide

aquifers
bodies of permeable rock containing groundwater

integrity
quality of being honest, whole, or upright

Reflecting

Answer the comprehension and vocabulary questions about the reading.

1. What is the main idea of this selection?
   a. Fracking provides access to huge quantities of natural gas.
   b. Fracking has been linked to increased earthquake activity.
   c. Fracking is being carefully examined in the New England states.

2. Which one of the following statements reflects evidence in support of the main idea?
   a. Wastewater from fracking seems to lubricate fault lines in dangerous ways.
   b. Fracking provides jobs for thousands of workers.
   c. Fracking in the U.S. occurs in densely populated areas.

3. Which best describes the voice or tone of the article?
    a. Opinionated and outspoken
    b. Informative and factual
    c. Uncertain and questioning

4. Study the word parts in *geophysicists* and how the word is used in the reading. Then choose the most accurate definition of the word.

   Geophysicists (paragraph 2)
   Geo + physic + ists
   (*Hint:* "Geo" also appears in words like *geography* and *geology*.)

    a. Scientists dealing with the stars and other heavenly bodies
    b. Scientists dealing with weather and climate
    c. Scientists dealing with the physical forces and movements of the Earth

5. Study how the word *severity* is used in the reading, and then choose the most accurate definition of the word.

   Severity (paragraph 8)

    a. Quality of being bright and cheery
    b. Quality of being fair or valuable
    c. Quality of being harsh or strict

Summarizing

Write a summary paragraph of the article using the guidelines from this chapter. Remember to use your own words and to focus only on the key ideas in the text.

Critical Thinking

- Does the author describe both pros and cons of fracking? How so? Is the treatment fair and balanced?
- Do you consider the supporting details reliable or unreliable? Explain.
- How does this reading illustrate the delicate balance between environmental protection and energy production?
- Which would you prefer: paying less for energy produced in a manner that may harm the environment or paying more for energy produced in a manner that is environmentally safe? Explain your choice.

Writing for Enrichment

What follows are possible writing activities to complete in response to the reading.

Prewriting

Choose one of the following writing ideas, or decide upon an idea of your own related to the reading.

1. Explain your own relationship with the environment. How do you interact with it? To what extent should it be protected?

2. Read another article about hydraulic fracturing, and write a summary of the article.

3. Compare and contrast oil, coal, and natural gas as providers of energy. Which option is cheaper? Cleaner? More effective?

4. Take a stand on hydraulic fracturing. Write an essay in which you argue for or against the procedure.

5. Explain why this contrast matters in the debate over energy: *Earth's natural resources are both bountiful and finite (limited).*

When planning . . .

- Research your topic as needed, taking thorough notes as you go along.
- Establish a main idea about the topic to emphasize.
- Review your notes for key ideas to support your main idea.
- Decide on the details that you will use to develop it.

When writing . . .

- Include a beginning, middle, and ending in your essay.
- Present your main idea in the beginning part.
- Support it in the middle paragraphs.
- Close your essay with final thoughts about your topic.

When revising and editing . . .

- Carefully review your first draft.
- Ask at least one peer to review your writing as well.
- Improve the content as needed.
- Then edit your revised writing for style and correctness.

Shots Studio, 2017 / Used under license from Shutterstock.com

Chapter 3

Critical Thinking and Viewing

You may have heard the common expression of "going through the motions." It refers to acting without putting much thought into your efforts. Going through the motions is perfectly acceptable for some actions, such as preparing a simple lunch or walking a dog. But what if you are reading a textbook chapter or planning an important writing assignment? For activities like these, you need to think more carefully and critically.

This chapter provides information that will help you understand critical thinking and use it in your course work. In the first part, you will learn about the two basic thinking patterns followed in almost all texts. Then you will learn about more specific, deeper levels of thinking, with special emphasis given to *analyzing* and *evaluating*. In the second part of the chapter, you will learn how to read and analyze visuals effectively.

Chapter Outline

- Considering Basic Thinking Patterns
- Accessing Deeper Thinking
- Analyzing Visuals

3.1 Considering Basic Thinking Patterns

Nearly all texts communicate ideas using one of two basic patterns of thinking. **Deductive thinking** begins with a general idea or principle (usually stated in a topic sentence or a thesis) and follows with specific details. It is the most common pattern of thinking that you will read and use. Conversely, **inductive thinking** moves from specific facts and details to a general conclusion. **Figure 3.1** shows how the two patterns of thinking move in different directions.

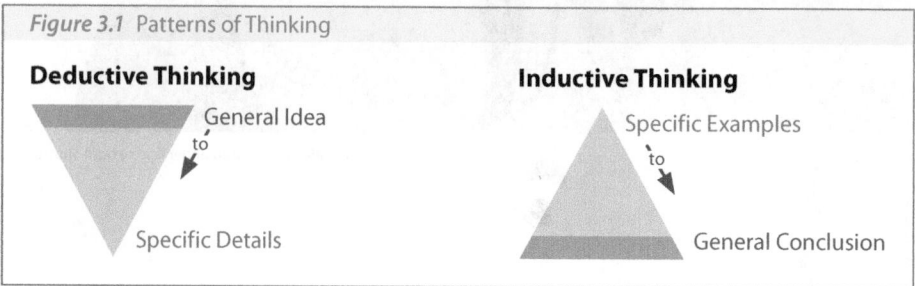

Figure 3.1 Patterns of Thinking

Deductive Thinking

General Idea
to
Specific Details

Inductive Thinking

Specific Examples
to
General Conclusion

Recognizing whether an academic selection is written deductively or inductively helps you analyze and evaluate the text for two reasons.

1. It helps you locate the main idea of the paragraph or essay.
2. It helps you trace the author's logic or way of supporting the main idea.

Deductive Thinking

The following paragraph is arranged deductively. The main idea (underlined) is followed by specific details. As you can see, when a text is arranged deductively, the main idea appears at the beginning of the text.

> It's hard to say how humpback whales find their way. They may rely on their excellent sense of hearing to pick up low-frequency sound waves that bounce off common ocean features such as rock and coral. Scientists also believe that they may look for familiar landforms. Two researchers recently detected a small amount of magnetic material in humpbacks, which may allow them to migrate by sensing the earth's magnetic field. This may explain why whales get stranded. Some researchers think it's because they are drawn to coasts with low magnetic forces, thinking these coasts are clear waterways. This would also explain how they could follow such precise migration paths.

These questions can help you check for deductive thinking. If you can answer "yes" to the questions, the text follows deductive logic.

- Does the text start with a topic sentence or thesis (main idea or claim)?
- Do the details logically support or follow from the thesis?
- Does the conclusion restate or summarize the main idea?

Inductive Thinking

The following paragraph is arranged inductively. It begins with specific examples leading to a general conclusion (underlined). With this pattern of thinking, the main idea comes at the end of the text.

> Arctic air masses dipped repeatedly across the nation's midsection. The results were reported on the nightly news. In the Texas panhandle, pipes burst as cloudless skies brought a rare hard freeze. In Tennessee, some 200 cars piled up in a dense fog, and many lives were lost. Many people were injured and one was killed in New York City as a short circuit caused by melting snow led to an underground train derailment. In California, old-timers couldn't remember a colder spell than the one that this year ruined nearly 85 percent of the citrus crop and most of the avocados, the strawberries, and the broccoli. <u>The winter of 2000-01 will be remembered as a costly one.</u>

These questions can help you check for inductive thinking. If you can answer "yes" to the questions, the text follows inductive logic.

- Does the text start with a series of facts, examples, and explanations?
- Do they logically lead up to the general conclusion?
- Does the general conclusion make sense in terms of the preceding evidence?

Practice 3.1 Read the paragraphs closely. Then fill in the blank with the type of thinking used—deductive or inductive thinking.

1. A good indicator of the influence and extent of globalization is the spread of English. In 1600, English was the mother tongue of between 4 and 7 million people. Not even all people in England spoke it. Today, about 1.5 billion people worldwide speak English, more than half as a second language. English is the most widespread language on earth. Most of the world's technical and scientific periodicals are written in English. English is the official language of the Olympics, of navigation in the air and on the seas, and of the World Council of Churches.

What pattern of thinking is used? _____

2. Mounds of paperwork, cluttered office desks, long lines of complaining citizens, and indifferent clerks who quietly shuffle papers—this image of bureaucracy can be found in all modern and postmodern societies. Few people are without a story or two of frustrating struggles against one bureaucracy or another. Most movies depict bureaucracy as perpetually mired in red tape and as an impersonal, soulless machine. *Ikiru*, directed by the Japanese filmmaker Akira Kurosawa, is a profound portrait of the individual versus bureaucracy.

What pattern of thinking is used? _____

Writing Deductively and Inductively

In most academic writing, you will use deductive thinking, moving from a general thesis to specific supporting details. Deduction is effective for exploring and expanding on ideas that are generally agreed upon. Therefore, deduction is popular in explanatory or expository writing. The following writing prompts call for a deductive response.

- Explain why World War II helped create conditions for an economic boom in 1950s America.

- Plunging readership and advertising rates have forced massive staff layoffs at newspapers across the country. Analyze the causes and effects of the decline in the newspaper industry.

Inductive conclusions, on the other hand, are often based on observations and experiences. Therefore, induction is a common feature in personal essays and narratives, where a writer may draw from personal experiences to come to a general conclusion.

When you write inductively, your goal is to provide enough evidence to improve the probability of your general conclusion. The following writing prompts could elicit an inductive response.

- What conditions in your childhood helped shape the person you have become?

- Trace the main character's development from the beginning to the end of a novel. Pay special attention to events and actions that have a significant effect on this character.

Some academic writing will use a mix of inductive and deductive thinking. While the main thesis may be supported deductively, a supporting idea within an essay may be organized inductively.

Practice 3.2 Review the following writing situations. Then fill in the blank with the type of thinking—deductive or inductive—that the writer should use.

1. For a writing assignment in Sociology, Prim will provide examples of time-honored customs in her native Thailand before coming to a conclusion about expectations for women in that society.

   Prim should use _____ thinking.

2. For a writing assignment in Environmental Science 203, Jackson will identify the most serious environmental issue in his community and give specific details (evidence) to support his main idea.

   Jackson should use _____ thinking.

3.2 Accessing Deeper Thinking

An educational psychologist named Benjamin Bloom classified thinking skills, moving from simple thinking to deeper levels of thinking. (See Table 3.1.) All of these levels of thinking are important, but two of the deeper levels—analyzing and evaluating—are especially significant when it comes to college coursework.

To **analyze** means to break down a subject into its essential parts and recognize the ways they work together. Comparing and classifying are examples of analytical thinking. To **evaluate** means to judge the value of a text and consider its strengths and weaknesses. Arguing for or against something is an example of evaluating.

Table 3.1 Bloom's Revised Taxonomy of Thinking Skills

	Reading	Writing
Remember	Collect basic information, identify key terms, and remember main points.	Recall basic information about a topic (facts, ideas, examples, definitions).
Understand	Draw inferences and conclusions about the topic based on what you know about it.	Explain what you have learned, give examples, and restate information.
Apply	Identify the main idea and crucial details; model or show understanding.	State a thesis about the topic and outline key supporting points.
Analyze	Carefully examine the topic and organization, classify the key points, show cause-effect relationships, and make comparisons.	Carefully examine all parts of the topic, recognize relationships between the parts, and choose an appropriate approach.
Evaluate	Judge the value of information and identify a text's strengths and weaknesses.	Judge the value and logic of other people's ideas as well as your own ideas, organization, and voice.
Create	Develop something new from what you have learned.	Develop new ideas and create a draft that draws from your learning, understanding, and analysis of the topic.

Analyzing

When you analyze a text, you study all of its parts separately and consider how they fit together. To analyze a text, first identify the essential parts. Then examine each part separately.

Understanding the Three Basic Parts

All paragraphs and essays consist of three basic parts: a beginning, a middle, and an ending. Each of these parts functions similarly in paragraphs and essays. See Figure 3.2.

Figure 3.2 Basic Three-Part Structure

	Paragraphs	Essays
Beginning	The topic sentence introduces the topic and states the focus of the paragraph.	The first paragraph (or paragraphs) introduces the topic, explains why the topic is important, and states the main idea of the essay in a thesis statement.
Middle	The middle sentences provide details about the topic and focus.	The middle paragraphs support the thesis statement with details and evidence. Each middle paragraph focuses on a different supporting idea and includes its own beginning, middle, and ending parts.
Ending	The last sentence provides a concluding point or summarizes the information that came before it.	The ending paragraph sums up why the topic is important and restates the main idea.

Seeing the Parts in an Essay

Here is an essay by John W. Fitzpatrick, a professor of ecology and an ornithologist (an expert on birds). The side notes explain the essay's three basic parts.

From "How Birds Can Save the World"

By John W. Fitzpatrick

Beginning
The opening introduces the topic and states the main idea (underlined).

Birds motivate us to keep the world healthy for them, and they teach us what we have to accomplish in order to do this. <u>In short, birds can help us save the world.</u>

Middle
1st supporting paragraph: *Birds signal health of the earth.*

Dramatic population recoveries such as those of Wood Ducks attest to the power of scientifically informed ecological restoration. But how can we know how well we are doing without having a reliable measure to gauge our results? The answer, of course, lies in the birds, whose numbers help us detect insidious long-term changes before their cumulative effects are irreversible. Indeed, birds are such accessible indicators of ecological health that many national governments have formal procedures for using birds to assess environmental well-being.

2nd supporting paragraph: *Migratory birds cover the world.*

Sometimes, whole communities of birds speak to us with a single voice about the earth, and about environmental threats. At least a third of the world's bird species are migratory, moving from one place during their breeding season to another place, where their job is to stay alive and replenish their bodies' fat and nutrient reserves.

3rd supporting paragraph: *Birds give a clear picture of nature.*

It is both fun and informative to recognize that each one of these mobile individuals represents a tiny but extraordinarily fit warm-blooded creature that treats the world as a single, interconnected place. Together, these hundreds of millions of migratory birds represent a true "heartbeat" of our planet's natural cycles.

Ending
Restates the main idea

Birds are so ubiquitous, so variable, so easily visible, and so darn charming that they will always be among our most important models and sources of information for how nature works. For hundreds of years, the most influential articles and textbooks in ecology, evolution, and conservation biology have used data gathered from the study of birds to demonstrate principles in the life sciences. As humans work toward the ideal of a stabilized planet, careful study of birds will always be in the forefront of this effort.

From *The Living Bird: 100 Years Of Listening To Nature* by Gerrit Vyn and the Cornell Lab Of Ornithology

Evaluating

When you evaluate a text, you judge its strengths and weaknesses. You may judge a text on a variety of factors, including credibility, relevance, and quality.

Considering Credibility

Credibility refers to the trustworthiness of a text's ideas and information. To evaluate a text's credibility, ask questions about key factors.

- **Authorship:** A piece written by an established writer or subject-matter expert is usually trustworthy. A text authored by an organization for commercial purposes or an author writing for personal gain may not be trustworthy.

  Authorship questions: Is the author an expert on the topic? What is the person's background? Does the author have an established reputation?

- **Source:** In general, scholarly and peer-reviewed books and journals provide more credible information than basic Web resources. Likewise, information in newspaper articles is considered more credible than social media posts.

  Source questions: What person or organization published the text? Is the source scholarly? Is the text published in print or on the Web?

- **Balance:** A balanced text presents information neutrally, meaning it covers an issue fairly and is free of bias. Biased information is one sided—it presents information in a manner that is partial to one point of view.

  Balance questions: Does the text cover different sides of the issue? Are different voices and perspectives represented? Is there any bias? Does the author seem overly emotional about the topic? Does the author ignore or misrepresent a certain viewpoint?

- **Accuracy:** The information should be correct, and sources should be cited within the text. If any facts or details seem suspicious, search for other sources that either confirm or contradict the details.

  Accuracy questions: Is the information true and accurate? Are sources cited within the text? Does any information seem suspicious?

- **Purpose:** Informative texts are typically more credible than those that are meant to entertain or persuade. Texts written to persuade readers to do something or feel a certain way should be read with a particularly critical eye.

  Purpose questions: What is the purpose of the text? To inform? To persuade? To entertain? Is the text trying to sell me something, either a product or an idea?

Checking for Relevance

Relevance refers to how well a text fulfills your reading purpose. If you're reading to learn something new, a relevant text may simply be one that contains accurate and timely information about an interesting topic. If you're reading for a research project, a relevant source will contain accurate information related to your topic of study. Consider these factors when evaluating a text for relevancy.

- **Timeliness:** The information is current and up-to-date.
- **Applicability:** The information fulfills your needs as a reader.
- **Accuracy:** The information is correct, and sources are cited within the text.
- **Completeness:** The coverage of the topic is thorough, meaning information that is needed to understand the topic is not missing.

If the text fails to meet any of these factors, you may need to find a different text with information more relevant to your reading purpose.

SPECIAL NOTE: *Timeliness* alone does not always make a text relevant. An older text may be more relevant than a new one. For example, a three-year-old study on vaccinations may be outdated, while a 50-year-old biography may still contain valid information.

Assessing Quality

Quality refers to the overall excellence of a text's information, readability, and design. To help you assess quality, ask and answer critical questions about those important factors.

- **Information:** A quality text contains accurate, balanced, and complete information.
  Information questions: Is the information accurate, up-to-date, and rich in details? Is the information comprehensive and complete? Is the information free of bias, and does it address all sides of the issue? Does the writing credit sources of information?

- **Readability:** A quality text is easy to read and free of writing errors.
  Readability questions: Do the sentences flow smoothly, making the writing easier to read? Is the writing free of obvious errors in spelling, grammar, punctuation, and usage?

- **Design:** A quality text looks clean and professional and is easy to navigate.
  Design questions: Does the design look clean and professional? Do design features like headings and subheadings make the writing easy to navigate? Do the font (type style) and type size improve the text's readability?

Read the following news release from NASA. Then review how one student evaluated the text for credibility, relevance, and quality.

West Antarctic Glacier Loss Appears Unstoppable

By Carol Rasmussen, *NASA Earth Science News Team*

A new study by researchers at NASA and the University of California, Irvine, finds a rapidly melting section of the West Antarctic Ice Sheet appears to be in an irreversible state of decline, with nothing to stop the glaciers in this area from melting into the sea. [1]

The study presents multiple lines of evidence, incorporating 40 years of observations that indicate the glaciers in the Amundsen Sea sector of West Antarctica "have passed the point of no return," according to glaciologist and lead author Eric Rignot of UC Irvine and NASA's Jet Propulsion Laboratory in Pasadena, California. The new study has been accepted for publication in the journal *Geophysical Research Letters*. [2]

These glaciers already contribute significantly to sea-level rise, releasing almost as much ice into the ocean annually as the entire Greenland Ice Sheet. They contain enough ice to raise the global sea level by four feet (1.2 meters) and are melting faster than most scientists had expected. Rignot said these findings will require an upward revision to current predictions of sea level rise. [3]

"This sector will be a major contributor to sea-level rise in the decades and centuries to come," Rignot said. "A conservative estimate is it could take several centuries for all of the ice to flow into the sea." [4]

Three major lines of evidence point to the glaciers' eventual demise: the changes in their flow speeds, how much of each glacier floats on seawater, and the slope of the terrain they are flowing over and its depth below sea level. In a paper in April, Rignot's research group discussed the steadily increasing flow speeds of these glaciers over the past 40 years. This new study examines the other two lines of evidence. [5]

The glaciers flow out from land to the ocean, with their leading edges afloat on the seawater. The point on a glacier where it first loses contact with land is called the grounding line. Nearly all glacier melt occurs on the underside of the glacier beyond the grounding line, on the section floating on seawater. [6]

Just as a grounded boat can float again on shallow water if it is made lighter, a glacier can float over an area where it used to be grounded if it becomes lighter, which it does by melting or by the thinning effects of the glacier stretching out. The Antarctic glaciers studied by Rignot's group have thinned so much they are now floating above places where they used to sit solidly on land, which means their grounding lines are retreating inland. [7]   Courtesy of NASA/JPL-Caltech

Consider Credibility: Is the reading credible? What factors prove its credibility or lack thereof?

The text is written by Carol Rasmussen, a writer for NASA. NASA is a government agency with a respected reputation in the science community. The source is a news release from the NASA website. It contains information about a study that was accepted for publication in a peer-reviewed journal, so the study itself must be credible. However, since the news release was written by a NASA employee on behalf of a NASA study, some bias may occur in the writing. Likewise, not many alternative perspectives are presented in the release. In general, the information seems accurate and well supported by sources and expert testimony. Overall, I find the reading credible, but I will need to do additional research to find alternative perspectives about the study.

Checking for Relevance: Is the reading timely, accurate, applicable, and complete?

The article displays all of the characteristics of relevancy. It describes a recent study of glaciers. It provides accurate and detailed information that relates to my research project on rising sea levels. The article does not describe the complete details of the study, but it answers all of my basic questions about it.

Assessing for Quality: Does the reading contain quality information, readability, and design?

This is a quality text. The information is accurate, complete, and up-to-date. It contains a lot of details and credits the sources of information. Though some bias may have crept into the release, the information seems well supported with accurate details. The article is easy to read, and the writing is free of errors. Lastly, the design looks clean and professional, though additional headings could make it easier to navigate. Overall, the source's credibility, relevance, and quality make the information appropriate to cite in my research paper.

oksix, 2017 / Used under license from Shutterstock.com

3.3 Analyzing Visuals

Visuals form their own special language, just like words. Indeed, images often carry more meaning than words can alone. But to understand the language of visuals, you need to "read" them closely. Critical viewing skills are especially important in today's highly visual and screen-based culture.

Many of your academic texts—both in print and online—will include visual information in the form of charts, graphs, figures, illustrations, maps, diagrams, photographs, and drawings. Knowing how to read these types of visuals and how to create visuals of your own will help you read and write successfully in college.

Visuals such as photographs are compelling storytelling devices, because often they convey emotion, actions, and events better than words can. Sometimes visuals accompany a reading. Other times they convey a story all by themselves. To derive meaning from visuals, follow the steps in the critical viewing process.

Critical Viewing Process

1. **Scan** the whole visual. What catches your eye? This is the focal point of a photo and often the most important part. What else catches your attention? How does it make you feel?

2. **Analyze** the visual by dividing it into smaller sections and studying each section closely. Small clues may hint at a larger meaning.

3. **Ask** critical questions about the visual.
   - **Creator:** Who created the visual? Why did the person create it?
   - **Message:** What does the visual show? What is the subject?
   - **Medium:** Where did the visual appear? When did it first appear there?
   - **Viewer:** Who was supposed to see this visual? Why am I viewing it?
   - **Context:** What is this visual meant to do? How is it supposed to make viewers feel? Why does it appear in this specific medium? How does it relate to the surrounding text?

4. **Associate** the visual to its title, caption, or surrounding text. Also consider associations between the visual and your own knowledge and experiences. Ask, what do I know about the subject of the photo? What memories does it evoke? In what ways can I relate to the image?

5. **Interpret** what the visual means. Use what you learned in steps 1–4 to help you come to a decision. Most visuals are open to multiple interpretations.

Review the following analysis, which applies the critical-viewing process to Figure 3.3.

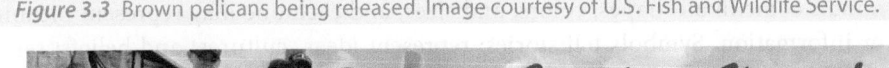

Figure 3.3 Brown pelicans being released. Image courtesy of U.S. Fish and Wildlife Service.

By U.S. Fish and Wildlife Service [Public domain], via Wikimedia Commons

1. **Scan.** The image focuses on three large brown pelicans on a pier. One pelican has its wings spread, as if it's ready to fly away. The other two look out to the water. There are people standing on the pier watching the pelicans. One person is holding a cage. The door of the cage is open, which might mean the pelicans were in it earlier. The right side of the picture is dominated by gray clouds reflecting off placid water.

2. **Analyze.** One pelican has red tags wrapped around its legs, which indicates that the birds have been cared for by human handlers. The people look happy and proud. The woman holding the cage and two of her fellow observers are wearing uniforms that a park ranger might wear. The other observers are wearing military-like garb, as if they work for the Coast Guard.

3. **Ask.**
   - **Creator:** U.S. Fish and Wildlife Service, as indicated by the caption
   - **Message:** The subjects are three pelicans on a pier preparing to fly away, while a group of people observes them.
   - **Medium:** *Carolina Visitor's* magazine
   - **Viewer:** Readers of the magazine, most likely tourists of North or South Carolina
   - **Context:** The purpose might be to show a wildlife refuge program.

4. **Associate.** The caption reads "Brown pelicans being released." This confirms my inferences; however, the caption doesn't provide many details.

5. **Interpret.** The image was created presumably by the U.S. Fish and Wildlife Service. The pride on the faces of the people indicate that this is a fulfilling moment. Based on its placement in a visitor's magazine, the photo may also be meant to show off the good environmental work being done in North or South Carolina.

Understanding Symbols

Symbols come in all shapes, colors, and sizes, and each one may represent meaningful ideas or information. Symbols tell stories; represent ideas, cultures, and beliefs; sell ideas and products; and give directions and commands. Critically viewing symbols can lead to surprising insights. You can discover a symbol's meaning by closely viewing its parts and making personal associations to it. To do so, consider the symbol's denotative and connotative meanings.

Denotative Meaning

Denotative meaning is a symbol's literal meaning. This meaning is taken from the symbol's shapes, colors, and images. For example, the "no smoking" symbol in **Figure 3.4** has a very clear denotative meaning. A large red circle with a line crossing through a smoldering, black cigarette warns that smoking is not permitted.

Find denotative meanings by scanning the symbol and analyzing its individual parts.

To view symbols for denotative meaning, ask:

- What does the symbol tell me to do?
- What features catch my eye?
- What shapes, colors, and images are included?

Connotative Meaning

Connotative meaning is much more subjective. It comes from the personal feelings, connections, and associations you make with the symbol. Your interpretations are greatly influenced by your knowledge and life experiences. Not surprisingly, someone else may view a symbol in a much different regard than you do. For example, a non-smoker might feel relief seeing a "no smoking" symbol on a patio outside a restaurant. The black cigarette may solidify the belief that smoking is dangerous and is associated with lung cancer. A smoker might interpret it differently.

Figure 3.4 No Smoking Symbol

Leigh Prather, 2017; yukipon, 2017 / Used under license from Shutterstock.com

To view symbols for connotative meaning, ask:

- How does the symbol make me feel?
- What do I already know about the symbol?
- What ideas do I associate with it?
- How might somebody with a different background, culture, or age view the symbol?

Review the sample analysis of Figure 3.5.

Denotative Meaning: What meaning can I interpret from the symbol's physical features?

Figure 3.5 Olympic Rings

The Olympic symbol (Figure 3.5) features five interlocking rings, representing the five continents, or regions, of the world. They are interlocked to show unity. The rings' individual colors—blue, yellow, black, green, and red—represent the colors found on all national flags.

Connotative Meaning: What feelings, associations, or connections does the symbol bring to mind?

I associate the symbols with great athletic feats. It also brings to mind mixed feelings about the unity of the world. On one hand, it makes me think about those glamorous opening and closing ceremonies, where everyone celebrates each other's cultures and applauds each other's flags. On the other hand, the Olympic rings make me disappointed that the goodwill doesn't endure in everyday life. The rings also have the negative connotation associated with some of the tragedies of the Olympics, specifically the events in Munich when 11 Israeli athletes were taken hostage by terrorists. The symbol makes me feel hopeful about the world, but sometimes it feels like false hope.

Practice 3.3 The statements below are responses to Figure 3.6. Fill in the blank after the statement with a *D* if it is a denotative response and a *C* if the response is connotative.

1. I associate the recycling symbol with personal responsibility. _____

2. The symbol also reminds me about the environment. _____

3. The three-arrow symbol indicates that an object is capable of being recycled. _____

4. But the arrows do not indicate that the object will be accepted at all recycling systems. _____

5. The three connecting arrows graphically represent or show "recycling." _____

6. I also can't help but think about all the waste that consumers create. _____

7. Sometimes a percentage is given in the middle of the symbol to indicate how much of the object is made from recycled material. _____

8. If only we could recycle everything. _____

Figure 3.6 Recycling Symbol

Reading Graphics

Graphics are visual representations of data. They can add value to a text because they communicate statistical trends and visual information better than words can. To understand and evaluate a graphic, you need to study its parts by following these steps.

- **Scan the graphic.** Consider it as a whole to get an overall idea about its message. Note its type (bar graph, pie graph, diagram, line graph, map, or illustration), its topic, labels, features, and level of detail.

- **Study the specific parts.** Start with the main heading or title. Next, note any additional labels or guides (such as the horizontal and vertical guides on a bar graph). Then focus on the actual information displayed in the graphic.

- **Evaluate the graphic.** Does it address an important topic? What is its purpose (to make a comparison, to show a change)? What is the source of the information? Is the graphic out of date or biased in any way?

- **Reflect on its effectiveness.** Explain in your own words the main message of the graphic. Then consider its effectiveness, how it relates to the surrounding text, and how it matches up to your previous knowledge of the topic.

Scan the bar graph in Figure 3.7. Then read the discussion to learn how all of the parts work together.

- **Study:** This bar graph compares the labor force in 2001 to the labor force in 2016 for five specific age groups. The heading identifies the subject or topic of the graphic. The horizontal line identifies the different age groups, and the vertical line identifies the percentage of the labor force for each group. The key in the upper right-hand corner of the graphic explains the color-coded bars.

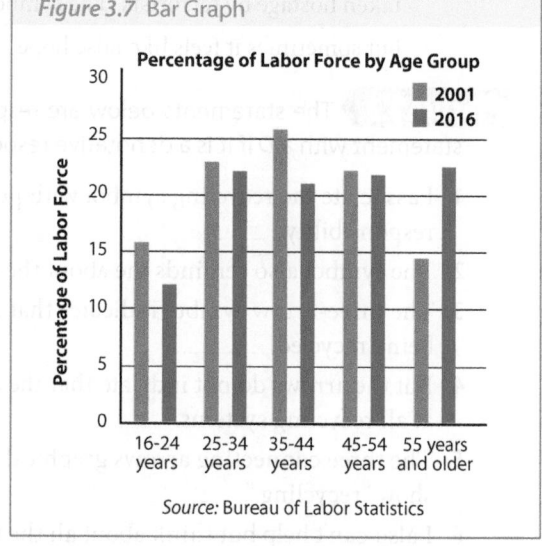

Figure 3.7 Bar Graph

Percentage of Labor Force by Age Group

Source: Bureau of Labor Statistics

- **Question:** The graphic addresses a relevant topic—labor force by age group. Its purpose is to show the changes in the ages of the labor force through time. The data comes from the Bureau of Labor Statistics. The information is not completely up-to-date since it ends in 2016.

- **Reflect:** The graphic reads quite clearly—and many interesting comparisons can be made. The most noteworthy comparison is that many more people over the age of 55 remained in the workforce in 2016 as compared to 2001.

Practice 3.4 Read the graphic in Figure 3.8 and answer the analysis questions about it.

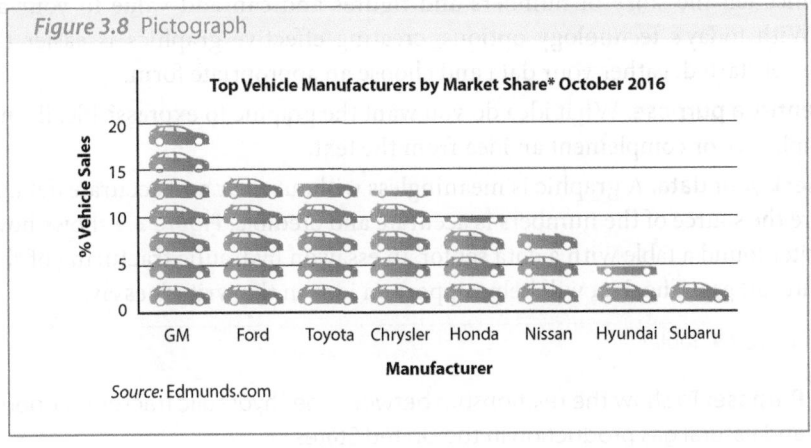

Figure 3.8 Pictograph

Top Vehicle Manufacturers by Market Share* October 2016

Source: Edmunds.com

1. Figure 3.8 is called a pictograph rather than a bar graph. What makes it a pictograph?
   a. The use of color.
   b. The *x* and *y* axes are different.
   c. The use of pictures in place of bars.

2. What is the topic of Figure 3.8?
   a. Top Hatchback Manufactures by Market Share October 2016
   b. Top Vehicle Manufactures by Market Share October 2016
   c. Top Vehicle Manufactures by Market Share October 2015

3. What information is provided on the vertical line?
   a. Percentage of Vehicle Sales
   b. Manufacturers
   c. Gas Mileage

4. Which manufacturer had the top market share of vehicle sales in October 2016?
   a. Honda
   b. Ford
   c. GM

5. What is the purpose of the graphic?
   a. To inform
   b. To persuade
   c. To entertain

Using Graphics in Writing

Graphics tell the story of numbers and figures and can add value to your academic writing. With today's technology options, creating effective graphics is easier than ever before. To get started, gather your data and choose an appropriate form.

- **Identify a purpose.** What idea do you want the graphic to express? Ideally, it should emphasize or complement an idea from the text.

- **Check your data.** A graphic is meaningless without clear and accurate data. Make sure the source of the numbers is accurate and credible. Figure 3.9 shows how one writer found a table with a data set for an essay on hydraulic fracturing of shale (natural) gas. The data will help support an idea in the writer's essay.

Figure 3.9 Table

Purpose: To show the relationship between the "hydraulic fracturing boom" and natural gas production in the United States

Data: The data set comes from the U.S. Energy Information Administration.

U.S. Natural Gas Production (billion cubic feet)

Year	Total Natural Gas	Shale Gas
2009	21,647	3,110
2010	22,381	5,336
2011	24,036	7,994
2012	25,283	10,371
2013	25,562	11,415
2014	27,497	13,447
2015	28,752	15,213

- **Understand your options.** Different types of graphics serve different purposes.

Line graphs show changes in amounts over time. (See Figure 3.10.) A scatter plot serves a similar purpose, but it doesn't connect its data points with a line, like a line graph does.

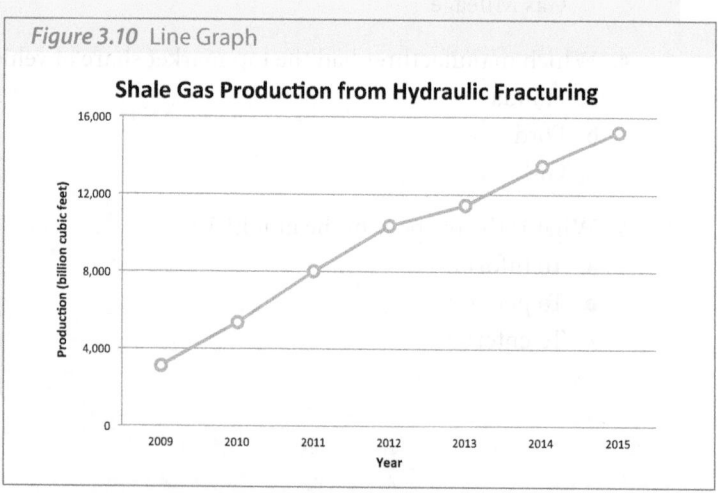

Figure 3.10 Line Graph

Shale Gas Production from Hydraulic Fracturing

Bar graphs show comparisons between amounts of something or the number of times something occurs (see Figure 3.11).

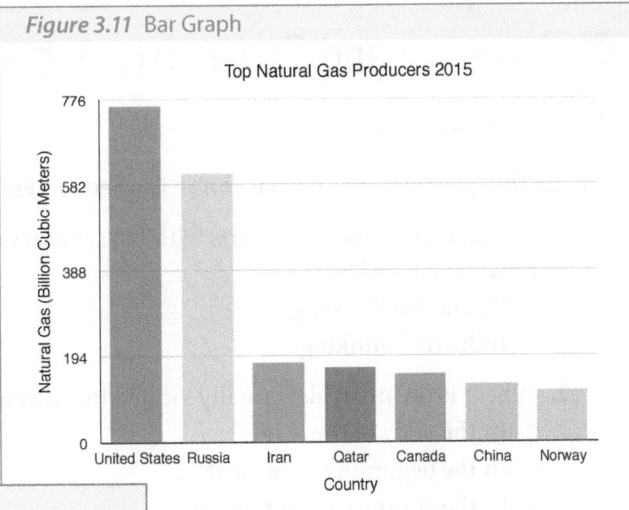

Figure 3.11 Bar Graph

Top Natural Gas Producers 2015

Pie charts show how something is divided up. The whole pie represents the whole sample, while the wedges represent the different parts (see Figure 3.12).

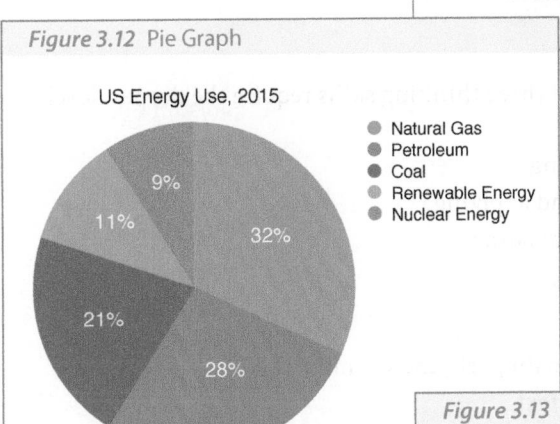

Figure 3.12 Pie Graph

US Energy Use, 2015

- Natural Gas
- Petroleum
- Coal
- Renewable Energy
- Nuclear Energy

Information maps use colors and symbols to show relationships between geographic data (see Figure 3.13).

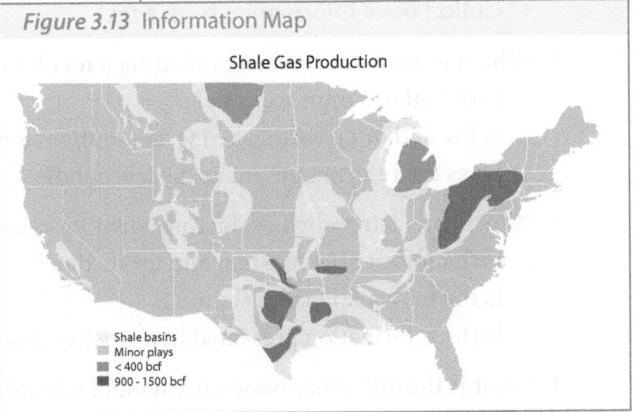

Figure 3.13 Information Map

Shale Gas Production

Shale basins
Minor plays
< 400 bcf
900 - 1500 bcf

- **Check your focus.** Your graphic should focus on one main idea.
- **Create a title and label the axes.** The title should summarize what the graphic shows. Label the *x* and *y* axes and any important data points. If necessary, add a separate legend to identify icon sets, colors, or data bars (see Figure 3.13).
- **Choose reader-friendly design features**, including colors, type size and font, and graphics. Use white space wisely and avoid clutter.

☑ Review and Enrichment

Chapter Review Quiz

Answer the questions about what you've learned in this chapter.

1. Which type of thinking starts with facts, observations, or details that lead to a general conclusion?
   a. Deductive thinking
   b. Inductive thinking

2. Where is the main idea usually located in a deductive text?
   a. In the body of the text
   b. In the beginning of the text
   c. In the closing part of the text

3. According to Benjamin Bloom, what three thinking skills require the deepest levels of thinking?
   a. Analyzing, evaluating, and creating
   b. Remembering, understanding, and applying
   c. Understanding, applying, and evaluating

4. What does it mean to analyze a text?
   a. To judge the value of a text
   b. To break down a subject into its main parts and examine them
   c. Collect basic information from a text

5. Which is *not* a factor when evaluating a text for credibility or trustworthiness?
   a. Is the information accurate?
   b. Is the author an established writer and/or subject-matter expert?
   c. Does the information make me feel good?

6. Which is a factor when evaluating a text for relevancy or usefulness?
   a. Is the information current and up-to-date?
   b. Is the information entertaining?
   c. Is the information presented in a creative design?

7. What is the difference between a symbol's denotative and connotative meaning?
   a. Denotative meaning is literal; connotative meaning is subjective or personal.
   b. Denotative meaning is temporary; connotative meaning is permanent.
   c. Denotative meaning is subjective; connotative meaning is literal.

8. Which type of graphic shows changes in amounts over time?
   a. Pie chart
   b. Information map
   c. Line graph

Reading for Enrichment

You will be reading a selection entitled "MyPlate" from *Nutrition Now*, a college textbook on health and wellness. MyPlate refers to the United States Department of Agriculture's recommendations for healthy eating, which are presented online for general use. The selection identifies the key features of this governmental website. Be sure to follow the steps in the reading process to help you gain a full understanding of the text. (See Section 2.1.)

About the Author

Judith E. Brown is a Professor Emerita of Nutrition at the School of Public Health and the Department of Obstetrics and Gynecology at the University of Minnesota. Dr. Brown is a registered dietician and the author of *Everywoman's Guide to Nutrition*, *Nutrition for Your Pregnancy*, and *What to Eat Before, During, and After Pregnancy*.

Prereading

The idea "you are what you eat" has been around a long time. It was, in fact, used as early as the 1820s. The idea suggests that to be fit and healthy you should eat fresh, healthy food. To help you gauge your own eating habits, consider these questions.

- Do you try to make healthy food choices?
- How does your lifestyle reflect your eating habits?
- Is there one food type that you should remove from your diet?
- Is there one food type that you should add to your diet?

Before you read, use the **STRAP** strategy to identify the main parts of the text. Also, consider listing a few questions that you hope the reading will answer.

Subject:	What specific topic does the reading address?
Type:	What form (*essay, narrative, textbook selection*) does the reading take?
Role:	What position (*student, professor, journalist*) does the writer assume?
Audience:	Who is the intended audience?
Purpose:	What is the general goal of the reading (*to inform, to persuade, to share*)?

Reading and Rereading

As you read, be sure to (1) check again the author's purpose and audience, (2) identify the main idea or thesis of the text, and (3) note the evidence that explains or supports the main idea. Consider annotating the text and/or taking notes as you read. Follow these annotating tips:

The Reading Process

Prereading — Rereading

Reading — Reflecting

- Underline, bracket, or highlight important information. Comment on these ideas in the margin.
- Write questions in the margin.

- Circle words that you are unsure of. Then define them.

Reread as needed to examine more closely important ideas and to make sure you understand the key points in the text.

MyPlate

Food group guides from the USDA have [1] been available in the United States since 1916. Known by such names as the Basic Four Food Groups, and the Food Guide Pyramid, these guides are **periodically** updated to reflect advances in knowledge about foods, diets, and health. The latest revision of USDA's food guidance materials is called MyPlate and is represented by the MyPlate logo. **Figure 3.14** shows this logo and a plate of foods set up to match its messages.

Figure 3.14 MyPlate logo

ChooseMyPlate.gov/USDA

The MyPlate logo is intended to give consumers a visual reminder of the types [2] and **proportions** of food that make up healthy meals. The logo shows a plate with four sections in different colors representing the proportion of vegetables, fruits, grains, and protein foods that should be on your plate. Next to the plate is a circle that represents a dairy product such as low-fat milk or other low-fat dairy product. The types of foods included on the plate are basic and nutrient dense.

ChooseMyPlate.gov Healthy Eating Messages

ChooseMyPlate.gov supports the healthy [3] eating messages in the Dietary Guidelines by offering the following key pieces of advice:

- Make at least half your plate fruits and vegetables.
- Enjoy your food but eat less.
- Make half your grains whole grains.
- Eat fewer foods that are high in saturated fat, added sugar, and sodium.
- Avoid oversized portions.

Figure 3.15 Sample Meal

Judith Brown, 2011

- Switch to fat-free or low-fat milk.
- Drink water instead of sugary drinks.
- Compare sodium in foods like soup, bread, and frozen meals and choose the foods with lower numbers.

The importance of consuming enough calories for growth and health while not eating extra calories and gaining weight is also stressed. Regular physical activity (60 minutes per day for children and adolescents and 2.5 hours or more per week of moderate-intensity activity for adults weekly) is stressed because it contributes to weight control and provides many other health benefits.

Healthy U.S.-Style Dietary Pattern

Portion Sizes and Food Measure Equivalents Unlike previous food group guides, the current version does not recommend serving sizes or numbers of servings individuals in general should consume from the food groups. This information is provided if requested using a personalized interactive tool on menu planning such as the Daily Food Plan. The personalized information generated shows amounts of each food group to consume and food portion sizes that correspond to that amount.

Information on amounts of basic foods recommended for different levels of calorie need in the ChooseMyPlate materials are based on cup- and ounce equivalents. Figure 3.16 provides a listing of cup and ounce equivalents for the food groups. You can get additional examples of serving size equivalents by highlighting a food group shown on the Daily Food Plan output and clicking on "What counts as an ounce?" or "What counts as a cup?"

Figure 3.16 How much food counts as a cup or an ounce?

Vegetables and Fruits: 1 cup equivalent (c-eq)	=	1 cup raw or cooked vegetables or fruit, 1 cup vegetable or fruit juice, or 2 cups leafy salad greens, ½ cup dried vegetable or fruit
Dairy: 1 cup equivalent (c-eq)	=	1 cup milk, yogurt, or fortified soy milk, or 1½ ounces natural or 2 ounces processed cheese
Grains: 1 ounce equivalent (oz-eq)	=	1 slice of bread, ½ cup cooked rice, cereal, or pasta; or 1 ounce ready-to-eat cereal (about 1 cup flaked cereal)
Protein: 1 ounce equivalent (oz-eq)	=	1 ounce lean meat, poultry, or seafood; 1 egg; 1 Tbsp peanut butter; ½ ounce nuts or seeds; ¼ cup cooked dried beans or peas

Sample Menus What does an eating pattern based on USDA's food group guidelines look like? Seven days of menus based on a 2,000-calorie diet that meet

Figure 3.17 Sample menus for a 2,000 calorie food pattern.

Sample Menus for a 2000 Calorie Food Pattern

DAY 1

BREAKFAST
Creamy oatmeal (cooked in milk):
- ½ cup uncooked oatmeal
- 1 cup fat-free milk
- 2 Tbsp raisins
- 2 tsp brown sugar
Beverage: 1 cup orange juice

LUNCH
Taco salad:
- 2 ounces tortilla chips
- 2 ounces cooked ground turkey
- 2 tsp corn/canola oil (to cook turkey)
- ¼ cup kidney beans*
- ½ ounce low-fat cheddar cheese
- ½ cup chopped lettuce
- ½ cup avocado
- 1 tsp lime juice (on avocado)
- 2 Tbsp salsa
Beverage:
1 cup water, coffee, or tea**

DINNER
Spinach lasagna roll-ups:
- 1 cup lasagna noodles(2 oz dry)
- ½ cup cooked spinach
- ½ cup ricotta cheese
- 1 ounce part-skim mozzarella cheese
- ½ cup tomato sauce*
1 ounce whole wheat roll
- 1 tsp tub margarine
Beverage: 1 cup fat-free milk

SNACKS
2 Tbsp raisins
1 ounce unsalted almonds

DAY 2

BREAKFAST
Breakfast burrito:
- 1 flour tortilla (8" diameter)
- 1 scrambled egg
- ⅓ cup black beans*
- 2 Tbsp salsa
½ large grapefruit
Beverage:
1 cup water, coffee, or tea**

LUNCH
Roast beef sandwich:
- 1 small whole grain hoagie bun
- 2 ounces lean roast beef
- 1 slice part-skim mozzarella cheese
- 2 slices tomato
- ¼ cup mushrooms
- 1 tsp corn/canola oil (to cook mushrooms)
- 1 tsp mustard
Baked potato wedges:
- 1 cup potato wedges
- 1 tsp corn/canola oil (to cook potato)
- 1 Tbsp ketchup
Beverage: 1 cup fat-free milk

DINNER
Baked salmon on beet greens:
- 4 ounce salmon filet
- 1 tsp olive oil
- 2 tsp lemon juice
- ⅓ cup cooked beet greens (sauteed in 2 tsp corn/canola oil)
Quinoa with almonds:
- ½ cup quinoa
- ½ ounce slivered almonds
Beverage: 1 cup fat-free milk

SNACKS
1 cup cantaloupe balls

DAY 3

BREAKFAST
Cold cereal:
- 1 cup ready-to-eat oat cereal
- 1 medium banana
- ½ cup fat-free milk
1 slice whole wheat toast
- 1 tsp tub margarine
Beverage: 1 cup prune juice

LUNCH
Tuna salad sandwich:
- 2 slices rye bread
- 2 ounces tuna
- 1 Tbsp mayonnaise
- 1 Tbsp chopped celery
- ½ cup shredded lettuce
1 medium peach
Beverage: 1 cup fat-free milk

DINNER
Roasted chicken:
- 3 ounces cooked chicken breast
1 large sweet potato, roasted
½ cup succotash (limas & corn)
- 1 tsp tub margarine
1 ounce whole wheat roll
- 1 tsp tub margarine
Beverage:
1 cup water, coffee, or tea**

SNACKS
¼ cup dried apricots
1 cup flavored yogurt (chocolate)

ChooseMyPlate.gov/USDA

USDA's food group recommendations and nutrient needs are available from the "Sample Menus and Recipes" link on the ChooseMyPlate.gov homepage. Three days of the menus are shown in **Figure 3.17**. The menus are intended to give consumers specific and general ideas about the types of foods to include in meals on a daily basis.

USDA's Interactive Diet Planning Tools   Do you want to lose weight? Want to learn about healthful foods for your preschooler or when you are pregnant? Do you need to look up information on the calorie value of different foods or keep track of your food intake? You can access this information and more from the ChooseMyPlate.gov site. To help lose weight, for example, access the Daily Food Plan interactive tool. This feature can be used to identify the amount of food from each group you should consume daily based on your age, sex, weight, height, and physical activity level. An allowance for teaspoons of oil, and an "empty calorie" allowance for extra fats and sugars are included in the Daily Food Plan results

ChooseMyPlate's SuperTracker can help you plan, analyze, and track your diet [9] and physical activity. Access SuperTracker by searching the term SuperTracker My Reports and you will see six interactive tools for diet, weight management, meal planning, and physical activity planning, assessment, and analysis.

- **Food-A-Pedia** enables you to identify and compare the nutrient content of foods.

- **Physical Activity Tracker** can be used to compare your level of physical activity to the Physical Activity Guidelines for Americans. It can also be used to plan your activities and evaluate progress in meeting your physical activity goals.

- **My Weight Manager** provides tips for weight loss and helps you track progress in meeting weight-loss goals.

- **My Top 5 Goals** presents 19 options for goals related to weight management, physical activity, calorie intake, food group intake, and nutrient intake. You can select and track progress on meeting up to five of these goals. For example, you can set a weight goal and receive a calorie intake plan that will help you reach the goal. Graphs on changes in weight over time and tips for weight loss can be generated by this tool.

- **My Reports** can be used to track changes in food group, calorie, and nutrient intake; and changes in physical activity level. Over 40 different reports can be generated. The reports automatically compare your results to the appropriate recommendations.

Several other useful planning tools are also accessible from the [10] ChooseMyPlate home page:

- **Healthy Eating on a Budget** features tips for saving money on food purchases and preparing healthy low-cost meals, and provides a two-week budget-friendly menu plan with recipes and a grocery-list builder.

- **MyPlate Kids' Place** offers fun educational materials for educators and parents. At this site you will find healthy eating-related games, activity sheets, videos, and songs that can be used as part of a curriculum or by parents.

- **What's Cooking?** An interactive tool that can help with healthy meal planning, cooking, and grocery shopping, this site features a searchable database of healthy recipes, options to save recipes to a cookbook, print recipe cards, and share recipes via social media.

Limitations of MyPlate Materials available from MyPlate are almost entirely   11
made available on the Internet, making the information inaccessible to people
who do not use computers or have access to the Internet. MyPlate does not provide
specific recommendations for infants, individuals on **therapeutic** diets, or vegans.

Menus suggested by MyPlate interactive tools may not correspond to   12
individual food preferences and contain relatively few ethnic foods. As with past
food guides, planning and evaluating how mixed dishes (such as stews, soups,
salads, and various types of pizza) fit into food groups can still be **perplexing**.

From Brown, Judith. *Nutrition Now*, 8th Edition. Copyright 2017. Cengage Learning.

---

periodically
regularly

proportions
a part or number in comparison to the whole

correspond
have a close similarity or match

curriculum
course of study

therapeutic
concerned with the treatment of disease

Reflecting

Answer the comprehension and vocabulary questions about the reading.

1. What is the main idea of this selection?
   a. Explanation of the USGA's latest guide for exercise and fitness
   b. Explanation of the USGA's latest food guidance resources
   c. Explanation of nutrition as a career choice

2. Which one of the following statements is an important supporting detail?
   a. The MyPlate website can help you plan, analyze, and track your diet.
   b. The MyPlate website provides dietary recommendations for ethnic foods.
   c. The MyPlate website explains how much soda you can drink per week.

3. Which basic thinking pattern is used to communicate the ideas in this text?
   a. Deductive thinking
   b. Inductive thinking

4. What factors support the credibility of the reading?
   a. The author is a professor of nutrition.

b. The text includes a lot graphics.

c. The reading comes from a college textbook on health and wellness.

d. Both *a* and *c*.

5. Which choice best describes the presentation of the text?

a. A personal account of diet and fitness

b. An informative text combined with visuals

c. A persuasive text encouraging a change

6. Which graphic in the selection is a pie chart?

a. Figure 3.14

b. Figure 3.16

c. Figure 3.17

7. Study the word parts of the word *equivalent* and how it is used in the reading. Then choose the most accurate definition of the word.
Equivalent (paragraph 6)   Equi + vale + (e)nt
(*Hint:* "Equi" is the root of *equal* and "vale" is the root of *evaluate*.)

a. Having different worth or value

b. Having the same worth or value

c. Having the same distance between

8. Study how the word *perplexing* is used in the reading, and then choose the most accurate definition of the word.
Perplexing (paragraph 12)

a. Puzzling

b. Easy to understand

c. Possible

Summarizing

Write a summary paragraph of the selection using the guidelines in Section 2.4 for help. Remember to use your own words and to focus only on the key ideas.

Critical Thinking

- Did you find the reading credible? Why or why not?
- How would you evaluate the helpfulness of the text? (Consider its relevance and quality.)
- Do you think the text fulfills its purpose?
- What surprised you about the information?
- How could you apply the information to your own life?
- Overall, how important are the graphics in the text?

Writing for Enrichment

Prewriting

Choose one of the following writing ideas, or decide upon an idea of your own related to the reading.

1. Explore in a personal journal or blog your attitude about food choices, diets, and/or fitness.

2. Review the MyPlate website (www.choosemyplate.gov), and report on what you discovered.

3. Compare and contrast your eating habits with those of a friend, family member, or acquaintance.

4. Take a stand on fast food. Write an essay in which you argue for or against a particular fast food chain or food type at one particular chain.

5. Analyze your food consumption for a week. Report on your findings in a summary paragraph.

The Writing Process

Prewrite → Revise → Publish

Write — Edit

When planning . . .
- Research your topic as needed, taking notes as you go along.
- Identify a main idea about the topic to emphasize.
- Review your notes for details to support your main idea.
- Decide on an order to present these details.

When writing . . .
- Include a beginning, middle, and ending in your writing.
- Present your main idea in the beginning part.
- Support the main idea in the middle part.
- Close your writing with final thoughts about your topic.

When revising and editing . . .
- Carefully review your first draft.
- Ask at least one peer to review your writing as well.
- Improve the content as needed.
- Then edit your revised writing for style and correctness.

Part 2:

Reading and Writing Essays

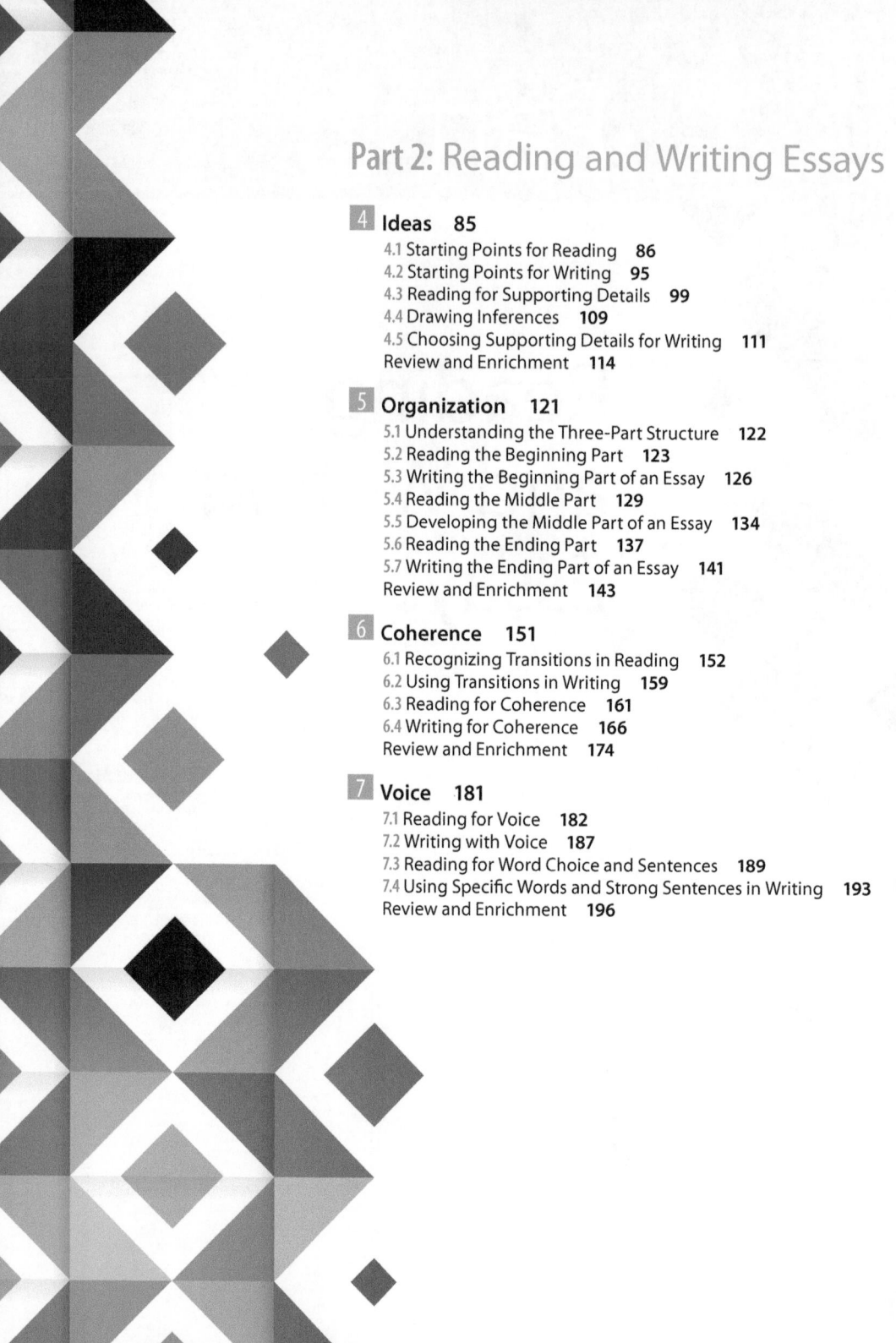

Part 2: Reading and Writing Essays

Falconia, 2017 / Used under license from Shutterstock.com

Chapter 4

Ideas

Ideas are the key element behind every selection that you read and write. That is, a text needs a topic, a main idea that puts the topic into focus, and details that support the main idea. Other elements such as organization, voice, and word choice depend on the ideas. A text without ideas would be like a recipe without any ingredients or a building plan without any building materials—there would be nothing to work with.

In this chapter, you will study the development of ideas in academic reading and writing. First, you will learn about identifying topics and main ideas in reading selections and for your own writing. Then you will learn about reading for supporting details and using different types of details in your writing.

Chapter Outline

- Starting Points for Reading
- Starting Points for Writing
- Reading for Supporting Details
- Drawing Inferences
- Choosing Supporting Details in Writing

4.1 Starting Points for Reading

All pieces of writing need to be about something, and that something is called the **topic**. A topic can be a person *(Michelle Obama)*, a place *(the Lorraine Motel)*, an object *(vinyl records)*, an idea *(fake news)*, or an animal *(coyotes)*. Recognizing the topic is the important first step when carrying out a reading assignment. Simply put, you need to know the topic to know what the text is about.

Identifying the Topic

In almost all texts, the topic is identified in the title, in the first few sentences, or in the first few paragraphs. A writer would have to have a very good reason not to make the topic clearly identifiable early on in a text. These examples show common placements of the topic.

Topic Stated in a Heading and First Sentence:

Harm

For most crimes to occur, some harm must have been done to a person or to a property. A certain number of crimes are actually categorized depending on the harm done to the victim, regardless of the intent behind the criminal act. Take two offenses, both of which involve one person hitting another in the back of the head with a tire iron. In the first instance, the victim dies, and the offender is charged with murder. In the second, the victim is only knocked unconscious, and the offender is charged with battery. Because the harm in the second instance was less severe, so was the crime with which the offender was charged.

From Gaines/Miller, *Cengage Advantage Books: Criminal Justice in Action,* 6E. © 2011 Cengage Learning.

Topic Stated in the First Sentence:

Every language has a logical structure. When people encounter an unfamiliar language for the first time, they are confused and disoriented, but after becoming familiar with the language, they eventually discover its rules and how the various parts are interrelated. All languages have rules and principles governing what sounds are to be used and how those sounds are to be combined to convey meaning. . . .

From Ferraro/Andreatta, *Cultural Anthropology,* 9E. © 2012 Cengage Learning.

Topic Stated at the End of the First Paragraph in an Essay:

Imagine a room containing a large group of people all working hard toward the same goal. Each person knows their job, does it carefully, and cooperates with other group members. Together, they function efficiently and smoothly—like a well-oiled machine. Then one worker stops his work and steps into someone else's workstation, using those materials to make little reproductions of himself. Soon the reproductions spill into other workstations, get in the way, and continue to multiply. A human body is like this room, and the body's cells are like these workers. If the body is healthy, each cell has a necessary job and does it correctly. When a cell begins to function abnormally, it can initiate a process that results in cancer.

Delayed Identification of a Topic:

In two days Kamal would have been four years old, but his wasted body now lies under a pile of rocks behind his family's hut.

Why did Kamal die? The too-easy answer is malnutrition. A lack of vitamins and protein opened him to intestinal infection and diarrhea. He could have been saved with a simple solution of boiled water, salts, and sugar, which the UNICEF distributes in a free kit called "oral rehydration therapy" (ORT). But Kamal's mother, forced to work 18-hour days at home and in the fields, had missed the rural health-care worker's demonstration in the village.

Why was Kamal malnourished in the first place? He and his six brothers and sisters had known hunger all their lives. His father and mother scraped at five dry acres of government land, earning no more than $500.00 (U.S.) even in a good year. For the past seven years, an unrelenting drought had dried up the wells and withered the crops.

Around the world, according to Roy Prosterman (*The Hunger Project Papers*), 18 children like Kamal die of hunger every 60 seconds. In the two minutes it may have taken you to read these words, another 36 children died. Of all of today's global problems, none can be more tragic than childhood deaths by starvation and disease.

Practice 4.1 ▶ Underline the topic in the following texts.

1.   Ethnicity can be a powerful draw in terms of customer loyalty and community development. Restaurants identified as purveyors of ethnic foods may appeal to members of a cuisine's ethnic group as well as to others who are interested in enjoying foods from different cultures. Ethnically based food service offers comfort and familiarity by providing foods that are considered to be part of a culture.

From Chon/Maier, *Welcome to Hospitality,* 3E. © 2010 Cengage Learning.

2.   We Have Been Here Before

Columbus, an Italian, arrived in the New World with a crew of more than 100 composed of Spaniards, Portuguese, some Jews who had been expelled from Spain, some convicts, and an Arab brought along to translate anticipated conversations with Chinese and Japanese—remember where Columbus thought he was going. Now, about this new American thing, "diversity."

Concerning which, Michael Barone says, "We have been here before." As when Benjamin Franklin, a worrywart, doubted that the Germans who were 40 percent of Pennsylvanians could be assimilated [made similar]. It is generally wise to believe Barone, the author every two years of "The Almanac of American Politics" and now of a new book, *The New Americans: How the Melting Pot Can Work Again.* To those who say that traditionally white-bread America has suddenly become multigrain, Barone says: Fiddlesticks.

America, he says, has always been multigrain. . . .

From "We Have Been Here Before" by George Will, *Newsweek,* June 11, 2001.

3.   Bridewealth is the compensation given upon marriage by the family of the groom to the family of the bride. According to Murdock's "Ethnographic Atlas" (reported in Stephens 1963: 211), approximately 46 percent of all societies give substantial bridewealth payment as a normal part of the marriage process. Although bridewealth is practiced in most regions of the world, it is perhaps most widely found in Africa. . . .

From Ferraro/Andreatta, *Cultural Anthropology,* 9E. © 2012 Cengage Learning.

Identifying the Main Idea

Writers don't expect to say everything about a topic in their writing. If they did, their writing could go on and on. Instead, they focus their attention on a **main idea**—a special feature, part, or claim about the topic that they want to emphasize. The main idea in most paragraphs is stated first in the **topic sentence**. In most essays and articles, the main idea is stated in a **thesis statement** in one of the opening paragraphs.

There are times, however, when the main idea is expressed in a summary statement near the end of the text. Then again, the main idea in some essays may be implied or suggested rather than directly stated, and some longer, more complex essays may have more than one main idea. The main idea can tell you a lot about a piece of writing. Consider these examples:

- In an **expository essay** the main idea tells you what feature of the topic will be explained.

  > Hybrid and electric cars are the two main alternatives to traditional gas guzzlers.

  Or it may indicate that a particular pattern of organization (*process, cause-effect*, etc.) will be used to discuss the main idea.

  > Research in sociology is a process that involves six steps.

- In an **argument essay** the main idea identifies the claim about a topic that the writer will argue for.

  > The city of Chicago should build barriers to prevent invasive fish from invading the Great Lakes.

- In a **narrative** the main idea may tell you how the writer feels about the topic, which will be autobiographical (something about the writer) or biographical (something about another person).

  > This is the tale of two sisters from Calcutta, who have lived in the United States for some 35 years but who find themselves on different sides in the current debate over the status of immigrants.

SPECIAL NOTE: The wording of a statement may signal it as the main idea: "Study after study has shown that . . . ," "The city of Chicago should . . . ," or "This is a tale of two sisters who . . ."

Steps for Finding the Main Idea

The following steps can help you identify the main idea or thesis in an essay, an article, or a chapter. In paragraphs, you usually need to look no further than the first sentence or the last sentence.

1. Review the title, headings, and the first and last paragraphs of the text.

2. Read the opening part, perhaps the first few paragraphs, to gain a general understanding of the topic.

3. Look for a sentence or two in one of the opening paragraphs that seems to direct the writing. (Often, this sentence comes at the end of one of these paragraphs.)

4. Underline this sentence, highlight it, or write it down. If you can't find such a sentence, try to state the main idea in your own words.

5. Continue your initial reading to see if this statement makes sense as the main idea. Each new paragraph should support or develop it with evidence, such as examples.

6. If your thinking changes, identify or write down what you now consider to be the main idea.

Topic Sentence in a Paragraph

A paragraph is a group of related sentences sharing details about a main idea stated in the topic sentence. The sentences in the body of the paragraph explain the main idea. The topic sentence in the paragraph that follows is underlined.

All the flavors that a person can taste are made up of a few taste sensations. In the Western world, people are used to thinking about four tastes: salty, sweet, sour, and bitter. The salty taste comes from substances that include sodium, such as snacks like potato chips or pretzels. The sweet sensation comes from sugars, whether in processed foods like sweetened cereals or naturally occurring in fruit or honey. Sour tastes come from acidic foods such as lemons and grapefruits, and bitter tastes come from alkaline foods such as coffee or dark chocolate. But in the Eastern world, two other taste sensations are recognized. A savory taste comes from amino acids, which are a basic part of meats and proteins. And a spicy taste comes from substances like the capsaicin in hot peppers. With all the sensations to appeal to, chefs can make every dish a unique and tasty work of art.

Thesis Statement in an Essay

An essay is a multi-paragraph text sharing details about a thesis statement. The paragraphs that follow explore or explain the thesis statement. The underlined sentence in "What Is Emotional Intelligence?" answers the question in the title, which suggests that it is the thesis statement.

What Is Emotional Intelligence?

Many experts believe that intelligence takes many forms. Rather than a narrow definition of intelligence, they believe in Multiple Intelligences: Linguistic,

Logical-Mathematical, Spatial, Kinesthetic, Musical, Interpersonal, Intrapersonal, and Naturalistic. Emotional intelligence may well be a combination, at least in part, of **intrapersonal** and **interpersonal** intelligences.

Emotional intelligence is a set of skills that determines how well you cope with the demands and pressures you face every day. How well do you understand yourself, **empathize** with others, draw on your inner resources, and encourage the same qualities in people you care about? Emotional intelligence involves having people skills, a positive outlook, and the capacity to adapt to change. Emotional intelligence can propel you through difficult situations.

The bottom line? New research links emotional intelligence to college success, and learning about the impact of EI in the first year of college helps students stay in school.

As you read about the five scales of emotional intelligence, begin thinking about yourself in these areas. As each scale is introduced, ask yourself whether you agree or disagree with the sample statement from a well-known emotional intelligence instrument as it pertains to you.

From Staley/Staley, *FOCUS on College and Career Success*, 1E. © 2012 Cengage Learning.

---

intrapersonal
having to do with a person's inner thoughts and feelings

interpersonal
having to do with the relationships between people

empathize
imagine what another person feels

Practice 4.2 Underline the thesis statement in each of the following essays.

1.   One-of-a-Kind Character(s)

Mystery books are hugely popular. In fact, they are so popular that a reader can find a mystery set in just about any time and place. There are mysteries that seem very real, and others that are more imaginative. What all mysteries have in common is a main detective or investigator who leads the reader through the mystery. The most famous mysteries have a one-of-a-kind main character leading the investigation.

Many mystery experts feel that Arthur Conan Doyle created the most famous detective of all, Sherlock Holmes. The mysterious Holmes hides out in his flat on Baker Street in London where he conducts experiments, reads, and occasionally goes into a funk (and smokes opium). His only friend and companion is the understanding Dr. Watson. Holmes is a very serious man with dark hair and piercing eyes, and he uses his great powers of observation and deduction to solve each mystery.

Another British writer, Agatha Christie, invented the famous amateur detective Jane Marple in the 1920s. Miss Marple is an elderly woman residing in a small village in England with the personality of a sweet aunt or grandmother. Miss Marple is a loner like Holmes, but she is very personable and understanding in social situations. While Holmes busies himself in his laboratory, Miss Marple works in her garden. Christie develops each mystery so Miss Marple just happens to appear at the site of crime. She snoops around, listens, asks questions, and eventually solves each crime.

These examples show that the most popular mysteries begin and end with a special investigator. Each new mystery allows this individual to put special talents into action to solve a crime that no one else can figure out. Readers enjoy each new opportunity to see how their favorite investigator does the job.

2.   Thinking Like Breathing

Which is more important for a successful career, critical thinking or creative thinking? It's a trick question. I may as well ask which is more important, breathing out or breathing in? Creative and critical thinking are two halves of a cycle: inspiration and expiration, and the interchange between the two is the key to success.

Creative thinking draws in possibilities. It is an expansive process, filling you with new ideas from the outside. Creativity reaches beyond what is known and into the unknown . . . to discover something new. Creativity is not necessarily discerning. You don't separate nitrogen from oxygen before you breathe it in. Your chest simply expands, and in it comes. Creative thinking floods you with new possibilities.

Critical thinking, on the other hand, sorts through the possibilities to do something practical. Critical thinking analyzes, applies, and evaluates. It categorizes, compares, contrasts, and traces causes and effects. It's like separating oxygen from the air to enrich your cells, or extracting the carbon dioxide from your blood to get rid of the waste.

Implied Main Ideas

There are times when the main idea is implied, or not directly stated. You will know that this is the case if no one or two sentences seem to direct the writing. When this occurs, follow these steps to identify the **implied main idea**:

1. Identify the topic.
2. Pay close attention to each set of details.
3. Write down the important idea that covers all of the details.
4. Read the text again to make sure that this idea accurately covers the details. Revise the statement as needed.

The following narrative paragraph describes the conditions of an eating disorder, but the main idea about this topic is not stated. Read the text and then see how one reader identified the implied main idea.

> Every fiber and cell of my body was obsessed with the numbers on the scale and how much fat I could pinch on my thigh. I fought my sisters for control of the TV to do my exercise programs. The cupboards were stacked with cans of diet mixes, the refrigerator full of diet drinks. Hidden in my underwear drawer were stacks of diet pills that I popped along with my vitamins. At my worst, I would quietly excuse myself from family activities to turn on the bathroom faucet full blast and vomit into the toilet. Every day I stood in front of the mirror, a ritual not unlike brushing my teeth, and carefully studied my body. I was never, ever small enough.

Topic: _Eating disorder (anorexia)_

Key details: _Weight a worry, insistent about exercise, using diet products, trips to the bathroom to vomit, ritually checking body_

Idea that covers the details: _The person suffered from a serious eating disorder._

Implied main idea: _Many signs indicated I was suffering from anorexia._

Practice 4.3 Carefully read the following excerpts. Then identify the implied main idea by filling in the information that follows each excerpt.

1. The most frequently thrown pitch is a fastball. As its name suggests, fastballs travel at the highest velocity of any pitch. Generally speaking, a fastball travels on a straight line. A second type of pitch, a changeup, is used to trick hitters into thinking it is a fastball. However, a changeup is thrown much slower and tails slightly downward. The curveball is a third pitch. It is hard to hit because it travels with topspin that it causes it to break sharply both laterally and downward. A curveball is slower than a fastball but faster than a changeup. Another common pitch called the slider breaks laterally and downward. However, its break is shorter than a curve, and it is faster. A skilled pitcher will master at least two of these pitches.

Topic: _____

Key details: _____

Idea that covers the details: _____

Implied main idea: _____

2. The word *ethics* derives from the Greek word *ethos*, meaning the guiding spirit or traditions that govern a culture. Part of America's culture is the unique protection offered to journalists by the First Amendment of the U.S. Constitution, so any discussion of ethics and the American media acknowledges the cultural belief that the First Amendment privilege carries with it special obligations. Among these obligations are professional ethics, the rules or standards governing the conduct of the members of a profession. . . . When journalists make the wrong ethical choices, the consequences can be very damaging and very public. "It may well be that if journalism loses touch with ethical choices, it will then cease to be of use to society and cease to have any real reason for being," writes media ethics scholar John Hulteng. "But that, for the sake of all of us, must never be allowed to happen." Journalists sometimes make poor ethical judgments because they work quickly, and their actions can be haphazard because the lust to be first with a story can override the desire to be right. . . .

From Biagi. *Media Impact: An Introduction to Mass Media*, 10E © 2011 Cengage Learning.

Topic: _____

Key details: _____

Idea that covers the details: _____

Implied main idea: _____

4.2 Starting Points for Writing

Ideas are the fuel that powers your writing, beginning with a topic. Some assignments will tell you specifically what you should write about. But in most cases, they will identify a general subject area that serves as a starting point for a topic search. If, for some reason, the general subject of the writing is not clear to you, consult with your instructor before you get started.

Selecting a Topic

Always try to select a topic that interests you and seems specific enough (or broad enough) for the assignment. **Figure 4.1** shows how the selecting process should work, moving from the general assignment and subject area to a specific topic. Keep in mind that you might identify more than one potential topic. If one doesn't work out, you can always try another one of your choices.

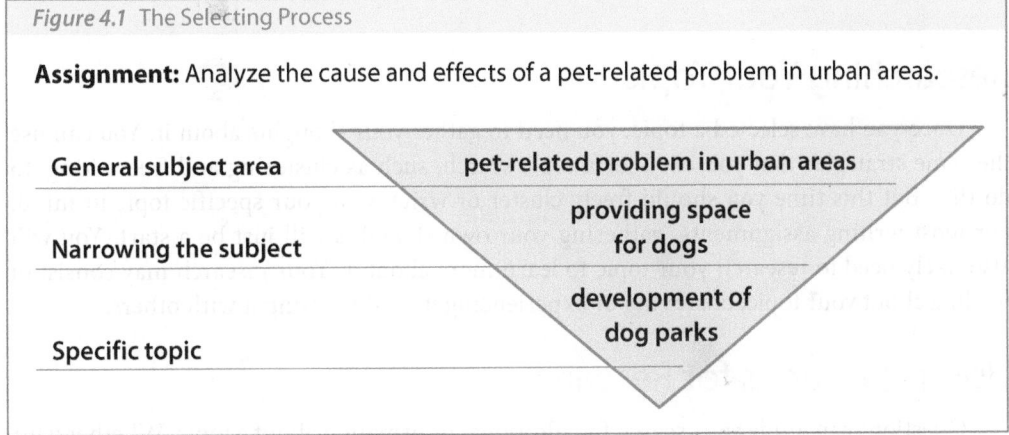

Figure 4.1 The Selecting Process

Assignment: Analyze the cause and effects of a pet-related problem in urban areas.

General subject area — pet-related problem in urban areas

Narrowing the subject — providing space for dogs

Specific topic — development of dog parks

Brainstorming Strategies

If you are having trouble selecting a specific topic, review your class notes or search the Internet for topics. The following strategies may also help you identify possible topics.

- **Freewriting:** Write nonstop for 5–10 minutes about your assignment to discover possible topics. Begin by jotting down a particular thought about the assignment. Then write whatever comes to mind without stopping to judge, edit, or correct your writing.
- **Five W's of Writing:** Answer the five W's (*who? what? when? where?* and *why?*) to identify basic information about your topic. Add *how?* to the list for more coverage.
- **Listing:** Rapidly list your thoughts about the assignment. Record ideas nonstop for as long as you can.

- **Clustering:** Begin a cluster with the general subject area or a narrowed subject. Cluster related words around it. Write about one of these ideas. See Figure 4.2.

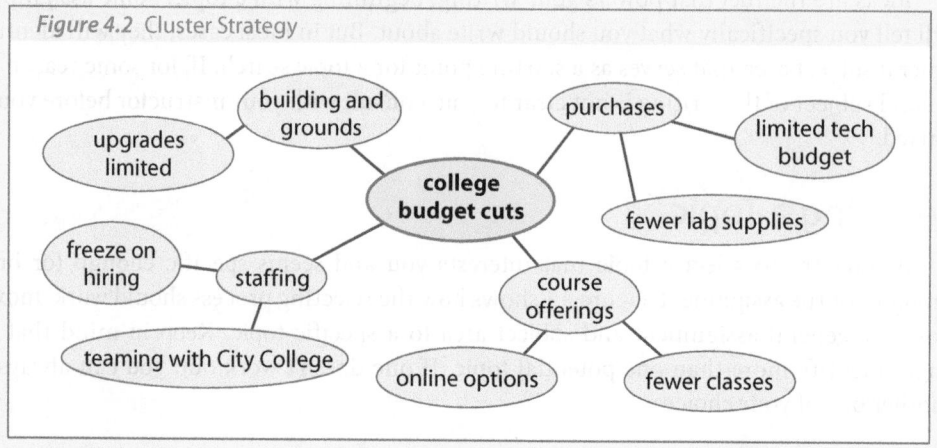

Figure 4.2 Cluster Strategy

Researching Your Topic

Once you have selected a topic, you need to gather your thoughts about it. You can use the same strategies that you used for a topic search, such as clustering and freewriting, to do this. But this time you should freely cluster or write with your specific topic in mind. For most writing assignments, gathering your own thoughts will just be a start. You will also likely need to research your topic to learn more about it. Your research may consist of reading about your topic, observing or experiencing it, or discussing it with others.

Using Questions for Research

Questions can guide your search for additional information about a topic. Whether your topic is a problem (*college budget cuts*), a policy (*graduation requirements*), or a concept (*a weight-training program*), the questions in Table 4.1 will lead you to related facts and details.

Table 4.1 Categories of Questions

	Description	Function	History	Value
Problems	What is the problem?	Who or what is affected by it?	What or who caused it?	What is its significance?
Policies	What are the most important features?	What is the policy meant to do?	What brought this policy about?	What are its advantages and disadvantages?
Concepts	What is the concept or idea?	Why is it important?	When did it start?	What value does it have?

Establishing a Main Idea

A skilled photographer focuses or centers a subject before taking a photograph. You should do the same once you have gathered enough information about your topic. A strong main idea or focus helps you decide what information to include in your writing and in what order. Suppose you are planning an essay about the effects of the Gulf oil spill on the shrimping industry. Your focus could be the effects that the spill had on one particular family business.

- **Topic:** *Effects of the Gulf oil spill on the shrimping industry*
- **Focus:** *The plight of one particular family business*

Without a clear main idea, writing can go on and on, in a number of different directions. For example, a personal essay that shares all sorts of details about a local music festival lacks focus. But one that shares the writer's impression of the listeners immediately around him is much more in focus.

Forming a Thesis Statement

A thesis statement is the controlling idea in an essay. The following formula can be used to write a thesis statement or a topic sentence. You may have to write multiple versions of a thesis statement before it says what you want it to say.

A specific topic	a particular feature, part, or claim	an effective thesis statement
Wind power	+ provides an important energy source in the Plains states	= Wind power provides an important energy source in the Plains states.

Qualities of an Effective Thesis Statement

To be effective, a thesis statement should meet four main standards. It should . . .

- identify a specific topic,
- clearly state a main idea about the topic,
- be supported by your research, and
- suggest a pattern of organization for the essay.

You may have to write two, three, or even four versions of a thesis statement before it meets these goals. What follows is an analysis of two sets of thesis statements to show you the difference between weak and strong ones.

Weak thesis statement: *Many large animals are endangered.*

- *Many large animals* is too general to serve as a topic for an essay. How many endangered animals are considered "large"?

- *Are endangered* is an ineffective main idea because it is too general. What exactly would a writer focus on in this essay?

Strong thesis statement: *Mountain gorillas can now be classified as an endangered species.*

- *Mountain gorillas* is specific enough to serve as a topic for an essay.

- *Can now be classified as an endangered species* is an effective main idea because it focuses on the endangerment classification. The writer could go through the requirements for classification, one by one.

Weak thesis statement: *Wearing hijab is common among Islamic women.*

- *Wearing hajib* is specific enough to serve as topic for an essay.

- However, *is common among Islamic women* is too general to serve as a main idea. It simply states a fact. What would there be to explain or develop in the essay?

Strong thesis statement: *To wear hijab—Islamic covering—is to invite opposing feelings.*

- *To wear hijab* is specific enough to serve as a topic for an essay.

- *Is to invite opposing feelings* is an effective main idea because it focuses on an interesting part of the topic. The writer could first explain the positive aspects of wearing hijab and then turn to the negative ones.

Practice 4.4   Read each pair of thesis statements. Then select the stronger thesis statement.

1. a. Human trafficking happens everywhere.
   b. Human trafficking is a difficult concept to define properly.

2. a. There are many ways to exercise.
   b. Regular bike spinning provides four main benefits.

3. a. Fatherlessness has become a common theme in America.
   b. Many families lack fathers.

4. a. Africa will prosper when women become part of the decision-making process.
   b. Africa needs help from its women.

5. a. General McClellan's overcautious methods prolonged the Civil War.
   b. General McClellan was a slow decision-maker.

4.3 Reading for Supporting Details

While the main idea or thesis provides a focus for a text, the supporting details and ideas support and develop the main idea. Supporting details can include examples, stories, explanations, quotations, statistics, and any other information that helps clarify and reinforce the text's main idea.

Differentiating Major and Minor Details

Writers use major and minor details to develop their main ideas. **Major details** explain or illustrate a main idea or main point. **Minor details** make major details clearer. Read the following passage and explanation of major and minor details to see how they fit together:

> As a significant method of energy production, nuclear power does offer distinct advantages. First, nuclear power plants do not release the harmful emissions that coal-burning plants do. As a result, nuclear power does not contribute greatly to global warming (Evans 15). Second, a single nuclear power plant can produce a large amount of energy, making it an efficient source ("Pros and Cons"). In fact, according to Robert Evans, "The amount of thermal energy released from just one kilogram of U235 undergoing fission is equivalent to that obtained by burning some 2.5 million kilograms, or 2500 tonnes, of coal" (116). . . .

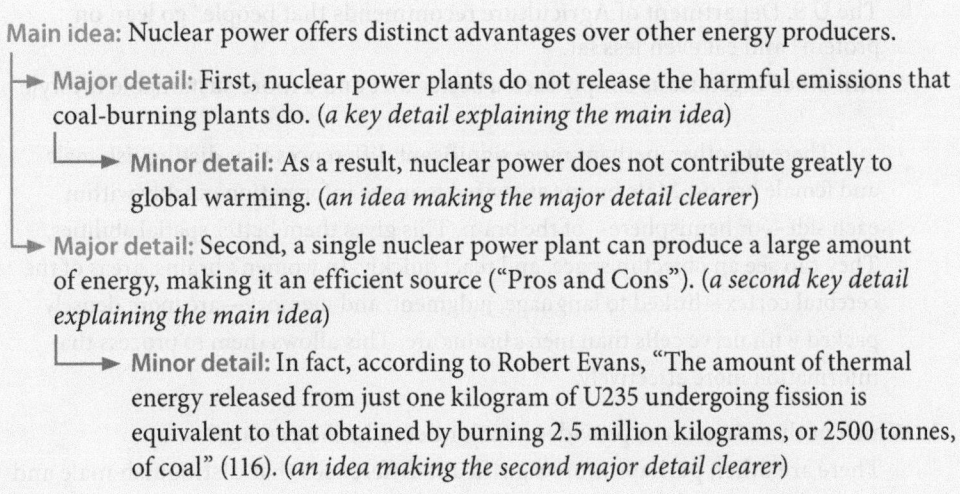

Main idea: Nuclear power offers distinct advantages over other energy producers.

➤ **Major detail:** First, nuclear power plants do not release the harmful emissions that coal-burning plants do. (*a key detail explaining the main idea*)

➤ **Minor detail:** As a result, nuclear power does not contribute greatly to global warming. (*an idea making the major detail clearer*)

➤ **Major detail:** Second, a single nuclear power plant can produce a large amount of energy, making it an efficient source ("Pros and Cons"). (*a second key detail explaining the main idea*)

➤ **Minor detail:** In fact, according to Robert Evans, "The amount of thermal energy released from just one kilogram of U235 undergoing fission is equivalent to that obtained by burning 2.5 million kilograms, or 2500 tonnes, of coal" (116). (*an idea making the second major detail clearer*)

Look for clue words to help you identify major and minor details. "Distinct advantages" in the main idea indicates that example advantages will follow. Sentences beginning with "first" and "second" indicate that they are examples (major details). Sentences beginning with "as a result" and "in fact" indicate that they are minor details clarifying or completing what comes before them. The breakdown of major and minor details will not always be so balanced and clear in the texts you read. One text may have many major details and few minor details. Another text may have a few major details but many minor details.

Practice 4.5 Answer the questions about major and minor details for the following readings.

Every vegetarian has unique reasons for eating what they eat. Many vegetarians see animals as creatures with intelligence and feelings. So they don't like the idea of killing animals for food, especially not in the overcrowded and inhumane factory farms of today. Other vegetarians reject modern American eating habits, with too much meat and too few vegetables. The U.S. Department of Agriculture recommends that people "go lean on protein" and eat even less fat. Still other vegetarians simply seek a better diet and a more sustainable lifestyle. And for some, it's just a matter of personal preference. They just would rather have a salad.

1. Which of these sentences provides a major detail in the passage?
   a. Every vegetarian has unique reasons for eating what they eat.
   b. Many vegetarians see animals as creatures with intelligence and feelings.
   c. So they don't like the idea of killing animals for food, especially not in the overcrowded and inhumane factory farms of today.

2. Which of these sentences provides a minor detail in the passage?
   a. Others vegetarians reject modern American eating habits, with too much meat and too few vegetables.
   b. The U.S. Department of Agriculture recommends that people "go lean on protein" and eat even less fat.
   c. Still other vegetarians simply seek a better diet and a more sustainable lifestyle.

There are other, perhaps more significant differences that distinguish male and female brains. Male brains are wired to move information quickly within each side—or hemisphere—of the brain. This gives them better spatial abilities. They can see an object in space, and react quickly. In women's brains, areas of the cerebral cortex—linked to language, judgment, and memory—are more densely packed with nerve cells than men's brains are. This allows them to process that information more effectively.

3. Which of these sentences provides a major detail in the passage?
   a. There are other, perhaps more significant differences that distinguish male and female brains.
   b. This gives them better spatial abilities.
   c. Male brains are wired to move information quickly within each side—or hemisphere—of the brain.

4. Which of these sentences provides a minor detail in the passage?
   a. In women's brains, areas of the cerebral cortex—linked to language, judgment,

and memory—are more densely packed with nerve cells that men's brains are.

b. This allows them to process the information more effectively.

c. There are other, perhaps more significant differences that distinguish male and female brains.

Recognizing Types of Support

Consider the following types of details commonly included in writing. The examples come from the article "Yes, Accidents Happen. But Why?" by Robert Strauss. A text may contain any number and combination of these types of details.

- **Facts and statistics** provide numbers and data to support something about the main idea. This type of information usually requires research to discover.

  > Drivers ages 18 to 20 were up to four times more likely to have an inattention-related accident than older drivers.

- **Anecdotes** provide a brief personal story to illustrate a key point.

  > When Fred Mannering takes his vintage MG sports car out for a spin, he always leaves plenty of room between the car in front of him and the MG. He brakes slowly and deliberately. He rarely speeds, and if he were to go fast, it would be only on a superhighway with little traffic.

- **Quotations** share the specific thoughts of people knowledgeable about the main idea. When used successfully, quotations offer an effective level of support.

  > "My other car is newer, with good antilock brakes and air bags, so I don't take nearly as much care," said Dr. Mannering, a Purdue University professor of civil engineering who studies the causes and results of traffic accidents.

- **References** to experts or studies provide authoritative support in the development of a thesis.

  > Dr. Mannering's study of accidents in Washington State from 1992 to 1997, a period during which air bags and antilock brakes became prevalent, showed that . . .

- **Analysis** shows the author's critical thinking about the topic or main idea.

  > In that way, he may reflect the behavior of the average driver, governed by hard-to-quantify influences.

■ **Explanations** discuss, clarify, demonstrate, interpret, or expound upon a key point.

> Insurance companies, carmakers, inventors, safety advocates and drivers themselves all have an interest in learning about what might reduce the number of accidents.

■ **Examples** demonstrate or show something.

> For example, a driver is unlikely to tell an officer that he was using a cell phone, especially if he thinks it will increase his liability.

■ **Definitions** explain complex terms.

> The one thing you might conclude—it's called an offset hypothesis—is that people have an acceptance of a level of safety. If they felt safer because of the air bags and brakes, then maybe they drove faster. . . .

■ **Reasons** answer the question "Why?" about something.

> Drinking alcohol certainly causes crashes, but to what extent? That has been difficult determine. Part of the problem stems from the limitations of researchers' information.

■ **Reflections** offer the writer's personal thoughts or feelings about the topic or main idea.

> Now the technology is available to separate out things like alcohol and different kinds of distractions. It is a long time coming, but soon we'll know what really does cause car accidents.

■ **Descriptions** provide details about how something or someone appears.

> Her orange track pants are worn and faded, her T-shirt is far too big, and her powder blue sweatshirt is tied around her waist. Her face and teeth are stained, hair greasy and unkempt.

Practice 4.6 Circle the type of detail represented by each of the following underlined ideas.

1. Plants can't run away from a threat, but they can stand their ground. "<u>They are very good at avoiding getting eaten</u>," said Linda Walling of the University of California, Riverside.
                                                                              —Natalie Angier

    a. Definition

    b. Quotation

    c. Reason

    d. Reflection

2. In short, Rosa Parks didn't make a spur-of-the-moment decision. She was part of a movement for change when success was far from certain. There is no way to diminish her historical importance, but it reminds us that this powerful act might never have taken place without the humble, frustrating work that preceded it.
   a. Facts and statistics
   b. Anecdote
   c. Definition
   d. Analysis

3. Nearly 2,000 Pakistanis have lost their lives to terrorism in this year alone, including 1,400 civilians and 600 security personnel ranging in rank from ordinary soldier to three-star general.
   a. Quotation
   b. Description
   c. Reason
   d. Facts and statistics

4. Slavery in the United States is the granting of that power by which one man exercises and enforces a right of property in the body and soul of another. The condition of a slave is simply that of the brute beast. . . .
   —Frederick Douglass
   a. Reason
   b. Definition
   c. Anecdote
   d. Example

5. All vegetarians are unique, with unique reasons for eating what they eat. For example, many see animals as more than meat—as creatures with intelligence and feelings.
   a. Definition
   b. Quotation
   c. Reference
   d. Example

6. The sun's rays do not present an unmitigated threat. As it falls on the skin, sunshine converts a fatty substance in the epidermis into vitamin D. The blood carries vitamin D from the skin to the intestines, where it plays a vital role in the absorption of calcium.
   a. Explanation
   b. Quotation
   c. Statistic
   d. Definition

Details Working Together

The number and types of details used by writers will vary from text to text, depending on the purpose of the writing and the nature of the topic. However, some types of details logically work together. For instance, specific examples often follow an explanation, an analysis often follows key statistics, and an explanation or analysis generally follows a quotation. The passages that follow illustrate this working relationship. (The main idea is underlined in each one.)

Explanations

Although some roles (jobs) are played by both women and men throughout the world, many others are associated with one gender or the other. Women generally tend crops, gather wild foods, care for children, prepare food, clean house, fetch water, and collect cooking fuel. Men, on the other hand, hunt, build houses, clear land for cultivation, herd large animals, fish, trap animals, and serve as political functionaries. There are exceptions

Examples for final explanation

to these broad generalizations about what constitutes men's and women's work, however. In some parts of traditional Africa, for example, women carry much heavier loads than men, work long hours in the fields, build houses, and even serve as warriors. And among the Northwest Coast peoples, such as the Tlingit, it is the women who collect shellfish, thereby attaching a stigma to the task. In Tlingit culture a man who collects shellfish is considered lazy because it is believed that men should be out hunting or fishing and not taking the easy way out by collecting shellfish.   From *Cultural Anthropology*, 9E. © 2012 Cengage Learning.

Statistics

The main source of drug data is the National Survey on Drug Use and Health, conducted annually by the National Institute on Drug Abuse. According to the survey, only about 9 percent of those questioned had used an illegal drug in the past month. Even so, this means that a significant number of Americans—nearly 23 million—are regularly using illegal drugs, and the figure mushrooms when users of legal substances such as alcohol (131 million users) and tobacco (70 million users) are included. Drug abuse often leads to further

Analysis

criminal behavior in adolescents. And in general, the growing market for illegal drugs causes significant damage both in the United States and in countries such as Mexico that supply America with its "fix."

From *Criminal Justice in Action*, 6E. © 2011 Cengage Learning.

Quotation

Earth-focused philosophers say that to be rooted, each of us needs to find a sense of place—a stream, a mountain, a yard, a neighborhood lot—any place of the earth with which we feel as one. According to biologist Stephen Jay Gould, "We will not fight to save what we do not love." When we become part

Explanation

of a place, it becomes a part of us. Then we are driven to defend it from harm and to help heal its wounds.   From *Living in the Environment*, 17E. © 2012 Cengage Learning.

Practice 4.7 Carefully read each of the following passages. Then choose the types of details used to support the main idea (underlined).

1. One troublesome aspect of capital punishment is that a black defendant is much more likely to be sentenced to death for killing a white victim than a white defendant is for killing a black victim. Indeed, looking at the general statistics, a bleak picture of minority incarceration emerges. Even though African Americans make up only 13 percent of the general population in the United States, the number of black men in state and federal prisons (561,000) is significantly larger than the number of white men (452,000). In federal prisons, one in every three inmates is Hispanic, a ratio that has increased dramatically over the past decade as law enforcement has focused on immigration law violations.

From GAINES/MILLER, *Cengage Advantage Books: Criminal Justice in Action*, 6E. © 2011 Cengage Learning.

a. Definition   c. Statistics
b. Quotations   d. Reflections

2. Reports show that many Burmese pythons have been imported into the United States, some of which end up in homes of irresponsible pet owners. "All of the Burmese pythons that we see in the park are a product of the international pet trade," said Skip Snow, a biologist at Everglades National Park. The problem is many pet owners don't fully understand the responsibility of caring for a python. Often the python, which grows to between 10 and 20 feet, becomes too big and too expensive to be kept in a home, and the owner releases the pet into the wild.

a. Reflection   c. Reasons
b. Quotation   d. Both *b* and *c*

3. Throughout its long history, Islam has witnessed periodic episodes of revivalism. Sometimes, especially during times when Islam was in crisis, these developments took a decidedly fundamentalist and violent form. At other times, as was the case in the late 1800s, they assumed the character of movements of reform and **accommodation**. A modern example of the former violent reaction was Wahhabism, a militant reform begun in the late 1700s when a desert **shaykh**, Muhammed ibn Abd al-Wahhab, joined forces with a tribal leader, Muhammed ibn Saud. Together they fought a jihad to purge Islam of Sufis, Shi'ites, and all others whom they accused of introducing innovations.

From Adler/Pouwels, *World Civilizations*, 6E. © 2012 Cengage Learning.

a. Example   c. Explanation
b. Quotation   d. Both *a* and *c*

---

revivalism	accommodation	shaykh
a desire to make strong again	settle or resolve	head of an Arab family or village

Evaluating Details

You can trust the details in your textbooks and other assigned readings because the authors are, for the most part, experts in their respective fields, and their writing has been carefully reviewed by other experts to assure that the details are accurate and trustworthy. Dr. Dickson Despommier is the author of *The Vertical Farm*. Dr. Despommier spent 38 years as a professor of microbiology and public health in environmental health sciences at Columbia University, so when he discusses the value of vertical farming, you can assume that he knows what he is talking about. Therefore, when you read this paragraph from his book, you can trust that the supporting details are accurate and authentic.

> As populations grew and urban life became the norm, our habit for producing mountains of waste began to take its toll. Garbage provided sustenance for a wide variety of **peri-domestic** diseases that emerged and then became **endemic**. For example, in the twelfth century, trash of all kinds, strewn carelessly across the European landscape by returning crusaders from the Middle East, attracted hordes of rats. These vermin harbored the plague bacillus, a flea-borne infection. As the rats died, the fleas soon found human hosts to feed on, igniting the first outbreak of the Black Death in Europe. It killed more than one-third of all those living there. **Cholera** came to Europe in 1836 by way of trading vessels from the Bay of Bengal, first to London, England. Because of the high nutrient content of the Thames River, due mostly to garbage dumping, cholera became endemic, killing thousands of Londoners every year until John Snow figured out its **modus operandi**.

peri-domestic living in or around humans	cholera disease of the small intestines
endemic common to one area	modus operandi how something acts or works

But what if Despommier had been trained in sociology or marketing? You wouldn't (or shouldn't) feel as confident in his information about vertical farming. Likewise, you wouldn't feel confident in the text if Despommier discussed urban waste using vague details like these:

> As cities grew, waste became more of a problem. And the growing piles of garbage brought on all sorts of diseases. For example, there was the Black Death that nearly wiped out European cities during Medieval times. Then later cholera caused by dumped garbage did that same kind of thing.

While the details in your textbooks and assigned readings will be reliable, the same might not be true in some other texts. For example, the details on some websites may be questionable; the same may hold true for information in some popular magazines or in books that may, for example, be out of date or written by people promoting a particular cause.

A reading's details are most likely trustworthy if the text meets these factors:

1. The source is a textbook, a book from a respected publisher, an essay in a respected periodical, or a website article with a reliable domain such as *.edu, .org,* or *.gov.*
2. An author is identified and writing in their field of expertise. In addition, the text is in line with material written by other experts in the field.
3. The topic is covered in depth. The information seems balanced and timely, and it is easy to follow and logical.

Read the extended definition of the term *utopia* and the evaluation of the supporting details that follows it.

Looking for Utopia

Everyone wishes to find a perfect place—a utopia that has no crime and no disease, where everyone is happy, healthy, wealthy, and wise. In fact, the word "utopia" would seem to mean "good place," coming from the Greek "eu" (good) and "topos" (place). However, the prefix in Greek is not "eu" but "ou," which means "not" or "no." That's right; "utopia" means "no place." Sir Thomas More coined the term in 1516, writing a book about a perfect place that didn't exist. His book was a satire, trying to show that a utopia wasn't possible. That didn't stop a number of utopian movements from springing up. In fact, one utopian community established in New Harmony, Indiana, proudly announced that it was based on ideas commended by Sir Thomas More. This 2,000-person communal city banned money but quickly dissolved due to quarreling. Nathaniel Hawthorne tells in *The Scarlet Letter* why such utopians are bound to fail: "The founders of any new colony, whatever Utopia of human virtues and happiness they originally project, have invariably recognized it among their earliest practical necessities to allot a portion of the virgin soil as a cemetery, and another portion as the site of a prison." In other words, no utopia can exist as long as any humans are in it.

1. What is the main idea of the reading? _Everyone wishes to find a perfect place._

2. What types of details support it? _The initial support is a definition. Next, a reference to an expert (Sir Thomas More) is offered. An example utopian community follows. Then a quotation from Nathaniel Hawthorne adds further support and authority._

3. Do the details seem reliable and trustworthy? Explain. _Yes, the information appears reliable and trustworthy. Facts and definitions can be checked._

4. What questions do you still have about the main idea? _Have other attempts at utopia been made? What caused disharmony within the experimental groups?_

Practice 4.8   Carefully read "Support Wind Farm Energy." Then choose the correct answer for each of the evaluation questions that follow.

Support Wind Farm Energy

To counteract its dependence on fossil fuels, the United States must invest in wind farms for its energy needs. A wind farm is made up of a group of large wind turbines, which convert wind into energy. The benefits of wind farms are numerous. First, wind is a free and renewable source of energy. In comparison, fossil fuels like oil and coal are limited in supply and cost money to extract from the earth. Second, wind farms are a clean energy source. Unlike power plants, which emit dangerous pollutants, wind farms release no pollution into the air or water, meaning less smog, less acid rain, and fewer greenhouse emissions. And then there's this: The American Wind Energy Association reports that running a single wind turbine has the potential to displace 2,000 tons of carbon dioxide, or the equivalent of one square mile of forest trees. But despite being the fastest growing energy source in the U.S., wind energy accounts for only 1.5 percent of power supplied in the country. If the United States wants to limit carbon emissions and lessen its dependence on fossil fuels, it must act now and invest more money in wind farms. The answer is in the air.

1. What is the main idea of the reading?
   a. In comparison, fossil fuels like oil and coal are limited in supply and cost money to extract from the earth.
   b. To counteract its dependence on fossil fuels, the United States must invest in wind farms for its energy needs.
   c. But despite being the fastest growing energy source in the U.S., wind energy accounts for only 1.5 percent of power supplied in the country.

2. What types of details support the main idea?
   a. Facts and statistics
   b. Reference and analysis   d. Both *b* and *c*
   c. Quotations and anecdotes   e. Both *a* and *b*

3. How would you rate the details?
   a. Unreliable and   b. Vague and general   c. Reliable and
      untrustworthy   trustworthy

4. What questions do you still have about the main idea?

_____

4.4 Drawing Inferences

An **inference** is a logical conclusion that you make about something that is not actually said or stated. A thoughtful inference results from a careful reading of a text. To make thoughtful inferences, follow these steps:

1. **Carefully read and reread the text**, using the reading process. See Section 2.1.
2. **Identify the main idea and supporting details.**
3. **Then ask yourself:** *What other conclusions can I draw from the reading?*

The following passage comes from the Bureau of Labor Statistics. Among other things, this government body provides economic news releases summarizing regional and state unemployment and employment figures. This passage was written in 2013, a time when the country was recovering from a recession (a period of low national employment). Note the inferences that were drawn after a careful reading of the passage.

Regional and state unemployment rates were little changed in February. Twenty-two states had unemployment rate decreases, 12 states had increases, and 16 states and the District of Columbia had no change, the U.S. Bureau of Labor Statistics reported today. Thirty-seven states and the District of Columbia had unemployment rate decreases from a year earlier, 10 states had increases, and three states had no change. The national jobless rate, 7.7 percent, edged down from January and was 0.6 percentage point lower than in February 2012.

In February, the West continued to have the highest regional unemployment rate, 8.5 percent, while the South had the lowest rate, 7.3 percent. No region had a statistically significant over-the-month unemployment rate change.

From Bureau of Labor Statistics "Regional and State Employment and Unemployment—February 2013"

1. What is the main idea in the passage? *Regional and state unemployment did not change much in February 2013.*

2. What details support the main idea? *(1) While 22 states had lower unemployment, 12 states had increases and 16 states plus DC had no change. (2) There was only a 0.6 percentage decrease in February compared to January.*

3. What inferences can you draw from the passage? *(1) The recovery from a major recession is a slow process. (2) All parts of the country, to some degree, are feeling the effects of unemployment due to the recession.*

Practice 4.9 Carefully read this passage. Then choose the correct answer to the questions that follow.

> The report documents for the first time an emerging "app gap" in which affluent children are likely to use mobile educational games, while those in low-income families are the most likely to have televisions in their bedrooms.
>
> The study, by Common Sense Media, a San Francisco nonprofit group, is the first of its kind since apps became widespread and the first to look at screen time from birth. It found that almost half the families with incomes above $75,000 had downloaded apps specifically for their young children, compared with one in eight of the families earning less than $30,000. More than a third of those low-income parents said they did not know what an "app"—short for application—was.
>
> From Biagi. *Media Impact: An Introduction to Mass Media,* 10E © 2011 Cengage Learning.

1. What is the main idea of the text?
   a. More than a third of those low-income parents said they did not know what an "app" was.
   b. The report found that almost half the families with incomes above $75,000 had downloaded apps specifically for their young children.
   c. The report documents for the first time an emerging "app gap" in which affluent children are likely to use mobile educational games, while those in low-income families are the most likely to have televisions in their bedrooms.

2. What type of supporting detail is *not* used to support this idea?
   a. Quotation
   b. Statistic
   c. Reference

3. Which of the following is *not* a logical inference (conclusion) that could be drawn from this passage?
   a. In some ways, technology is increasing the learning gap between the haves and have-nots.
   b. Early childhood intervention needs to be an important part of a complete education program.
   c. High-income families are the cause of the learning gap.

4.5 Choosing Supporting Details for Writing

When planning a piece of writing, you are making decisions about the ideas you will develop. First, you select a topic. Next, you gather details about the topic, taking careful notes as you go along. After reviewing your notes, you form a main idea for your writing. Then you are ready to decide how best to use the details you have collected. Suppose a student is planning an essay about the technology-driven sharing economy, and his main idea is its simplicity of use.

- **Topic:** sharing economy
- **Focus:** simplicity leads to growth
- **Main Idea:** The sharing economy (*topic*) thrives because users value its simplicity (*focus*).

Here are the writer's notes about his topic. The annotations (in red type) reflect his thoughts as he reviews his notes.

Notes About the Sharing Economy

"The People Who Share" website
"What is the sharing economy?" by Benita Matofska

First off, I should define "sharing economy."

- "a socio-economic system built around the sharing of human and physical assets"
- includes shared production, distribution, trade, and consumption of goods by different people and organizations
- includes swapping, exchanging, purchasing, collaborative consumption, re-distribution, renting

Forbes **website – 7/30/2013**
"What Is the New Sharing Economy?" by James Gardner

Then I will stress the simplicity and ease of use.

- possible because of advances in technology
- human need—strive for simplicity
- ease of use—access resources when we need

Airbnb

- started in San Fran in 2008 by 2 people with a spare bed and inability to meet the rent

I'll follow with some popular examples.

- now operating in 191 countries
- make spare room or spare house available to rent

ZipCar

- gives people access to a car for as long as they need it
- book car online, select one nearby, unlock it with mobile, and drive away

TaskRabbit

- formed by Leah Busque in 2008
- people for hire pick up laundry, do the shopping, etc.
- post job online and TaskRabbit will bid for work

Time website

"Today's Smart Choice: Don't Own—Share" by Bryan Walsh, 3/17/11

- sharing replacing ownership society
- "ownership" just about ruined the economy
- has a green element
- Rachel Botsman, co-author of *What's Mine Is Yours: The Rise of Collaborative Consumption*: "It works because people can trust each other."

I'll consider its future at the end.

New York News & Politics website

"The Sharing Economy Isn't About Trust; It's About Desperation" by Kevin Roose

- shared economy succeeds because digital tools enable and encourage trust; also because economy is struggling
- Sarah Kessler (*Fast Company*): "Hard to make it in the sharing economy."

After reviewing these notes, the student decided on these supporting details to support the thesis about the sharing economy.

1. **Define the sharing economy** (to make sure readers understand what it is).

2. **Explain its simplicity and ease of use** (to segue into the focus of the essay).

3. **Provide examples** (to illustrate the simplicity).

4. **Consider its future** (to conclude the essay).

Next, he identified the details that support each point. He would also note if he needed to gather additional details to support any of these idea.

1. **Define the sharing economy.**

   from "People Who Share" website

   - "a socio-economic system built around the sharing of human and physical assets"
   - includes shared production, distribution, trade, and consumption of goods by different people and organizations

   from SearchCIO website TechTarget

   - also known as collaborative consumption

2. **Explain its simplicity and ease of use.**

from *Forbes* **website – 7/30/2013**

- possible because of advances in technology
- human need—strive for simplicity
- ease of use—access resources when we need them

from *Time* **website**

- sharing replacing ownership society
- "ownership" just about ruined the economy

3. **Provide examples.**

from *Forbes* **website – 7/30/2013**

Airbnb

- started in San Fran in 2008 by 2 people with a spare bed and needing cash
- now operating in 192 countries; 10 million nights booked in 5 years

ZipCar

- gives people access to a car for as long as they need it
- book car online, select one nearby, unlock it with mobile, and drive away

TaskRabbit

- people for hire pick up laundry, do the shopping, etc.
- post job online and TaskRabbit will bid for work

4. **Consider its future.**

from **"The People Who Share" website**

- future—built for the long term

from *Time* **website**

- one of 10 ideas that will change the world according to *Time*
- young consumers leading to different forms of consumption
- has a green element

from *New York News & Politics* **website**

- Sarah Kessler (*Fast Company*): "Hard to make it in the sharing economy."
- no benefits, little money

Moving from Planning to Drafting

Once the writer has crafted a main idea (thesis) and put together a list of supporting details, she is ready to write the first draft of her essay. Her goal should be to get all of her ideas on paper, using her planning notes as a guide. If everything goes well, the first draft will develop as planned. Then again, she may discover that she needs to do more research for one part of her paper or even rethink her main idea. This is all part of the writing process.

☑ Review and Enrichment

Chapter Review Quiz

Answer the questions about what you've learned in this chapter.

1. Where should you look in a reading selection to find the topic?
   a. In the middle part of the reading
   b. In the title, first few sentences, or first few paragraphs
   c. In the ending paragraph

2. What is the main idea in a reading selection?
   a. A special feature, part, or claim about a topic that will be emphasized
   b. A conclusion that can be drawn from a text
   c. The introduction of the topic in the first two sentences

3. In an essay, the main idea is stated in the _____ .
   a. Topic sentence
   b. Thesis statement
   c. Supporting detail

4. What is an implied main idea?
   a. A main idea stated as a question
   b. A main idea that is not directly stated in the text
   c. A main idea that lacks effective support

5. Why is it important to decide on a main idea for your writing?
   a. A main idea gives your writing direction so you know what to say about your topic.
   b. A main idea helps you end your essay.
   c. A main idea offers you countless choices for supporting details.

6. What is the difference between major and minor details?
   a. Major details are very important and minor details are unimportant.
   b. Major details appear in the beginning paragraphs, and minor details appear in the final paragraphs.
   c. Major details explain a main idea, and minor details make the major details clearer.

7. What is an inference?
   a. A concluding statement that sums up the major details in a text
   b. A logical conclusion that you make about something that is not actually stated in a text
   c. A key question that you have after reading a selection

8. Why is it important to include plenty of strong details in your writing?

    a. Details are needed to support or explain the main idea.

    b. Details are needed to make your writing longer.

    c. Details are needed to explain everything about a topic.

Reading for Enrichment

You will be reading excerpted pages from *Empire of the Summer Moon*, the story behind an important evolution in the history of Comanche Native Americans, a tribe living in the warm and dry climate of the American West. Be sure to follow the steps in the reading process to help you gain a full understanding of the text. (See Section 2.1.)

About the Author

S.C. Gwynne is an award-winning journalist writing for *The Dallas Morning News*. He also has served as a correspondent and editor for *Time* and as executive editor for *Texas Monthly*. His book *Empire of the Summer Moon* was a finalist for the Pulitzer Prize and the National Book Critics Circle Award.

Prereading

S.C. Gwynne states that more than 250 years ago the Comanche tribe experienced a "transformative technology"—or a technology that significantly affected their lives, just as steam and electricity affected the rest of the world. Consider what this technology might have been, especially when thinking about how the Comanches lived in a rather primitive way. Then consider a few technologies that have significantly transformed your own life.

Before you read, use the STRAP strategy to identify the main parts of the text. Also, consider listing a few questions that you hope the reading will answer.

Subject:	What specific topic does the reading address?
Type:	What form (*essay, book excerpt, textbook selection*) does the reading take?
Role:	What position (*student, professor, journalist*) does the writer assume?
Audience:	Who is the intended audience (*general readers, students, journalists*)?
Purpose:	What is the general goal of the reading (*to inform, to persuade, to share*)?

Reading and Rereading

As you read, be sure to (1) identify the main idea of the essay, (2) follow the details that develop this idea, and (3) look for answers to the questions you may have listed. Consider annotating the text and/or taking notes as you read. Then reread as needed to form a clear understanding of the text.

The Reading Process

Incredible Transformation

What happened to the Comanche tribe between roughly 1625 and 1750 was   *1*
one of the great social and military transformations in history. The agent of this
astonishing change was the horse. Or, more precisely, what this backward tribe
of Stone Age hunters did with the horse, an astonishing piece of transformative
technology that had as much of an effect on the Great Plains as steam and
electricity had on the rest of civilization. . . .

No one knows exactly how or when the Comanche bands in eastern Wyoming   *2*
first encountered the horse, but that event probably happened somewhere near the
midpoint of the seventeenth century. Since the Pawnees, who lived in the area we
now call Nebraska, were known to be mounted by 1680, the Comanches almost
certainly had horses by that time. There were no witnesses to this great coming
together of Stone Age hunters and horses, nothing to record what happened when
they met or what there was in the soul of the Comanches that understood the horse
so much better than everyone else did. Whatever it was, whatever sort of accidental
brilliance, whatever the particular, **subliminal** bond between warrior and horse, it
must have thrilled these dark-skinned **pariahs** from the Wind River country.

The Comanches adapted to the horse earlier and more completely than any   *3*
other plains tribe. They are considered, without much debate, the **prototype**
horse tribe in North America. No one could outride them or outshoot them from
the back of a horse. Among other horse tribes, only the Kiowas fought entirely
mounted, as the Comanches did. Pawnees, Crows, even the Dakotas used the horse
primarily for transport. They would ride to the battle, then dismount and fight.
No tribe other than the Comanches ever learned to breed horses—an intensely
demanding, knowledge-based skill that helped create enormous wealth for the
tribe. They were always careful in the **castration** of the herd; almost all riding
horses were **geldings**. Few other tribes bothered with this. It was not uncommon
for a Comanche warrior to have one hundred to two hundred mounts, or for a chief

to have fifteen hundred. (A Sioux chief might have forty horses, by comparison.) They were not only the richest of all tribes in sheer horseflesh, their horses were also the main medium through which the rest of the tribes became mounted. . . .

Colonel Richard Dodge, whose **expedition** made early contact with Comanches, believed them to be the finest light cavalry in the world, superior to any mounted soldiers in Europe or America. [George] Catlin also saw them as incomparable horsemen. As he described it, the American soldiers were dumbfounded at what they saw. "On their feet they are one of the most unattractive and **slovenly** looking races of Indians I have ever seen, but the moment they mount their horses, they seem at once **metamorphosed**," wrote Catlin. "I am ready, without hesitation, to pronounce the Comanches the most extraordinary horsemen I have seen yet in all my travels." *4*

Children were given their own horses at four or five. Soon the boys were expected to learn tricks, which included picking up objects on the ground at a gallop. The young rider would start with light objects and move to progressively heavier objects until finally, without assistance and at a full gallop, he could pick up a man. Rescuing a fallen comrade was seen as one of the most basic obligations of a Comanche warrior. Women could often ride as well as men. One observer watched two Comanche women set out at full speed with lassoes and each rope a bounding antelope on the first throw. Women had their own mounts, as well as mules and gentle horses for packing. *5*

When they were not stealing horses or breeding them, they were capturing them in the wild. General Thomas James told a story of how he had witnessed this in 1832, when he had visited the Comanches as a horse buyer. He watched as many riders headed bands of wild horses into a deep ravine where a hundred men waited on horseback with coiled **lariats**. When the "terrified wild horses reached the ambush," there was a good deal of dust and confusion as the riders lassoed them by the neck or forefeet. But every rider got an animal. Only one horse got away. *6*

The Comanches pursued him, and in two hours he came back "tamed and gentle." Within twenty-four hours one hundred or more wild horses had been captured "amid the wildest excitement" and appeared to be "as subject to their masters as farm horses." They would chase a herd of mustangs for several days until the animals were exhausted, making them easy to capture. Comanches waited by water holes for parched horses to gorge themselves so they could barely run, then captured them. . . .

In the late 1600s, Comanche mastery of the horse had led them to migrate   7 southward out of the harsh, cold lands of the Wind River and into more temperate climates. The meaning of the migration was simple: They were challenging other tribes for supremacy over the single richest hunting prize on the continent, the buffalo herds of the southern plains.

subliminal
subconscious, hidden

pariah
a person rejected by others

castration
removal of testicles

geldings
castrated male horses

expedition
a journey with a specific purpose

slovenly
unclean or shabby

metamorphosed
changed to something wholly different

lariats
a noosed rope used to catch horses

Reflecting

Answer the comprehension and vocabulary questions about the reading.

1. What is the main idea of this selection?
   a. The horse served as a transformative technology for the Comanche bands.
   b. The buffalo became the Comanches' main food source.
   c. The Comanche bands could shoot an arrow while on the move.

2. What is the main type of supporting detail used in paragraph 2?

   a. Statistics
   b. References
   c. Explanation

3. What is the main type of supporting detail used in paragraph 4?
   a. Statistics
   b. References
   c. Definitions

4. The following sentence comes from paragraph 5: *"The young rider would start with light objects and move to progressively heavier objects until finally, without assistance and at a full gallop, he could pick up a man."* Is this selection an example of a major or a minor detail?
   a. Major detail
   b. Minor detail

5. In paragraph 6, General Thomas James shares a story. What type of supporting detail does this represent?
   a. Analysis
   b. Anecdote
   c. Reflection

6. Study how the word *prototype* is used in the reading, and then choose the most accurate definition of the word.
   Prototype (paragraph 3)
   a. Surprising example
   b. Final product
   c. Original model

Summarizing

Write a summary paragraph of the selection using the guidelines in Section 2.4 for help. Remember to use your own words and to focus only on the key ideas.

Critical Thinking

- How is there an element of mystery or uncertainty in this essay? And does it in any way diminish its effectiveness?
- How does this selection show the connectedness of people and places in history?
- Can you relate, in any way, what happened to the Comanche bands to any people in the modern world?

Writing for Enrichment

Choose one of the following writing ideas, or decide upon an idea of your own related to the reading. Be sure to follow the steps in the writing process to develop your work.

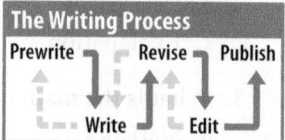

1. Explain how the horse was considered a "transformative technology" for the Comanches in the same way that steam and electricity were transformative for other civilizations of the time.

2. Explain the Comanche lifestyle before and after the tribe's introduction to the horse.

3. Write a brief biography of one of the most famous Comanche warriors, Quanah Parker.

4. Analyze the transformative impact of a particular technology in your own life.

When prewriting and planning . . .

- Research your topic as needed, taking thorough notes as you go.
- Establish a thesis for your essay.
- Review your notes for key ideas to support your thesis.
- Decide on the details that you will use to develop these ideas.

When writing . . .

- Include a beginning, middle, and ending in your essay.
- Present your thesis in the beginning part.
- Support the thesis in the middle paragraphs with plenty of major and minor details.
- Close your essay with final thoughts about your thesis.

When revising and editing. . .

- Carefully review your first draft, making sure that you develop each key point with sufficient details.
- Ask at least one peer to review your writing.
- Improve the content as needed.
- Then edit your revised writing for style and correctness.

bopav, 2017 / Used under license from Shutterstock.com

Chapter 5

Organization

Ideas and organization work together to create a meaningful text. For example, the directions in manuals are organized chronologically so they can be followed, just as the explanations in textbooks are organized logically so they can be understood. It would be almost impossible to understand any piece of writing if the ideas weren't thoughtfully organized. Ideas need form and structure to create meaning.

In terms of basic organization, a text needs a clearly developed beginning, middle, and ending to form a meaningful whole. Within the body of a text, the ideas and details must be arranged according to an appropriate pattern of organization such as cause-effect or time order. In this chapter, you will learn how to recognize and appreciate the organization in reading selections and how to effectively organize the ideas in your own essays.

Chapter Outline

- Understanding the Three-Part Structure
- Reading the Beginning Part
- Writing the Beginning Part of an Essay
- Reading the Middle Part
- Developing the Middle Part of an Essay
- Reading the Ending Part
- Writing the Ending Part of an Essay

5.1 Understanding the Three-Part Structure

Figure 5.1 identifies the basic structure of paragraphs and essays (and other multi-paragraph informational texts). When you are reading and writing academic texts, keep this three-part structure in mind.

Figure 5.1 Three-Part Structure

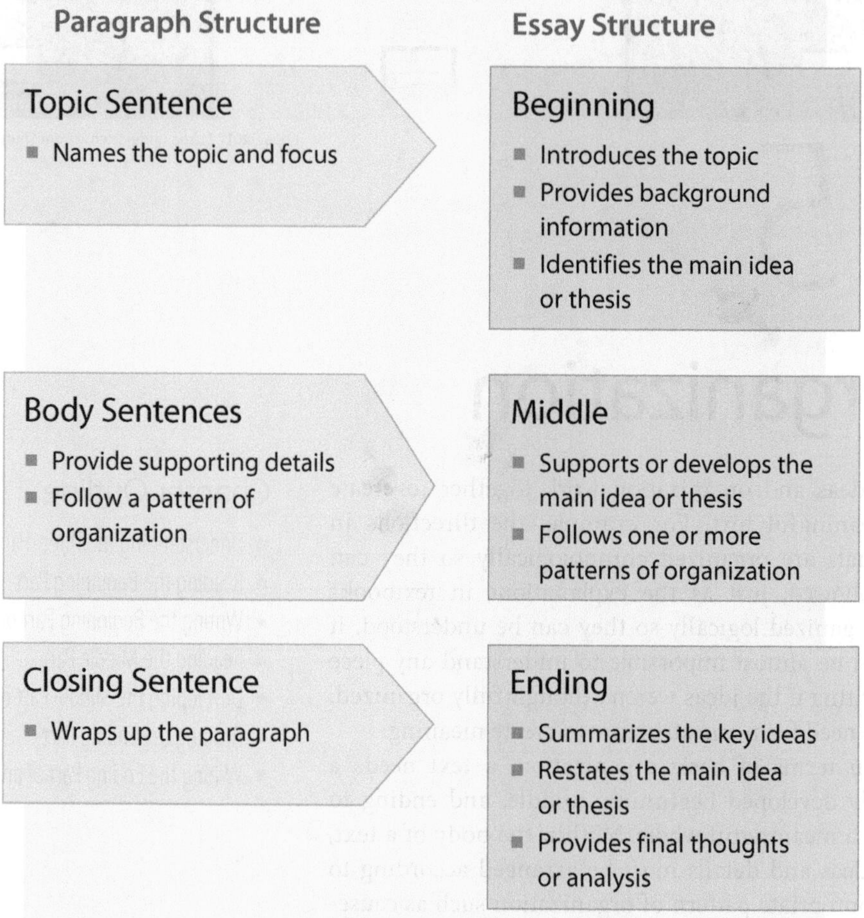

Paragraph Structure

Topic Sentence
- Names the topic and focus

Body Sentences
- Provide supporting details
- Follow a pattern of organization

Closing Sentence
- Wraps up the paragraph

Essay Structure

Beginning
- Introduces the topic
- Provides background information
- Identifies the main idea or thesis

Middle
- Supports or develops the main idea or thesis
- Follows one or more patterns of organization

Ending
- Summarizes the key ideas
- Restates the main idea or thesis
- Provides final thoughts or analysis

5.2 Reading the Beginning Part

Generally speaking, the beginning part of an informational reading introduces the topic and provides background information that leads up to the thesis statement. The thesis statement usually completes the beginning part of an essay. Reading an academic text can be challenging when the beginning part does not lead up to the thesis. Here is the beginning of an essay entitled "Shrouded in Contradiction" by Gelareh Asayesh, who grew up in Iran before moving to Florida.

> I grew up wearing the miniskirt to school, the veil to the mosque. In the Tehran of my childhood, women in bright sundresses shared the sidewalk with women swathed in black. The tension between the two ways of life was **palpable**. As a schoolgirl, I often cringed when my bare legs got leering or **contemptuous** glances. Yet, at times, I long for the days when I could walk the streets of my country with the wind in my hair. When clothes were clothes. In today's Iran, whatever I wear sends a message. If it's **chador**, it embarrasses my Westernized relatives. If it's a skimpy scarf, I risk being accused of stepping on the blood of the martyrs who died in the war with Iraq. Each time I return to Tehran, I wait until the last possible moment, when my plane lands on the tarmac, to don the scarf and long jacket that many Iranian women wear in lieu of a veil. To wear hijab—Islamic covering—is to invite contradictions.

palpable
noticeable, intense

contemptuous
showing disrespect

chador
a traditional garment worn by Muslim and Hindu women that covers the body from head to foot, including all or part of the face

- **Topic:** A young woman's clothing when returning to Tehran, Iran
- **Background information:** The writer first describes how she dressed as a girl in Tehran. Then she describes how she must dress now upon returning there for visits.
- **Thesis:** "To wear hijab—Islamic covering—*(topic)* is to invite contradictions *(focus).*"

Here is the beginning part of an essay from a college textbook entitled "Cyber Crime."

> The Craigslist advertisement—offering $300 a week and a free trailer to "watch over a 688-acre patch of hilly farmland and feed a few cows"—acted like a beacon to the unemployed and the desperate. The ad drew more than one hundred responses, and four men traveled to the property in rural southern Ohio

for a final "interview." Only one of them survived, a man who alerted local law enforcement after a close escape on November 6, 2011. The bodies of the three other men were found in shallow graves, leaving authorities perplexed as to the motives of the two suspects in the crime, Richard J. Beasley and high school student Brogan Rafferty.

Using false names, Beasley and Rafferty were allegedly able to attract applicants from across the United States for a job that did not exist on land they did not own. Access and **anonymity** are two of the hallmarks of Internet technology, which has transformed daily life in the twenty-first century. Nearly three-fourths of all American households now own a computer, and the **proliferation** of handheld Internet devices has made it possible to be online at almost any time or in any "place." Furthermore, nearly every business in today's economy relies on computers to conduct its daily affairs and to provide consumers with easy access to its products and services. In short, the Internet has become a place where large numbers of people interact socially and commercially. As in any such environment, wrongdoing has an opportunity to flourish.

From GAINES/MILLER, *Cengage Advantage Books: Criminal Justice in Action*, 6E. © 2011 Cengage Learning.

---

anonymity	**proliferation**
quality of being unknown	drastic increase

- **Topic:** Cyber crime
- **Background information:** The essay begins with a dramatic example of cyber crime, followed by observations about technology's role in modern life.
- **Thesis:** "In short, the Internet has become a place where large numbers of people interact socially and commercially *(topic)*. As in any such environment, wrongdoing has an opportunity to flourish *(focus)*."

Practice 5.1 Carefully read these two beginnings, and answer the questions after each one.

When you go to buy a box of Valentine's Day candy, what color will the box be? Green? Blue? The answer, of course, is red. What is the most popular color of women's lipstick? Yellow? Brown? Again, the answer is red. Red has been the most popular lipstick color since the construction of the pyramids in ancient Egypt. At a traffic light, the color red means *stop*. But when it comes to sexual attraction, the color red is more likely to mean *go*.

From Rathus, *Psych5*. © 2018 Cengage Learning

1. What is the topic?
   a. The spectrum of colors
   b. Lipstick
   c. The color red

2. What is the main background information?
   a. The color red is associated with Valentine's Day and lipstick.
   b. All colors have specific associations.
   c. Colors have a long history.

3. What is the main idea (thesis)?
   a. Red has been the most popular lipstick color since the construction of the pyramids in ancient Egypt.
   b. But when it comes to sexual attraction, the color red is more likely to mean *go*.
   c. At a traffic light, the color red means *stop*.

> For several years a picture of Warren Spahn of the Milwaukee Braves (now the Atlanta Braves) hung on my closet door, one leg poised in midair before he delivered a smoking fastball. Time passed and Spahn's picture gave way to others: Elvis, John F. Kennedy, Carl Jung, Joseph Campbell, Ben Hogan. Like serpents, we keep shedding the skins of our heroes as we move toward new phases in our lives.
>
> Like many of my generation, I have a weakness for hero worship. At some point, however, we begin to question our heroes and our need for them. This leads us to ask: What is a hero? Despite immense differences in cultures, heroes around the world generally share a number of traits that instruct and inspire people.
>
> From *Is a Hero Really Nothing but a Sandwich?* by Ted Tollefson

4. What is the topic?
   a. Weaknesses
   b. Heroes
   c. Phases of life

5. What is the main background information?
   a. Anecdotes (stories) about the author's personal heroes
   b. Questions we have about our heroes
   c. The pitching delivery of Warren Spahn

6. What is the main idea (thesis)?
   a. Our heroes change as we change.
   b. Heroes around the world share a number of traits.
   c. People around the world need heroes.

5.3 Writing the Beginning Part of an Essay

The beginning part of an essay, usually consisting of one or two paragraphs, should (1) introduce the topic in an interesting and/or important way; (2) provide background information, if needed, leading up to the thesis; and (3) state the thesis (main idea).

Strategies for Introducing a Topic

First impressions are important—say, for instance, when you're interviewing for a job or introducing yourself to a roommate or a work supervisor. First impressions are important in writing as well. The first few sentences should introduce the topic in an interesting and/or important way and set the tone and direction for the rest of the piece. Here are strategies to fulfill this function:

Surprising or Little-Known Facts

To gain your reader's attention, you can open with a surprising or little-known fact about your topic. This strategy works well if readers are unfamiliar or perhaps uninterested in a topic. In an essay about fetal alcohol syndrome, the writer provides this surprising opening idea.

> Thousands of babies are born each year with alcohol-related defects, making fetal alcohol syndrome one of the leading causes of mental retardation.

Important or Challenging Questions

Asking an important or challenging question will naturally lead your readers into the text because they will expect an answer to follow. In an essay about people experiencing homelessness, the writer poses this thought-provoking question.

> What exactly do the signs held up by people experiencing homelessness tell us?

Quotation from an Expert

A revealing quotation from an expert can also be used to provide an immediate level of authority to an essay. In an essay about the sharing economy, a writer uses a telling quotation about his topic.

> Thomas Friedman is a prize-winning journalist who, among other things, is interested in trends shaping the global economy. He states, "The sharing economy is producing both new entrepreneurs and a new concept of ownership."

Brief, Dramatic Stories (Anecdotes)

Readers are naturally attracted to interesting stories, even if they are very brief, so sharing a story can be an effective way to introduce a topic. In a family history piece, the writer shares a dramatic story about his great-grandmother's city of birth.

> It was May 1945; World War II had just ended, and Yugoslavia had been overtaken. The town of Vrhnika, Yugoslavia, was no longer safe for my great-grandmother and her family. Russian troops were breaking into houses, taking what they wanted, and even killing.

Bold Statements

A bold statement can effectively gain a reader's interest about a topic. In a problem-solution essay, the writer introduces her topic, childhood malnourishment, with this dramatic statement.

> Dry weather may be to blame for the unrelenting drought in parts of Africa. But cruel government politics have created a devastating famine.

Identifying the Main Idea

At times, the best way to begin may be to state the main idea and get on with the rest of the text, especially if the topic really doesn't need an introduction. In a descriptive essay about kayaking, the writer simply stated his main idea.

> On most summer mornings, I kayak on Castle Rock Lake for exercise and enjoyment.

Practice 5.2 ▶ Identify the opening strategy used for each item.

1. When people outside the Netherlands think of the Dutch, what do they envision?
   a. Surprising or little known fact
   b. Important or challenging question
   c. Brief, dramatic story

2. Jackie Thomas, Nike's associate director of sports marketing, usually spends her lunch hour on the sports-shoe company's basketball courts charging for the basket, always outnumbered by male colleagues. "I hold my own," boasts the 33-year-old executive.
   a. Bold statement
   b. Identifying the main idea
   c. Brief, dramatic story

Completing the Beginning Part

Suppose you are writing an informational essay about Legg-Calve-Perthes (pronounced leg-cal-VAY-PER-theez), a rare, degenerative bone disease. You could share *a brief, dramatic story* to introduce your topic and then state the thesis (underlined).

> Allie Mason acted like a typical coed. She was bubbly, energetic, and friendly. She was also a conscientious student, belonging to the Honors Art Club in high school. What set Allie apart was a physical condition that caused one of her legs to be noticeably shorter that the other one. As a result, she had to endure endless medical procedures and missed out on physical activities such as running and dancing. She also has had to endure more than her share of cruel remarks. She remembers one girl complaining to the gym teacher, "Hey, it's not fair that Allie doesn't have to run the mile and we do." The reason for Allie's suffering has been Legg-Calve-Perthes, a painful, degenerative bone disease that truly challenges the sufferer.

If you were explaining the process of water purification, you could introduce your topic with *surprising facts* and *statistics* before stating your thesis (underlined).

> One of the most overlooked luxuries of living in the United States is access to clean drinking water. Statistics show roughly one-eighth of the world's population lack access to safe water supplies, while as many as 2.5 billion people live without sanitized water. Untreated water is full of dangerous chemicals and contaminants that can lead to debilitating and sometimes fatal diseases, including dysentery and diarrhea. What is needed worldwide are dependable purification systems that make water safe to drink.

If you were writing about the sharing economy, you might introduce your topic with a *revealing quotation* and then expand on the quotation to lead up to the thesis (underlined).

> Thomas Friedman is a Pulitzer prize-winning author who is interested in trends shaping the global economy. He states, "The sharing economy is producing both new entrepreneurs and a new concept of ownership." Brian Chesky and Nathan Blecharczyk, who created Airbnb, and Leah Busque, who created TaskRabbit, are three such entrepreneurs who are changing the way we conduct business. These businesses connect people directly and promote sharing rather than buying. The sharing economy is thriving because users value its simplicity.

5.4 Reading the Middle Part

The details that support the thesis (main idea) of an essay often follow one main pattern of organization. For example, an essay explaining a process will almost always follow the chronological pattern. Within such an essay, however, other patterns of organization may be employed as well, but in a secondary role. For example, a process essay may contain a comparison and/or a detailed description. Knowing how the patterns of organization work will help you follow the supporting details in a reading selection.

Chronological Order

Narratives that recall experiences and essays that explain how something works or how to do something follow chronological, or time, order. This paragraph explains the process for making cheese. The highlighted words show that **chronological order** is used.

Cheese Making

Cheese making starts by heating the milk to kill off any unsafe bacteria. Once the milk is heated, a starter culture is added to curdle it. The culture contains different enzymes and bacteria that give cheese its unique flavor. Next, the cheese sits for a day, until the milk has curdled into solids. The solids are called *curds*, while the leftover liquid is called *whey*. After the cheese maker separates the curds from the whey, the process continues by reheating the curds, letting them settle, and stirring away as much liquid as possible. This step is repeated until the cheese maker believes the cheese is sufficiently solid. When the cheese solidifies, it is poured into molds of different shapes and sizes. Finally, the cheese is placed in cooler temperatures so that it can ripen.

Cause-Effect

Textbooks commonly explain the relationship between causes and effects. For example, a science text may explain the causes and effects of suburban expansion on the environment, or a history text may discuss the causes and effects of an important event. The following paragraph discusses the causes and effects of hypothermia. The highlighted words show that **cause-effect organization** is followed. A secondary pattern is used as well because there is a process involved in the effects of the condition.

Hypothermia

Even a slight drop in the normal human body temperature of 98.6 degrees Fahrenheit causes hypothermia. Often produced by accidental or prolonged exposure to cold, the condition forces all bodily functions to slow down. The heart rate and blood pressure decrease. Breathing becomes slower and shallower.

As the body temperature drops, these effects become even more dramatic until it reaches somewhere between 88 and 82 degrees Fahrenheit and the person lapses into unconsciousness. When the temperature reaches between 65 and 59 degrees Fahrenheit, heart action, blood flow, and electrical brain activity stop. Normally such a condition would be fatal. However, as the body cools down, the need for oxygen also slows down. A person can survive in a deep hypothermic state for an hour or longer and be revived without serious complications.

Logical Order

Texts that simply present information in a sensible order are organized logically. The supporting details essentially follow one another in a reasonable way to create a coherent text. One idea or detail logically leads to the next one. This passage logically discusses the skill of listening.

Listen Hard!

It's estimated that college students spend 10 hours per week listening to lectures.   1

Instructors can speak 2,500-5,000 words during a 50 minute lecture. That's a lot of words flying by at breakneck speed, so it's important to listen correctly. But what does that mean?

Think about the various situations in which you find yourself listening. You   2
often listen to empty chit-chat on your way to class. "Hey, how's it going?" when you spot your best friend in the hallway is an example, right? Listening in this situation doesn't require a lot of brainpower.

You also listen in challenging situations, some that are emotionally charged;   3
for example, a friend needs to vent, relieve stress, or express her anxieties. Most people who are blowing off steam aren't looking for you to fix their problems. They just want to be heard and hear you say something like "I understand" or "That's too bad."

Listening to chit-chat and listening in emotionally charged situations   4
require what are called soft listening skills. You must be accepting, sensitive, and nonjudgmental. You don't have to assess, analyze, or conclude. You just have to be there for someone else.

When you're listening to new information, as you do in your college classes,   5
you have to pay close attention, think critically, and ultimately make decisions about what you're hearing. When you're listening to a person trying to inform you or to persuade you, you need hard listening skills. In situations like these you must evaluate, analyze, and decide.

From *FOCUS on College and Career Success*, 1E. © 2012 Cengage Learning

Comparison

Texts that show the similarities and differences between two topics follow one of the comparison patterns of organization. One text may make a topic-by-topic comparison, discussing one topic completely and then the other topic. Another text may discuss all of the similarities between the two topics and then their differences. Still another text may make a point-by-point comparison of the two topics. This paragraph makes a topic-by-topic comparison of the two main legal representatives in the British legal system.

Solicitors and Barristers

In the British legal system, both solicitors and barristers serve the public, but they do so in different ways. Someone in Great Britain seeking legal help contacts a solicitor, who will usually be part of a law firm. A solicitor then serves as a client's legal representative, providing legal guidance and advice. When a client needs specialized legal help before the high court, a solicitor will contact his legal partner, a barrister. Unlike a solicitor, a barrister has no attachment to any firm but instead is a member of chambers, a group of barristers that share legal aides and office help. A barrister's main responsibility is to argue a client's case before a judge and jury. This legal division of power has served the British public well for ages, though solicitors are now gaining more responsibility before the courts.

Problem-Solution

Texts that explore a particular problem often follow the problem-solution pattern of organization. Usually, the parts of the problem are identified and analyzed, followed by a discussion of possible solutions. Sometimes the best solution is addressed in detail. Cause-effect is a common secondary pattern of organization when problems are discussed. This passage follows the problem-solution pattern regarding lead poisoning, a serious health problem in the young.

Lead Poisoning

(Problem) Lead poisoning is a serious health problem for young children. According to the Alliance for Healthy Homes, the problem is especially serious for inner-city children living in homes still containing lead-based paints, the major source of the problem. Young children may ingest peeling paint or breath in the dust from the paint; both are potentially harmful. Lead poisoning can lead to headaches and nausea, as well as more deep-seated problems such as learning disabilities and behavioral problems.

(Solutions) Tragically, no complete cures to lead poisoning exist. The best immediate solution is for home dwellers to carry out daily house cleanings and to regularly wash their hands. For the long term, walls covered in lead paint should be repainted with a safer paint, but without any sanding beforehand. In addition, renters must know they have rights for protecting their health and safety. Landlords by law are required to find and address sources of lead.

Practice 5.3 Carefully read each of the following texts. Then decide which pattern of organization is used: *chronological, logical, cause-effect, comparison,* or *problem-solution.*

1.   Each year, more people experiencing homelessness roam the largest cities in the United States. Many experts point to the shortage of affordable housing as the reason for this. According to Peter Marcuse in a recent *Nation* article, the 2 percent vacancy rate of affordable housing in the U.S. is not great enough to fill the need. So what is the solution? First of all, the federal government must accept responsibility for sheltering people without permanent housing and increase production of affordable housing. Secondly, the government must ensure that the proper housing is made available through temporary emergency shelters as well as transitional shelters and affordable permanent housing. With the proper housing, homelessness could become a matter of choice rather than necessity.

Pattern of organization: _____

2.   The recent uptick in earthquakes in Texas, Oklahoma and several other central US states raises an obvious question: What is causing all of this seismicity?

Several factors can promote the occurrence of earthquakes. There are natural changes caused by the shifting of Earth's plates, the advance and retreat of glaciers, the addition or removal of surface water or ground water, and the injection or removal of fluids due to industrial activity.

Studies, including two reports issued in April, indicate that human activities, including activities related to oil and gas extraction, are beginning to play a significant role in triggering earthquakes in the central US.

Extracting oil and gas from shale rock involves cracking, or fracturing, a layer of underground rock with a high-pressure mix of water, sand, and chemicals. As the oil and gas are released, those injection fluids and briny water also come up. That wastewater is later disposed of in what are called injection wells, or sometimes disposal wells.

From "Why is oil and gas activity causing earthquakes? And can we reduce the risk?" *The Conversation* theconversation.com

Pattern of organization: _____

3.   When the researchers compared the three generations on work values, they found that differences are small, subtle and not readily divisible into three periods. For example, millennials valued the extrinsic rewards of work, such as money and status, slightly less than Gen-Xers and only slightly more than boomers.

Similarly, millennials were only marginally less invested in the intrinsic rewards of work, such as its opportunities for skill development and creativity, than earlier generations. They valued work that was directly helpful to others and socially worthwhile to a lesser extent than 18-year-old boomers and Gen-Xers.

Indeed, the magnitude of these differences was consistently tiny. On average, roughly 45% of millennials went against the overall pattern of generational differences   From "Millennials in the workplace: not as different as you think" *The Conversation* theconversation.com

Pattern of organization: _____

4.   Born in 1533, [Elizabeth I] was only three years old when her mother was executed. Her mother was declared illegitimate by order of the Henry, who had wished for a son. But after her father's death, Parliament established Elizabeth as third in line to the throne behind her half-brother, Edward, and her Catholic half-sister, Mary. During Mary's reign (1553-1558), Elizabeth was imprisoned, but she was careful to stay clear of the hectic Protestant-Catholic struggles of the day. By doing so, she managed to stay alive until she could become ruler in her own right.

Her rule began amid many internal dangers. The Catholic party in England opposed her as a suspected Protestant. The Calvinists opposed her as being too much like her father, Henry, who never accepted Protestant theology. The Scots were becoming rabid Calvinists who despised the English's halfway measures in religious affairs. On top of this, the government was deeply in debt.

Elizabeth showed great insight in selecting her officials and maintained good relations with Parliament. She conducted diplomatic affairs with farsightedness and found she could use her status as an unmarried queen to definite advantage.

In 1588, after long negotiations failed, Philip of Spain sent the Spanish Armada to punish England for aiding the rebellious Dutch Calvinists across the Channel. The queen rallied her sailors in a stirring visit before the battle. The resulting defeat of the Armada not only signaled England's rise to naval equality with Spain but also made Elizabeth England's most popular monarch.

From Adler/Pouwels, *World Civilizations*, 6E. © 2012 Cengage Learning.

Main pattern of organization: _____

Second pattern: _____

5.5 Developing the Middle Part of an Essay

After identifying your thesis, you need to determine how to organize the details that support it. Usually, the thesis will suggest a pattern of organization to follow. For example, the thesis statement "I am Korean, but I am American, too" suggests that the writer will compare the two cultures. The thesis statement "A fresh approach is needed to fix the gender wage gap" suggests that the writer will focus on the problem and solutions to income inequality between men and women. The thesis statement "The sharing economy thrives because users value its simplicity" suggests that the writer will present the support logically, moving sensibly from one key point to the next.

Here are three planning strategies for arranging the supporting information after identifying an appropriate pattern of organization:

- **Make a quick list** of key points.
- **Create an outline**—an organized arrangement of key points and supporting details. (See Section 2.4.)
- **Fill in a graphic organizer**, arranging key points and details in a chart or diagram. (See Section 1.5.)

Making a Quick List

A **quick list** works well for shorter essays or when your planning time is limited. For an essay organized chronologically, list the key supporting details according to time. For an essay organized spatially, list the key details from left to right, top to bottom, or near to far. For an essay organized logically, decide which supporting details go together; then determine what key point they make. Figure 5.2 illustrates a quick list for an essay that follows logical order.

> *Figure 5.2* Quick List
>
> **Thesis statement:** The sharing economy thrives because users value its simplicity.
>
> **1.** Define the sharing economy.
>
> **2.** Explain its simplicity and ease of use.
>
> **3.** Provide examples.
>
> **4.** Consider its future.

Using an Outline

An outline carefully arranges ideas for your writing. The ideas in a topic outline are expressed in words and phrases; the ideas in a sentence outline are expressed in sentences. In a traditional outline, if you have a "I," you should have at least a "II." If you have an "A," you should have at least a "B," and so on. Each new division represents another level of detail. You can also change or simplify the form to meet your writing needs. Figure 5.3 is the first part of a simplified outline that includes key points in complete sentences and supporting details in phrases.

Figure 5.3 Simplified Outline

Thesis statement: Charlotte Perkins Gilman rejected common beliefs about male dominance.

1. Gilman's beliefs did little to prepare her for married life.
    - in 1884, married Charles W. Stetson
    - gave birth to a daughter
    - visited CA shortly after to mentally and emotionally heal
    - wrote a book about a pregnant woman locked in a room

2. During the next stage in her life, Gilman became a leading feminist.
    - delivered speeches on women's rights
    - edited *Impress* for Women's Press Associate
    - from 1895-1900, continued lecturing
    - in 1896, a delegate to the National Socialist and Labor Congress in London

---

Using a Graphic Organizer

A graphic organizer (see **Figures 1.3–1.10**) helps you map out your writing using a chart, table, or diagram. For example, you can use a line diagram to organize information for an essay that identifies three examples of the topic. **Figure 5.4** shows an example.

Figure 5.4 Sample Line Diagram

Thesis statement: The most famous mysteries have a one-of-a-kind main character leading the investigation.

Writing the Middle Part

In the middle paragraphs, you develop the key points that support your thesis statement. Use your quick list, outline, or graphic organizer as a general guide. Also consider these writing tips:

- **Keep your thesis statement in mind** as you write. All of your key points should support or explain this statement.

- **Develop each key point in a separate paragraph** (or two). State the key point in the form of a topic sentence, and follow with details that support it.

- **Fully explain each point.** Use the evidence you gathered during your research.

- **Use your own words,** except on those few occasions when you use the exact words from one of your sources. Credit the source of the information.

- **Be open to new ideas** as they occur to you as you write.

The paragraphs in the middle part of your essay should, among other things, *define, explain, describe, show,* and *analyze* your topic and thesis. In an informational essay about the degenerative bone disease Legg-Calve-Perthes, the writer developed one middle paragraph using this part of his outline.

> 1. Legg-Calve-Perthes is both rare and mysterious
>   – affects 5 out of 100,000 children (5 to 12)
>   – boys affected more frequently, 4 to 1
>   – believed not to be genetic
>   – factor—lessening blood flow to hip joint
>   – distorts femur fitting into hip (Allie's doubled in size)

Legg-Calve-Perthes is both rare and mysterious. The disease affects only five of every 100,000 children, usually when they are between the ages of five and twelve. Boys suffer from the disease far more frequently than girls do by a ratio of 4 to 1. When girls do develop Legg-Calve-Perthes, they tend to suffer more severely from it. At this point, researchers are not really sure of the cause of the disease. They are, however, fairly certain that it is not genetic. They also know that a reduction of blood flow at the hip joint contributes to the disease and causes the bone tissue to collapse or react in other strange ways. Usually, the rounded part of the femur bone that fits into the hip joint becomes deformed. In Allie's case, the top of her femur bone grew to double its normal size, a condition that produced extreme pain when she tried to walk. It's hard to imagine how Allie or anyone else is able to deal with this condition during the active childhood years.

5.6 Reading the Ending Part

The ending, of course, brings an informational text to a close. In this part, a writer may restate the thesis, summarize the main supporting details, and/or offer a final thought to keep the reader thinking about the topic. The ending of an essay is usually the final paragraph, but it may consist of the final few paragraphs. It may even begin with a transitional phrase such as *in summary, in conclusion,* or *as I have just shown.*

Think of the ending as the ribbon that secures and wraps up the reading. It should reinforce, enhance, or broaden what you have learned in the main part of the writing. For example, the ending paragraph (paragraph 4) in this brief essay reinforces the thesis (underlined) and adds additional information.

> As much as puppies or pandas or even children, dolphins are universally   *1*
> beloved. They seem to play and frolic anytime. Their mouths are fixed in what
> looks like a state of perpetual merriment, and their behavior and enormous brain
> suggests an intelligence approaching that of humans—even, some might argue,
> surpassing it.
>
> Dolphins are turning out to be exceedingly clever, but not in the loving,   *2*
> utopian-socialist manner that sentimental Flipperophiles may have hoped.
> Researchers who spent thousands of hours observing the behavior of bottle-nosed
> dolphins off the coast of Australia have discovered that the males form social
> alliances that are far more sophisticated and devious than seen in any animals
> other than human beings. In these sleek submarine partnerships, one team of
> dolphins will recruit the help of another band of males to gang up against a
> third group, a sort of multi-tiered battle plan that requires considerable mental
> calculus.
>
> The purpose of these complex alliances is not exactly sportive. Males collide   *3*
> with their peers in order to steal fertile females from competing bands. And after
> they succeed in spiriting a female away, the males remain in their tight-knit group
> and perform a series of feats, at once spectacular and threatening, to guarantee
> that the female stays in line. Two or three males will surround her, leaping and
> bellyflopping, swiveling and somersaulting, all in perfect synchrony. Should the
> female be so unimpressed by the choreography as to attempt to flee, the males will
> chase after her, bite her, slap her with their fins, or slam into her with their bodies.
> The scientists call this effort to control females "herding," but they acknowledge

that the word does not convey the aggressiveness of the act. As the herding proceeds, the sounds of fin swatting and body bashing rumble the waters, and sometimes the female emerges with deep tooth rakes on her side.

Although biologists have long been impressed with the intelligence and social complexity of bottle-nose dolphins—the type of porpoise often enlisted for marine mammal shows because they are so responsive to trainers—they were nonetheless surprised by the Machiavellian flavor of the males' stratagems. Equally impressive, the multipart alliances among dolphins seemed flexible, shifting from day to day depending on the dolphins' needs, whether one group owed a favor to another, and the dolphins' perceptions of what they could get away with. The creatures seem to be highly opportunistic, which meant that each animal was always computing who was friend and who was foe.

From *The Beauty and the Beastly* by Natalie Angier, Houghton Mifflin, 1995.

utopian-socialist
peaceful means to harmony and well-being

calculus
difficult undertaking

sportive
playful

synchrony
things occurring at the same time

Machiavellian
selfish, secretive, without moral principles

stratagems
plans or strategies

Practice 5.4 Carefully read the essay. Then answer the questions that follow it.

A Penny for Your World-Saving Thoughts

Most people in the developed world think of technology as the newest $300 cell phone or the best $50,000 hybrid vehicle or one of our many $40,000,000 predator drones. In the developing world, however, a whole different breed of entrepreneurs is working on technologies that cost very little and use materials as simple as corncobs and discarded two-liter bottles. These inventors don't care so much about the future as about the present, in which more than a billion people live without access to safe drinking water (World). With a rare combination of creativity and compassion, a generation of inventors is fixing the world's worst problems with the simplest solutions.

For example, Amy Smith, an instructor at MIT, works in the Peruvian Andes to turn corncobs into charcoal. Like 800 million others in the world, the locals of

El Valle Sagrado de los Incas currently heat their homes with agricultural waste products such as dung, straw, and corncobs. These fuels produce a great deal of smoke, which causes respiratory infections, the leading cause of death for those under five in such homes. By turning corncobs into charcoal, Smith converts a high-smoke fuel to a low-smoke one, not only heating homes but saving lives. Her process involves corncobs, matches, a 55-gallon drum with a lid, and patience. She jokingly calls her creations "carbon macro-tubes" (Ward).

Also, a man called "Solar Demi" is working to bring light to the slums of Manila, Philippines. In these tight-packed quarters, electricity is scarce, and most people live in total darkness. Demi takes discarded two-liter bottles, strips off their labels, cleans them, and fills them with a mixture of distilled water and bleach. He then cuts a hole in the roof of a home and fits the bottle in place with a watertight flange. This simple arrangement costs $1 per installation and produces 55 watts of free solar lighting. The Liter of Light Project aims to bring solar bottle lighting into one million homes in the Philippines (Ambani). 3

In South Africa, the problem is not lack of light but lack of water. Traditionally in many tribes, women and girls carry water in containers on their heads, a technique that requires numerous trips (keeping girls out of school) and causes stress injuries to necks. To solve this problem, architect Hans Hendrikse and his brother Piet have developed a wheel-shaped plastic drum that can hold up to 50 liters and is durable enough to roll across the ground behind a person. Four trips for water turn into one, and backbreaking loads turn into an easy stroll with a sloshing drum behind. By working with global partners, the Hendrikses are providing the Q-drum cheaply to those who need it most (Hendrikse). 4

Throughout the developing world, unsafe drinking water is a huge problem. It causes diarrhea, which kills 1.5 million children every year—more than AIDS and malaria combined. The company Vestergaard Frandsen wants to put a stop to it, so it has developed the LifeStraw—a compact filtering device that is about the size of a fat ballpoint pen. Children can carry this straw with them and drink surface water without fear of getting waterborne diseases. The straw costs about $20 in the developed world, but Vestergaard Frandsen is working with international partners to provide the straw affordably to those elsewhere who do not have safe supplies of water ("LifeStraw"). 5

It's become fashionable to talk about how the future belongs to the   6
innovators, and people who say such things are often thinking about space
elevators and the like. But the present also belongs to the innovators—those who
make corncob coal and soda-bottle lights and drums and straws that deliver
water. All of these inventions are simple, elegant solutions to the world's oldest
problems. With thinking like this, not only is our future bright, but our present
can be as well.

---

respiratory
pertaining to breathing

durable
strong and sturdy

1. Which sentence in the opening paragraph states the thesis or main idea of the piece?
   a. With a rare combination of creativity and compassion, a generation of inventors
      is fixing the world's worst problems with the simplest solutions.
   b. Most people in the developed world think of technology as the newest $300
      cell phone or the best $50,000 hybrid vehicle or one of our many $40,000,000
      predator drones.
   c. These inventors don't care so much about the future as about the present, in
      which more than a billion people live without access to safe drinking water.

2. What pattern of organization does paragraph 4 follow?
   a. Chronological
   b. Comparison
   c. Problem-solution

3. Which sentence or sentences in the closing paragraph restate the main idea or thesis
   of the essay?
   a. It's become fashionable to talk about how the future belongs to the innovators,
      and people who say such things are often thinking about space elevators and
      the like.
   b. But the present belongs to the innovators . . . . All of these inventions are simple,
      elegant solutions to the world's oldest problems.
   c. In the developing world, however, a whole different breed of entrepreneurs is
      working on technologies that cost very little.

4. What additional information is shared in the closing paragraph?
   a. The author shares a final thought about the future and the present.
   b. The author makes a call to action to other entrepreneurs.
   c. The author wishes that in the past more could have been done for the poor.

5.7 Writing the Ending Part of an Essay

While the opening part of your writing offers important first impressions, the closing part offers important final impressions. More specifically, the closing helps the reader better understand and appreciate the importance of the topic and thesis.

Consider these strategies when writing your closing. In most cases, you will want to use more than one of these strategies, but whatever you choose to do, the ending must flow smoothly from your last middle paragraph.

- **Remind the reader of the thesis.**

  > Legg-Calve-Perthes is like a cancer in how it affects an individual and her family.

- **Summarize the main points** or highlight one or two of them.

  > By removing dirt and sludge through pretreatment and coagulation, then filtering the lingering particles, and finally disinfecting with chlorine and other chemicals, water purification plants make certain that the water our bodies desperately need to survive will do the job.

- **Reflect on the explanation or argument** you've presented in the main part of your essay.

  > Many factors contribute to a person's level of physical activity. Depending on the time of year, a person may live a moderate physical lifestyle one week and a sedentary lifestyle the next week. What's most important, though, is to live a healthy lifestyle, and a healthy lifestyle requires some form of exercise.

- **Offer a final idea** to keep the reader thinking about the topic.

  > Trust is the foundation of a source-reporter relationship. Journalists Williams and Fainaru-Wada knew this. They decided against revealing their source and would have served jail time if the source had not confessed. But the next journalist might not be so lucky. It's time to pass a federal shield law.

In this closing paragraph of an essay about choosing a vegetarian diet, the writer reminds the reader about the thesis and reflects on the explanation presented in the main part.

> The vegetarian lifestyle offers numerous physical and spiritual benefits to a person who chooses it. But the lifestyle isn't for everyone. People with poor impulse control will have a hard time resisting society's penchant for eating meat. Besides that, growing children and adolescents must be careful to get enough of the proteins and fats they need to keep growing. The vegetarian lifestyle doesn't work for everyone.

In the closing paragraph of an essay about the degenerative bone disease Legg-Calve-Perthes, the writer reminds the reader about the thesis, reflects on the explanation provided in the main part of the essay, and provides an important final thought.

> Legg-Calve-Perthes is like a cancer in how it affects an individual and her family. In Allie's case, the debilitating effects started with her painful efforts to walk and have continued with attempts to address the condition with operations, therapy, and braces. Through all of this, she and her family have missed out on so much. Her mother had to quit her job, and her sister felt ignored. As Allie recalled, "My sister has always felt jealous of all of the attention I get from my parents." But knowing that the condition should, in time, resolve itself certainly must help sufferers like Allie meet each new challenge. It must also help them to know that young people suffering from Legg-Calve-Perthes usually do quite well in the long term. Unfortunately, the chance of permanent hip damage exists as well.

In the closing paragraph of an essay about life-threatening stress, the writer reminds the reader about the thesis and anecdote included in the beginning part. Then she highlights key points in the middle part before offering a final idea about "the second step—learning how to manage stress."

> Because stress is so common, many people fail to recognize its potential danger. They go about their day without much awareness of how their stress affects their health and interactions. For example, Jan, the student described in the beginning, was certainly aware that she experienced stress while bustling through her busy morning. However, if she is like most college students, she wasn't aware that excessive stress could lead to serious illness and early death. Learning about stress's causes and effects is an important first step that they must take. After that, they will be ready for the second step—learning how to manage stress.

NOTE: Because the ending leaves an important final impression, try out a variety of possible endings. Read each one out loud, and choose the one that flows best with the main ideas that come before it. Reading your writing out loud will also help you discover a natural stopping point to conclude your essay. Once you find it, don't tack on another idea.

☑ Review and Enrichment

Chapter Review Quiz

Answer the questions about what you've learned in this chapter.

1. What type of information is usually provided in the beginning part of a text?
   a. The topic, background information, and supporting details
   b. The topic, background information, and the main idea (thesis)
   c. The main idea (thesis), supporting details, and summary

2. What are two effective strategies for introducing the topic in your writing?
   a. Provide surprising or little-known facts or make a bold statement
   b. Include a major detail followed by minor details
   c. Offer an effective chart or photo

3. How are details arranged in a logical pattern of organization?
   a. Details are arranged by time.
   b. Details are arranged in a sensible manner.
   c. Details are arranged by similarities and differences.

4. What pattern of organization shows similarities and differences between two topics?
   a. Cause-effect
   b. Problem-solution
   c. Comparison

5. When your time is limited, what is the best way to plan an essay?
   a. Create an outline.
   b. Fill in a graphic organizer.
   c. Make a quick list.

6. Which writing tip refers to developing the middle part of an essay?
   a. Always keep your thesis statement in mind.
   b. Summarize your main points.
   c. Make a bold statement.

7. How does the ending reinforce what is said in the main part of an essay?
   a. It may restate the thesis and summarize the main supporting points.
   b. It may introduce a new topic in an interesting way.
   c. It may offer a key supporting detail.

8. What should be your goal when developing the ending part of an essay?
   a. Leave the reader with questions about your topic.
   b. Share important information that you forgot to include in the middle part.
   c. Help the reader better understand the importance of your topic and thesis.

Reading for Enrichment

You will be reading an essay in which the writer takes a surprising, and perhaps unpopular, position on a crisis receiving frequent national attention. Be sure to follow the steps in the reading process to help you gain a full understanding of the text.

About the Author

Nick Gillespie is editor for Reason.com and Reason.tv and the coauthor of *The Declaration of Independents: How Libertarian Politics Can Fix What's Wrong with America*. His writing has appeared in *The New York Times*, the *Los Angeles Times*, and *The Wall Street Journal*. And he has appeared on NPR, PBS, CNN, C-SPAN, and Fox News. The essay here first appeared in *The Wall Street Journal*.

Prereading

We often hear of students bullied in schools, employees harassed in the workplace, and servicemen and -women bullied in the military. We even hear of bullying in professional football locker rooms. As you probably know, digital technology has contributed to these problems because it allows bullies to harass and intimidate anonymously. In "Stop Panicking About Bullies," Gillespie responds specifically to bullying in our schools. Explore your own thoughts by freewriting about bullying. Try to write for at least five to eight minutes without stopping.

Before you read, use the STRAP strategy to identify the main parts of the text. Also, consider listing a few questions that you hope the reading will answer.

Subject: What specific topic does the reading address?
Type: What form (*essay, narrative, textbook selection*) does the reading take?
Role: What position (*student, professor, journalist*) does the writer assume?
Audience: Who is the intended audience?
Purpose: What is the general goal of the reading (*to inform, to persuade, to share*)?

Reading and Rereading

As you read, be sure to (1) note the main idea of the essay, (2) identify the three main parts of the text, and (3) look for patterns of organization used to arrange the supporting details. Consider annotating the text and/or taking notes as you read. Then reread as needed to form a clear understanding of the text.

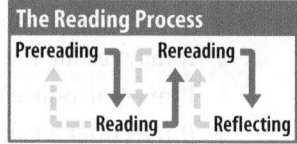

The Reading Process
Prereading · Rereading
Reading · Reflecting

Stop Panicking About Bullies

Is America really in the midst of a "bullying crisis," as so many now claim? I   1
don't see it. I also suspect that our fears about the **ubiquity** of bullying are just the
latest in a long line of well-intentioned yet **hyperbolic** alarms about how awful it is
to be a kid today.

I have no interest in defending the bullies who dominate sandboxes, extort   2
lunch money, and use Twitter to taunt their classmates. But there is no growing
crisis. Childhood and adolescence in America have never been less brutal. Even
as the country's overprotective parents whip themselves up into a moral panic
about kid-on-kid cruelty, the numbers don't point to any explosion of abuse. As
for the rising wave of laws and regulations designed to combat meanness among
students, they are likely to lump together minor slights with major offenses. The
antibullying movement is already **conflating** serious cases of gay-bashing and
vicious harassment with things like name calling.

How did we get here? We live in an age of helicopter parents so pushy and   3
overbearing that Colorado Springs banned its annual Easter-egg hunt on account
of adults jumping the starter's gun and scooping up treat-filled plastic eggs on
behalf of their **winsome** kids. The Department of Education in New York City—
once known as the town too tough for Al Capone—is seeking to ban such words as
"dinosaurs," "Halloween," and "dancing" from citywide tests on the grounds that
they could "evoke unpleasant emotions in the students," it was reported this week.

Now that schools are peanut-free, latex-free, and soda-free, parents,   4
administrators, and teachers have got to worry about something. Since most kids
now have access to cable TV, the Internet, unlimited talk and texting, college, and
a world of opportunities that was unimaginable even 20 years ago, it seems that
adults have responded by becoming ever more overprotective and thin-skinned.

Kids might be fatter than they used to be, but by most standards they are safer 5
and better behaved than they were when I was growing up in the 1970s and '80s.

Infant and adolescent mortality, accidents, sex, and drug use—all are down from their levels of a few decades ago. Acceptance of homosexuality is up, especially among younger Americans. But given today's **rhetoric** about bullying, you could be forgiven for thinking that kids today are not simply reading and watching grim, **postapocalyptic** fantasies like *The Hunger Games* but actually inhabiting such terrifying terrain, a world where *Lord of the Flies* meets *Mad Max 2: The Road Warrior*, presided over by Voldemort.

One thing seems certain: the focus on bullying will lead to more lawsuits against schools and bullies, many of which will stretch the limits of **empathy** and patience. Consider, for instance, the current case of 19-year-old Eric Giray, who is suing New York's Calhoun School and a former classmate for $1.5 million over abuse that allegedly took place in 2004. Such cases can only become more common.

6

Which isn't to say that there aren't kids who face terrible cases of bullying. The immensely powerful and highly acclaimed documentary *Bully*, whose makers hope to create a nationwide movement against the "bullying crisis," opens in selected theaters this weekend. The film follows the harrowing experiences of a handful of victims of harassment, including two who killed themselves in desperation. It is, above all, a damning **indictment** of ineffectual and indifferent school officials. No viewer can watch the abuse endured by kids such as Alex, a 13-year-old social misfit in Sioux City, Iowa, or Kelby, a 14-year-old lesbian in small-town Oklahoma, without feeling angry and motivated to change youth culture and the school officials who turn a blind eye.

7

But is bullying—which the stopbullying.gov website of the Department of Health and Human Services defines as "teasing," "name-calling," "taunting," "leaving someone out on purpose," "telling other children not to be friends with someone," "spreading rumors about someone," "hitting/kicking/pinching,"

8

"spitting," and "making mean or rude hand gestures"—really a growing problem
in America?

Despite the rare and tragic cases that rightly command our attention and   9
outrage, the data show that things are, in fact, getting better for kids. When it
comes to school violence, the numbers are particularly encouraging. According to
the National Center for Education Statistics (NCES), between 1995 and 2009 the
percentage of students who reported "being afraid of attack or harm at school"
declined to 4% from 12%. Over the same period, the victimization rate per 1,000
students declined fivefold.

When it comes to bullying numbers, long-term trends are less clear. The   10
makers of *Bully* say that "over 13 million American kids will be bullied this year,"
and estimates of the percentage of students who are bullied in a given year range
from 20% to 70%. NCES changed the way it tabulated bullying incidents in 2005
and cautions against using earlier data. Its **biennial** reports find that 28% of
students ages 12-18 reported being bullied in 2005; that percentage rose to 32%
in 2007, before dropping back to 28% in 2009 (the most recent year for which
data are available). Such numbers strongly suggest that there is no epidemic afoot
(though one wonders if the new anti-bullying laws and media campaigns might
lead to more reports going forward).

The most common bullying behaviors reported include being "made fun   11
of, called names, or insulted" (reported by about 19% of victims in 2009) and
being made the "subject of rumors" (16%). Nine percent of victims reported being
"pushed, shoved, tripped, or spit on," and 6% reported being "threatened with
harm." Though it may not be surprising that bullying mostly happens during the
school day, it is stunning to learn that the most common locations for bullying
are inside classrooms, in hallways and stairwells, and on playgrounds—areas
ostensibly patrolled by teachers and administrators.

None of this is to be celebrated, of course, but it hardly paints a picture of   *12*

contemporary American childhood as an unrestrained Hobbesian nightmare.

Before more of our schools' money, time, and personnel are diverted away from

education in the name of this supposed crisis, we should make an effort to

distinguish between the serious abuse suffered by kids in *Bully* and lower-level

sorts of harassment.

ubiquity
being everywhere, especially at the same time

hyperbolic
exaggerated

winsome
sweet and charming

rhetoric
outspoken language

empathy
the ability to identify with someone else's feelings

indictment
accusation or charge

biennial
happening every two years

Hobbesian
related to Thomas Hobbes, who argued that citizens must submit to the power of a supreme ruler to maintain a civil society

Reflecting

Answer the comprehension and vocabulary questions about the reading.

1. What is the main idea of this selection?
   a. Bullying is on the rise.
   b. The bullying crisis is exaggerated.
   c. Bullying needs to be addressed more vigorously.

2. How does the author introduce his topic?
   a. By making a bold statement
   b. By quoting an expert
   c. By asking an important question

3. What pattern of organization is used to organize the supporting details in the middle part?
   a. Logical
   b. Chronological
   c. Comparison

4. What statement best describes the nature of the supporting details?
   a. Based entirely on the personal thoughts of the writer
   b. Based on personal thoughts backed up with effective evidence
   c. Based entirely on published reports

5. What is the focus of the ending paragraph?
   a. To surprise readers
   b. To summarize the main points in the essay
   c. To add a new, important detail

6. Study how the word *conflating* is used in the reading, and then choose the most accurate definition of the word.
   Conflating (paragraph 2)
   a. Uniting or blending
   b. Increasing
   c. Reducing

7. Study the word parts of the word *postapocalyptic* and how it is used in the reading. Then choose the most accurate definition of the word.
   Postapocalyptic (paragraph 5)   Post + apocalyp(se) + ic
   (*Hint:* "post" also appears in words like *postpone* and *postwar.*)
   a. Before the destruction of the world
   b. During an important time
   c. After the destruction of the world

Summarizing

Write a summary paragraph of the selection using the guidelines in Section 2.4 for help. Remember to use your own words and to focus only on the key ideas.

Critical Thinking

■ The author is a libertarian, a person who essentially believes that individuals should be allowed to say or do what they want, but within reason. How might this belief influence his argument?

■ Ultimately, whose responsibility is it to address the problem of bullying? Why?

■ The media make sure that we always have something to worry about. How would you respond to this claim?

■ Some schools and businesses have programs in place to address issues like bullying. Do you have any experience with such a program, and if so, how effective has it been?

Writing for Enrichment

What follows are possible writing activities to complete in response to the reading.

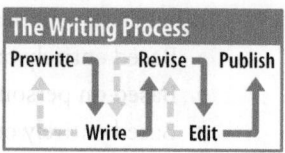

Prewriting

Choose one of the following writing ideas, or decide upon an idea of your own related to the reading.

1. Describe an act of bullying you have experienced or witnessed.
2. Explain the most reasonable solutions to the problem of bullying.
3. Develop your own position on bullying in school, the workplace, or the military.
4. Analyze the causes of bullying.
5. Compare in-person bullying to cyberbullying (technology-based bullying) as well as the approaches for preventing both types.
6. Interview someone involved in this problem, and report on what you have learned.

When planning . . .

- Research the topic as needed, taking thorough notes as you go.
- Establish a thesis for your essay.
- Review your notes for key ideas to support your thesis.

When writing . . .

- Develop effective beginning, middle, and ending parts in your essay.
- Present your thesis in the beginning part.
- Support the thesis with plenty of details in the middle part.
- Close your essay with final thoughts about your thesis.

When revising and editing . . .

- Carefully review your first draft.
- Ask at least one peer to review your writing as well.
- Rewrite the content as needed.
- Then edit your revised writing for style and correctness.

Tyler Olson, 2017 / Used under license from Shutterstock.com

Chapter 6

Coherence

Many years ago, poet and essayist Matthew Arnold gave this wise advice to authors: "Have something to say and say it clearly as you can." Arnold's recommendation is the ultimate test of any informational text you read: Does it clearly present important and/or useful information? And does it form a complete and unified whole? If the answer to these questions is "Yes," then the author has created a coherent text.

Likewise, your goal as a writer is to create coherent essays and reports. That is, you must "have something to say" and express your ideas clearly and completely. This chapter will help you recognize coherency in a variety of informational texts and help you achieve it in your writing. Special attention is given to the use of transitions in the first part of the chapter.

Chapter Outline

- Recognizing Transitions in Reading
- Using Transitions in Writing
- Reading for Coherence
- Writing for Coherence

6.1 Recognizing Transitions in Reading

The supporting details in informational texts are arranged according to patterns of organization, including chronological, spatial, cause-effect, comparison-contrast, and logical. Certain transitional words and phrases are commonly associated with the different patterns. For example, in an essay explaining a process, chronological transitions such as *first, second,* and *next* are often used to signal each new step. Transitions help unify a text by connecting ideas from sentence to sentence and paragraph to paragraph.

Recognizing the transitions will alert you to the type of text you are reading (for instance, a narrative or comparison essay) and help you follow the development of the ideas. This section identifies common transitions used with the different patterns.

Chronological Transitions

Table 6.1 includes common chronological transitions. These transitions are often used in narrative and process essays and signify time order.

Table 6.1 Common Chronological Transitions

after	next	in the future	now
second	today	during	for several years
yesterday	after that	then	in the past
meanwhile	before	sometime after	one night
over the past decade	later	in the beginning	first
	tomorrow	several years ago	third
as soon as	currently	finally	last

This paragraph uses transitional phrases (underlined) to establish the time frame of a discussion about a Salvadoran gang.

> Over the past decade, Salvadoran politicians passed a series of *mano dura,* or "firm hand," laws designed to crack down on criminal gang activity. These laws made it easier for police to detain suspects who exhibited certain characteristics such as having gang tattoos or loitering in known gang areas. Still, several years ago, MS-13 (the Mara Salvatrucha gang) members fired on two crowded buses in San Salvador, the country's capital, killing seventeen people and intensifying public outrage over gang violence. Three months later, in response, Salvadoran president Mauricio Funes signed the country's harshest antigang legislation to date. Under the new law, merely belonging to a gang is punishable by four to six years in prison, even if no other criminal activity is proved.

From GAINES/MILLER, *Criminal Justice in Action*, 6E. © 2011 Cengage Learning.

Spatial Transitions

Table 6.2 includes common spatial transitions. (Spatial means "of or relating to space.") These transitions are used to arrange the details in descriptions. Descriptions of a specific person, place, or thing usually appear within a larger text, such as a narrative or informational essay.

Table 6.2 Common Spatial Transitions

top, on top of	beside	on the right	in the distance
below	on the left	across	behind
up close	in one place	down	over
in the middle	above	in front of	under
next, next to	between	high above	diagonally
beneath	in back of	along	far and near

Mark Twain's *Life on the Mississippi* is an autobiography in which Twain recalls his training experiences as a riverboat pilot. This particular passage from the book describes one particular stunning sunset on the Mississippi River. The transitions Twain uses (underlined) help organize the description spatially, or by location.

I still keep in mind a certain wonderful sunset, which I witnessed when steamboating was new to me. A broad expanse of the river was turned to blood; in the middle distance the red hue brightened into gold, through which a solitary log came floating black and **conspicuous**; in one place a long, slanting mark lay sparkling upon the water; in another [place] the surface was broken by boiling, tumbling rings that were as many tinted as an opal; where the ruddy flush was faintest was a smooth spot that was covered with graceful circles and radiating lines, ever so delicately traced; the shore on our left was densely wooded, and the somber shadow that fell from this forest was broken in one place by a long, ruffled trail that shone like silver; and high above the forest wall a clean-stemmed dead tree waved a single leafy bough that glowed like a flame in the unobstructed splendor that was flowing from the sun. There were graceful curves, reflected images, woody heights, soft distances; and over the whole scene, far and near, the dissolving lights drifted steadily, enriching it every passing moment with new marvels of coloring.

From *Life on the Mississippi* by Mark Twain. Used under the public domain.

---

conspicuous
easily seen or noticed

Example Transitions

Table 6.3 includes common transitions used to announce or introduce new examples in essays that explain, classify, and illustrate. Identifying these transitions will help you find the key points in a reading selection.

Table 6.3 Common Example Transitions

also	one example	still another	one reason
for instance	a second strategy	in addition	yet another way
for example	one approach	further, moreover	a third step
first	another	other	the next example

This passage from an environmental textbook uses transitions (underlined) to identify each new approach or strategy to reduce forest fires.

Ecologists and forest fire experts have proposed several strategies for reducing fire-related harm to forests and to people who use the forests. One approach is to set small, contained surface fires to remove flammable small trees and underbrush in the highest-risk forest areas. Such prescribed burns require careful planning and monitoring to keep them from getting out of control. As an alternative to prescribed burns, local officials in populated parts of fire-prone California use herds of goats (kept in moveable pens) to eat away underbrush.

A second strategy is to allow some fires on public lands to burn, thereby removing flammable underbrush and smaller trees, as long as the fires do not threaten human structures and life.

A third strategy is to protect houses and other buildings in fire-prone areas by thinning a zone of about 60 meters (200 feet) around them and eliminating the use of highly flammable construction materials such as wood shingles.

A fourth approach is to thin forest areas that are vulnerable to fire by clearing away small fire-prone trees and underbrush under careful environmental controls. Many forest fire scientists warn that such thinning operations should not remove economically valuable medium-sized and large trees for two reasons. First, these are the most fire-resistant trees. Second, their removal encourages dense growth of more flammable young trees. . . .

From Miller, *Living in the Environment*, 17E. © 2012 Cengage Learning

Cause-Effect Transitions

Table 6.4 includes common transitions used in cause-effect essays, one of the most important patterns of organization in informational writing. Some essays will focus more attention on the causes or effects of a problem. Other essays will give equal treatment to each.

Table 6.4 Common Cause-Effect Transitions

Causes:	since	the reason is	the main cause is
	because	the main reason is	in fact
	results from		
Effects:	therefore	along with	hence
	consequently	as a result	thus
	as a consequence	the main effect is	then

This passage from a media textbook uses transitions (underlined) to identify a main cause and the resulting effects of the failure of magazines in the technology age.

Today, only one in three new magazines will survive more than five years. The reason most magazines fail is that many new companies do not have the money to keep publishing long enough to be able to refine their editorial content, sell advertisers on the idea, and gather subscribers—in other words, until the magazine can make a profit.

All magazines are vulnerable to changing economic and even technology trends. In 2005, *TV Guide* announced that it was discontinuing the magazine's role as a publisher of local TV schedules and, instead, re-launching the magazine in a new format exclusively devoted to celebrity news. Changing technology and the expansion of TV channels made it too hard for the magazine to keep up with TV programming, so the magazine chose to focus on the most popular part of the magazine—celebrity features. . . .

As a result, today's changing economic outlook means that people are less willing to buy magazines when they believe they can find most of the information they want for free on the Internet. In 2009, when he announced that Condé Nast Publications was shutting down several popular magazines, including *Gourmet* and *Modern Bride*, CEO Chuck Townsend said, "In this economic climate it is important to narrow our focus to titles with the greatest prospects for long-term growth."

From Biagi, *Media/Impact: An Introduction to Mass Media*, 11E. © 2014 Cengage Learning

Comparison-Contrast Transitions

Table 6.5 includes common transitions used in essays that compare and/or contrast. Some comparison-contrast essays focus more attention on the comparisons of the two topics; others focus more attention on the contrast of the topics. Still others are balanced in their treatment. Identifying the transitions will help you to follow any approach.

Table 6.5 Common Comparison-Contrast Transitions

Comparing:	also	similarly	just as
	both	likewise	so is
	in the same way	in comparison	in addition
	similar	as well	
Contrasting:	although	however	in contrast
	even though	yet	on the other hand
	but	while	
	or	despite	

This passage from a psychology textbook uses transitions (underlined) to help establish a discussion of the contrasts between the two sides of the brain. This passage would lack coherence without these transitions.

Right Brain/Left Brain . . . The brain divides its work in interesting ways. Roughly 95 percent of us use our left brain for language (speaking, writing, and understanding). In addition, the left hemisphere is superior in math, judging time and rhythm, and coordinating the order of complex movements, such as those needed for speech.   1

In contrast, the right hemisphere can produce only the simplest language and numbers. Working with the right brain is like talking to a child who can say only a dozen words or so. To answer questions, the right hemisphere must use nonverbal responses, such as pointing at objects.   2

Although it is poor at producing language, the right brain is especially good at perceptual skills, such as recognizing patterns, faces, and melodies, putting together a puzzle, or drawing a picture. It also helps us express emotions and detect the emotions that other people are feeling (Borod et al., 2002; Stuss & Alexander, 2000).   3

Even though the right hemisphere is nearly "speechless," it is superior at some aspects of understanding language. If the right side of the brain is damaged, people lose their ability to understand jokes, irony, sarcasm, implications, and other nuances of language.   From Coon/Mitterer. *Psychology*, 12E. © 2012 Cengage Learning   4

Logical Order Transitions

Some reading selections simply present information in a sensible order, moving logically from one point to the next. Table 6.6 includes transitions that are commonly used to clarify ideas in essays that follow logical order.

Table 6.6 Common Logical Order Transitions

however	besides	insofar as	yet
other	in other words	nevertheless	every now and then
after all	for this reason	whenever	most of the time
moreover	but	while	sometimes

In this paragraph from a sociology textbook, the transitions (underlined) indicate that the details progress logically or sensibly from one point to the next.

> Nobody can disagree with supporting fatherhood and stable family life. However, one problem with pro-fatherhood policies is that they are often intended to replace welfare programs, which are simultaneously being cut by both the federal and state governments. Moreover, critics of pro-fatherhood policies argue that what is essential for the healthy development of children is not just the father or, for that matter, even the mother. As psychologists have shown, what is essential is a lasting and loving relationship with at least one adult (Silverstein and Auerbach, 1999). In other words, it is not necessarily the presence of a nuclear family that ensures healthy family life. Insofar as the Fatherhood Initiative supports only one kind of family, it devalues other forms of family life, including single-parent households, homosexual couples, and so on.

From BRYM/LIE, *Sociology*, 2E. © 2007 Cengage Learning

Practice 6.1 Underline the transitions used in each of the following texts based on the pattern of organization identified in bold print.

1. **Examples:** Marriageable men were in short supply for years afterward, and the imbalance between men and women aged 20 to 35 influenced what was considered acceptable sexual conduct. For instance, after the war it proved impossible to put young men and women back into the tight customary constraints of prewar society.

In addition, the many millions of [drafted soldiers] in the armies had been torn out of their accustomed and expected slots in life. For better or worse, many—especially rural youth—never returned to their prewar lifestyles. . . .

From Adler/Pouwels, *World Civilizations*, 6E. © 2012 Cengage Learning

2. **Cause-Effect:** Even anthropologists whose fieldwork experience is less traumatic encounter some level of stress from culture shock, the psychological **disorientation** caused by trying to adjust to major differences in lifestyles and living conditions. Culture shock, a term introduced by anthropologist Kalervo Oberg (1960), ranges from mild irritation to out-and-out panic. This general psychological stress occurs when the anthropologist tries to play the game of life with little or no understanding of the basic rules. Due to this lack of understanding, the fieldworker, struggling to learn what is meaningful in the new culture, never really knows when the person may be committing a serious social **indiscretion** that might severely jeopardize the entire fieldwork project, such as using the wrong hand when sharing food, or speaking out of turn.

Consequently, when culture shock sets in, everything seems to go wrong. You may become irritated over minor inconveniences. You may begin to view things critically and negatively. For example, you might think the food is strange, the people don't keep their appointments, no one likes you, everything seems **unhygienic**, people don't look you in the eye, and on and on.

From Ferraro/Andreatta, *Cultural Anthropology*, 9E. © 2012 Cengage Learning

disorientation	indiscretion	unhygienic
confusion	lack of good judgment	not healthful, unsanitary

3. **Logical:** When my husband fasts, our relationship becomes a bland, lukewarm concoction that I find difficult to swallow. I'm not proud of this fact. After all, he isn't the only one in our house with a spiritual practice: I stumble out of bed in the dark most mornings and meditate in the corner of our room with my back to him, trying to find that bottomless truth beyond words. Once in a great while, I'll drag him to church on Sunday. Whenever I suggest we say grace at the table, he reaches willingly for my hand, and words of gratitude flow easily from him. He has never criticized my practices, even when they are wildly inconsistent or contradictory. But Ramadan is not ten minutes of meditation or an hour-long sermon; it's an entire month of deprivation. Ismail's God is the old-fashioned kind, omnipresent and stern, uncompromising with his demands. During Ramadan this God expects him to pray on time, five times a day—and to squeeze in additional prayers of forgiveness as often as he can.

Excerpted from Krista Bremer's *My Accidental Jihad: A Love Story.* Copyright 2014.

6.2 Using Transitions in Writing

When you develop your writing, use transitions as needed to create a clear and unified piece of writing. Very often, your assignments will identify the pattern of organization for your writing, so you will know which type of transitions to use.

Identify the Pattern of Organization

Suppose your instructor created this assignment: *Describe a favorite location in the city, using plenty of sensory details. Arrange the details in an orderly way to help the reader visualize this setting.* In this assignment, it is clear that you are creating a description, so you would use spatial transitions to organize your details.

Or suppose you were given this assignment: *Explain the causes and effects of the Haymarket Riot of 1886. In your explanation, cite at least two sources provided in the reading list about this event.* It is clear in this assignment that you will be developing a cause-effect essay, so you would use transitions that identify causes and effects.

However, not all of your assignments will clearly identify a pattern of organization, such as this assignment: *Landscaping in cold climates poses specific challenges. Report on the best use of one type of plant as a cold-climate design feature.* For assignments like this, an organizing pattern usually emerges after you research your topic and establish a main idea for your writing. For example, if you decided to focus on the types of trees that work in cold climates, you could use example transitions (*one example, another example, also*) to organize the details (the trees) in the report.

Be Selective with Transitions

A piece of writing may sound forced or awkward if it contains too many transitions, so use them selectively. Transitions should be used as needed to help establish the organization of the text. This passage illustrates what can happen if a writer uses too many transitions. The transitions (underlined) actually bring undue attention on themselves and sound forced.

> Americans made many sacrifices during the 1973 energy crisis. First, homeowners voluntarily turned down their thermostats by an average of two degrees. Second, businesses voluntarily shortened the work week and cut back on energy use. Third, unneeded lights were turned off in homes and businesses. Fourth, slower driving was encouraged, and fifth, Sunday driving was discouraged.

Practice 6.2 Fill in the blank with the appropriate transitions to complete each text.

1. Narrative following chronological order

Jammed in our aging royal blue Chevy Astro with limited legroom, my family journeyed along historic Route 66 near the New Mexico-Arizona border on our way to the Grand Canyon. This was not exactly my idea of a fun time. _____ the air conditioner was on the blink, so beads of sweat trickled down my brow and my back. That I was jammed between my two brothers, who generated their own heat, made the situation almost unbearable. _____ I noticed the low-battery sign blinking on my smartphone. Considering we were six hours from our destination, I would be soon without music to distract me while we motored along this godforsaken stretch of scrubland. How would I survive? _____ what happened seemed like a scene from a bad comedy movie. Grayish smoke billowed from under the hood of the van, blocking my dad's view of the road. Dad pulled off the road, and a bad vacation _____ became the worst vacation ever.

2. Information essay providing examples

Different people pursue different levels of physical activity. _____ a person with a sedentary lifestyle exercises fewer than three times per week. This type of lifestyle is linked to weight gain and an increased risk of developing diseases such as type 2 diabetes.   *1*

_____ level of physical activity is simply known as "lifestyle active." This level describes a person who performs everyday lifestyle activities, such as walking to and from the store, doing yard work, or playing pick-up basketball. Engaging in regular lifestyle activities can help control cholesterol levels and reduce body fat.   *2*

Still _____ level called the "moderate physical lifestyle" describes someone who follows a cardio-respiratory exercise program of 20 to 60 minutes of activity, three to five days per week. Such a person might be a regular runner, weight lifter, or power walker. A moderate physical lifestyle helps a person become fit while reducing the risk of chronic disease.   *3*

The highest level of physical activity is a "vigorous lifestyle." People on this level exercise 20 to 60 minutes most days of the week and follow a routine of aerobic exercises, strength training, and stretching exercises. A vigorous physical lifestyle achieves the same benefits as moderate physical activities while promoting a greater level of fitness.   *4*

6.3 Reading for Coherence

Your assigned readings will be easy to follow if they display coherency. A coherent text exhibits the following characteristics:

- The details explain or support a clearly identifiable topic and main idea.
- The supporting information is organized and built sensibly from sentence to sentence, paragraph to paragraph, and section to section.
- Key points are clarified and expanded upon to ensure understanding.
- Important words and phrases are repeated to connect ideas.
- Pronoun references help connect ideas (for example, *it* for *automobile*).
- Transitions such as *in addition* or *in contrast* help readers follow the text.

In short, your readings will be clear, complete, and unified if they follow these characteristics. This selection from a cultural anthropology textbook illustrates important features of a coherent paragraph.

> Language, which is found in all cultures of the world, is a symbolic system of sounds that, when put together according to a certain set of rules, conveys meanings to its speakers. The meanings attached to any given word in all languages are totally **arbitrary**; that is, the word *cow* has no particular connection to the large bovine animal that the English language refers to as a cow. The word *cow* is no more or less reasonable as a word for that animal than would be *kaflumpha, sporge,* or *four-pronged squirter*. The word *cow* does not look like a cow, sound like a cow, or have any particular physical connection to a cow. The only explanation for the use of the word is that somewhere during the evolution of the English language the word *cow* came to be used to refer to a large, milk-giving, domesticated animal. Other languages use different, and equally arbitrary, words to describe the very same animal. From Ferraro/Andreatta, *Cultural Anthropology,* 9E. © 2012 Cengage Learning.

---

arbitrary
not planned or chosen for a particular reason

Here are the key features that contribute to the coherence of the above paragraph:

- **The paragraph is built around an identifiable topic** (*language*) **and main idea** (*is a symbolic system of sounds . . .*).
- **The information is well organized.** The paragraph follows logical order.
- **Ideas are clarified or expanded upon to aid in understanding.** For example, the sentence "The only explanation for the use of . . ." expands upon the sentence before it.
- **Repeated words and phrases connect ideas and help the text progress sensibly.** Some of the repeated elements are underlined in the text.

This two-paragraph selection, which compares Chinese and American attitudes about the home, illustrates coherence within each paragraph and between the paragraphs.

Chinese Place, American Space

Americans have a sense of space, not of place. Go to an American home in exurbia, and almost the first thing you do is drift toward the picture window. How curious that the first compliment you pay your host inside his house is to say how lovely it is outside the house! He is pleased that you should admire his vistas. This distant horizon is not merely a line separating earth from the sky; it is a symbol of the future. The American is not rooted in his place, however lovely; his eyes are drawn by the expanding space to a point on the horizon, which is his future. $_1$

By contrast, consider the traditional Chinese home. Blank walls enclose it. Step behind the spirit wall and you are in a courtyard with perhaps a miniature garden around a corner. Once inside his private compound, you are wrapped in an ambiance of calm beauty, an ordered world of buildings, pavement, rock, and decorative vegetation. But you have no distant view; nowhere does the space open out before you. Raw nature in such a home is experienced only as weather, and the only open space is the sky above. The Chinese [man] is rooted in his place. When he has to leave, it is not for the promised land on the terrestrial horizon, but for another world altogether along the vertical, religious axis of his imagination. $_2$

Yi-Fu Tuan, "Chinese Place, American Space."

exurbia	spirit wall	ambiance
a region beyond suburbs	a wall around a courtyard to keep out evil spirits	a feeling or mood associated with a place

These features contribute to the coherency of "Chinese Place, American Space":

- **The excerpt is built around an identifiable topic** (*the American and Chinese sense of home*) **and main idea** (*is significantly different*).
- **The information is well organized.** The comparison pattern is used—the first paragraph analyzes one topic; the next paragraph analyzes the second topic.
- **Ideas are clarified or expanded upon to aid in understanding.** For example, the sentence "The American is not rooted in place . . ." clarifies the idea that comes before it.
- **Repeated words and phrases link ideas and help the text progress sensibly.** A few of the repeated words and phases are underlined in the text.
- **Pronoun references also help link ideas.** For example, the pronoun "his" in the third sentence in paragraph 1 connects with "your host" in the same sentence.
- **Transitions alert readers to a condition or a change in the direction of the text.** For example, *by contrast* at the start of paragraph 2 announces a change in direction of the text.

Practice 6.3 After reading each text, answer the coherency questions.

1.   Mammals do have the largest brains of all animals. But we humans are not   *1*
the mammalian record holders. That honor goes to whales, whose brains tip the
scales at around 19 pounds. At three pounds, the human brain seems puny—until
we compare brain weight with body weight. We then find that a sperm whale's
brain is 1/10,000 of its weight. The ratio for humans is 1/60. And yet, the ratio for
tree shrews (very small squirrel-like insect-eating mammals) is about 1/30. So our
human brains are not noteworthy in terms of either **absolute weight** or **relative
weight** (Coolidge & Wynn, 2009).

While a small positive correlation exists between intelligence and brain size,   *2*
overall size alone does not determine human intelligence (Johnson et al., 2008;
Witelson, Beresh, & Kigar, 2006). In fact, many parts of the brain are surprisingly
similar to corresponding brain areas in smaller animals, such as lizards. It is your
larger **cerebral cortex** that sets you apart.

The cerebral cortex covers most of the brain with a mantle of gray matter   *3*
(spongy tissue made up mostly of cell bodies). The cortex in small animals, like
rats, is small and smooth. In humans it is twisted and folded, and it is the largest
brain structure. The fact than humans are more intelligent than other animals is
related to this corticalization, or increase in the size and wrinkling of the cortex.

From Coon/Mitterer. *Psychology*, 12E. © 2012 Cengage Learning

---

absolute weight	relative weight	cerebral cortex
weight of a body in a vacuum, or on its own	weight of a body in relation to a particular range	outer layer of the brain

1. How is this text organized?
   a. Chronologically
   b. Logically
   c. Spatially

2. What is an example of a sentence that clarifies or expands upon the sentence
before it?
   a. While a small positive correlation exists between intelligence and brain size, . . .
   b. In fact, many parts of the brain are surprisingly similar to corresponding brain
   areas in smaller animals, . . .
   c. The cerebral cortex covers most of the brain with a mantle of gray matter.

3. What are two examples of key words repeated in the selection?
   a. Human and brain
   b. Shrews and intelligence
   c. Lizards and structure

4. What transitional words or phrases are used to help the reader follow the text?
- a. *And yet* and *while*
- b. *In* and *or*
- c. *Such as* and *with*

5. What noun does the pronoun "it" refer to in this sentence from the passage? "The cortex in small animals, like rats, is small and smooth. In humans it is twisted and folded, and it is the largest brain structure."
- a. Animals
- b. Cortex
- c. Humans

2.   Mate Selection: Whom Should You Marry?

Every society defines a set of kin with whom a person is to avoid marriage and sexual intimacy. In no society is it permissible to mate with one's parents or siblings (that is, within the nuclear family), and in most cases the restricted group of kin is considerably wider. Beyond this notion of incest, people in all societies are faced with rules either restricting their choice of marriage partners or strongly encouraging the selection of certain people as highly desirable mates. These are known as the rules of **exogamy** (marrying outside of a certain group) and **endogamy** (marrying within a certain group).   *1*

Rules of Exogamy

Because of the universality of the incest taboo, all societies have rules about marrying outside a certain group of kin. These are known as rules of exogamy. In societies such as the United States and Canada, the exogamous group extends only slightly beyond the nuclear family. It is considered either illegal or inadvisable to marry one's first cousin, and in some cases, one's second cousin, but beyond that one can marry other more distant relatives and encounter only mild disapproval. . . .   *2*

Rules of Endogamy

In contrast to exogamy, the rules of endogamy require a person to select a mate from within one's own group. Hindu castes in traditional India are strongly endogamous, believing that to marry below one's caste would result in serious ritual pollution. Caste endogamy is also found in a somewhat less rigid form among the Rwanda and Banyankole of eastern central Africa. . . .   *3*

Even though there are no strongly sanctioned legal rules of endogamy in the   *4*

United States, there is a certain amount of marrying with one's own group based on class, ethnicity, religion, and race. This general **de facto** endogamy found in the United States results from the fact that people do not have frequent social contacts with people from different backgrounds. . . .

Arranged Marriages

Individuals in most contemporary Western societies are free to marry anyone   5
they please. In many societies, however, the interests of the family are so strong that marriages are arranged. Negotiations are handled by family members of the prospective bride and groom, and for all practical purposes, the decision of whom one will marry is made primarily by one's parents or other influential relatives. In certain cultures, such as parts of traditional Japan, India, and China, future marriage partners are betrothed while they are still children. . . .

From Ferraro/Andreatta, *Cultural Anthropology*, 9E. © 2012 Cengage Learning

exogamy	endogamy	de facto
a rule requiring marriage outside of one's own social or kinship group	a rule requiring marriage within a specified social or kinship group	in effect, in practice

6. What helpful design element is *not* included in this passage?
  a. Title
  b. Headings
  c. Bulleted list

7. How is the main part of the text generally organized?
  a. Using the comparison-contrast pattern
  b. Using chronological order
  c. Using the spatial pattern

8. What transitional words or phrases suggest this pattern of organization?
  a. *Beyond* and *because*
  b. *In contrast* and *even though*
  c. *However* and *such as*

9. What key word is repeated in the first paragraph?
  a. Intimacy
  b. Rules

10. What is an example of a sentence that clarifies or expands upon the sentence before it in the final paragraph?
  a. In many societies, however, the interests of the family are so strong that marriages are arranged.
  b. Negotiations are handled by family members of the prospective bride and groom . . .

6.4 Writing for Coherence

Producing a coherent piece of writing takes time and effort. But if you're like many students, you may have a difficult time staying with a piece of writing long enough to do your best work. Here are some tips that can help you address this problem:

- **Write about topics that interest you.** If you're truly interested in a topic, you will naturally take more care when you write about it.
- **Approach your writing as a process, developing it step by step.** Then you will not try to get everything right in your first draft, which will only lead to frustration and poor results.
- **Share your writing as it develops.** Try to have at least one or two other people review your writing as you develop it. Reviewers will help you see ways to improve the clarity and quality of your writing that you might miss.
- **Be willing to experiment or take risks.** One of your experiments may lead to a clearer or more complete explanation.
- **Remember the end game.** A coherent piece of writing should form a meaningful whole—with fully developed beginning, middle, and ending parts.

Checking for Overall Coherence

Your essays will be coherent in terms of overall structure if they form a unified whole. Each successive draft that you develop and each revision that you make should improve upon the clarity, completeness, and unity of each part. This is how experienced writers develop coherent writing. Even the most accomplished authors fail to get everything right the first, second, or even the third time. Use Figure 6.1 as a basic guide when you check the overall structure of your writing for coherency.

Figure 6.1 Structure of Coherent Writing

The **beginning** part should . . .	<ul><li>effectively introduce the topic,</li><li>provide background information, and</li><li>state the thesis.</li></ul>
The **middle** part should . . .	<ul><li>support the thesis,</li><li>explain each key point with specific details, and</li><li>follow an appropriate pattern of organization.</li></ul>
The **ending** part should . . .	<ul><li>remind the reader of the thesis,</li><li>summarize the key supporting points, and/or</li><li>offer a final idea about the topic.</li></ul>

This student narrative is labeled and assessed for general coherence to help you see how to use **Figure 6.1** as a guide.

Paddling Bliss

Beginning

Thesis (underlined)

Early in the morning, a light grey fog blanketed the lake. I could just make out the boats docked in the marina and a faint outline of trees to the side. Not a sound could be heard. But now, a few hours later, the fog has lifted, which means it's time to get on the water. Most mornings, I kayak for exercise and enjoyment. ¹

To get started, I push off just 30 yards from my grandfather's cottage in O'Dell's Bay. By habit, I check the water quality soon after I start, looking for any patches of nasty algae that sometimes blooms on the surface. At its best, the lake water is a very light brown color, almost looking like root beer in the wake of a motorboat. At its worst, in the dog days of August, the water can shimmer with smelly, blue-green algae. ²

Middle

Supporting details organized chronologically (transitions underlined)

Once I'm out of the bay, I usually turn left, staying fairly close to the shoreline. On a good day, I'll see a lot of fish jumping, or at least I'll hear their splash and see the circular ripples that they've caused. Last year, for the first time, I saw a bald eagle flying away from its nest, which looked pretty much like a junk pile in the tree. I once came upon a crane with a fish in its mouth. As I paddled closer, it would move on, a few yards at a time. We played tag like this for a few moments before the crane had enough and took to the air to find a quiet spot for dinner. ³

After awhile, I'll mark out a spot, say a boat docked 50 yards away, and paddle like crazy until I reach that spot. This really gets my heart pumping and gives my upper body a good workout. Then, for a time, I'll just lazily drift along, taking in the quiet and calm that can be felt only on the water. ⁴

The lake is big enough that it makes me feel pretty small sometimes. When the wind picks up, the waves can build up a lot of power, making kayaking feel more like riding a roller coaster. And I swear that the sky is bigger here than it is back in the city. I like it best when it is partly cloudy, because the clouds look huge against the blue sky. ⁵

Ending

Offering final idea

Once I reach Half Moon Bay, I usually turn around and head back. The trip home might be easier or harder, depending on the wind's direction. I almost always focus less on nature and more on exercise on the return trip. I guess that's because I'm seeing the same things for a second time. When I finally make my last paddle and glide to a stop on the beach, I'm tired but happy for the trip. ⁶

Line-by-Line Writing Moves

Writing coherently may start at the general level, making sure that you have fully developed beginning, middle, and ending parts. But as you develop your essays, there are a number of line-by-line writing moves you can make to establish and maintain coherence. These moves are listed in Figure 6.2.

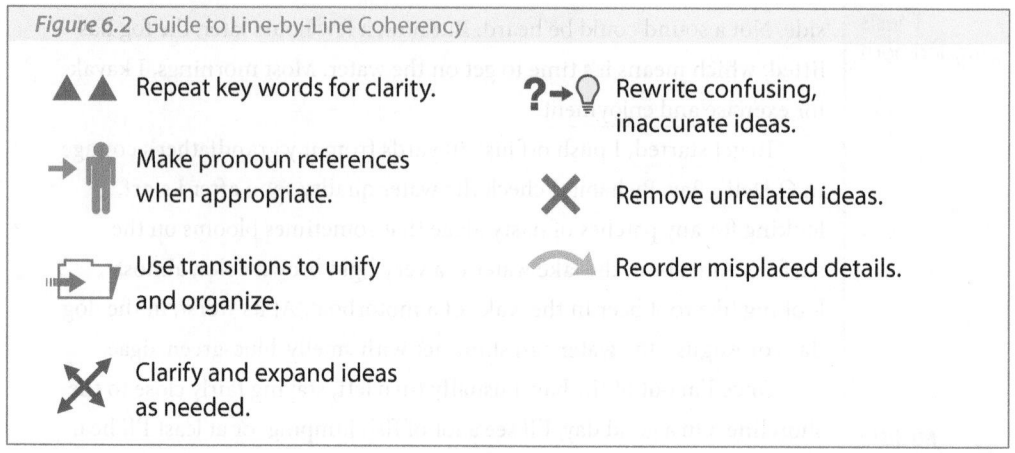

Figure 6.2 Guide to Line-by-Line Coherency

▲ ▲ Repeat key words for clarity.

→ 👤 Make pronoun references when appropriate.

↦ Use transitions to unify and organize.

✗ Clarify and expand ideas as needed.

? → 💡 Rewrite confusing, inaccurate ideas.

✗ Remove unrelated ideas.

↝ Reorder misplaced details.

Each of the writing moves identified in Figure 6.2 is illustrated in the examples that follow. As you will see, each example helps establish or maintain coherence.

Repeat Key Words for Clarity

The repetition of key words is an essential feature of coherent writing. If, for example, the topic of your essay is clean drinking water, you would naturally repeat the word "water" as needed to ensure clarity as is done in this opening paragraph:

> One of the most overlooked luxuries of living in the United States is access to clean drinking water. Statistics show roughly one-eighth of the world's population lack access to safe water supplies, while as many as 2.5 billion people live without sanitized water. Untreated water is full of unhealthy chemicals and contaminants that, if consumed, lead to uncomfortable and sometimes fatal diseases, including dysentery and diarrhea. Purification plants remove these harmful impurities to make the water drinkable.

As you revise your writing, make sure the key words are repeated enough, but not too often. A word repeated too often can disrupt the flow of writing.

Make Pronoun References

If you repeat a key word too often, your writing may sound forced and awkward. When that happens, replace the key word with a pronoun. Suppose in an essay identifying famous detectives in crime fiction, you wrote this paragraph about Philip Marlowe.

In the late 1930s, mystery writer Raymond Chandler created one of the first great American private investigators, Philip Marlowe. Marlowe is a hard-drinking tough guy who works in Los Angeles. Marlowe carries a gun and is not afraid of a fight, but he is also very intelligent. Marlowe learned to be an investigator by working for the district attorney and an insurance company. He often puts his life at risk against some real lowlifes during his investigations.

After reviewing the paragraph, you realize that you have at least one too many "Marlowe" references, so you substitute a pronoun for one of them to improve the readability.

In the late 1930s, mystery writer Raymond Chandler created one of the first great American private investigators, Philip Marlowe. Marlowe is a hard-drinking tough guy who works in Los Angeles. He carries a gun and is not afraid of a fight, but he is also very intelligent. Marlowe learned to be an investigator by working for the district attorney and an insurance company. He often puts his life at risk against some real lowlifes during his investigations.

Use Transitions to Unify and Organize

Transitions are words or phrases that link ideas and alert the reader to a change or addition in a text (see Sections 6.1 and 6.2). Suppose you are describing a typical laundry day, and while planning, you list the steps in your "process":

- haul laundry bags into basement laundry room
- sort the laundry for different washers
- study or read while waiting
- wrestle the heavy clothes into the dryers
- continue waiting
- fluff and fold dry clothes

To identify the steps, you would use chronological transitions (underlined).

When you're a college student, doing laundry is a chore. I happen to clean my dirty clothes in the basement of my apartment building. First, I haul my two laundry baskets down four flights of stairs to the laundry room. Next, I go through the process of sorting the dirty clothes into two or three washers, depositing my quarters, and starting the machines. Then I either wait in an uncomfortable plastic chair in the room, studying or playing a game on my iPhone, or I head back to my apartment for 20 minutes or so. Upon return, I pry the wet clothes out of the washers and wrestle them into dryers. . . .

Explain and Clarify as Needed

A coherent piece of writing is clear and complete. To be complete, every detail in the writing must be fully explained. Suppose you are writing an essay about Ulysses S. Grant's unexpected rise to power, and you started it this way:

> A surprising story in the Civil War is the rise to power of U. S. Grant. At the start of the war, Grant was a clerk in his father-in-law's leather shop before signing on as lowly brigadier general in the Illinois Volunteers. But in a few years, he was appointed by President Lincoln to lead all of the troops in the Union Army. Grant earned this position by succeeding in three important battles in the West.
>
> Grant's first important victory came in February of 1862 at the Battle of Fort Donelson in Tennessee. The Confederate troops had entered the fort to regroup after a battle at Fort Henry. But before long, the Confederate troops agreed to Grant's terms of an unconditional surrender. After that, the "U.S." in U.S. Grant was said to stand for "unconditional surrender."

After reviewing this part, you realize that a key detail in the second paragraph is not complete enough, so you expand upon it (in *italics*):

> Grant's first important victory came in February of 1862 at the Battle of Fort Donelson in Tennessee. The Confederate troops had entered the fort to regroup after a battle at Fort Henry. *Grant ordered his men to make minor attacks on the fort, and they also stopped an attempt by the Confederacy to break out.* But before long, the Confederate troops agreed to Grant's terms of an unconditional surrender. After that, the "U.S." in U.S. Grant was said to stand for "unconditional surrender."

Rewrite Confusing, Inaccurate Ideas

Any ideas that are confusing or awkward must be revised until they are clear and smooth reading. Let's say you are explaining the cheese-making process, and one part reads as follows.

> After the cheese maker separates the curds from the whey, the process continues by reheating the curds, letting them settle, and stirring away as much liquid as possible. This step is repeated until you believe the cheese is sufficiently solid. When the cheese solidifies, it is poured into molds of different shapes and sizes. Then the cheese is placed in cooler temperatures so that it can ripen.

Upon review, you see that the second sentence is written in the second person (*you*) while the other sentences are in the third person (*he, she,* or *they*). You rewrite the sentence to correct this error:

> This step is repeated until the cheese maker believes the cheese is sufficiently solid.

Remove Unrelated Ideas

Delete any details in your writing that do not directly relate to the main idea of your writing. Suppose you started an essay about head injuries in the NFL in this way.

> New studies conclude that concussions can lead to long-term, crippling brain damage. As a result, the National Football League (NFL) has improved its baseline testing for players who suffer head injuries during a game. The National Hockey League is also concerned about the long-term effects of head injuries on hockey athletes. Before gaining permission to re-enter an NFL game, the player in question must pass a lengthy test (six to eight minutes) that measures memory, balance, and concentration. The NFL is also cutting back on practice time and off-season programs, as well as limiting full-contact practices during the season.

Upon reviewing your work, you remove a detail (*crossed out*) because it is unrelated to the NFL and thus disrupts the unity of this part.

> New studies conclude that concussions can learn to long-term, crippling brain damage. As a result, the National Football League (NFL) has improved its baseline testing for players who suffer head injuries during a game. ~~The National Hockey League is also concerned about the long-term effects on head injuries on hockey athletes~~. Before gaining permission to re-enter an NFL game, the player in question must pass a lengthy test (six to eight minutes) that measures memory, balance, and concentration. The NFL is also cutting back on practice time and off-season programs, as well as limiting full-contact practices during the season.

Reorder Misplaced Ideas

Always check the details in your writing to make sure that they are arranged in the best order. Let's say you're writing about a motorcycle trip, and in one passage you describe the soil along the open road:

> Even the color of the dirt changes as you travel. Missouri's soil, for example, is red clay, with lots of crumbly white rock in it. Illinois has rich, black dirt that fades to a dark gray when it's dry. Get to Arizona, and the "dirt" is yellow-gray dust or sand.

During revision, you realize the description would make better sense if it moved spatially from north to southwest.

> Even the color of the dirt changes as you travel. <u>Illinois</u>, for example, has rich, black dirt that fades to a dark gray when it's dry. <u>Missouri's</u> soil is red clay, with crumbly white rock in it. Get to <u>Arizona</u>, and the "dirt" is yellow-gray dust or sand.

Practice 6.4 Answer the coherence-based questions after each of the following texts.

The earth's biodiversity is a vital part of the natural capital that helps keep us alive and supports our economies. With the help of technology, we use biodiversity to provide us with food, wood, fibers, energy from wood and biofuels, and medicines. Biodiversity also plays critical roles in preserving the quality of the air and water, maintaining the fertility of topsoil, decomposing and recycling waste, and controlling populations that humans consider to be pests. Biodiversity should not be confused with biomes. In carrying out so many services, biodiversity helps us to sustain life on earth.   From Miller, *Living in the Environment*, 17E. © 2012 Cengage Learning

1. What key word is repeated throughout the paragraph?
   a. Earth
   b. Biodiversity
   c. Biofuels

2. What sentence disrupts the unity of the paragraph?
   a. With the help of technology, we use biodiversity to provide us with food. . . .
   b. Biodiversity should not be confused with biomes.
   c. In carrying out so many services, biodiversity helps us to sustain life on earth.

Scientists first survey the globe to predict which strains of the influenza virus will dominate the next flu season. The following steps help decide which strains to put in a flu vaccine. Next, the World Health Organization confirms the dominant strains and submits its recommendation to the Food and Drug Administration (FDA). The FDA then distributes seeds of the three strains to manufacturers for production.

3. What sentence move would make the paragraph coherent?
   a. Move the first sentence after the second sentence
   b. Move the second sentence after the third sentence
   c. Move the first sentence after the third sentence

4. What key word is repeated throughout the text?
   a. Vaccine
   b. Strains
   c. Flu

The Economist, a London-based news magazine, reports that vertical farms make good sense. One reason is vertical farms need no soil. Crops are grown hydroponically, in a solution of essential minerals dissolved in water. The plants' roots absorb nutrients directly from this liquid. Second, since crops are grown in a controlled environment, few pesticides or herbicides are needed. Everything is recycled, so vertical farming uses far less water and nutrients than traditional farms use. Vertical farms will provide food to local areas, which saves on transportation costs ("Does It Really Stack Up?").

5. What pattern of organization is used in this passage? **Hint:** Consider the transitions *one reason is* and *second.*
   a. Chronological
   b. Examples
   c. Cause-effect

6. What transition would you use at the start of this sentence if you were to add the sentence to the end of the paragraph: "Everything is recycled, so vertical farming uses far less water and nutrients than traditional farms use"?
   a. Likewise
   b. However
   c. Third

Even a slight drop in the normal body temperature of 98.6 degrees Fahrenheit causes hypothermia. Often caused by accidental or prolonged exposure to cold, hypothermia forces bodily functions to slow down. The heart rate and blood pressure decrease. Breathing becomes slower and shallower. Mountain climbers risk hypothermia. As the body temperature drops between 86 and 82 degrees Fahrenheit, the person lapses into unconsciousness.

7. What pattern of organization is used in this passage?
   a. Chronological
   b. Examples
   c. Cause-effect

8. What sentence disrupts the unity of the paragraph?
   a. Mountain climbers risk hypothermia.
   b. The heart rate and blood pressure decrease.
   c. Breathing becomes slower and shallower.

☑ Review and Enrichment

Chapter Review Quiz

Answer the questions about what you've learned in this chapter.

1. When are spatial transitions often used?
   a. In descriptions organized by location
   b. In arguments organized logically
   c. In personal narratives organized by time

2. Which of these transitions are typically used in comparison-contrast writing?
   a. *After all* and *besides*
   b. *Similarly* and *even though*
   c. *In other words* and *whenever*

3. What type of transitions would you likely use for this assignment: Report on the best uses of a certain food type for meals that would interest your peers?
   a. Transitions that show cause-effect
   b. Transitions that indicate different examples
   c. Transitions that show logical order

4. Why should you use transitions selectively?
   a. They are hard to understand.
   b. They add very little to the writing.
   c. They make writing sound forced when overused.

5. How do you know if a text that you read is coherent?
   a. A coherent text is clear, complete, and unified.
   b. A coherent text is brief and direct.
   c. A coherent text contains familiar information.

6. What is *not* a feature of a coherent text?
   a. The supporting details are clearly organized.
   b. Key words are seldom repeated.
   c. Transitions are used as needed for clarity.

7. When does a text form a unified whole?
   a. When the overall structure is complete and unified
   b. When the text contains a beginning part and a middle part
   c. When the writer completes a first draft

8. What will help you do your best writing?
   a. Keep risk taking or experimenting to a minimum.
   b. Write about topics that interest you.
   c. Focus on the end product rather than the process.

Reading for Enrichment

In this section, you will read an essay entitled "Call Me Crazy, But I Have to Be Myself." Be sure to follow the steps in the reading process to help you gain a full understanding of the text.

About the Author

Mary Seymour had this personal essay published in *Newsweek*'s "My Turn" column. At the time of publication, she was an alumni-magazine editor.

Prereading

Mental illnesses such as bipolar disorder or post-traumatic stress disorder are complicated and painful topics frequently discussed on talk shows and in newspapers and magazines. In the magazine essay you are about to read, the author reflects on her experiences with depression. Explore your own thoughts about mental illness by freewriting about it for five minutes. Consider what you know about the subject and what you would like to find out.

Also, before you begin reading, use the **STRAP** strategy to identify the main parts of the text. Consider listing a few questions that you hope the reading will answer.

Subject:	What specific topic does the reading address?
Type:	What form (*essay, personal narrative, textbook chapter*) does the reading take?
Role:	What position (*personal commentator, professor, journalist*) does the writer assume?
Audience:	Who is the intended audience (*general readers, students, administrators*)?
Purpose:	What is the general goal of the reading (*to inform, to persuade, to share*)?

Reading and Rereading

As you read, be sure to (1) identify the main idea of the essay, (2) follow the details that develop this idea, and (3) note how the author maintains coherence throughout the essay. Consider annotating the text and/or taking notes as you read. Then reread as needed to form a clear understanding of the text.

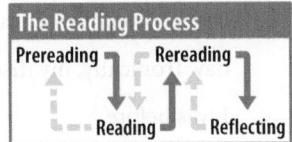

Call Me Crazy, But I Have to Be Myself

Nearly every day, without thinking, I say things like "So-and-so is driving   1
me crazy" or "That's nuts!" Sometimes I catch myself and realize that I'm not
being sensitive toward people with mental illness. Then I remember I'm one of the
mentally ill. If I can't throw those words around, who can?

Being a functional member of society and having a mental disorder is an   2
intricate balancing act. Every morning I send my son to junior high school, put
on professional **garb**, and drive off to my job as alumni-magazine editor at a
prep school, where I've worked for six years. Only a few people at work know I'm
manic-depressive, or bipolar, as it's sometimes called.

Sometimes I'm not sure myself what I am. I blend in easily with "normal"   3
people. You'd never know that seven years ago, fueled by the stress of a failing
marriage and fanned by the genetic inheritance of a manic-depressive grandfather,
I had a **psychotic** break. To look at me, you'd never guess I once ran naked
through my yard or shuffled down the hallways of a psychiatric ward. To hear me,
you'd never guess God channeled messages to me through my computer. After my
breakdown at 36, I was diagnosed as bipolar, a condition marked by moods that
swing between elation and despair.

It took a second, less-severe psychotic episode in 1997, followed by a period   4
of deep depression, to convince me I truly was bipolar. Admitting I had a disorder
that I'd have to manage for life was the hardest thing I've ever done. Since then, a
combination of therapy, visits to a psychiatrist, medication, and inner **calibration**
have helped me find an even keel. Now I manage my moods with the vigilance of
a mother hen, nudging them back to center whenever they wander too far. Eating
wisely, sleeping well, and exercising regularly keep me balanced from day to
day. Ironically, my disorder has taught me to be healthier and happier than
I was before.

Most of the time, I feel lucky to blend in with the crowd. Things that most 5 people grumble about—paying bills, maintaining a car, working 9 to 5—strike me as incredible privileges. I'll never forget gazing through the barred windows of the psychiatric ward into the parking lot, watching people come and go effortlessly, wondering if I'd ever be like them again. There's nothing like a stint in a locked ward to make one grateful for the freedoms and burdens of full citizenship.

Yet sometimes I feel like an **impostor**. Sometimes I wish I could sit at the 6 lunch table and talk about lithium and **Celexa** instead of "Will & Grace." While everyone talks about her fitness routine, I want to brag how it took five orderlies to hold me down and shoot me full of sedatives when I was admitted to the hospital, and how for a brief moment I knew the answers to every infinite mystery of the blazingly bright universe. I yearn for people to know me—the real me—in all my complexity, but I'm afraid it would scare the bejesus out of them.

Every now and then, I feel like I'm truly being myself. Like the time the 7 school chaplain, in whom I'd confided my past, asked me to help counsel a severely bipolar student. This young woman had tried to commit suicide, had been hospitalized many times, and sometimes locked herself in her dorm room to keep the "voices" from overwhelming her. I walked and talked with her, sharing stories about medication and psychosis. I hoped to show by example that manic-depression did not necessarily mean a diminished life. At commencement, I watched her proudly accept her diploma; despite ongoing struggles with her illness, she's continuing her education.

I'm able to be fully myself with my closest friends, all of whom have similar 8 **schisms** between private and public selves. We didn't set out to befriend each other—we just all speak the same language, of hardship and spiritual discovery and psychological awareness.

What I yearn for most is to integrate both sides of myself. I want to be part 9 of the normal world but I also want to own my identity as bipolar. I want people to know what I've been through so I can help those traveling a similar path. Fear has kept me from telling my story: fear of being **stigmatized**, of making people uncomfortable, of being reduced to a label. But hiding the truth has become more uncomfortable than letting it out. It's time for me to own up to who I am, complicated psychiatric history and all. Call me crazy, but I think it's the right thing to do.

intricate
having many parts

garb
clothes

psychotic
mental breakdown

imposter
to pretend to be someone you are not

Celexa
antidepressant

stigmatized
treated with disapproval

Reflecting

Answer the comprehension and vocabulary questions about the reading.

1. What is the main idea of this selection?
   a. That the author makes it a point to hide her disorder
   b. That functioning in society with a mental disorder is a balancing act
   c. That most people do not really understand mental disorders

2. What statement best describes the nature of the supporting details?
   a. Based almost entirely on the personal thoughts and experiences of the writer
   b. Based generally on the thoughts and feelings of her friends and family members
   c. Based generally on published reports

3. What type of detail is used to support the topic sentence in paragraph 7?
   a. Quotation from an expert
   b. Reasons
   c. A brief illustrative story (anecdote)

4. Transitions such as "Most of the time," "Yet," and "Every now and then" introduce paragraphs in this essay. What pattern of organization do these transitions suggest?

a. Logical

b. Spatial

c. Comparison-contrast

5. What is the function or purpose of the sentence "Eating wisely, sleeping well, and exercising regularly keep me balanced from day to day" in paragraph 4?

a. It clarifies or expands on the sentence before it.

b. It adds a completely new idea.

c. It repeats what is said before it.

6. Study how the word *calibrations* is used in the reading, and then choose the most accurate definition of the word.
Calibrations (paragraph 4)

a. Adjustments

b. Conflicts

c. Scoldings

7. Study how the word *schisms* is used in the reading, and then choose the most accurate definition of the word.
Schisms (paragraph 8)

a. Likenesses

b. Divisions

c. Connections

Summarizing

Write a summary paragraph of the selection using the guidelines in Section 2.4. Remember to use your own words and to focus only on the key ideas.

Critical Thinking

- What are your thoughts about the title of the reading? Did your attitude about it change after reading the essay? Explain.

- The writer starts with one label for herself ("mentally ill") and then quickly adds another ("functional member of society"). How does the second label redefine the first?

- In what ways is the author the intended audience of the essay?

- How has this essay added to your understanding of mental illness? And how has it prompted you to learn more about the topic?

- In the chapter introduction, this famous writing advice is quoted: "Have something to say and say it as clearly as you can." Does this essay meet these two standards? Explain.

Writing for Enrichment

Choose one of the following writing ideas, or decide upon an idea of your own related to the reading. Use the writing process to help you develop your work.

1. In a personal blog post, explore your thoughts and feelings about mental illness in general, or about a specific topic related to the subject.

2. Write a reflective personal essay modeled after the essay by Mary Seymour. (The topic doesn't necessarily have to be about mental illness.)

3. Research a particular mental disorder and report on your findings. Consider the causes and characteristics of the disorder as well as its diagnosis and treatment.

4. Compare Seymour's essay with another essay written by someone living with a mental disorder.

5. Research careers in the mental health field and report on one or two of the careers that interest you.

When planning . . .

- Choose a topic that interests you and that you can easily learn about.
- Research your topic as needed.
- Establish a main idea (thesis) after reviewing your notes.
- Decide on the details that you will use to develop your main idea and an appropriate pattern of organization.

When writing . . .

- Include a beginning, middle, and ending in your writing.
- Present your thesis in the beginning part.
- Support your thesis in the middle part.
- Close your writing with final thoughts about your thesis.

When revising and editing . . .

- Review your first draft for overall and line-by-line coherence.
- Ask at least one peer to review your writing as well.
- Revise your writing until it forms a clear, complete, and unified whole.
- Edit your revised writing for style and correctness.

Chapter

7

Voice

Voice or tone refers to the special way a writer speaks to the reader. Most informational texts will speak in one of three ways: Writers of professional material will use a serious, academic voice to share important facts and details. Essayists and bloggers will use a more relaxed, personal voice as they share their thoughts and experiences with the reader. And when the occasion calls for it, certain essayists may use a satiric voice to criticize someone or something.

Recognizing voice is an important part of understanding and appreciating a text. It involves identifying the author's attitude about her topic through the words and sentences she uses. Writing with voice involves choosing words and sentences that help you speak in an appropriate way. This chapter explores key aspects of reading and writing for voice.

Chapter Outline

- Reading for Voice
- Writing with Voice
- Reading for Word Choice and Sentences
- Using Specific Words and Strong Sentences in Writing

7.1 Reading for Voice

Think of voice as the personality projected in a piece of writing. Some texts require a straightforward, serious personality. Other texts require more personal contact with the reader. To establish an appropriate voice, authors must consider the purpose and the intended audience for their writing. The ability to identify the purpose and intended audience for a selection will help you approach and understand your reading.

Considering the Purpose

Purpose is the specific reason for a reading selection. A reading's purpose may be *to inform, to persuade, to criticize, to share,* or *to entertain.* For example, the purpose of a textbook is to inform readers about an academic subject such as biology or political science. With this purpose in mind, the author will project a serious, academic voice, explaining new concepts as clearly and completely as possible.

Writers of professional journals and scholarly nonfiction will also use a serious, **academic voice** because they, too, are writing to inform their respective audiences. The purpose of argument essays, editorials, and position papers is usually to persuade and inform, so they will project a serious, academic voice as well. If any of the texts just mentioned sound too casual to the reader, they will not seem trustworthy.

Some newspaper columnists and nonfiction essayists write strictly to inform, so they use a more formal, academic voice; others write to entertain or engage as well as to inform the reader, so they speak more informally. Writers of memoirs and autobiographies write to share their thoughts about their lives, so they almost always use a **personal voice**. Most readers would have a difficult time maintaining interest in a narrative, memoir, or autobiography that was academic in voice or tone.

Occasionally, skilled essayists will write to criticize an event or individual using humor and/or indirection (saying one thing but meaning something else). When they do this, they are using a **satiric voice**. In order for a satiric piece to succeed, writers must be sure that they are not so indirect that they confuse the reader.

Considering the Audience

Audience is the intended readership for a text. Students, of course, are the intended audience for textbooks, but there are different levels of textbooks with different students in mind. For example, a freshmen biology textbook introduces readers new to the discipline, whereas an advanced biology text addresses readers who already have a strong understanding of the subject. While both texts will project an academic voice, the level of language and complexity of the content in each will differ.

The audience for professional journals and other scholarly texts are people with a thorough interest in the subject matter, so writers of articles in those publications must speak with a level of expertise about the subject. For students just beginning their higher-level education, such scholarly texts may be challenging to read.

The audience for local newspapers is the general citizenry who subscribe to the paper, whereas newspapers such as *The New York Times* and *Washington Post* address national and international audiences, as do news magazines such as *Time*.

Authors of autobiographies and memoirs may have a particular audience in mind (football fans, millennials, political junkies), but, in truth, they want their writing to appeal to a wide range of readers. Table 7.1 encapsulates the voice authors typically project for different purposes and audiences.

Table 7.1 Purpose, Voice, and Audience

	Purpose	**Audience**	**Voice**
Textbooks	to inform	students	academic
Professional texts	to inform	professionals	academic
Syndicated columns and essays	to inform and/or entertain	general readership	academic or personal
Memoirs/autobiographies	to share	audience varies	personal
Satires	to criticize	audience varies	academic or personal

Practice 7.1 Identify the purpose and audience for each of the following types of reading selections.

1. A chapter in a chemistry textbook
   a. To inform students
   b. To praise professional scientists
   c. To entertain a general audience

2. A report in a medical journal
   a. To entertain students
   b. To share with a general audience
   c. To inform medical professionals

3. An autobiography by a former president
   a. To criticize students
   b. To share with a varied audience
   c. To share with professionals

4. A newspaper editorial outlining the benefits of increasing taxes
   a. To persuade general readers
   b. To criticize professionals
   c. To entertain students

Types of Voice

The texts you read in and out of the classroom will generally follow one of three types of voice: academic, personal, or satiric.

Academic Voice

An academic voice is used in textbooks, professional journals, and research projects. An academic voice follows **formal English**, which sounds serious and sticks to the facts. Essays in textbooks and professional journals may contain brief personal introductions and/or snippets of personal reflection but overall maintain an academic voice. This passage from a psychology textbook uses an academic voice. Notice that it relies heavily on important research, which adds a level of authority and formality in the text.

> Does marijuana produce physical dependency? Yes, according to recent studies (Filbey et al., 2009; Lichtman & Martin, 2006). Frequent users of marijuana find it very difficult to quit, so dependency is a risk (Budney & Hughes, 2006), but marijuana's potential for abuse lies primarily in the realm of psychological dependency, not physical addiction.
>
> For about a day after a person smokes marijuana, his or her attention, coordination, and short-term memory are impaired (Pope, Gruber, & Yurgelun-Todd, 1995). Frequent marijuana users show small declines in learning memory, attention, and thinking abilities (Solowij et al., 2002). When surveyed at age 29, nonusers are healthier, earn more, and are more satisfied with their lives than people who smoke marijuana regularly (Ellickson, Martino, & Collins, 2004).
>
> People who smoke five or more "joints" a week score 4 points lower on IQ tests. This is enough to dull their learning capacity. In fact, many people who have stopped using marijuana say they quit because they were bothered by short-term memory loss and concentration problems.
>
> From Coon/Mitterer. *Psychology,* 12E. © 2012 Cengage Learning

Personal Voice

A personal voice is used in personal narratives and essays, blogs, columns in magazines, and memoirs. A personal voice uses **informal English**, which often sounds somewhat relaxed, and includes the writer's thoughts and feelings. This passage from a memoir uses a personal voice.

> Once my mom came to this country, she was pretty much on her own, facing new people, a new culture, even new weather. She got along fine with my dad's

family, but it was not the same as having her own family and friends close by. There were many times, early on, when she wondered what the hell she was doing here.

I remember coming home one day when I was eight or nine, seeing her leaning against the stove, crying. She had just received a letter informing her that my grandfather had died. Even though Edwin had made her life miserable, the news still shocked and hurt her. He was her father. And once she left England, she never saw him again, probably never talked to him again, and she wasn't able to attend the funeral. We just didn't have that kind of money.

She saw her mother only three or four times after coming here and didn't attend her funeral either. So she was essentially cut off from all that she had known. But once she had my sister and me, she had to make a go of it here. And that is what she did.

Satiric Voice

A satiric voice is used in essays and commentaries in which the writer speaks sarcastically or humorously about a topic. In his eighteenth-century essay "A Modest Proposal," Jonathan Swift, in all apparent seriousness, offers a "solution" to the burden caused by poor children in Ireland—that they be sold as food to the rich. Swift, of course, is not serious. He is using satire to make a point about the treatment of Ireland's poor. Here is a passage from this famous satire.

I have been assured by a very knowing American of my acquaintance in London, that a young healthy child well nursed at a year old makes a most delicious, nourishing, and wholesome food, whether stewed, roasted, baked, or boiled; and I make no doubt that it will equally serve in a **fricassee** or a **ragout**.

A child will make two dishes at an entertainment for friends; and when the family dines alone, the fore and hind quarters will make a reasonable dish, and seasoned with a little pepper or salt will be very good boiled on the fourth day, especially in winter.

---

fricassee
method of cooking meat

ragout
well-seasoned meat and vegetables in a thick sauce

Practice 7.2 Carefully read each passage. Then decide which voice is used in each one: *academic*, *personal*, or *satiric*.

1. Growing up, you never saw pea-shoot fried rice on a restaurant menu. It had no protein! There weren't even eggs! What up with the scallions?

   Voice: _____

2. Public housing was built in Chicago because of the Great Migration, the name given to the movement of African Americans from the South to the North. The mechanical cotton picker, introduced in the 1920s, replaced field hands in the cotton fields of the South. . . .

   Voice: _____

3. First, and I cannot believe I have to say this, but shooting people in real life is not cool and it's not great. It's super not those things. In fact, it's one of the worst real-life things you can do to someone, somewhere below *shooting someone whom that person loves*, which is definitely worse, and somewhere above *not returning a text message*, which is definitely a bad thing to do to someone but not as bad as shooting them. So don't do it. Shooting people is stupid. Guns are stupid.

   Voice: _____

4. General Sherman and his men devised ingenious methods for the wrenching of the Southern railroad. They first used a portable rail-lifter that consisted of a chain with a hook on one end and a large iron ring on the other. The hook would be placed under the rail and a small pole put through the ring. Bracing the pole in the ground, a group of soldiers could lift the rail from the ties. . . .

   Voice: _____

5.   We all have problems and barriers that block our progress or prevent us from moving into new areas. Often, the way we respond to our problems places limitations on what we can be, do, and have.

       Problems often work like barriers. When we bump up against one of our problems, we usually turn away and start walking along a different path. And all of a sudden—bump!—we've struck another barrier. And we turn away again. . . .

       If we respond to problems by loving them instead of resisting them, we can expand the boundaries in which we live our lives.

   From ELLIS, *Becoming a Master Student*, 13E. © 2011 Cengage Learning

   Voice: _____

7.2 Writing with Voice

Voice is the way you express yourself or sound in your writing. To project the appropriate voice in your writing, always consider the purpose and audience of the assignment.

Considering Purpose and Audience

- **Narrative Writing:** Whenever you are assigned a personal narrative, a memoir, or a personal essay, your purpose is to share and perhaps to entertain or to inform, and your audience will be your instructor and classmates unless otherwise directed. For narrative assignments, you should use a personal voice because you will be exploring your personal thoughts and experiences.
- **Expository Writing:** Whenever you are assigned expository essays, research reports, and summaries, your purpose is to inform, and your audience is your instructor and your classmates. For these types of assignments, you should use a formal academic voice, presenting your ideas and details clearly and completely.
- **Argument Writing:** Whenever you are assigned an argument essay, your purpose is to persuade and perhaps to inform, and your intended audience is your instructor and classmates. As such, you should use a formal, academic voice in your writing.

Personal Voice

A personal voice reads like an informed conversation with a classmate. It is used most often in autobiographical writing and personal essays. Writing in a personal voice will often include using the following elements:

- **First-person point of view**, meaning that you relate information in the first person, using first-person pronouns—*I, me, my, we, us.*

  > I love spicy food. In fact, I believe food gets better the closer I get to the equator.

- **Subjective writing**, meaning that it will naturally include your personal thoughts and feelings.

  > Why do I order Szechuan chicken extra hot? Partly because I like to see the look of horror on my friends' faces when I start sweating.

- **Easy-to-read sentences** to give the writing the feel of a conversation.

  > At the poles, people eat seal blubber and lutefisk. But at the equator, people eat tacos and teriyaki.

- **Familiar words** to help establish a level of informality.

  > I've really grown to love hot food, partly for the benefits I get from eating it.

Academic Voice

An academic voice is used in most expository essays and research papers. Academic voice includes the following:

- **Third-person point of view,** meaning that you relate all information in the third person, using third-person pronouns, such as *he, she, his, her, they, them*.

  > A key spokesperson for vertical farming is Dickson Despommier, a professor at Columbia University in New York city. At *Verticalfarm.com*, he talks about agricultural techniques.

- **Objective writing,** meaning that you do not include your personal thoughts and feelings.

  > Vertical farms require no soil. Crops are grown hydroponically in a solution of essential minerals dissolved in water.

- **Carefully constructed sentences** to establish a level of formality.

  > There are no stacked greenhouses yet, as Despommier has envisioned them. As a matter of fact, environmental scientists and engineers have serious questions about the efficiency of vertical farming.

- **Content-related words** to reflect knowledge of the topic.

  > Two key technologies already exist for vertical farming—greenhouses and hydroponics.

- **Research if so directed** to credit sources of information used in the writing.

  > Dr. Ted Caplow, a pioneer in rooftop greenhouses, believes vertical farming will work only if it uses natural light ("Does It Really Stack Up?").

- **Avoiding informal expressions** such as familiar sayings, slang, and contractions.

  > Powered by solar panels, it will [not *it'll*] produce 30 tons of vegetables per year.

- **Adhering to the conventions for Standard English,** the established dialect of English used in all academic writing.

  > The roots of plants absorb [not *absorbs*] nutrients directly from this liquid.

7.3 Reading for Word Choice and Sentences

You read informational texts for their explanations, arguments, and ideas. In doing so, you don't generally give careful attention to every noun or verb or sentence. Rather, you're interested in understanding ideas and gaining information. However, paying attention to the author's word choice, or diction, and the way she shapes certain sentences will add to your appreciation and understanding of a text.

Word Choice

Word choice is closely connected to voice in that the words used help create the writer's voice. For example, textbook writers use specific nouns, verbs, and modifiers related to their area of expertise. These words help create the academic voice in the text. Personal essayists, on the other hand, usually rely on more familiar words, which help create a personal or conversational voice.

Word Choice in Academic Texts

Three common features of the words used in textbooks include the following: nominalizations, technical terms, and carefully constructed language.

Nominalizations Academic texts often contain nominalizations—word forms in which verbs, adjectives, or other parts of speech are used as nouns. These words give a text an academic tone and may make a selection more challenging to read.

> **Nominal Constructions**
> - "In all societies, people apply *imagination* . . ."
>   (In more direct terms, "In all societies, people imagine . . .")
> - "The various types of artistic *expression* include . . ."
>   (In more direct terms, "People express themselves artistically by . . .")
> - "Among Latinos, Spanglish *conversations* often flow easily from . . ."
>   (In more direct terms, "Latinos often converse in . . .")

Technical Terms Academic texts will also contain content-related technical terms. Many texts provide definitions of these words either on the page where they occur or in a glossary. Otherwise, you can refer to a dictionary to learn what such terms mean. Here is a passage from an academic text discussing the genetic makeup of a certain group of people. The technical terms used in this passage are underlined.

> Despite centuries of <u>admixing</u>, a modern Catawba Indian was found to be, on average, 50 percent white and 50 percent Native American in <u>genetic composition</u> (Pollitzer et al., 1967). The results of the study surprised many who expected the percentage of <u>white genetic attributes</u> to be much higher. . . .

Carefully Constructed Language In academic texts, writers should choose their words carefully to maintain a certain level of formality. In addition, academic writers will use very few personal pronouns and few, if any, contractions. In the box that follows, compare how a similar idea is stated with carefully constructed language versus personal language.

- **Academic, Formal Language:** One of the best ways to maintain well-being, researchers found, is self-compassion, a healthy form of self-acceptance of individual impediments.

- **Personal, Informal Language:** Researchers have found that we could be happier if we'd only learn how to accept and deal with setbacks in life.

Word Choice in Personal Texts

The language in narratives, personal essays, and feature articles is often relaxed and informal, reflecting the writer's purpose—to share personal thoughts, feelings, and/or experiences.

Relaxed Language Most personal texts will sound somewhat friendly in tone and make the reader feel comfortable and at ease. They may include personal pronouns, in particular first-person pronouns (*I, we, us*), contractions (*it's, can't, weren't*), and perhaps some familiar expressions (*Of course* and *It's too bad that . . .*). Overall, the words will be recognizable to most readers. Notice how easy it is to follow this passage from a personal essay:

- **Personal, Informal Language:** Of course, those were old memories. By the time I reached college, Grandpa wasn't as active anymore. Tired and overworked from his years of hard labor at the steel yard, his back eventually gave out and his joints swelled up with arthritis. And so I sat there, staring at the ceiling and thinking about him. Sure, I had a lump in my throat, and tears filled my eyes; but I also felt thankful for the times we had together and hopeful that one day I could be as good a grandfather as he had been to me. I owed him that much.

Practice 7.3 Carefully read each of the following passages. Then identify the word choice as *academic* or *personal*.

1. This was not exactly my idea of a fun family vacation. Sweat beads trickled down my brow, and a feeling of dread washed over me as I noticed my phone was running out of battery.

   Word Choice: _____

2. While vertical farming may seem futuristic, it has roots in the past. A classic example is the Hanging Gardens of Babylon built in 600 BC. These gardens consisted of a series of stackable terraces.

   Word Choice: _____

3. When a paragraph is coherent, the parts stay together. A coherent paragraph flows smoothly because the writer uses devices such as repetition and transitions to connect ideas.

Word Choice: _____

4. And then there was Martha. She was a talker, talking openly and frequently, usually about her family—where they were all living and what they were doing. She'd get very excited anytime a relative came to visit.

Word Choice: _____

5. I try to be supportive of Ismail's fast, but it's hard. The rules seem unnecessarily harsh to me, an American raised in the seventies by parents who challenged the status quo.

Word Choice: _____

Sentences

All sentences are built with the same parts—nouns, verbs, and modifiers. How an author works with these parts depends on his purpose for writing and his intended audience. Academic authors take special care that their sentences communicate content with a proper level of formality and depth. Authors of personal pieces are generally more interested in writing sentences that engage and/or entertain the reader.

Sentences in Academic Texts

Academic texts are characterized by longer sentences with multiple layers of meaning. Longer sentences often reveal careful thought and reflection on the part of the writer, who needs to share information thoroughly and accurately. Consider these examples from academic texts. In each one, the core sentence is underlined. Notice all of the additional information added to each one.

> Once a country's forests are gone, the companies move on to another country, leaving ecological devastation behind.

> In Indonesia, Malaysia, and other areas of Southeast Asia, tropical forests are being replaced with vast plantations of oil palm, which produces an oil used in cooking, cosmetics, and biodiesel fuel for motor vehicles (especially in Europe).

> Anorexia nervosa is an eating disorder in which a person who has access to food does not eat enough to keep her weight within 15 percent of normal.

Sentences in Personal Texts

For the most part, the sentences in personal texts are relaxed and conversational. As such, they are usually simple in structure, easy to follow, and move along at a quicker pace than sentences in academic texts. Notice how easy it is to read the following passages from personal narratives.

> Mr. Lucarelli was the principal at Jefferson School. He was a roly-poly, hot-tempered Italian. And he tried to teach us to square dance.

> Dad discovered the engine had overheated, and we were stuck. "Is this thing going to blow up?" asked my sister Michelle. "I have a bunch of clothes in the trunk."

> On a good day, I'll see a lot of fish jumping, or at least I'll hear their splash. Last year, for the first time, I saw a bald eagle flying away from its nest.

Practice 7.4 Carefully read the following sentences. Then fill in the blank to identify each one as either *academic* or *personal* in structure.

1. I love watching the cranes fishing in the river. They look so ancient. It's too bad that they visit for such a short time.

Sentence style: _____

2. While executions historically demand a certain degree of morbid curiosity, the last meals of the condemned seem to stimulate heightened interest.

Sentence style: _____

3. Her face was dirty. Her hair greasy and matted. A part of me felt sorry for her.

Sentence style: _____

4. The basic unit of the Braille system is called a "cell," which is two dots wide and three dots high.

Sentence style: _____

5. Take, for example, the big bang, the flash that brought our universe into existence.

Sentence style: _____

6. Admitting I had a disorder was the hardest thing I've ever done. Now I manage my moods very carefully.

Sentence style: _____

7.4 Using Specific Words and Strong Sentences in Writing

Your words and sentences must fit the type of writing that you are doing. The language and sentences you use in a summary or report will likely be different from the language you use in a personal blog or narrative.

Choosing Specific Words

In most cases, specific words (*Pickett's infantry charged*) are better to use than general ones (*the general's men advanced*). In addition, a more colorful modifier such as *belly* in *belly laugh* can be more desirable than a general modifier such as *loud* in a *loud laugh*.

It's especially important to use specific nouns and verbs because they carry the most meaning in your writing. Table 7.2 shows different examples of general versus specific nouns and verbs.

Table 7.2 General vs. Specific Words

General nouns:	hybrid	idea	headache	writer
Specific nouns:	Prius	memory	migraine	Mark Twain
General verbs:	talk	move	think	draw
Specific verbs:	debate	slink	reflect	sketch

What to Watch for with Words

If the words you use help to create clear and interesting paragraphs, essays, and reports, then you have probably used the right ones. Look for opportunities to replace the following word problems:

- **Vague adjectives** (modifiers of nouns) such as *neat, big, pretty, small, cute, fun, bad, nice, good, great,* and *funny.* Use more specific adjectives instead.

  Vague adjective: Gerald delivered a nice tribute to his mother.

  Specific adjective: Gerald delivered a heartwarming tribute to his mother.

- **Too many adjectives in general.** Being "adjective happy" detracts from rather than adds to writing.

  Too many adjectives: Part-time help can complete high-profile, high-impact workplace tasks without adding full-time employees.

  Fewer adjectives: Part-time help can complete important tasks without adding full-time employees. (simpler and clearer)

■ **Too many "be" verbs** (*is, are, was, were*). Instead, use specific action verbs.

> **"Be" verb:**   Carlos is a persuasive debater about politics.
>
> **Specific action verb:**   Carlos debates persuasively about politics.

■ **Words used incorrectly.** Words such as *their, there,* and *they're* are often misused.

> Presidents consult with their (not *they're* or *there*) advisors.

Writing Strong Sentences

Writing clear, correct sentences leads to effective paragraphs and essays. A simple sentence expresses a complete thought and contains a subject and a verb. But not all sentences are "simple." There are compound sentences and complex sentences, as well as other types.

The most common sentence errors include fragments (*incomplete sentences*), comma splices (*two sentences connected only with a comma*), and run-on sentences (*two sentences joined without punctuation or a connecting word*). (See Table 7.3.)

Table 7.3 A Basic Guide to Sentences

Correct Sentences

Simple sentence:	Jackson chews his fingernails. (*one complete idea*)
Compound sentence:	Max watches the presentation, but his mind is really somewhere else. (*two complete ideas*)
Complex sentence:	Sonja takes quick notes, while Connie sketches tiny flowers. (*one main idea and one subordinate or lesser idea*)

Sentence Errors

Fragment:	Popcorn all over the floor. (*no verb*)
Complete:	Popcorn spilled all over the floor. (*verb added*)
Fragment:	Couldn't help laughing. (*no subject*)
Complete:	We couldn't help laughing. (*subject added*)
Comma Splice:	Josie and I ordered coffee, we decided to split a cookie. (*missing a connecting word or end punctuation*)
Correct:	Josie and I ordered coffee, and we decided to split a cookie. (*connecting word added*)
Run-on:	Taking my dog for a walk frustrates me he has to sniff every tree and shrub in front of him. (*no punctuation*)
Correct:	Taking my dog for a walk frustrates me. He has to sniff every tree and shrub in front of him. (*punctuation added*)

What to Watch for with Sentences

Understanding basic sentence structure and common errors is a critical first step when it comes to writing effective sentences. Also, watch for these problems:

- **Short, choppy sentences.** Too many short sentences in a row sound choppy. To correct this problem, combine some of the ideas.

Choppy sentences:	A Harley roared past us. The cycle was jet black. It stopped in front of a food truck. The food truck sells fresh fish tacos.
Combined sentences:	A jet-black Harley roared past us and stopped in front of a food stand that sells fresh fish tacos.

- **Sentences with the same beginning.** This problem often creates writing that sounds too elementary. To correct this problem, vary some of the beginnings.

Sentences with no variety:	Keeping a daily planner is important. It keeps track of your schedule. It lists your assignments. It helps you plan your time.
Varied sentences:	Keeping a daily planner is important. In addition to keeping track of your schedule, it lists your assignments and helps you plan your time.

- **Sentences with passive verbs.** With a passive verb, the subject is acted upon rather than doing the action. Such sentences produce sluggish and awkward writing. To fix this problem, change the passive verbs into active ones.

Passive verb:	Regular walks, biking, and yard work are performed by people with active lifestyles.
Active verb:	People with active lifestyles regularly walk, bike, and do yard work.

Sentence-Revision Review

These strategies can help you identify and fix common sentence errors:

1. **List the opening words in your sentences.** Decide if you need to vary some of your sentence beginnings. You don't want too many of your sentences starting in the same way.

2. **Count the number of words in each sentence.** Decide if you need to vary some sentence lengths. You don't want too many of your sentences structured in the same way.

3. **Identify the main verbs in your sentences.** Decide if too many of them are "be" verbs (*is, are, was, were*). Your sentences will sound more interesting, and carry more meaning, if you substitute specific action verbs for some of the "be" verbs.

☑ Review and Enrichment

Chapter Review Quiz

Answer the questions about what you've learned in this chapter.

1. What is the purpose of satire?
   a. To use humor or sarcasm to make a point
   b. To argue for a certain point of view
   c. To share a memorable personal experience

2. Who is the intended audience for college-level introductory textbooks?
   a. Professionals
   b. Students
   c. General readers

3. What is *not* a characteristic of an academic voice?
   a. Objective (sticking to the facts)
   b. Serious
   c. Conversational in style

4. What does it mean to use the third-person point of view in academic writing?
   a. To relate information in the third person, using third-person pronouns (*he, she, they, them*)
   b. To share information with three different people
   c. To have a three-party panel of experts approve the text

5. How is personal writing subjective?
   a. It uses sarcasm to make fun of someone.
   b. It includes the personal thoughts and feelings of the writer.
   c. It sticks to the facts.

6. Academic writing often contains nominalizations. What are nominalizations?
   a. Specific nouns such as *surgeon* (instead of *doctor*)
   b. Vivid action verbs such as *whisper* (instead of *talk*)
   c. Forms of verbs or adjectives used as nouns such as *expression* (from *express*)

7. What are two general characteristics of sentences in personal writing?
   a. They are conversational in tone and easy to follow.
   b. They are sarcastic and cruel.
   c. They are serious and complex.

8. What are three examples of vague adjectives to avoid in writing?
   a. Is, are, were
   b. Big, nice, good
   c. Their, its, your

Reading for Enrichment

You will be reading a personal essay in which the author, an acclaimed writer and college professor, provides advice for incoming minority students. Be sure to follow the steps in the reading process to help you gain a full understanding of the text.

About the Author

Nikki Giovanni is a poet, essayist, and a University Distinguished Professor of English at Virginia Tech. She has received many honors and awards for her writing and has, over the years, become a valued spokesperson in the African American community.

Prereading

Providing advice to incoming students is a common theme for educators and writers. There are texts helping students with time management, test taking, essay writing, and social skills. Some of these texts may be academic in voice. Most of them, though, are written with a more personal touch, such as "Campus Racism 101," in which Giovanni advises African American students who are entering predominantly White colleges. Before you begin reading, consider what advice you would like to receive as you begin your college education.

Then use the **STRAP** strategy to identify the main parts of the text. Also, consider listing a few questions that you hope the reading will answer.

Subject:	What specific topic does the reading address?
Type:	What form (*essay, personal narrative, textbook selection*) does the reading take?
Role:	What position (*student, professor, journalist*) does the writer assume?
Audience:	Who is the intended audience (*general readers, Black students, administrators*)?
Purpose:	What is the general goal of the reading (*to inform, to persuade, to entertain*)?

Reading and Rereading

As you read, be sure to (1) identify the main idea of the essay, (2) follow the details that develop this idea, (3) confirm the purpose and audience, and (4) identify characteristics of the author's writing voice. Consider annotating the text and/or taking notes as you read. Then reread as needed to form a clear understanding of the text.

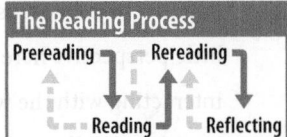

The Reading Process

Prereading → Rereading

Reading → Reflecting

Campus Racism 101

There is a bumper sticker that reads: *TOO BAD IGNORANCE ISN'T PAINFUL*. I like that. But ignorance is. We just seldom attribute the pain to it or even recognize it when we see it. Like the postcard on my corkboard. It shows a young man in a very hip jacket smoking a cigarette. In the background is a high school with the American flag waving. The caption says: "Too cool for school. Yet too stupid for the real world." Out of the mouth of the young man is a bubble enclosing the words "Maybe I'll start a band." There could be a postcard showing a jock in a uniform saying, "I don't need school. I'm going to the NFL or NBA." Or one showing a young man or woman studying and a group of young people saying, "So you want to be white." Or something equally **demeaning**. We need to quit it.

I am a professor of English at Virginia Tech. I've been here for four years, though for only two years with academic rank. I am tenured, which means I have a teaching position for life, a rarity on a predominantly white campus. Whether from **malice** or ignorance, people who think I should be at a **predominantly** Black institution will ask, "Why are you at Tech?" Because it's here. And so are Black students. But even if Black students weren't here, it's painfully obvious that this nation and this world cannot allow white students to go through higher education without interacting with Blacks in authoritative positions. It is equally clear that predominantly Black colleges cannot accommodate the numbers of Black students who want and need an education.

Is it difficult to attend a predominantly white college? Compared with what? Being passed over for promotion because you lack credentials? Being turned down for jobs because you are not college-educated? Joining the armed forces or going to jail because you cannot find an alternative to the streets? Let's have a little perspective here. Where can you go and what can you do that frees you from interacting with the white American mentality? You're going to interact; the only question is, will you be in some control of yourself and your actions, or will you be controlled by others? I'm going to recommend self-control.

What's the difference between prison and college? They both prescribe *4*
your behavior for a given period of time. They both allow you to read books and
develop your writing. They both give you time alone to think and time with your
peers to talk about issues. But four years of prison doesn't give you a passport to
greater opportunities. Most likely that time only gives you greater knowledge
of how to get back in. Four years of college gives you an opportunity not only to
lift yourself but to serve your people effectively. What's the difference when you
are called nigger in college from when you are called nigger in prison? In college
you can, though I admit with effort, follow procedures to have those students
who called you nigger kicked out or suspended. You can bring issues to public
attention without risking your life. But mostly, college is and always has been the
future. We, neither less nor more than other people, need knowledge. There are
discomforts attached to attending predominantly white colleges, though no more
so than living in a racist world. Here are some rules to follow that may help:

Go to class. No matter how you feel. No matter how you think the professor *5*
feels about you. It's important to have a consistent presence in the classroom. If
nothing else, the professor will know you care enough and are serious enough to
be there.

Meet your professors. Extend your hand (give a firm handshake) and tell them *6*
your name. Ask them what you need to do to make an A. You may never make an
A, but you have put them on notice that you are serious about getting good grades.

Do assignments on time. Typed or computer-generated. You have the syllabus. *7*
Follow it, and turn those papers in. If for some reason you can't complete an
assignment on time, let your professor know before it is due and work out a new
due date—then meet it.

Go back to see your professor. Tell him or her your name again. If an *8*
assignment received less than an A, ask why, and find out what you need to do to
improve the next assignment.

Yes, your professor is busy. So are you. So are your parents who are working *9*
to pay or help with your tuition. Ask early what you need to do if you feel you are

starting to get into academic trouble. Do not wait until you are failing.

Understand that there will be professors who do not like you; there may even be professors who are racist or sexist or both. You must discriminate among your professors to see who will give you the help you need. You may not simply say, "They are all against me." They aren't. They mostly don't care. Since you are the one who wants to be educated, find the people who want to help.   10

Don't defeat yourself. Cultivate your friends. Know your enemies. You cannot undo hundreds of years of **prejudicial** thinking. Think for yourself and speak up. Raise your hand in class. Say what you believe no matter how awkward you may think it sounds. You will improve in your **articulation** and confidence.   11

Participate in some campus activity. Join the newspaper staff. Run for office. Join a dorm council. Do something that involves you on campus. You are going to be there for four years, so let your presence be known, if not felt.   12

You will inevitably run into some white classmates who are troubling because they often say stupid things, ask stupid questions—and expect an answer. Here are some comebacks to some of the most common inquiries and comments: 13

Q: What's it like to grow up in a ghetto?   14

A: I don't know.   15

Q: (from the teacher): Can you give us the Black perspective on Toni Morrison, Huck Finn, slavery, Martin Luther King, Jr., and others?   16

A: I can give you my perspective. (Do not take the burden of 22 million people on your shoulders. Remind everyone that you are an individual, and don't speak for the race or any other individual within it.)   17

Q: Why do all the Black people sit together in the dining hall?   18

A: Why do all the white students sit together?   19

Q: Why should there be an African-American studies course?   20

A: Because white Americans have not adequately studied the contributions of Africans and African-Americans. Both Black and white students need to know our total common history.   21

Q: Why are there so many scholarships for "minority" students?   22

A: Because they wouldn't give my great-grandparents their forty acres and the   *23*
mule.

Q: How can whites understand Black history, culture, literature, and so forth?   *24*

A: The same way we understand white history, culture, literature, and so   *25*
forth. That is why we're in school: to learn.

Q: Should whites take African-American studies courses?   *26*

A: Of course. We take white-studies courses, though the universities don't call   *27*
them that.

Comment: When I see groups of Black people on campus, it's really   *28*
intimidating.

Comeback: I understand what you mean. I'm frightened when I see white   *29*
students congregating.

Comment: It's not fair. It's easier for you guys to get into college than for other   *30*
people.

Comeback: If it's so easy, why aren't there more of us?   *31*

Comment: It's not our fault that America is the way it is.   *32*

Comeback: It's not our fault, either, but both of us have a responsibility to   *33*
make changes.

It's really very simple. Educational progress is a national concern; education is   *34*
a private one. Your job is not to educate white people; it is to obtain an education.
If you take the racial world on your shoulders, you will not get the job done. Deal
with yourself as an individual worthy of respect, and make everyone else deal with
you the same way. College is a little like playing grown-up. Practice what you want
to be. You have been telling your parents you are grown. Now is your chance to act
like it.

---

demeaning
degrading or insulting

malice
desire to inflict injury, harm, or suffering

prejudicial
unreasonable opinion or feeling about a ethnic, racial,
social, or religious group

articulation
clear and polished way of speaking

Reflecting

Answer the comprehension and vocabulary questions about the reading.

1. Why is the title significant?
   a. It suggests that the essay is a guide for all students beginning their college careers.
   b. It suggests that college campuses can be racist, and the "101" indicates that the essay will describe the basic ways to deal with it.
   c. It suggests that college campuses are in need of change, and this essay will explain why.

2. What is the main idea of this selection?
   a. Black students should do just fine in majority White colleges if they study hard.
   b. Black students may find it challenging to attend a majority White college, but following certain rules will help.
   c. Black students should remember that they have no more or no less pressure on them than anyone else.

3. How would you describe Giovanni's writing voice in this essay?
   a. Honest, direct, and personal
   b. Academic and research-dominant
   c. Humorous and light-hearted

4. How would you characterize the sentence style in the essay?
   a. Complex and containing multiple levels of meaning
   b. Easy to follow, but power-packed
   c. Unclear and vague

5. In paragraph 4, Giovanni says, "But mostly, college is and always has been the future." What does she mean?
   a. That future generations of minority students will have easier college experiences
   b. That the knowledge that comes with a college education opens doors to future opportunities
   c. That colleges will be far different in the future, especially for minority students

6. What is the purpose of Giovanni's questions and answers starting with paragraph 14?
   a. To provide conversation starters for Black students when they introduce themselves to their professors
   b. To provide tips for conversing during important class projects
   c. To provide comebacks for ignorant questions they may receive from White classmates

7. Study the word parts of the word *predominantly* and how the word is used in the reading. Then choose the most accurate definition of the word.

Predominantly (paragraph 2)   Pre + domin + ant + ly

(*Hint:* "domin" is the root in a word like *dominate*.)

  a. Mainly, for the most part

  b. Before another part

  c. To be in control very early

8. Study the word parts of the word *discomforts* and how the word is used in the reading. Then choose the most accurate definition of the word.

Discomforts (paragraph 4)   Dis + comfort(s)

  a. Very comfortable

  b. Uncomfortable

  c. Unequal

Summarizing

Write a summary of "Campus Racism 101." Remember to use your own words and to focus only on the key ideas. (See Section 2.4 for help.)

Critical Thinking

- How does your race impact your reading of the essay?
- What audience do you think Giovanni is writing for?
- Why does Giovanni make the comparison between prison and college in paragraph 4?
- What are some of the most surprising statements that Giovanni makes? Why are they surprising?
- Have you been a target of racism in an educational environment? How did you respond? What impact did the experience have on your approach or attitude toward school and learning?
- In the closing paragraph, Giovanni says, "Educational progress is a national concern; education is a private one." What does she mean by making this distinction?

Writing for Enrichment

Next, you will review possible writing activities to complete in response to the reading. Use the writing process to help you develop your responses.

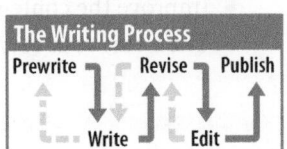

The Writing Process

Prewrite   Revise   Publish

Write   Edit

Prewriting

Choose one of these writing ideas or decide upon an idea of your own.

1. Giovanni identifies the following bumper-sticker message: TOO BAD IGNORANCE ISN'T PAINFUL. Explore this idea in a personal blog entry. Base your thoughts on your own experiences and observations.

2. Rewrite part of Giovanni's essay using an academic voice.

3. Agree or disagree with Giovanni's thesis or claim. Support your point of view with strong facts and details.

4. Explore Giovanni's claim that "college is and always has been the future."

5. Provide advice and/or rules to follow for another aspect of student life (paying for school, being a part of the LGBTQ community and maneuvering in the straight world, etc.).

When planning . . .

- Be clear about the audience and purpose of your writing.
- Collect plenty of details about your topic.
- Establish a thesis or claim for your essay.
- Review your details to make sure that you have sufficient information to support you thesis.
- Decide if you will use a personal or academic voice.

When writing . . .

- Develop effective beginning, middle, and ending parts in your essay.
- Present your thesis in the beginning part.
- Support the thesis in the middle part.
- Close your essay with final thoughts about your thesis.

When revising and editing . . .

- Carefully review your first draft for content and voice.
- Ask at least one peer to review your writing as well.
- Improve the content and/or voice as needed.
- Then edit your revised writing for style and correctness.

Part 3:

Types of Reading and Writing

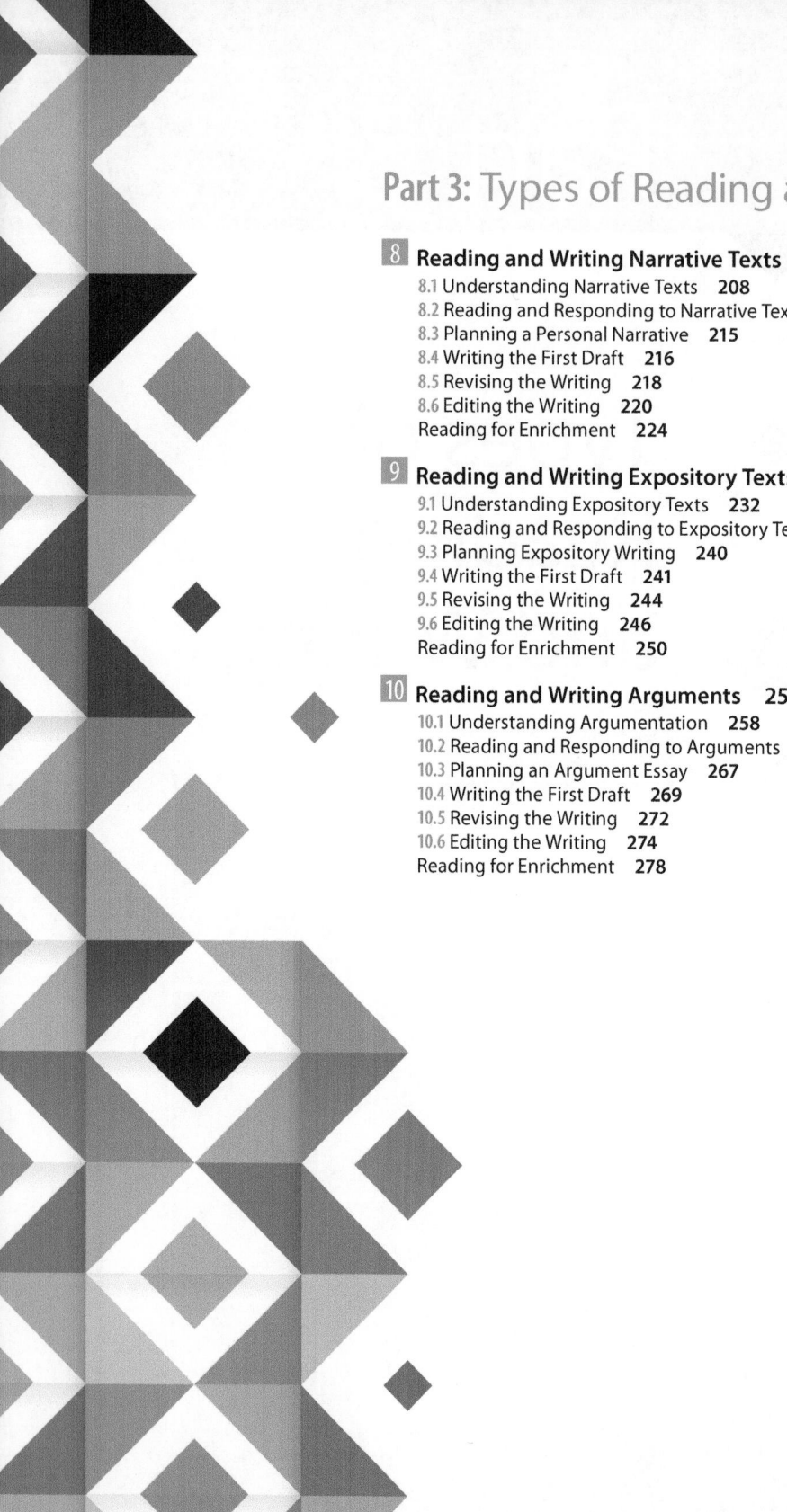

Part 3: Types of Reading and Writing

Erlo Brown, 2017 / Used under license from Shutterstock.com

Chapter

8

Reading and Writing Narrative Texts

In his book *On Writing Well,* William Zinsser says that the one subject all writers know better than anything or anyone else is themselves. Their thoughts and feelings about their past actions and present lives shape who they are and how they see the world.

When writing directly about their own experiences, writers are involved in narration. (To **narrate** means "to tell a story.") Narrative writing shares real or imagined events in the order that they happened. This chapter focuses on nonfiction or true narratives.

You will learn about different types of true narratives and read and respond to a professional narrative. Then you will plan and write a narrative about an experience in your own life. Through this process, you may learn something new about the experience and, more importantly, about yourself.

Chapter Outline

- Understanding Narrative Texts
- Reading and Responding to Narrative Texts
- Planning a Personal Narrative
- Writing the First Draft
- Revising the Writing
- Editing the Writing

8.1 Understanding Narrative Texts

A narrative usually shares an event in a writer's life that has some heightened importance, most often from a first-person point of view. ("*I* turned the key." "*We* reached the boat.") Surprises, setbacks, turning points—these are common subjects for personal narratives.

Depending on the topic, a narrative will draw out different responses. Some narratives will simply entertain readers. Others will encourage, inspire, or even shock readers. As a reader, it is enjoyable and informative to compare the writer's experience with your own: Have you experienced a similar event? Did you have the same feelings as the writer? Why or why not?

Here are some common forms of narrative texts:

Personal Narrative

A **personal narrative** focuses on recreating an experience by answering the 5 W's and H (*who? what? when? where? why?* and *how?*) about it. Typically, the narrative focuses on one event or experience using many sensory details.

> It was a Saturday morning when my uncle Elijah took me outside to buy my first car. He discovered it on Craigslist. Outside, the car was depressing. Its red paint had faded to a dusty, tomato-soup color that rubbed off on your fingers. Inside, the fake leather seats were cracked, and crumbly orange foam padding showed through. The interior stank of dirty motor oil and what smelled like old cheese. When my uncle said, "Start it up," I turned the key to the roar of a broken exhaust. When Elijah said, "We'll take it," I almost cried. I drove his car home, while he drove the junk heap to his house to work on. Later that night, he brought "Tomato Can" back to my house. I couldn't believe it was the same car. He had used a restoring wax, and the paint was now a deep, shiny red. A new exhaust pipe made the engine purr. New seat covers hid the old upholstery. I could still smell the cheese, but that would fade with time. I had my first set of wheels.

Personal Essay

A **personal essay** goes a step further by recreating the experience and explaining what it means. Though analysis may work its way into a personal essay, the writer's main purpose is still to recreate the story.

> The weirdest thing about living with your parents is having people constantly observing your every move: "Is that a second glass of wine?" "Who's calling?" "Are you going to put the cheese away?" "Why does the dog like you more than me?" "Haven't you already taken a shower today?" And on and on, world without end.
>
> After five years in New York, I decided it was time for a change. I packed up my Williamsburg apartment and moved across the country to the little island in

the **Puget Sound** where I was born. I had decided to go to nursing school, and I had also decided to live with my parents while I completed a year of **prerequisites** at the local community college. It's been four months.   Excerpted from "I Moved Back To My Parent's House At 29, And It Wasn't The End Of The World" by Ramona Emerson. Originally appeared in *BuzzFeed*.

Puget Sound
Semi-enclosed body of water outside of Seattle

prerequisites
classes needed to advance to other courses

Autobiography and Memoir

An **autobiography** provides a detailed account of the writer's own life. It is written in the first person. A memoir focuses on one specific aspect of the writer's life rather than the life in its entirety.

My mother taught me that reading is a kind of work, and that every paragraph merits exertion, and in this way, I learned how to absorb difficult books. Soon after I went to kindergarten, however, I learned that reading difficult books also brings trouble. I was punished for reading ahead of the class, for being unwilling to speak and act "nicely." I didn't know why I simultaneously feared and adored my female teachers, but I did know that I needed their attention, positive or negative, at all times. Tiny but determined, I navigated the confusing and unstable path of being what you are while knowing that it's more than people want to see.   Excerpted from *Lab Girl* by Hope Jahren.

Anecdote

Anecdotes are very brief narrative stories that are used to illustrate a point or draw attention to an idea. Anecdotes can be used in the opening paragraphs of expository or argumentative essays as a strategy for introducing a topic and leading up to the main idea.

I stopped eating pork about eight years ago, after a scientist happened to mention that the animal whose teeth most closely resemble our own is the pig. . . . A couple of years later, I gave up all **mammalian** meat, period. I still eat fish and poultry, however, and pour eggnog in my coffee. My dietary decisions are **arbitrary** and inconsistent, and when my friends ask why I'm willing to try the duck but not the lamb, I don't have a good answer. Food choices are often like that: difficult to **articulate** but strongly held. And lately, debates over food choices have flared with particular vehemence.

Excerpted from "Sorry, Vegans: Brussels Sprouts Like to Live, Too" by Natalie Angier.

---

mammalian
relating to a mammal

arbitrary
random

articulate
explain

8.2 Reading and Responding to Narrative Texts

When reading narratives, use a time line to keep track of the important events and a plot line to analyze the key parts in the story.

Using a Time Line

Part of the challenge when reading a narrative is keeping track of the key actions in the order that they occur. Placing the details in a time line (see **Figure 8.1**) works well for this purpose because narratives are almost always organized chronologically. When completing a time line, focus on the essential actions in a story. You don't need to include all the specific details.

Figure 8.1 Time Line

1 — Early morning phone call

2 — Mom says, "Grandpa died."

3 — Dropping on the couch

4 — Remembering good times

5 — Appreciating his good character

Following a Plot Line

A narrative is essentially a story. And like the plot in a fictional story, a personal narrative should create suspense as it moves along. **Figure 8.2** shows the parts of the plot and how the level of reader interest should build as the story progresses. Tracing a narrative's plot will direct you to the most important parts of the story.

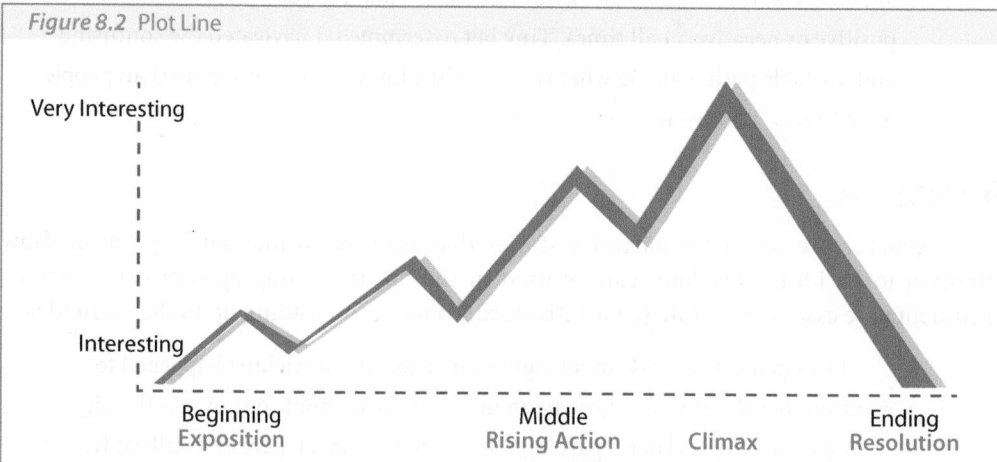

Figure 8.2 Plot Line

Very Interesting

Interesting

Beginning — Exposition

Middle — Rising Action

Climax

Ending — Resolution

- **Exposition:** The characters (people) are introduced, the setting (time and place of the action) is established, and a conflict or problem is identified.

- **Rising action:** A series of actions and conversations build suspense and interest.

- **Climax:** The main character faces the conflict, either overcoming it or learning from it. This is the most exciting part. The way the main character reacts to the climax may reveal the main point of the story.

- **Resolution:** The narrative wraps up quickly after the climax. Sometimes the climax and resolution are wrapped up in one action.

Reading and Reacting to a Professional Narrative

"Emery's Born" is a narrative within *Double Cup Love*, a memoir about a man at a crossroads between his past and future.

The Reading Process

Prereading → Rereading

Reading → Reflecting

About the Author

Eddie Huang is a chef, writer, and television personality. He is the author of the memoirs *Double Cup Love* and *Fresh Off the Boat*, the latter of which inspired a network sitcom by the same name. He is also the host of *Huang's World* on Viceland.

Prereading

Before you read, answer the STRAP questions to identify the main features of the reading.

Subject: What is the specific topic of the reading?
Type: What form (*essay, narrative, textbook selection*) does the reading take?
Role: What position (*student, subject, educator*) does the writer assume?
Audience: Who is the intended audience (*general readers, students, teachers*)?
Purpose: What is the goal of the reading (*to inform, to persuade, to entertain*)?

Reading and Rereading

As you read, consider completing a time line to identify the key actions in the narrative. Also, try to identify the different parts of the plot (see **Figure 8.2**) during your reading. Be sure to reread any parts as necessary.

Emery's Born

I didn't understand my dad back then and therefore I didn't like him. But on March 7, 1985, everything changed. Emery was born.   *1*

Dad came home from the hospital and picked me up. I remember he was very stern.   *2*

"Eddie, let's go see your mom."   *3*

"Is Mom still at the hospital?"   *4*

"Yeah, she just had your brother."   *5*

"Oh, cool! What's he look like?"   *6*

"He's big. Nine pounds, ten ounces. Fat baby."   *7*

"Awesome! He's gonna be tall!"   *8*

"Yeaaa, right!" He loved saying "yeaaa, right!"   9

We got in our Chevy Malibu station wagon and went off to the   10
hospital. I didn't say anything to my dad. He didn't say anything
to me. I just stared out the window at the trees. I liked the trees in
Northern Virginia, passing now in a blur as we drove up and down
the hills. It felt like we were on a roller coaster. Soon we pulled into
the drugstore.

"I thought we were going to the hospital?"   11

"We need to make a stop here. Let's go."   12

"OK."   13

My dad walked into the store and I walked alongside him. He   14
wasn't the kind of dad who would hold your hand or pat your head.
He was more like a boss. I just followed his lead whenever he was
around.

"Eddie, pick any toy you want."   15

"Really?"   16

"Yeah, but only one toy."   17

"What'd I do?"   18

"What do you mean?"   19

"Did I do something good?"   20

"No, not really."   21

I was suspicious. Was this a trap? My dad never did anything   22
nice. Even my mom never got me toys. Something was wrong.

"Why am I getting a toy, then?"   23

He was hiding something from me. I remember he looked away   24
and didn't make much eye contact.

"Eddie. Dad will always love you."   25

I didn't understand. He just kept staring at the wall of toys. If I   26
was with my mom, I'd be bouncing off the wall picking through the
toys, but I was careful around my dad. He always told me to walk
straight, chest out. I stood there as stiff as I could and stared at the
wall with him. Then he spoke again.

"Xiao Wen, your brother Emery is born today but I want you to   27 remember what I tell you. No matter what happens, no matter how much we love your brother, it doesn't change how we feel about you. Mom and Dad will always love you, OK? Nothing will ever change that."

"I know." 28

"How do you know?" 29

I shrugged. 30

"Really? You aren't worried that we may like Emery more?" 31

"No. I never thought about it. Emery is supposed to be my best 32
friend."

"Ha ha, who told you that?" 33

"Mom." 34

"Hmmm, she's right. You have a good mom. I didn't know she 35
already told you this."

"Yeah, I wanna go meet Emery." 36

"OK, well, pick a toy and then we go see Emery." 37

I knew exactly what toy I wanted. 38

"Dad, I want the green He-Man car." 39

But there was one problem with that choice. Just as my dad went 40
to grab it, I spoke up.

"But I don't have a He-Man, Dad." 41

He wasn't falling for it. 42

"You want the car or you want a He-Man?" 43

"I want the car." 44

"You sure? This is what Americans call put the car before the 45
He-Man."

"Yeah, I want the car." 46

"Why do you want the car?" 47

"The car is green. I like green. Plus, it's bigger, He-Man is just 48
. . . a man."

"Ha ha, OK, here's your car." 49

He handed me the car. 50

Thirty-two years later, it's still here: the green He-Man car 51

driven by a belief in **unconditional** love between a father and son.
Despite everything that's happened between us, I see myself as
privileged. My dad stopped the world on March 7, 1985, to remind
me that he loved me, and I'll never forget it.

Reflecting

Practice 8.1 Answer the comprehension and vocabulary questions about the reading.

1. Why does Eddie's father offer to buy him a new a toy?
   a. To reward Eddie for having a great attitude about his new brother
   b. So Eddie has a gift to give his newborn brother
   c. To remind Eddie he will always love him, even if his attention will be split between Eddie and his newborn brother

2. How are the details in "Emery's Born" organized?
   a. By time (chronologically)
   b. By order of importance
   c. By comparing and contrasting

3. How would you describe the author's voice?
   a. Informed and distanced
   b. Humorous and sincere
   c. Angry and critical

4. Study how the word *unconditional* is used in the reading, and then choose the most accurate definition of the word.
   Unconditional (paragraph 51)
   a. Fragile
   b. Absolute
   c. Limited

Critical Thinking

- In the final paragraph, Huang says his father "stopped the world on March 7, 1985." Why might he have chosen this specific phrase? How did his dad "stop the world"?
- What details from the text reveal Eddie's father's uneasiness about outwardly expressing his love for his son?

8.3 Planning a Personal Narrative

Now that you've read and reflected on a sample text, you're ready to plan your own narrative. Prewriting begins by thinking about personal events or experiences that you feel are worthy of being shared. Consider surprises, setbacks, or turning points in your life. Or more generally, recall events that represent something about you.

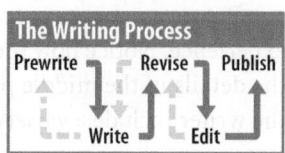

Brainstorm ideas to help identify a few events or experiences that you could write about. Ideally, you should think of events that cover brief spans of time. Then choose one for your narrative. Once you pick a topic, think about how the experience unfolded. If you have trouble recalling details, consider the following strategies:

- Talk about the experience with someone connected to the time and place.
- Review pictures or videos about the experience.
- Write for five minutes nonstop about the topic to see what details come to mind.

Then record the important details related to the experience. Think in terms of what happened first, second, third, and so on. It may be helpful to list these details in a time line. (See Figure 8.1.)

A Closer Look at Narrative Details

Narratives become memorable when they include a variety of details, including sensory details, dialogue, and personal reflections.

- **Sensory details** are the sights, sounds, smells, tastes, and textures (sensations) related to an experience. (Sights and sounds are usually of primary importance.)

  I wobbled over to my cushy leather couch. *(sight)*
  My cell phone buzzed. *(sound)*
  I was already awake, frying eggs in a skillet. *(smell)*
  He handed me a glass of bourbon that burned when I took a drink. *(taste)*
  I had a lump in my throat. *(sensation)*

- **Dialogue** shares conversations between people.

  "Are you awake?" she asked, her voice cracking.
  Sensing her distress, I asked, "What's wrong?"

- **Personal reflections** reveal your thoughts and feelings at the time.

  I felt thankful for the times we had together.

Think carefully about your narrative topic in terms of sensory details, dialogue, and personal reflections: What senses were important (sights, sounds, etc.)? What conversations do you recall? What thoughts and feelings were you having? Create a list of the different types of details that you could include in your first draft.

8.4 Writing the First Draft

Before you begin your own first draft, read this student narrative based on a memorable experience. Notice how the writer created effective opening and closing parts. Also consider the details in the middle part: Are they all arranged chronologically (by time)? Finally, does the writer include a variety of details—sensory details, dialogue, and personal reflections?

Remembering Gramps

Opening Paragraph

It was sometime after eight o'clock on a Saturday morning when I received the call about my grandfather's death. I was already awake, frying eggs in a skillet, when my cell phone buzzed on the countertop. A little early for a phone call, I thought. It was my mom. "Are you awake?" she asked, her voice cracking. Sensing her distress, I asked, "What's wrong?" She told me my grandfather had suffered a stroke during the night and didn't make it.

Middle Paragraph 1

After talking through the funeral plans, I wobbled over to my cushy, leather couch and stared blankly at the circulating blades on the ceiling fan. Memories of my grandfather spun around in my head, like the time he taught me how to throw a curveball, and the Canadian fishing trip we took together, and the day he thought he had poured me a Coke but instead handed me his glass of bourbon that burned my throat when I took a gulp.

Middle Paragraph 2

Of course, those were old memories. By the time I reached college, Grandpa wasn't as active anymore. Tired and overworked from his years of hard labor at the steel yard, his back eventually gave out and his joints swelled up with arthritis. He lived alone in the modest two-bedroom home he built for my grandmother after they married. But even after she was gone, he never lost the sparkle in his brown eyes. Nor did he lose his sense of humor, punctuated by a deep baritone laugh.

Closing Paragraph

And so I sat there, staring at the ceiling and reminiscing about Grandpa. Sure, I had a lump in my throat, and tears filled my eyes; but I felt thankful for the times we had together and hopeful that one day I could be as good a grandfather as he had been to me. I owed him that much—and so much more.

Developing an Opening Paragraph

The opening part should grab the readers' attention and lead them into the story. Here are three strategies for beginning a narrative:

- **Set the stage.**

  It was sometime after eight o'clock on a Saturday morning when I received the call about my grandfather's death.

- **Jump right into things.**

  Jammed in our aging royal blue Chevy Astro van with no air conditioning, no radio, and limited legroom sat my parents, my two sisters, and our dog, Max.

- **Offer an interesting thought.**

  I should have listened to my brother and never walked into that room.

Creating the Middle Paragraphs

In the middle part of your narrative, share the main details about the experience. In other words, this is where you tell your story. Here are some reminders:

- **Include explanations, sensory details, dialogue, and personal reflections** to recreate the experience and build your audience's interest.
- **When necessary, use transition words that show time:** *after, before, during, later, now, soon, suddenly, then, when, while, first, second, finally, lastly.*
- **Organize your details** so they are easy to follow.

Creating a Closing Paragraph

The closing part can wrap up the experience after the most exciting action has happened, or it can provide an analysis of the experience by explaining its value and importance. Here are three strategies to consider:

- **Offer a final analysis or reflection about the experience.**

  I felt thankful for the times we had together and hopeful that one day I could be as good a grandfather as he had been to me.

- **Include a final piece of dialogue.**

  We did eventually make it to the Grand Canyon, but not before Mom admitted, "A beach vacation sounds really nice right now."

- **Conclude with the last important action.**

  John and Dan triumphantly strolled home. Dan had John's jacket in his hand.

When you write the first draft of your narrative, be sure to follow this advice, and refer to the other narratives in this chapter for additional ideas. Keep writing until you have told the complete story.

8.5 Revising the Writing

Revising a first draft involves adding, deleting, rearranging, and reworking parts of the writing. Revision often begins with a peer review. Sharing your work with peers helps you gain a fresh perspective on your first draft, and the feedback will help you make changes to improve your narrative.

Here's an example of feedback the student writer received for "Remembering Gramps." Have at least one classmate or trusted friend read and react to your first draft. Have the peer reviewer use questions like these to help them respond to your narrative.

Peer Review Sheet

Narrative title: Remembering Gramps

Writer: Jody Parker

Reviewer: Shawn Wallis

1. Which part of the narrative works best—opening, middle, or closing? Why?

   Opening, because it makes you want to read the rest and find out what is going to happen.

2. Which part of the narrative needs work—opening, middle, or closing? Why?

   Middle, because I want more details about the relationship between the writer and the grandfather.

3. Which details in the story caught your attention? Name three.

   a. buzzing phone

   b. cracking voice

   c. modest two-bedroom home

4. Does the writer include appropriate dialogue? Explain.

   Yes, a short exchange between mother and son gets the reader's attention.

5. Identify a phrase or two that shows the writer's level of interest in their story.

   The first two sentences of the second paragraph

Adding Specific Verbs and Modifiers

Strengthen your narrative by replacing general verbs and modifiers with more specific ones as in **Figure 8.3**. Doing so will strengthen your writing and help readers better understand the story.

Figure 8.3 Specific Verbs and Modifiers

Verbs		Modifiers	
General	**Specific**	**General**	**Specific**
grew	swelled	baseball cap	flat-billed Yankees cap
came	advanced	curly hair	wavy auburn hair
run	sprint	deep laugh	baritone laugh
lives	roams	sweet sauce	tangy barbecue sauce
wear	don	dangerous pier	wobbly pier

Read aloud the first draft and then the revised version of the excerpt. Study how the specific verbs and adjectives add life to the writing.

> wobbled   cushy, leather   stared   circulating   ceiling
> I ~~walked~~ over to my couch and ~~looked~~ blankly at the blades on the fan.

Improve your first draft by replacing general verbs and modifiers with more specific ones. Also, use a revising checklist like the one in **Figure 8.4** to check your ideas, organization, and voice. Continue working until you can check off each item on the list.

Figure 8.4 Revising Checklist

Ideas

☐ Do I focus on one specific experience or memory?

☐ Do I include sensory details and dialogue?

☐ Do I use specific verbs and modifiers?

Organization

☐ Does the narrative have an opening, a middle, and a closing?

☐ Is the story organized chronologically?

☐ Have I used transitions to connect my sentences?

Voice

☐ Is my interest in the story obvious to the reader?

☐ Does my writing voice sound natural?

8.6 Editing the Writing

The main work of editing is correcting the revised first draft for sentence style, spelling, grammar, and usage. This step becomes important *after* you have made the important changes related to the ideas, organization, and voice in your first draft.

Quotation Marks and Dialogue

Most narratives include dialogue, which enlivens the story and reveals the personalities of its characters. When you write conversations between people using their exact words, place quotation marks before and after the **direct quotation**. However, when you write *about* what someone has said, not using the speaker's exact words, omit the quotation marks before and after the **indirect quotation**.

Direct Quotation

Before we left class, Mr. Lopez said, "Next week's final will cover the entire semester."

Indirect Quotation

Mr. Lopez told the class that the final will cover the entire semester.

Practice 8.2 Fill in the blank after each sentence with a *D* for direct quotation or an *I* for indirect quotation, depending on whether or not the speaker's exact words are used.

1. "I'm having the worst day," Jesse said. "I left my cell phone at home." _____

2. "Who is your favorite actress?" asked Veronica. _____

3. The salesperson suggested that I should take the truck for a short drive. _____

4. Frank said that if we want to make the game on time, we should leave by noon. _____

5. "Pull over to the side on the road," said the police officer. _____

6. After glancing at her test score, Jillian said, "Spring break can't come soon enough." _____

7. "And with this new model phone," said the salesperson, "you will save money on out-of-area calls." _____

8. Raul mentioned that running in a marathon is his next goal. _____

Punctuation of Dialogue

As you edit your narrative, check the dialogue for punctuation errors. Familiarize yourself with these three rules:

- **When a period or comma follows the quotation**, place the period or comma *before* the quotation mark.

  > "You should check your voice messages," advised Mr. Lee.

  > "As you will soon discover," Reggie said, "the wrap station in the cafeteria is the best choice for lunch."

- **When a question mark or an exclamation point follows the quotation**, place it before the quotation mark if it belongs with the quotation. Otherwise, place it after.

  > Sheryl asked, "Where can I get some good soul food?"

  > Did you hear Veronica say, "I quit"?

- **When a semicolon or colon follows the quotation**, place it *after* the quotation mark.

  > Trey simply said, "I have other plans"; he didn't mention his fear of heights.

Practice 8.3 Fill in the blank with a *C* if the dialogue in the sentence is correctly punctuated or an *I* if the sentence is incorrectly punctuated.

1. "Let's focus on solutions, not problems", offered Haley. _____

2. Jack promised he would "try my best to make it;" however, I know he's not coming. _____

3. "It's not the size of the dog in the fight," suggested Mark Twain ", it's the size of the fight in the dog." _____

4. "It's about time you showed up!" exclaimed Karen. _____

5. "Should I apply for the job"? asked my roommate. _____

6. What is meant by the saying, "There is more to the book than its cover?" _____

7. "We are doing everything in our power to regain your trust," said the company spokesperson. _____

8. "I've never received a parking or speeding ticket," bragged Franklin. _____

Editing a Narrative

Becoming an effective editor takes practice. You must train yourself to look for different types of errors. One helpful strategy is to check your writing one sentence at a time from the bottom up. Doing so will help you focus more effectively on each sentence. You can also use an editing checklist to help you find and fix any grammar or punctuation errors (see Figure 8.5). A checklist helps you focus on one type of error at a time.

Figure 8.5 Editing Checklist

Words

☐ Have I used specific verbs and modifiers?

☐ Have I used more action verbs than "be" verbs (*is, are, was, were*)?

Sentences

☐ Have I used sentences with varying beginnings and lengths?

☐ Have I avoided sentence errors, such as fragments and run-ons?

Conventions

☐ Do I use correct verb forms (*he saw*, not *he seen*)?

☐ Do my subjects and verbs agree (*she speaks*, not *she speak*)?

☐ Have I used the right words (*their, there, they're*)?

☐ Have I capitalized first words and proper nouns and adjectives?

☐ Have I used commas after long introductory word groups and to separate items in a series?

☐ Have I correctly punctuated any dialogue?

☐ Have I carefully checked my spelling?

Practice 8.4   The following essay contains a number of errors in capitalization, punctuation, and usage (*their, there*). Use proofreading marks to correct the essay. *Hint:* the essay includes five capitalization errors, three missing periods, and three misused words.

Whale Watchers

On a sunny afternoon off the coast of san diego, my friend Natalie and I set

off on our great whale-watching adventure. In the winter months, 20,000 gray

whales migrate through the Pacific waters and along the coast of california, and we wanted to see the majestic creatures in there natural habitat.

As we stepped aboard the 100-foot tour boat nicknamed *Night and day*, Natalie reminded me to take some medication to prevent seasickness Good thing she did, because the captain announced we would hit six-foot swells on our journey. Their were about 40 other passengers on board with us.

About 15 minutes off the shoreline, a passenger shouted, "There she blows!" Indeed, about 20 yards ahead of us, I saw a spray of white water rocket vertically from the ocean surface We had spotted our first whale! As the boat crept closer, we could see the bumpy, gray backs of two more whales rising above the waves. I was so excited that I high-fived Natalie so hard it made my hand sting

We ended up seeing five different gray whales, two packs of dolphins, and to many pelicans to count. Seeing this beautiful sea life in the wild was an experience I'll never forget. learning that the whales are endangered goes to show that we must boost our efforts to protect them from extinction.

Proofreading Marks

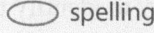 spelling   ⊙ add period   <u>d</u> capitalize   ^{word}∧ add word

When you edit your revised narrative, use the checklist in Figure 8.5 as a guide. Keep going until you can check off each question. Also, have a classmate check your writing for errors to make sure that you haven't missed anything.

Adding a Title

Finish the narrative by adding an attention-getting title. Here are three simple strategies:

- **Use a phrase from the piece:**

    Remembering Gramps

- **Use alliteration**, the repetition of a consonant sound:

    Whale Watchers

- **Use a play on words:**

    Tripped-Up Road Trip

☑ Reading for Enrichment

You will be reading short narratives by three New Yorkers reflecting on their experiences after the 9/11 terrorist attacks on the World Trade Center. Follow the reading process and refer to what you have learned about narratives in this chapter to help you gain a full understanding of the text. After reflecting on your reading, you will have an opportunity to write your own narrative.

About the Authors

Noel Maitland is a captain in the New York City Fire Department. Members of his company during 9/11 perished in the line of duty. **Diana Kane** is a television producer associated with various TV series and specials. **Pete Hamill** is an American journalist, novelist, editor, and educator. He is best known for his journalistic work in New York City.

Prereading

Some life experiences are so vivid and affecting that we will never forget where we were when they happened. For many Americans of a certain age (including the writers of "ZipUSA 10013"), 9/11 is one of these big moments. Other life-altering moments are more personal—perhaps the loss of a loved one; moving to a new city, state, or country; or getting married. What personal experiences, if any, would you consider life-changing? Think about their effect on you and others.

To prepare for your reading of "ZipUSA 10013," use the STRAP strategy to identify the main parts of the text. Also, consider listing a few of your own thoughts or questions about 9/11 before you start.

Subject:	What specific topic does the reading address?
Type:	What form (*essay, narrative, textbook selection*) does the reading take?
Role:	What position (*citizen, visitor, researcher*) does the writer assume?
Audience:	Who is the intended audience?
Purpose:	What is the general goal of the reading (*to persuade, to recall, to entertain*)?

Reading and Rereading

The three narratives in "ZipUSA 10013" are called Cantos I, II, and III. By definition, a "canto" is a self-contained part of a larger text, and the term has traditionally been used to mark the different parts in longer poem. Keep in mind that each canto tells a personal story related to 9/11.

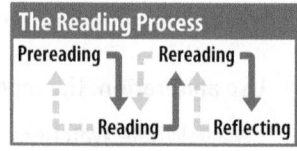

As you read, decide whether or not each writer tells a good story. That is, do the details build interest and suspense into the story (see **Figure 8.2**)? Reread as needed to make sure you haven't missed anything.

ZipUSA: 10013

Canto I

After the towers collapse, I arrive on the scene. There are no streets, only *1*
caverns of destruction, filled with sections of I beams, aluminum facade, dust,
paper, and mud. Buildings surrounding what will come to be known as **ground
zero** are gutted, burning fiercely, have hundreds of broken windows, or have been
ripped wide open by flying **girders**. The command system is shattered; a chief is
yelling orders from atop a rig. Every man seems to be from a different unit, and
most lack basic equipment. We stretch hose lines to control fires in the acres of
rubble, and pass stretchers, breathing masks, and forcible-entry tools over the
girders to try to rescue trapped firemen.

Later I find my company, Ladder 15, at a staging area, where they've set up *2*
chairs outside the shattered windows of an office building's backside, like some
war zone Parisian café.

After a few hours of awaiting orders, we split up to look for work. I find a *3*
large **contingent** of firefighters and police on the south side of Tower 2's remains,
snaking a hose line into the rubble's smoky darkness. I search for victims under
the wreckage. No sign of anyone.

From time to time the smoke lifts a little, showing six stories of uncollapsed *4*
steel girders and concrete flooring looming overhead. I keep searching, making
mental notes of what girder I'll duck under if the rest of the building gives way.

Men shout for relief at the end of the hose line. I follow the line into intense *5*
heat and choking smoke. About a half hour later I reach the end and offer to take
the nozzle, but the nozzleman refuses. "I'm not going anywhere until Duncan
comes back!" he yells. By tradition, a company keeps the nozzle until the fire is
out and firefighters from the house are safe. I help feed in hose, then start back to
get some tools. Suddenly I feel sick and dehydrated. Hundreds of hands steady me
as I clamber over rubble and down ladders that the brothers have laid across the
steepest sections.

In the **triage** center in the firehouse across the street, the nurses seem like angels with IVs. Before I fall asleep, I think back to the afternoon, when firefighters and construction workers fired up earthmoving equipment and started clearing the street. Only hours after the collapse of the towers, the recovery had begun.

—Noel Maitland

Canto II

You know my neighborhood. Last September, the sidewalk in front of my home became the backdrop for news reporters showing the world the devastation. My neighborhood, TriBeCa, just north of ground zero, also became a triage center when merchants threw open their doors to the injured and scared. It became a staging area for rescue workers searching for survivors in the smoldering rubble at the end of my street. And my corner was one where thousands streamed to pay final respects to those lost in a national tragedy that played itself out in an American neighborhood.

We had elementary schools and a canine day care center. We were also home to Miramax Films and some of the world's trendiest restaurants. We were an **eclectic** mix of artists, Wall Street brokers, and middle-class families. We are different now. Weary from the effort to recover and plagued by uncertainty, we are a neighborhood adrift.

Paul, a neighbor, was the son of "homesteaders," middle-class families attracted here by city **subsidies** after the towers were built in the mid-seventies. Like so many Americans, he decided to raise his own family where he grew up. A month after the attacks, he packed up and left. For how long? I asked. "Forever," he replied.

A friend from uptown offered to walk me home one night. As we walked down my street, he grabbed my arm in alarm. "I know that smell," he said, of the ever present smoke in the night air, reminder of the fires still burning deep inside that diminishing pile. "I grew up next to a cemetery," he said. It was the smell of the crematorium.

I watched one morning as a father walked his son to school down my street. Once proud skyscrapers stood vacant, their facades burned and stripped, their offices charred honeycombs. The son took his father's hand and asked, "Where is the future?" His father replied, "The future is everywhere around you, at all times." 11

—Diana Kane

Canto III

Weeks later, when the sirens had vanished from the night and we were no longer asked for passports, gas bills, and driver's licenses to prove that we lived in what we came to call the frozen zone, everything looked the same and everything felt different. 12

My wife, Fukiko, and I were lucky. We had been across the street when Tower 2 came down with the roaring sound of a steel-and-glass avalanche. We were engulfed by that cloud of dust that rose 25 stories above the street, a cloud so opaque that it looked like a solid. The cloud was made of pulverized floors, exploded glass, smashed desks, computers, food, file cabinets, and human beings. She and I were separated in the dust, found our way home separately, and celebrated the simple fact of being alive. 13

We were lucky in another way: In our loft 14 blocks north of ground zero, we had electricity. Television, telephones, the Internet all worked. So did we. For nine straight days, we wrote newspaper stories about the calamity. On the tenth day I wrote nothing and for the first time sat on a couch, thinking about the ruined world, and wept. 14

But life also provided its own consolations. In the streets we met some of our neighbors for the first time. We stood on street corners together, manual laborers and dot-com workers, mothers and children, all staring downtown at 15 the smoldering stumps of the towers. We asked about children, and dogs, and survivors. The emotions of awe, horror, rage were gone quickly, replaced by a shared sense of **vulnerability**.

That is what remains: vulnerability. And from vulnerability there has *16* emerged a tough **fatalism**. We all learned, that terrible morning, that we could die while reaching for a piece of toast at breakfast. Where I live, that knowledge has made us more human. Even on streets noisy again with traffic, strangers say good morning. Men kiss their wives more, and hug their children, and walk with them to the Hudson to embrace the sunset. But not one talks with utter confidence about tomorrow.

—Pete Hamill

Used by permission of *NATIONAL GEOGRAPHIC CREATIVE*.

ground zero
the site of the 9/11 terrorist attack

crematorium
a place where deceased bodies are burned into ash

girders
large support beams

pulverized
destroyed to dust

contingent
group or representation

vulnerability
capable of being wounded or hurt

triage
the process of identifying the level of urgency of the wounded

fatalism
acceptance of things and events as they are

subsidies
financial aid measures

Reflecting

Answer the comprehension and vocabulary questions about the reading.

1. How are the details in Canto I organized?
   a. By order of importance
   b. By time (chronologically)
   c. By comparing and contrasting

2. What is the focus of the Canto II narrative?
   a. Recalling the writer's neighborhood before and after the attack
   b. Recalling the writer's rescue after the attack
   c. Recalling the superhuman efforts of individuals before and after the attack

3. What do the three mini-stories at the end of Canto II show?
   a. That things are back to normal in the writer's neighborhood
   b. That the residents have decided to leave the area forever
   c. That people are scarred by the attack and uncertain of the future

4. In Canto III, which of these ideas is not mentioned?
   a. The writer and his neighbors felt it was time to move.
   b. The writer and his neighbors felt more vulnerable.
   c. The writer and his neighbors felt a heightened sense of appreciation for life.

5. Which types of details does the writer use in Canto III? (*Hint:* See Section 8.3 for help.)
   a. Dialogue and sensory details
   b. Sensory details and personal reflection
   c. Personal reflection and dialogue

6. Study how the word *eclectic* is used in the reading, and then choose the most accurate definition of the word.
   eclectic (paragraph 8)
   a. Wide-ranging
   b. Similar
   c. Opposite

7. Study how the word *opaque* is used in the reading, and then choose the most accurate definition of the word.
   opaque (paragraph 13)
   a. Transparent
   b. Unable to be seen through
   c. Blurry

Time Line

Create a time line for Canto I, identifying Noel Maitland's key actions following the attack. (See Figure 8.1 for an example.)

Critical Thinking

- What do the Cantos have in common and how are they different?
- Which Canto affected you the most and why?
- "Experience is a hard teacher because she gives the test first, the lessons afterward." How does this quote apply to these narratives?
- How do the Cantos illustrate that writing can be good therapy?
- What questions do you have about 9/11 after reading these stories?

Writing for Enrichment

Review the possible writing activities to complete in response to the reading.

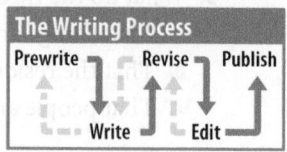

The Writing Process
Prewrite   Revise   Publish
Write   Edit

Prewriting

Choose one of the following writing ideas, or create your own idea related to the reading.

1. Explore in a personal blog post or journal a life-changing event from your life.

2. Think of a personal experience or event that impacted the way you view the world. Share this experience in a personal essay.

3. Write a personal narrative that is set in a place that made your senses come alive. Make the experience come to life for readers through sensory details.

4. Share a story recalling when you gained a great appreciation for a parent, sibling, or other close relative.

5. Write about an experience that made you more aware of a custom or culture different from your own.

When planning . . .

- Make sure that your topic is specific enough for a personal narrative.
- Use a time line to identify the key actions related to your topic.
- Consider what dialogue, sensory details, and personal reflections you might want to include in your writing.

When writing . . .

- If you have trouble getting started, write about the experience as if you are telling a friend or family member about it.
- Include a beginning, middle, and ending. (See Section 8.4 for help.)

When revising and editing . . .

- Be sure that your opening grabs the reader's attention, the middle shares the key details in an interesting way, and the ending wraps up the experience.
- Decide if the dialogue seems realistic.
- Edit your revised writing for style and correctness.

Reflecting on Narrative Writing

Consider these questions about your narrative reading and writing experiences.

1. Why do writers find it important to write about their personal experiences?

2. Which is the most helpful reading strategy in the chapter? Explain.

3. What do you like about your narrative? What part did you struggle with and why?

4. What is the most important thing you have learned about narrative writing?

Repina Valeriya, 2017 / Used under license from Shutterstock.com

Chapter

9

Reading and Writing Expository Texts

Expository writing explains or informs, and it helps readers learn about new topics and become informed about important issues. It is the type of writing found most often in newspapers, informational websites, textbooks, and other nonfiction resources. The best informational writing goes beyond just explaining. It informs and engages, making a reader say, "Wow, I didn't know that!"

Expository writing is built on a foundation of accurate and up-to-date information gathered from trustworthy sources. Writers build their text so that the information is clear and easy to follow. This usually means that the main idea or thesis comes first, followed by the details that explain it.

Expository texts should answer the key questions a reader may have about the topic and refrain from expressing personal opinions. This chapter will help you become a more informed reader and writer of expository texts.

Chapter Outline

- Understanding Expository Texts
- Reading and Responding to Expository Texts
- Planning an Expository Essay
- Writing the First Draft
- Revising the Writing
- Editing the Writing

9.1 Understanding Expository Texts

Since most of your academic reading and writing will be expository, it is important that you understand the different types of exposition. What follows are the common types, including illustration, definition, process, classification, cause-effect, and comparison-contrast. Some of these, such as process and classification, are also patterns for organizing details.

As you read these examples, you will get a better idea about how exposition is commonly developed. You can refer to them for guidance when you are assigned to write your own informational texts. Indeed, some longer forms of expository writing will use more than one of the patterns.

Illustration

An **illustration** explains or clarifies a main idea with specific reasons, facts, and details. As the name suggests, an illustration "paints a picture" for the reader, helping the person see the topic clearly.

> For over 2,000 years, audiences have enjoyed shadow-puppet shows in China. The stage is simple: a white cloth screen with a light shining behind it. The puppets, too, are simple: profile cutouts of princes, sages, soldiers, and queens with joints held together by thread, allowing movement. Five performers use these simple materials to bring a story to life. A puppeteer operates all of the puppets while a singer sings their story and adds voices to each character. The other three performers play instruments: a fiddle, a flute, and a drum. Traditionally, this entertainment began when Emperor Wu of the Han dynasty lost a favorite concubine. A minister arranged the first shadow puppetry using children's dolls behind a screen to remind the emperor of his lost love. From that time, the art of shadow puppetry has remained strong, though it now is in danger of dying out, like other traditional art forms.

Definition

A **definition** explores the meaning of an important word or concept. The writing may include synonyms, antonyms, etymology (history), examples, and comparisons.

> Culturally defined body weight and shape preferences change with time and in ways that have little to do with health. In the fifteenth century, culturally defined body shape standards in Europe favored thin, muscular men and plump women. In America in the early 1900s, moon-faced and pear-shaped women

and muscular men were the rage. It was not until that latter part of the twentieth century that ideal body shape took a turn in Europe and American toward thinness, and at times, to unhealthy levels of extreme thinness. In contrast, the culturally defined ideal weight status in some poor nations is overweight or obese.

From Judith E. Brown, *Nutrition Now*, 8E. © 2017 Cengage Learning.

Process

Some **process** texts focus on how something works, such as the process of amending the constitution or of transforming from a caterpillar to butterfly. Other process texts focus on what typically happens or how to do something. Process transition words (*first, second, then*) are often used in these texts.

> What happens when minority citizens are arrested for a crime? Bail is set higher for African Americans and Latinos than for Whites, and minorities have less success with plea bargains. Once on trial, minority defendants are found guilty more often than Whites defendants. At sentencing, African Americans and Hispanics are likely to get longer sentences than Whites, even when they have the same number of prior arrests and socioeconomic backgrounds as Whites. Once sentenced, they are less likely to be released on probation (Western 2007, 2014).

From Anderson, Taylor, and Logio, *Sociology: The Essentials*, 9E. © 2017 Cengage Learning.

Classification

A **classification** breaks a subject into categories, explaining each category and relating them to the larger whole. This type of text focuses on groups, types, varieties, and kinds, sorting them and organizing them in a structure sometimes called a **taxonomy**.

> The modern orchestra uses three basic types of instruments: strings, winds, and percussion. String instruments produce sound through bowing, plucking, or strumming tightened strings, which vibrate in response. Violins, violas, cellos, and basses are the most common string instruments in orchestras, though guitars also may be used. Wind instruments produce sound by vibrating a volume of air in a cylinder. Some winds, like flutes and piccolos, create sound by blowing across an opening; others, like clarinets and saxophones, do so by blowing over or through a reed; and still more do so by vibrating lips on a mouthpiece. Percussion instruments make sound by striking an object. This category includes drums, cymbals, triangles, and even the piano.

Cause-Effect

A **cause-effect** text identifies the reasons that a certain event, condition, or set of circumstances occurred and explores what resulted from it. The text links causes to effects, exploring chains of events.

> Lead is a naturally occurring element in the earth's crust, but it is also a deadly neurotoxin. The amount of exposure people have to natural sources of lead tends to be low, but human-made products and activities can make lead much more prevalent. Prior to 1978 in the United States, paint, toys, and gasoline often contained lead. To this day, some houses contain lead pipes or copper pipes soldered with lead. When lead is ingested—whether from water that runs through old pipes, chips of old paint, or flecks of soil contaminated by years of lead-laden exhaust—lead poisoning can occur. In children, lead poisoning often causes vomiting, diarrhea, loss of appetite, and weight loss and may result in developmental delays. In adults, lead poisoning can result in high blood pressure, memory loss, and mood disorders.

Comparison-Contrast

A **comparison-contrast** text explains how two or more subjects are alike and different. Some comparisons focus on similarities and others on differences. Some focus first on one subject and then the other, while others consider each subject point by point.

> When selecting an alternative to traditional gas guzzlers, consumers can choose between hybrid and electric vehicles. Hybrid cars have both electric and gasoline motors. They use electricity at slow speeds, with light payloads, and when traveling downhill, but hybrids shift to gasoline at high speeds, when hauling loads, or when climbing hills. The gasoline engine also helps to recharge the electric battery. Electric cars use electricity exclusively, getting their energy from wall sockets or swapping out their used batteries for fully-charged ones at charging stations. Hybrids have excellent fuel economy, averaging about 45 miles to the gallon. They also produce fewer emissions than regular gas-powered vehicles. Electric cars use no gasoline at all and produce no emissions. However, their batteries take four to eight hours to fully recharge, drawing on electricity that is often generated by burning fossil fuels such as coal. Hybrid vehicles can travel more than 500 miles without stopping to refuel, while electric vehicles have a range of 100 to 200 miles.

9.2 Reading and Responding to Expository Texts

When you read an expository text, your main goal is to identify the main idea (thesis) and the details that explain it. The main idea is usually stated in the beginning paragraph and the supporting details follow in the middle part of the text. The strategies that follow will help you keep track of the details during your reading.

Using a T Chart

A T chart is a note-taking strategy that helps you keep track of important sets of details that compare and/or contrast. Write the topic of the reading at the top. Then form the T chart and identify the subtopics for the two columns. List the important details under each label that show similarities and/or differences. Figure 9.1 shows a T chart that identifies some of the main differences between marriage customs in two cultures as explained in the essay "Is Marriage a Crime?"

Figure 9.1 T Chart

Topic: Two definitions of marriage

U.S. marriage customs	Iraq marriage customs
• voluntary act	• marriage arranged
• depends on mutual attraction and interests	• for the benefit of both families
• main objective: personal fulfillment and happiness	• main objective: protect bride and families

Recognizing Transition Words

Writers often use transition words or phrases to illustrate an idea, define a term, outline a process, distinguish categories, show cause and effect, or compare and contrast. As you read expository texts, watch for transition words like those in Table 9.1.

Table 9.1 Transition Words for Expository Texts

Illustrate	Define	Process	Classify	Cause	Compare
for example	means	first	type/kind	because	like
for instance	comes from	next	category	result	different
demonstrate	root word	then	group	reason	contrast
moreover	synonymous	after	variety	outcome	same

Reading and Reacting to a Professional Expository Essay

The following reading focuses on the different approaches to marriage in the United States and Iraq. The essay reveals that these differences raise serious questions about one of the country's marriage customs when put into practice in the other country. Use the reading process to gain a full understanding of this essay.

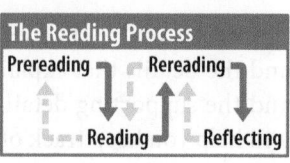

About the Authors

Gary Ferraro is an applied anthropologist who conducted research for extended periods of time in Kenya and Swaziland. He has served as a consultant/cross-cultural trainer for large organizations (USAID, the Peace Corps, the World Bank) and large international corporations such as IBM and G.E. Plastics. He currently works with businesses to help them cope with cultural differences at home and abroad.

Susan Andreatta is a past president of the Society for Applied Anthropology. She's educated in political economy and political ecology as applied to the environment and health. As an applied anthropologist, Andreatta conducts field research in the areas of tourism, migration, resettlement, health and nutrition, sustainable farming and fishing, and the marketing of fresh local produce and seafood.

Prereading

Before you begin reading, answer the STRAP questions to identify the main features of the reading selection.

Subject: What is the specific topic of the reading?

Type: What form (*newspaper article, narrative, textbook essay*) does the reading take?

Role: What position (*anthropologist, government official, human rights expert*) do the writers assume?

Audience: Who is the intended audience (*students, general readers, immigration officials*)?

Purpose: What is the goal of the reading (*to inform, to persuade, to entertain*)?

Reading and Rereading

As you read the text, make it your goal to identify the main idea and all the supporting details. Consider taking notes as you go along, perhaps in the form of a T chart. (See Figure 9.1). Reread the text as needed to gain a full understanding of its content.

Is Marriage a Crime?

Most Americans take considerable pride in the fact that theirs is a nation of immigrants. Since our earliest days as a nation, immigrants have come to our shores in search of a better life. They settled in urban neighborhoods, learned to speak English, worked hard, and eventually (after several generations) moved to the suburbs, where they joined the country club and became active in their homeowners associations. However, when immigrants first arrive, they may be surprised to discover that practicing their traditional cultural customs can put them on the wrong side of the laws of their new country.

In 1996 a recent Iraqi refugee was the proud father of two brides in a traditional double wedding ceremony for his two eldest daughters at their home in Lincoln, Nebraska (Terry 1996). An Islamic **cleric** was flown in from Ohio to perform the ceremony in front of more than a hundred friends and relatives. For all attending it was a festive social event celebrating the sacredness of matrimony. But for local authorities, it was the scene of a crime.

The problem stemmed from the fact that the two Iraqi brides, who were thirteen and fourteen years old, were marrying men who were twenty-eight and thirty-four. According to marital law in Nebraska, seventeen is the minimum legal age for marriage. Authorities charged the father with two counts of child abuse, while the mother was charged with contributing to the **delinquency** of a minor. Moreover it is illegal for anyone older than eighteen to have sexual relations with anyone younger than eighteen. Because the two grooms **consummated** their marriages on the night of the wedding, both men were charged with statutory rape, which carries a maximum sentence of fifty years in prison. Both the parents and their two sons-in-law were shocked when police came to arrest them.

The issue in this tragic case revolves around two very different definitions of marriage. According to both law and custom in the United States, marriage represents a voluntary union between two consenting individuals. The **criteria** for selecting a spouse in the United States include personal **compatibility**, physical attractiveness, and romantic love. And the major objectives of marriage in the United States are the happiness and personal fulfillment of the two principal players, the wife and the husband.

By way of contrast, marriage in traditional Iraqi society is based on an entirely   5 different set of cultural **assumptions**. Marriages are arranged by the parents, with little or no input from the prospective brides. Traditional Iraqi marriage is viewed more as a union between two large families than as a way of providing happiness and individual fulfillment for the husband and wife. In addition, traditional Iraqi parents fear that their daughters will engage in premarital sexual relations and thereby dishonor the entire family. To their way of thinking, the best way to protect their daughters and their families from such disgrace is to marry them off at an early age.

Clearly this case presented a real dilemma for Nebraska law enforcement   6 officials. The Iraqis, who were ignorant of marital law in Nebraska, had no intention of violating the law. Nevertheless their traditional marriage practices did violate some strongly held American values and some strongly **sanctioned** laws. Many Americans want to be sensitive to the cultural **pluralism** that has made our country unique. At the same time Americans need to be true to their core values of protecting the rights of women and children. Should culture be taken into consideration when dealing with civil and criminal cases, and if so, to what extent? How would you resolve this case if you were serving on the jury?

From Ferraro/Andreatta, *Cultural Anthropology: An Applied Perspective*, 2014 Edition. © 2014 Cengage Learning.

cleric
religious leader

delinquency
illegal behavior

consummated
completed the union of marriage by the first marital sexual intercourse

criteria
standards

sanctioned
approved or binding

pluralism
society in which different ethnic groups preserve their own customs

Reflecting

Practice 9.1 Answer the comprehension and vocabulary questions about the reading.

1. What is the main idea of the essay?
   a. That the U.S. is proud to be a country of immigrants
   b. That immigrants practicing their traditional customs in the U.S. could be breaking the law
   c. That marriage reflects a sacred trust between two people

2. What evidence supports the main idea?
   a. The authors cite several noteworthy examples.
   b. The authors refer to important scholarly research.
   c. The authors cite one example in detail.

3. How do the authors end the essay?
   a. By asking the reader important questions about the topic
   b. By coming to a specific conclusion about the topic
   c. By placing blame on an existing condition

4. Study how the word *compatibility* is used in the reading, and then choose the most accurate definition of the word.
   Compatibility (paragraph 4)
   a. Ability to improve as a person
   b. Ability to feel comfortable together
   c. Ability to survive combat situations

5. Study how the word *assumptions* is used in the reading, and then choose the most accurate definition of the word.
   Assumptions (paragraph 5)
   a. Beliefs or truths
   b. Answers
   c. Questions

Personal Response

Write freely for 5-10 minutes, exploring your thoughts and feelings about the essay.

Critical Thinking

- What conclusions can you draw from the facts in the text?
- What emotional response do you have to this essay—surprise, shock, anger? Explain.
- What makes the marriage example in the essay so unique for the United States?
- What questions do you still have about the topic?

9.3 Planning Expository Writing

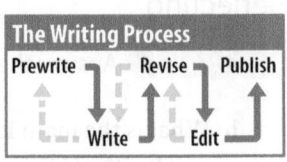

The Writing Process

Now that you've read and reflected on an expository text, you're ready to plan an essay of your own. Prewriting begins by thinking about specific topics to write about. There are many worthy topics related to general subject areas such as technology, fashion, entertainment, the environment, sports, health and fitness, science, or medicine.

Brainstorm ideas to help identify a general subject area to write about. Check online and in printed materials (magazines, newspapers, textbooks) and talk to your peers about possible writing ideas within the subject area. Then identify a possible topic that you could write about in your essay. For example, you might be interested in health and fitness, and within that subject, you specifically could explore how adrenaline functions in the body.

General Subject

health and fitness

Specific Topic

producing adrenaline highs

Selecting Sources and Gathering Details

With a specific topic in mind, the next step is to gather information about it. Occasionally, you may know enough about a topic to draw solely on your prior knowledge. Usually, though, you will need to conduct research. Consider both primary and secondary sources. Primary sources of information deal with direct experiences related to a topic. Secondary sources deal with reports about the topic in books, websites, and other media sources. (See Section 11.1 for more information.)

Primary Sources

- events or experiences
- interviews
- museum exhibits
- surveys/questionnaires
- letters/diaries/journals
- presentations or speeches

Secondary Sources

- textbooks
- magazine/journal articles
- news reports
- websites
- books
- documentaries

Create a list of important facts and details that you learned during your research. Unless you already know a lot about your topic, consult at least two or three different sources of information. Be sure to identify the sources in your notes; you may need to refer back to them as you write. (See Section 11.3 for help.)

Identifying a Main Idea and Thesis Statement

The next step is to choose the essay's main idea—the important, overall idea that you want to emphasize. A main idea may focus on a topic's value, its strength or weaknesses, its causes and effects, etc. The main idea is identified in an essay's thesis statement.

Specific Topic	**Main Idea**	**Thesis Statement**
adrenaline high	**+** its causes and effects	**=** The high a person gets from an adrenaline rush has many interesting causes and effects.

Create a main idea for your essay. To identify this idea, look for one feature or part of the topic that stands out in your mind. Then write your thesis statement using the formula above as a guide. (You will probably write two or three versions of this statement before it sounds right to you.)

An effective thesis helps a writer decide what information to include in the essay, and in what order. For example, the sample thesis statement about an adrenaline high indicates that the writer will first explain what an adrenaline high is, and then identify its causes and effects. (See Section 5.4 for general organizational patterns you can choose from.) You may also decide that you need to collect more information to develop your thesis.

Plan how you will develop your thesis statement. That is, how do you plan to arrange or present the details you have gathered to support your thesis? Will you show causes and effects, give examples, or organize your details in some other way? (See Section 5.4 for help.)

9.4 Writing the First Draft

After prewriting and planning, the next step is to write a first draft. But before you begin writing, read the following student essay. Notice how the beginning draws the reader into the text. Also, notice how the details in the middle part follow the arrangement established in the thesis statement. Lastly, consider how the closing provides readers with some interesting final thoughts.

Adrenaline Junkies

Opening Paragraph

What do you picture when you hear the phrase "adrenaline junkie"? A daredevil soaring through the air on a motorcycle? A mountain climber rapidly rappelling down the side of a mountain? A gambler stuffing quarters in a slot machine? Actually, all three qualify as adrenaline junkies if they do the activities to get their highs. The high a person gets from an adrenaline rush has many interesting causes and effects.

Middle Paragraph 1

Adrenaline is a hormone linked to the two glands located above the kidneys. Each gland has two parts: the outer portion called the cortex, and the inner portion called the medulla. When a person experiences unusual exertion or a crisis, the person's brain triggers the medulla, which releases little packets of adrenaline into the bloodstream (Nathan). The rush of adrenaline in the blood leads to increased blood pressure, heart rate, and muscle strength. All of these conditions cause an adrenaline high (Scheuller 2). *2*

Middle Paragraph 2

The level of stimulus that a person needs depends on the amount of protein in the person's medulla. A person with a higher level of protein in the medulla experiences an adrenaline release more easily than someone with a lower level of the protein (Scheuller 4). For example, a person with higher levels may get an adrenaline high by simply completing a research paper on time. A person with low levels may not get an adrenaline rush unless a more dramatic act such as skydiving is carried out. *3*

Middle Paragraph 3

An adrenaline high can be channeled for healthy effects. A person who gets a rush from meeting the due date for a research paper may work well as a research technician in a science lab. As long as the person avoids becoming all-consumed by the work, seeking the high won't be health threatening. Someone who gets high from skydiving may do well as a firefighter or even a brain surgeon, as long as the person gets periodic relief from tension. *4*

Middle Paragraph 4

On the other hand, getting the wrong type of adrenaline high, or seeking too many highs, can be harmful. Compulsive gambling, frequent drug use, and careless risk taking in business are examples of destructive highs. These negative pursuits may lead to bankruptcy, broken relationships, injury, addiction, and death (Lyons 3). *5*

Closing Paragraph

But in the end, maybe we shouldn't be overly worried about becoming adrenaline junkies. Instead, we should focus on the benefits that adrenaline highs can have for individuals and for the common good. Just as we know our blood pressure and our pulse rate, maybe we should know our adrenaline protein level so we can trigger and manage our adrenaline highs as needed. Then we can do our best work at just the right time. *6*

NOTE: The information in parentheses like *(Lyons 3)* indicates that the writer is citing a particular idea from a specific source from her research. (See **Section 11.3**.)

Developing an Opening Paragraph

The opening paragraph of an expository essay should identify the topic, gain the reader's interest, and state the thesis. Here are three strategies for gaining your reader's interest:

- **Ask engaging questions.**

   What do you picture when you hear the phrase "adrenaline junkie"? A daredevil soaring through the air on a motorcycle? A mountain climber rapidly rappelling down the side of a mountain?

- **Make an important or dramatic statement.**

   One special hormone lessens our pain and allows us to fight danger or flee, even when injured. This hormone is called adrenaline.

- **Share an interesting story (anecdote).**

   Marcie Handel vividly remembers the few moments leading up to her second driver's license test. Her heart began to race, her hands began to sweat, and she was just about ready to find an escape before her name was called. We have all had a similar response to a stressful situation, and it can be tied directly to the adrenaline hormone.

Creating the Middle Paragraphs

The middle paragraphs develop the explanation with facts and details that support the thesis. Follow these tips for developing this part:

- Follow the organizational pattern you identified during prewriting.
- Generally, develop one main point per paragraph.
- Provide enough information to make each point clear to the reader.
- Use transitions to help you move smoothly from one point to the next. (See Sections 6.1 and 6.2 for help.)

Creating the Closing Paragraph

The closing paragraph should restate the thesis, summarize the main supporting points, and/or provide a final thought or two. Here are two strategies to consider:

- **Provide a thought-provoking idea.**

   Just as we know our blood pressure and our pulse rate, maybe we should know our adrenaline protein level so we can trigger and manage our adrenaline highs as needed.

- **Provide a strong final quotation.**

   "As a child, I loved being on stage. I loved singing. I loved the lights. I loved the adrenaline," concludes actress Emma Watson. "I was completely obsessive."

When you write the first draft of your narrative, be sure to follow the advice given in **Section 9.4**. And refer to the other essays in the chapter for additional ideas. Keep going until you get all of your thoughts and ideas on paper.

9.5   Revising the Writing

Revising your first draft involves adding, deleting, rearranging, and reworking parts of your writing. Revision can begin with a peer review. Sharing your writing at various stages is important, especially when you review and revise a first draft. The feedback that you receive will help you improve and strengthen your essay.

Here is an example of feedback the writer received for "Adrenaline Junkies." Ask at least one classmate or trusted friend to read and react to your first draft. Have the peer reviewer use questions like these to help them respond to your writing.

Peer Review Sheet

Essay title: Adrenaline Junkies

Writer: Angel Castro

Reviewer: Larisa Klein

1. Which part of the essay seems to work best—opening, middle, or closing? Why?

   Opening, because the questions got me interested in the topic

2. Which part of the essay needs work—opening, middle, or closing? Why?

   Middle, because I would like to know more healthy ways to channel adrenaline

3. Do the middle paragraphs clearly explain the thesis? How so?

   Yes, the middle paragraphs explain what adrenaline is and then explore

   its causes and effects

4. Do you understand the topic after reading the essay?

   Yes, especially where and how adrenaline is produced in the body

5. Identify a line or two that show the writer's level of interest.

   The last sentences of the third paragraph: These lines give helpful examples

---

Adding Clarifying Details

In some cases, it may not be enough to simply state an idea and expect the reader to understand what you mean. You may need to add details before an idea becomes clear.

Key point: Courage means different things to different people.

Major detail: For my brother it means using the "river swing" on the Black River. *(Not clear enough)*

Minor detail: The platform to swing from is about 30 feet up in a huge oak tree, and the rope to grab onto is attached to an even higher tree. *(Clearer)*

Minor detail: Once you climb up to the platform, you must grab above a knot on the rope. Then, at the call of " Go," you swing way out and let go right at the top of your swing. *(Much clearer)*

Read aloud the unrevised and then the revised version of the following passage. Note how the added minor details make the information clearer.

> "Human trafficking" is a difficult term to define. To begin with, human trafficking, migration, and smuggling are distinct but related situations, and incorrect understanding of them could wrongly label people. ∧
>
> For example, Public Law 106-386 forbids the U.S. government from jailing victims of human trafficking. On the other hand, illegal immigration subjects may . . .

You can improve your writing using the revising checklist in **Figure 9.2** and your partner's comments on the Peer Review Sheet as a guide.

Figure 9.2 Revising Checklist

Ideas

☐ Do I focus on one specific, interesting topic to explain?

☐ Do I state the main idea of my essay in a thesis statement?

☐ Do I include different types of details to provide support?

☐ Do I explain each new main idea with enough details?

Organization

☐ Does my essay have effective opening, middle, and closing paragraphs?

☐ Have I arranged the supporting details in an effective pattern?

Voice

☐ Do I sound knowledgeable and interested?

9.6 Editing the Writing

The main work of editing is correcting your revised first draft. Errors can distract the reader and take away from the effectiveness of your writing.

Avoiding Fragments

A sentence has a subject and verb and expresses a complete thought. A group of words that lacks a subject or verb and does not express a complete thought is a sentence error called a **fragment**. To fix a fragment, supply the part that it is missing.

Fragments	Sentences
An adrenaline high. (lacks verb)	An adrenaline high **can be channeled for healthy effects.**
Qualify as adrenaline junkies. (lacks subject)	**All three** qualify as adrenaline junkies.
Linked to two glands. (lacks subject and verb)	**Adrenaline is a hormone** linked to two glands.
When someone experiences unusual exertion. (incomplete thought)	When someone experiences unusual exertion, **the person's brain triggers the medulla.**
Who feels a rush from skydiving. (incomplete thought)	**A person** who feels a rush from skydiving **may do well as a firefighter.**

Practice 9.2 Fill in the blank with *S* if the group of words is a complete sentence and *F* if the group of words is a sentence fragment.

1. Each gland has an outer cortex and an inner medulla. _____
2. The brain activates the medulla. _____
3. Which releases little packets of adrenaline. _____
4. High levels of protein in the medulla. _____
5. Adrenaline in the bloodstream can lead to added muscle strength. _____
6. Getting high by completing a big assignment. _____
7. Some people need a major adventure to trigger an adrenaline rush. _____
8. Who gets high from ice climbing and hang gliding. _____
9. Frequent drug use illustrates a harmful high. _____
10. To know more about adrenaline protein levels. _____

Avoiding Run-Ons and Comma Splices

When two sentences are short and express related ideas, you may want to combine them into a compound sentence. Place a comma after the first sentence, and use a coordinating conjunction (*and, but, or, nor, for, so, yet*) to connect it to the second sentence.

Two Sentences	Compound Sentence
Rob phoned Bill. Jean called Clare.	Rob phoned Bill, **and** Jean called Clare.
I swim. Lorna jogs.	I swim, **but** Lorna jogs.
I packed a lunch. We went out to eat.	I packed a lunch, **yet** we went out to eat.

However, two sentences joined *without* a comma or coordinating conjunction form a run-on sentence, which is an error. Two sentences joined with just a comma and no coordinating conjunction form a comma splice, another kind of error. To fix them, use both a comma and a coordinating conjunction to join two sentences.

Run-On Sentence	Corrected Sentence
Jana played sax I played piano.	Jana played sax, **and** I played piano.

Comma Splice	Corrected Sentence
A storm is coming, let's load the van.	A storm is coming, **so** let's load the van.

Practice 9.3 Fill in the blank with *C* if the group of words correctly expresses a compound sentence and *I* if the group of words incorrectly expresses a compound sentence and forms a run-on or comma splice.

1. Each culture has marriage customs, often they conflict with each other. _____

2. Western cultures value romantic love eastern cultures value family bonds. _____

3. Romance may be valued in a marriage, but it is not everything. _____

4. Trust is important in a marriage cooperation is essential, too. _____

5. In many cultures husbands are thought to hold the dominant role, yet in many marriages wives are really in control. _____

6. Both members can't be in charge of everything spouses have to split the duties and responsibilities. _____

7. Money problems create many stresses, so couples must agree about spending. _____

8. Abuse is never acceptable in relationships abuse can take many forms. _____

9. A marriage is a partnership, and the two people must work as a team. _____

10. Customs seek to control relationships, but in the end it's up to the people in the relationship. _____

Editing an Essay

Becoming a good editor takes practice. You must train yourself to look for different types of errors. One helpful strategy is to make a copy of your text separated into a list of individual sentences. Editing one sentence at a time is easier than editing a large block of copy. It also helps to use an editing checklist (see Figure 9.3) to ensure you find and fix any grammar or punctuation errors. A checklist also helps you focus on one type of error at a time.

Figure 9.3 Editing Checklist

Words

☐ Have I used specific verbs and modifiers?

☐ Have I used more action verbs than "be" verbs (*is, are, was, were*)?

☐ Have I used transitions or signal words to help my reader follow the ideas?

Sentences

☐ Have I used sentences with varying beginnings and lengths?

☐ Have I avoided fragments, run-ons, and comma splices?

Conventions

☐ Do I use correct verb forms (*he saw,* not *he seen*)?

☐ Do my subjects and verbs agree (*she speaks,* not *she speak*)?

☐ Have I used the right words (*their, there, they're*)?

☐ Have I capitalized first words and proper nouns and adjectives?

☐ Have I used commas after long introductory word groups and to separate items in a series?

☐ Have I used apostrophes correctly in contractions and to show possession?

☐ Have I checked for spelling?

Practice 9.4   The following essay contains a number of spelling, comma, and apostrophe errors. Use the given proofreading marks to correct the essay. *Hint:* The essay includes four misspelled words, three missing commas, and three missing apostrophes.

Trafficking in Slaves

At some point, most nations histories include periods of either being enslaved or enslaving others. Unfortunately, the condition continues today. In fact, different types of slavery exist today in developing countries as well as in prosperous countrys such as the United States. Current trends show that human trafficking or slavery is a very complex problem, with few realistic solutions.

"Human trafficking" is a difficult term to define. To begin with, human trafficking, migration, and smuggling are distinct but related situations, and an incorrect understanding of them could wrongly labal people. For example, Public Law 106-386 forbids the U.S. government from jailing victims of human trafficking yet illegal immigration subjects many people too criminal charges and possible deportation. Smuggling, the illegal transport of people into a country, is also considered a matter of immigration rather than human trafficking.

Human trafficking is different, for it abuses the victims and forces them to travel or work against there will. With this idea in mind, the United Nations has developed this definition of human trafficking: "The recruitment, transportation, transfer, harbouring or receipt of persons, by means of the threat or use of force or having control over another person for the purpose of exploitation." Under this definition, smuggling can become trafficking if a smugglers actions include any means of force or threats.

Due to globalization, theres probably no illegal activity more serious than human trafficking. Because of human trafficking in today's world millions of people experience multiple forms of slavery, from sexual slavery to debt slavery.

Proofreading Marks

 spelling    add comma $\vee$ insert an apostrophe $\overset{word}{\wedge}$ add word

When you edit your revised essay, use **Figure 9.3** as a guide. Keep going until you can check off each question in the checklist. Also, have a classmate check your writing for errors.

Adding a Title

Make sure to add an attention-getting title. Here are three strategies to try:

- **Pose a thought-provoking question:**
  Is Marriage a Crime?
- **Identify Your Topic:**
  Whale Watchers
- **Make a dramatic pronouncement:**
  Trafficking in Slaves

✅ Reading for Enrichment

You will be reading an expository selection from a sociology textbook. The selection addresses the failures of man-made flood-prevention systems in New Orleans in the wake of Hurricane Katrina. Follow the reading process and refer to what you have learned about expository essays in this chapter to help you gain a full understanding of the text. After reflecting on your reading, you will have an opportunity to write your own essay.

About the Author

Joel K. Bourne is an award-winning journalist and former senior editor at *National Geographic*. He has appeared on numerous television and radio programs, including CNN, NPR, and the National Geographic Channel.

Prereading

In August 2005, Hurricane Katrina ripped across the Gulf of Mexico, devastating coastal cities along its path. Among the hardest hit was New Orleans, where flooding led to more than 700 deaths and unprecedented property damage. In the end, 53 of the levees that were supposed to protect the city from flood damage failed. More than a decade later, New Orleans is still rebuilding, and many experts say the city is more vulnerable than ever to another natural disaster. Consider these facts as you prepare to read the essay.

Before you read, use the **STRAP** strategy to identify the main parts of the text. Also, briefly write down your personal thoughts and recollections of Hurricane Katrina and what you expect to learn from the essay.

Subject: What specific topic does the reading address?
Type: What form (*essay, narrative, textbook selection*) does the reading take?
Role: What position (*citizen, professor, reporter*) does each writer assume?
Audience: Who is the intended audience (*general readers, politicians, students*)?
Purpose: What is the general goal of the reading (*to persuade, to illustrate, to share*)?

Reading and Rereading

As you read, be sure you identify the main idea of the essay and the way in which the author supports this idea. Also, see if you can determine the type of exposition the author is using—illustration, process, etc. Reread the essay as needed to clarify your thinking about the text.

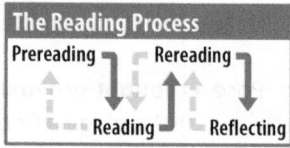

The Reading Process
Prereading — Rereading
Reading — Reflecting

New Orleans: A Perilous Future

Hurricane Katrina, the costliest natural disaster in United States history, was 1 also a warning shot. Right after the tragedy, many people expressed a **defiant** resolve to rebuild the city. However, among engineers and experts, that resolve is giving way to a growing awareness that another such disaster is **inevitable**, and nothing short of a massive and endless national commitment can prevent it.

Located in one of the lowest spots in the United States, the Big Easy is already 2 as much as 17 feet below sea level in places, and it continues to sink by up to an inch a year. Upstream dams and **levees** built to tame Mississippi River floods and ease shipping have starved the delta downstream of sediments and nutrients, causing wetlands that once buffered the city against storm-driven seas to sink beneath the waves. Louisiana has lost 1,900 square miles of coastal lands since the 1930s; Katrina and Hurricane Rita together took out 217 square miles, putting the city that much closer to the open Gulf. Most **ominous** of all, global warming is raising the Gulf faster than at any time since the last Ice Age thawed. Sea levels could rise several feet over the next century. Even before then, hurricanes may draw ever more energy from warming seas and grow stronger and more frequent.

The great tragedy of Katrina is that the hard lessons learned in earlier storms 3 were **blithely** forgotten by all. After the great Mississippi River flood of 1927 wreaked havoc all along its course and came within a few feet of spilling over the river levees and inundating New Orleans, the growing city clamored for additional protection. Over the coming decades, the federal government erected a vast network of levees and spillways along the river and around the city, while giant new dams along the Missouri—the Mississippi's longest tributary—created ponds all the way to South Dakota. The system was billed as a triumph of engineering over nature.

However, Gilbert F. White, considered the "father of floodplain 4 management," came to a far different conclusion, one that Katrina drove home with a vengeance. As a young University of Chicago geographer, White had studied the delta after the 1927 disaster and realized that much of the suffering could have been avoided. "Floods are 'acts of god,'" he wrote in 1942, "but flood losses are largely acts of man." White and his colleagues argued that dams, levees, and other flood protections may actually increase flood losses because they spur new development in the floodplain, which incurs catastrophic losses when manmade flood protections fail. The phenomenon became known as the "levee effect."

After Katrina taller, stronger floodwalls now glisten in the breaches, their   5
clean white concrete contrasting starkly with the still ruined neighborhoods behind them, while massive new black floodplains are poised to close the canals at the lakefront. The rebuilt hurricane protection system gives returning New Orleanians some sense of security. However, the **corps** has yet to fix what many see as the weakest link in the system, the 76-mile ship channel called the Mississippi River Gulf Outlet (MRGO), which the corps dug east of town in the late 1950s and early 1960s.

Residents of St. Bernard parish had been clamoring for years for the corps   6
to close the little-used channel they call the "hurricane highway." Touted as a shortcut to the port for ocean freighters, the channel instead destroyed tens of thousands of acres of wetlands. It brought in salt water that killed marsh plants, while the wakes of the few ships eroded the banks of the channel, widening it from 500 feet to almost a half mile in places. One lesson of Katrina is simple, says John Lopez of the Lake Pontchartrain Basin Foundation: Close MRGO.

The corps says it now intends to do so. However, when or how the channel   7
might be shut down is anyone's guess. Congress has yet to give a green light. "If we don't close MRGO," says Lopez, "it might be time to do what my wife says and move to Kansas."

Though the corps denies that the channel amplified Katrina's surge, everyone   8
agrees that its levees—St. Bernard's primary hurricane defense—failed miserably.

The corps insist the structures simply weren't high enough to withstand Katrina's 17 feet of surge and six-foot waves. Nevertheless, at many of the breaches, the levees were built of weak sand and shell dredged from the canal itself. Paul Kemp of Louisiana State University believes the shell-sand sections began to collapse as soon as the waves started breaking on them, long before the main surge hit. He also notes that where these levees were fronted by intact wetlands and trees, they survived. Where they ended directly in the water, they failed.

9   Old ways die hard in the bayou. Even after the dramatic failure of the shells and sand in the levees, independent investigators found corps contractors using the same material to rebuild them. Only after the discovery was made public did the corps barge in yellowish clay from the Mississippi to cap the levees. Additionally, parts of the new structures still have no buffer against erosion.

10   Nevertheless, many are rebuilding, regardless of what the experts say, with a typical New Orleans cocktail of denial, faith in the levees, and 100-proof love of home. Three months after the storm, when much of the city still lay in ruins, the mere suggestion by a blue-ribbon panel of planners from the Urban Land Institute to hold off rebuilding the lowest areas set off a howl of protests. Mayor C. Ray Nagin, who was in a tight election race at the time, dropped the notion of "shrinking the footprint" like a hot beignet, as did his opponent, Lieutenant Governor Mitch Landrieu. The mayor, however, fell short of promising every neighborhood city services.

11   To make matters even more confusing, the federal government declared it would offer flood insurance for most new or substantially rebuilt houses only if they were raised by several feet. However, the city government granted exemptions to many returning homeowners, grandfathering their houses at their prior elevations. The result has been an unplanned patchwork recovery, with some people raising their homes to protect against floods and others building right back where they were in the lowest sections of the city.

12   The reality remains daunting for those trying to rebuild, or trying to decide

whether to come back at all. The risk of catastrophic flooding is rising year by year with no end in sight—in no small part because the city is sinking.

From Joel K. Bourne. Article courtesy of *National Geographic Creative*.

---

defiant
bold and strong

levees
walls or embankments designed to control flooding

ominous
indicating something bad is coming

blithely
happily

corps
unit of the Army

beignet
a flaky, doughnut-like pastry famous to New Orleans

Reflecting

Answer the comprehension and vocabulary questions about the reading.

1. Based on your reading, how would you define the word "perilous" in the title?
   a. Secure
   b. Uncertain
   c. Favorable

2. What is the main idea of the reading?
   a. The city of New Orleans remains at risk from environmental disasters based on geographic location and ill-advised flood-prevention structures.
   b. The city of New Orleans is showing its resolve to rebuild in the wake of Hurricane Katrina.
   c. The city of New Orleans has learned from its past flood-prevention mistakes and is tackling flood prevention in new, innovative ways.

3. What is the "levee effect" described in paragraph 4?
   a. A phenomenon that shows manmade flood protections like levees discourage people from living in floodplains, because they don't want to risk those protections failing.
   b. A phenomenon that shows manmade flood protections like levees increase flood losses by encouraging more people to live in floodplains, thus putting more people at risk when those protections fail.
   c. A phenomenon that shows manmade flood protections like levees protect more people from flood loss by encouraging more people to live in floodplains.

4. Which of these best describes the overall pattern of organization for this reading?
  a. Comparison
  b. Cause-effect
  c. Chronological (time)

5. Study how the word *inevitable* is used in the reading, and then choose the most accurate definition of the word.
  Inevitable (paragraph 1)
  a. Unavoidable
  b. Avoidable
  c. Impossible

6. In paragraph 9, what major detail supports the main idea "Old ways die hard in the bayou"?
  a. Even after the dramatic failure of the shells and sand in the levees, independent investigators found corps contractors using the same material to rebuild them.
  b. Only after the discovery was made public did the corps barge in yellowish clay from the Mississippi to cap the levees.
  c. The corps insist the structures simply weren't high enough to withstand Katrina's 17 feet of surge and six-foot waves.

Summarizing

Write a summary of "New Orleans: A Perilous Future."

Critical Thinking

  ■ How much responsibility do you place on human activity for flood problems in New Orleans?
  ■ The author often contrasts the fixes the corps has made to fixes suggested by other experts. Why does the author offer this contrast of opinions? What does the contrast reveal about the corps' fixes?
  ■ What factors would lead someone to return to a city, even after it's been devastated by a flood or other natural disaster?
  ■ Do you think certain residential areas in New Orleans that are at greatest risk for future flood damage should be closed to residents? Why or why not?
  ■ What advice would you give to the people who feel uncertain about their future in New Orleans? Should they move? If they stay, what warnings or information do they need to know about?

Writing for Enrichment

Choose one of the following writing ideas, or decide upon an idea of your own related to the reading.

The Writing Process

Prewrite — Revise — Publish

Write — Edit

1. Write an expository essay that explains the circumstances around another city impacted by a natural disaster.

2. Research different safeguards cities or residents can take to prepare for potential natural disasters. Explain these safeguards with examples from places that suffered weather-related disasters. Were some safeguards more successful than others?

3. The frequency of monster storms—Category 4 and 5—has doubled since 1970. Write a cause-effect essay outlining the causes and effects of this sharp increase. (See Section 9.1.)

4. Write a classification essay that identifies types of natural disasters and explains the similarities and differences between the categories. (See Section 9.1.)

5. Research different approaches to controlling river flooding. Compare and contrast two main approaches, explaining how each approach works as well as its effectiveness. Use real examples to support your ideas. (See Section 9.1.)

When planning . . .
- Make sure that your topic is specific enough for an expository essay.
- Research your topic to gather plenty of details.
- Establish a main idea for your essay, and express it in a thesis statement. (See Section 9.3.)
- List your details in the best order to support your thesis.

When writing . . .
- Pay careful attention to each part of your essay—the opening, middle, and closing. (See Section 9.4.)
- Explain each of your main points clearly and completely.
- Use a variety of details to support your ideas.

When revising and editing . . .
- Decide if your essay answers key questions readers may have about your topic.
- Be prepared to do additional research if necessary.
- Add citations to give credit to the sources of key ideas you use in your writing. (See Section 11.3 for help using citations.)
- Ask at least one classmate or trusted friend to respond to your first draft.
- Revise and edit your writing for content, style, and correctness. Use the checklists in Figures 9.2 and 9.3 to help you improve your work.

imanolqs, 2017 / Used under license from Shutterstock.com

Reading and Writing Arguments

One definition of *argument* is "a quarrel or dispute," as when a brother and a sister engage in a shouting match with heated words. Another definition of *argument* is "a discussion aimed at demonstrating truth or falsehood." Levelheadedness rather than anger is important in this type of argument.

This chapter focuses on reasonable arguments that let the facts speak for themselves. A well-crafted argumentative essay informs and explains. It prompts logical thinking rather than emotion, guiding the reader toward informed conclusions about important, sometimes controversial issues.

In this chapter, you will learn about the working parts of strong arguments and the importance of analyzing arguments for their logic and completeness. Then you will write an argumentative essay of your own.

Chapter Outline

- Understanding Argumentation
- Reading and Responding to Arguments
- Planning an Argument Essay
- Writing the First Draft
- Revising the Writing
- Editing the Writing

10.1 Understanding Argumentation

In ancient Greece and Rome, anyone lucky enough to receive an education was trained in **argumentation**. The belief was (and still is) that those who develop argumentative skills become clear thinkers and leaders. Believe it or not, the basic structure used to build arguments in those ancient civilizations is still used today.

An argument is only as good as the thoughts and ideas that go into it. A strong argument develops a logical or reasonable claim (the thesis) with solid evidence (the support). It acknowledges important opposing points of view and either counters (disputes) them or concedes (admits) their value. Overall, an argument provides a meaningful and logical examination of an issue. Arguments, of course, are made about issues of which people have differing points of view. There's nothing to argue about if everyone agrees on something.

Arguments are weakened by **logical fallacies** or false statements. These appear unintentionally in quickly fashioned persuasive texts or intentionally in manipulative arguments, such as advertisements: "Temptrol is the best cold medicine in the world!" or "One call to my law office will take care of all of your bankruptcy problems!"

You'll encounter argumentation in each of the following forms of writing.

Editorial

An **editorial** presents a point of view on a currently debated topic. Traditionally, editorials have often been written by editors of newspapers or magazines. You may find them in the "Opinions" sections of those periodicals.

> You've seen the anti-vaccine slogans: "If you mixed mercury, aluminum phosphate, ammonium sulfate, and formaldehyde with viruses, then got a syringe and injected it into your child, you would be arrested and sent to jail for child endangerment and abuse. Then why is it legal for a doctor to do it?"
>
> You may have also seen these parody slogans. "If you burst into the bedroom of children you didn't know while wielding an axe, then forcibly carried them away, you would be arrested. So why are firefighters allowed to do it?" "If you packed scores of people into a pressurized metal tube, then used refined kerosene to launch them 35,000 feet into the air, you would be arrested. So why are airlines allowed to do it?" Endless variations are possible.
>
> The point is clear. The anti-vaccine movement is alarmist, ill-informed, and downright silly. It has been with us ever since Jonas Salk invented the first polio vaccine—you know, the one that virtually wiped polio off the face of the planet. Yet today it makes less sense than ever before. . . .

Personal Commentary

Like editorials, **personal commentaries** present an opinion. But while editorials are officially approved by the editorial staff of a periodical and are usually written by those editors, a personal commentary may appear nearly anywhere, from blogs to book prefaces to professional essays. Similarly, while editorials tend to discuss current events, personal commentaries may deal with nearly any topic.

> We live in a time of chaos and uncertainty. Every day we are bombarded with news of strife and tragedy somewhere in the world. Stories of terrorist strikes and military counterstrikes are commonplace. At times it appears the world is coming apart at the seams. This is when the lessons of history become essential. By comparing conflict and crime in the world today with that of earlier times, we see a pattern emerging. It is a pattern of progress and of hope. . . .

Problem-Solution Essay

A **problem-solution essay** is a particular type of argument that seeks to explain a problem and provide a convincing solution or set of solutions for it. This sort of essay involves argumentation in that the writer seeks to convince the reader to take a particular course of action. In explaining the problem, a problem-solution essay may also need to persuade the reader to accept specific causes.

> Texting while driving is undeniably dangerous. Studies have shown that this distraction is as much an impairment as driving while intoxicated. Yet people are tempted to respond whenever their cell phone gives an alert.
>
> Given how "smart" phones are now, one solution is to make them incapable of texting while moving at driving speeds. A phone's GPS could simply freeze its texting apps, perhaps except when use is voice activated and hands free. . . .

Position Paper

Many college courses, especially those in the humanities—from literature to history to philosophy—ask students to write **position papers** on a regular basis. The purpose of these essays is to demonstrate a student's thoughts about the material being covered in class or readings related to it.

> Some critics complain that *Crime and Punishment*'s epilogue doesn't fit the rest of the novel. They claim that it just continues to dwell on Raskolnikov's moral confusion, which has already been thoroughly treated in the story. Others complain about the sudden change of direction in the final paragraph, as if Dostoevsky planned to write a sequel but never lived to do so.
>
> My own feeling is that this ending is perfectly suited to the novel. It gives meaning to the mental suffering throughout by offering a hint of better things to come. It shows the strength of Sofia's faithfulness. And it does so without stooping to a "fairy-tale" ending. . . .

Analyzing Parts of an Argument

The goal of an argument essay is to get the reader to accept or see the value in a particular point of view. Careful reading of these texts is necessary for making informed decisions about whether to accept or dismiss the writer's position.

To understand an argument, you need to recognize its basic parts. Studying the parts and their functions will help you follow the author's thinking.

- **Main Claim:** The main claim (or thesis) generally appears early in the essay, usually in one of the first paragraphs, after background information about the topic. A claim presents a viewpoint about the topic that cannot be directly proven true like a fact can be. However, a claim can be strengthened by evidence:

  > Laws should be enacted to reduce our dependence on nitrogen-based fertilizers and detergents.

- **Supporting Claims (Reasons):** A supporting claim is a statement that provides a reason for accepting the main claim. Body paragraphs in essays of argumentation often begin with a new supporting claim. Each claim is then supported with evidence.

  > Nitrogen runoff in our waterways leads to algal blooms and red tides, blocking sunlight to other water plants and staining our shorelines.

- **Evidence:** A claim succeeds or fails based on its supporting evidence. The evidence in a strong argument can be checked, backed up, and relied upon. Common types of evidence include the following:

  - **Facts and statistics:** According to a 2011 study by the DNR, a murky bottom predicts an algae cover greater than 80 percent.
  - **Examples:** Lake Erie experienced an unusually high buildup of algae in 2014.
  - **Expert testimony:** Sarah Follet, a water resource official, stated, "There are . . ."

- **Counterarguments:** A strong argument addresses opposing points of view, either conceding or countering them. A **concession** admits the value of an opposing point. A **counter** shows why the opposing point lacks value. Opposing points of view may be introduced with words or phrases such as *admittedly, granted, it is true that, I accept that,* and *no doubt.*

  - **Opposing point of view:** It is true that the appearance of the algae is limited to late summer, and according to some people, it occurs only if the weather is windless and hot.
  - **Counter:** In saying this, people are simply ignoring the problem. The algae will still be there regardless of the weather, just waiting to bloom.
  - **Concession:** Fixing the algae problem is admittedly a pricey endeavor.

- **Call to Action:** Many arguments end by requesting that the reader respond to the argument by thinking or acting in a certain way.

  > We must demand that our elected officials address this harmful side effect of nitrogen-based fertilizers and detergents.

Analyzing Logic

The strength of an argument depends on its logic. **Logic** is the science of reasonable and accurate thinking. An argument is logical if it contains important and provable evidence to support a reasonable claim.

Reliable and Logical Evidence

Different types of evidence provide different types of support for an argument. The best evidence is fact-based, meaning it is provable. Opinions, which are personally held attitudes, are not provable and are not reliable forms of evidence.

- **Fact:** Nuclear power is a nonrenewable energy source. *(You can check this statement for accuracy.)*
- **Opinion:** I think nuclear power is unsafe. *(This simply offers a personal feeling.)*

For an essay that argues "Nuclear power is not an appropriate source of energy," the following types of evidence would be provable:

- **Observations:** Ugly nuclear reactors litter the countryside in Europe.
- **Quotations:** Former Japan Prime Minister Naoto Kan says, "Nuclear arms and atomic power represent a technology in which coexistence with man is extremely difficult."
- **Facts and Statistics:** The explosion of the nuclear reactor at the Chernobyl Nuclear Power Plant in Ukraine exposed more than 600,000 people to the effects of radiation poisoning.
- **Comparisons:** Using fossil fuels for energy is much less expensive than uranium.
- **Explanations:** The World Nuclear Association points out that although the Fukushima Daiichi nuclear accident caused no deaths or sickness from radiation, more than 100,000 people had to be evacuated from their homes, and 1,000 people died as a result of the evacuation.
- **Inferences:** Scientific discovery, such as nuclear fission, can have unintended consequences for mankind.

The quantity of evidence used is not the only factor that makes an argument logical. The quality and variety of the evidence are similarly important factors. When analyzing the supporting evidence for an argument, make sure the evidence is:

- **Accurate:** Do most experts agree on the information? Is it up to date?
- **Complete:** Does the evidence tell the "whole story"? Or do some legitimate counterarguments seem to be ignored?
- **Relevant:** Is all evidence related to the main argument?

Faulty Logic

A logical fallacy is a misleading or false statement that weakens or distorts an argument. Avoid logical fallacies in your own writing, and be aware of them while reading argumentative texts.

Common Logical Fallacies

■ **Exaggerating the Facts:** This fallacy distorts facts in order to make an extreme claim.

> Eating chocolate can cause all kinds of diseases, even if you eat only one or two pieces a day.

■ **Offering Extremes:** This fallacy offers extreme or outlandish consequences for not acting a certain way.

> Either people should give up chocolate, or we are going to face incredible increases in heath-care costs.

■ **Half Truths:** A half truth contains part but not the whole truth. It fails to tell "the whole story," making it both true and false simultaneously.

> The increase in tuition is a good idea because it will lower taxes for county residents. (But the increase might hurt low-income residents.)

■ **Appealing to Popular Position:** Also known as "bandwagoning," this fallacy argues for something on the basis that many other people like it.

> The new tuition increase is a good idea because everyone at the last board meeting voted for it.

■ **Straw Man:** This logical fallacy distorts an issue by exaggerating or misinterpreting an opponent's position.

> Those who consider themselves caring people cannot approve of the death penalty.

■ **Broad Generalization:** This logical fallacy makes an all-or-nothing claim based on little evidence. The claim will often include an intensifier, such as *all*, *every*, or *never*.

> All professional athletes will cheat if that is the only way they can maintain their competitive edge.

■ **Impressing with Numbers:** In this case, a writer attempts to overwhelm the reader with a deluge of statistics, some of which may be unrelated to the issue at hand.

> At 35 ppm, CO levels factory-wide are an insignificant 10 ppm above the OSHA guideline of 25 ppm. This "pollution" pales in comparison to such things as "noise pollution" in other industries, where a dBA as high as 115 is allowed.

■ **Red Herring:** This fallacy presents an observation or detail to distract the reader from the actual claim.

> Although the student parking problem is real, and the proposed solutions seem valid, we already have a full agenda of other topics to discuss.

■ **Ad Populum:** This fallacy appeals to the reader's emotions instead of to logic.

> The fashion industry is essentially corrupt. Hugo Boss designed Nazi uniforms.

10.2 Reading and Responding to Arguments

When reading an argument essay, you need to identify the main parts of the text and then decide if they provide a thoughtful and reasonable discussion of the topic. You can use a line diagram to help you analyze the author's argument.

Using a Line Diagram

At the top of the diagram, identify the main claim. In the second level of the diagram, name the supporting claims (reasons), and in the third level, identify evidence used to strengthen each supporting claim. Generally speaking, each middle paragraph or two will provide a new supporting claim. **Figure 10.1** shows parts of a line diagram for the essay "A Necessary Protection."

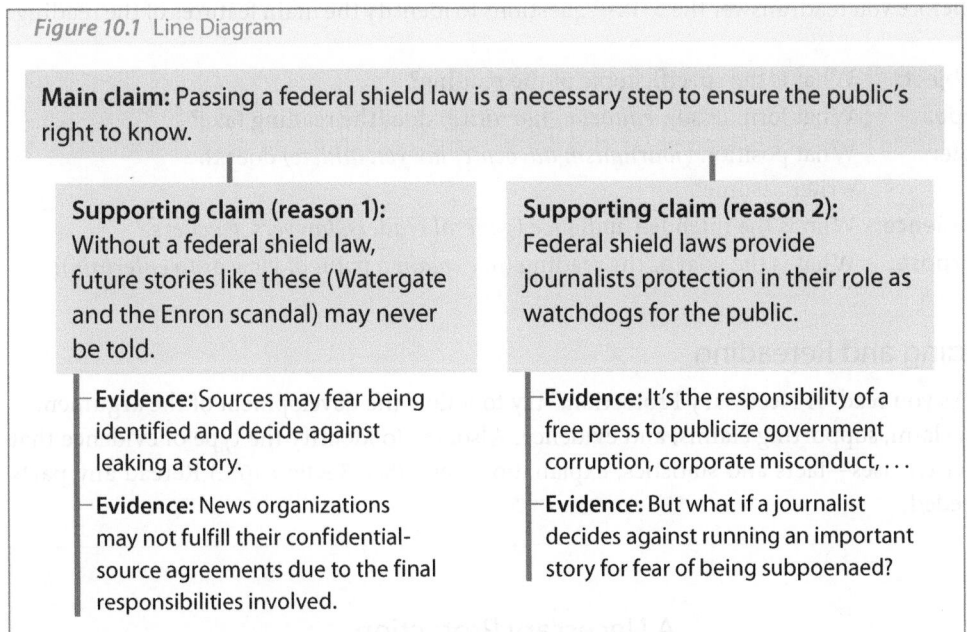

Figure 10.1 Line Diagram

Main claim: Passing a federal shield law is a necessary step to ensure the public's right to know.

Supporting claim (reason 1): Without a federal shield law, future stories like these (Watergate and the Enron scandal) may never be told.

Evidence: Sources may fear being identified and decide against leaking a story.

Evidence: News organizations may not fulfill their confidential-source agreements due to the final responsibilities involved.

Supporting claim (reason 2): Federal shield laws provide journalists protection in their role as watchdogs for the public.

Evidence: It's the responsibility of a free press to publicize government corruption, corporate misconduct, . . .

Evidence: But what if a journalist decides against running an important story for fear of being subpoenaed?

Understanding the Voice

Voice refers to the author's writing personality and attitude toward the topic and the reader. Use these questions as a guide for judging voice in an argument.

- Does the author seem honest and sincere?
- Does the author make a reasonable, informed claim?
- Does the author seem respectful and understanding?
- Does the author focus on issues rather than personalities?
- Does the author engage readers, rather than lecture them?

Reading and Reacting to a Professional Argument

"A Necessary Protection" is an essay written in response to an important federal case involving two journalists investigating steroid use in professional sports.

The Reading Process

About the Author

Tim Kemper is a graduate of Butler University with training in journalism and communications. He is currently managing editor of Thoughtful Learning, a publishing company specializing in literacy and business communication.

Prereading

Before you read, answer the **STRAP** questions to identify the main features of the reading.

Subject: What is the specific topic of the reading?

Type: What form (*essay, editorial, narrative*) does the reading take?

Role: What position (*journalism advocate, lawyer, athlete*) does the writer assume?

Audience: Who is the intended audience (*general readers, lawyers, teachers*)?

Purpose: What is the goal of the reading (*to explain a point of view* or *to entertain*)?

Reading and Rereading

As you read "A Necessary Protection," try to follow the development of the argument—main claim, supporting claims, and evidence. Also, try to identify the type of evidence that the writer uses—facts and statistics, explanations, etc. (See **Section 10.1**.) Reread any parts as needed.

A Necessary Protection

In the summer of 2006, investigative journalists Lance Williams and Mark   *1*

Fainaru-Wada of the *San Francisco Chronicle* faced a dilemma: either reveal the

source who leaked **confidential** information for their story about steroid use

in professional baseball or refuse and be found in **contempt** of court, with an

18-month prison sentence potentially facing them. At the heart of the matter were

shield laws.

A shield law gives reporters protection from being forced to reveal   *2*
confidential information or **anonymous sources** in a courtroom. Currently,
49 states, including California, offer shield laws of varying degrees. However,
Williams and Fainaru-Wada's source was involved in a federal investigation,
and no federal shield law exists. So the journalists were in a **vulnerable** position.
They authored important news but were perceived by the courts as breaking the
law in doing so. To remedy this situation, a federal shield law is needed. Then
journalists like Williams and Fainaru-Wada can do their jobs and the public can
be rightly informed.

Some of the most important stories in American history have surfaced due   *3*
to anonymous **whistle-blowers**, including the Watergate and Enron scandals.
Without a federal shield law, future stories like these may never be told for two
reasons. First, sources may fear being identified and decide against leaking a
story of corruption or scandal. Second, news organizations may not fulfill their
confidential-source agreements due to the financial responsibilities connected to
fighting a case in court. Either one hurts news gathering.

Furthermore, a federal shield law would provide journalists with the basic   *4*
protections they need to be watchdogs for the general public. It's the responsibility
of a free press to alert citizens to government corruption, corporate misconduct,
and threats to public health and safety by unearthing important stories. But what
if a journalist decides against running an important story with an unnamed
source for fear of being **subpoenaed**? Then, of course, the free press will not be
able to function effectively.

Admittedly, a federal shield law should not provide journalists with   *5*
unlimited protections. For example, if an unnamed source is a threat to national
security or could cause bodily harm, the journalist should be **compelled** to
reveal the source. However, in almost all other cases where an unnamed source
is absolutely necessary, reporters shouldn't have to fear imprisonment for
honoring confidentiality.

Trust is the foundation of a source-reporter relationship. Williams and   6
Fainaru-Wada knew this. They decided against revealing their source and would
have served jail time if the source had not confessed. The next journalist might
not be so lucky without a federal shield law.

contempt
willful disregard for the rules of a court

anonymous sources
people interviewed by a reporter who ask not to be
named in the article the reporter writes

vulnerable
unprotected

whistle-blowers
people who make a public disclosure of corruption or
wrongdoing done by someone else

subpoenaed
required to be submitted to the court

Reflecting

Practice 10.1   Answer the comprehension and vocabulary questions about the reading.

1. Where in the essay is the main claim stated?
   a. In the second paragraph
   b. In another middle paragraph
   c. In the first paragraph

2. What is the main type of evidence included in the essay?
   a. Many statistics
   b. Quotations from experts
   c. Explanations plus a few statistics and facts

3. In what paragraph does the writer concede a point about shield laws?
   a. Paragraph 1
   b. Paragraph 3
   c. Paragraph 5

4. How would you describe the author's voice?
   a. Informed and sincere
   b. Somewhat interested
   c. Angry and critical

5. Study how the word *confidential* is used in the reading, and then choose the most accurate definition of the word.

Confidential (paragraph 1)

a. Intended to be revealed

b. Intended to be kept secret

c. Intended to be used in court

6. Study how the word *compelled* is used in the reading, and then choose the most accurate definition of the word.

Compelled (paragraph 5)

a. Allowed

b. Forced

c. Asked

Critical Thinking

- Does this essay provide enough information to make an informed opinion about the topic? Explain.
- Do you consider the evidence to be reliable and logical?
- What else would you like to know about shield laws?
- Does this essay change your thinking about the press? If so, how?
- What connections, if any, are their between unnamed sources and fake news?

10.3 Planning an Argument Essay

The starting point for a strong argument essay is a debatable topic—one in which people have differing points of view. A topic like smoking is not debatable because smoking is harmful and everyone knows it, including smokers. On the other hand, topics related to gun control or immigration are clearly debatable and worthy of examining.

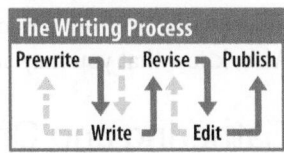

Brainstorm a list of three or four debatable topics that interest you and that you could write about in an argument essay. Consider issues that affect your education (graduation requirements) or community (on-street parking) as well as issues that have more national or global importance (high-speed rails). If you can't think of worthy topics, review newspapers, magazines, and websites for ideas. Then select one of the topics for your essay.

Not Debatable	Debatable
People need access to health care.	All Americans should be entitled to health care.

Making a Claim

A strong argument essay results from a clear interest and understanding of a topic, so becoming familiar with your topic is the next key step in the planning process.

If your essay will include a research component, consult a few reliable sources of information (books, websites, etc.) and, if possible, talk with other people who know about the topic. Make sure to record important facts, details, and positions related to the topic. Then after reviewing these notes, write down a position (point of view) that you would like to develop in your essay.

An argument essay is built around a main claim about the topic. Once you establish a claim, you can continue your planning and research the claim to support it. A main claim identifies the topic plus your position about it. The formula in **Figure 10.2** shows how a main claim is constructed.

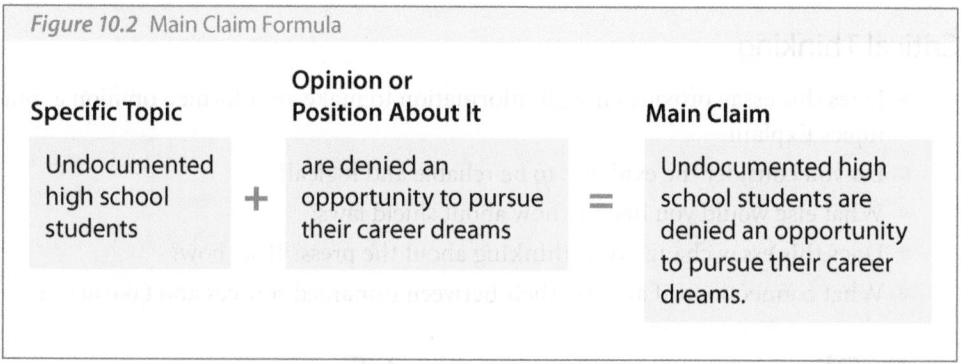

Figure 10.2 Main Claim Formula

Specific Topic		Opinion or Position About It		Main Claim
Undocumented high school students	+	are denied an opportunity to pursue their career dreams	=	Undocumented high school students are denied an opportunity to pursue their career dreams.

Create the main claim for your essay using the formula above as a guide. You may need to write two or three versions of this statement before it says exactly what you want it to say. Also, know that you may adjust or change your claim as you continue to plan your essay.

Gathering and Organizing the Support

To build a convincing argument, you need strong support for your main claim. For an essay like "The Problems of the Social Media Echo Chamber" (see **Chapter 10: "Reading for Enrichment"**), that means identifying effective supporting claims (reasons) and evidence (facts, details, explanations). Other argument essays like "Dream Act May Help Students Fight for Residency" (see **Section 10.4**) state a problem in the main claim and provide one or more reasonable solutions as the support.

No matter what form your argument takes, make sure to gather plenty of convincing supporting evidence to present in your essay. Consider using a line diagram (see **Figure 10.1**) to keep track of your support if it comes in the form of reasons or a problem-solution web (see **Figure 1.8**) if your support comes in the form of solutions to a problem.

Once you have gathered your support, decide on the best way to arrange it. A common pattern of arrangement is **order of importance**. With this pattern of arrangement, you present your supporting reasons in one of two ways—either from the most important one to the least important one or the other way around. In a problem-solution essay, you either explain one main solution or lead up to the best solution. Once you have gathered your supporting details and decided how to organize your essay, create an outline or quick list or use a graphic organizer to create a visual of your thesis and supporting details (see Section 5.5).

Considering Opposing Points of View

You can actually strengthen your argument by responding to main objections or concerns a reader may have to it. Generally speaking, your response should be in the form of a concession or counterargument.

- To **concede** means to admit the value of another point of view.
- To **counter** means to show why the opposing point lacks value.

You can introduce opposing viewpoints with words and phrases such as *admittedly, granted, it is true, I accept that, unfortunately,* and *no doubt*. It is usually best to address objections early or late in your argument.

10.4 Writing the First Draft

After prewriting and planning, the next step is to write a first draft. But before you begin, read this student essay. Notice how the beginning draws the reader into the text. Also, notice how the details in the middle part explain a possible solution to the problem stated in the main claim. Lastly, notice how the closing makes a call to action.

Dream Act May Help Students Fight for Residency

Opening paragraph

Facts

Attending college, joining the military, creating a career path: these are [1] dreams for most U.S. high school graduates. But for Maria Lopez, a senior at San Marshall High School who has lived in the U.S for seven years, her only legal next step is to return to Mexico. She, like nearly 65,000 young people each year, is an undocumented high school student and has no way to achieve legal residency here. As a result, Maria and other undocumented students are denied an opportunity to pursue their career dreams.

Thesis statement

The only legal route for residency for these young people is to go back to [2] their country of birth, file the proper paperwork, and then return to the U.S. Unfortunately, attempts to return legally are often difficult, with roadblocks such as a ten-year restriction on re-entering the U.S. However, one piece of proposed federal legislation could offer a solution for these young people:

Thesis statement (continued)

The Development, Relief, and Education for Alien Minors Act (S. 729), better known as the Dream Act.

Support Paragraph 1

The current version of this bill would grant eligible immigrant students six years of conditional residency during which they could earn full citizenship. To be eligible, a student must: (1) graduate from a U.S. high school or obtain a GED, (2) be of good moral character, (3) have arrived in the U.S. under the age of 16, (4) have proof of residence in the U.S. for at least five consecutive years since the arrival date, and (5) be between the ages of 12 and 35 at the time of the bill's enactment.

3

Support Paragraph 2

Explanations

To gain full citizenship, the student must do one of the following during a residency: (1) complete at least two years of work toward a four-year college degree, (2) earn a two-year college degree, or (3) serve in the military for two years. If, within the six-year period, a student does not complete one of these requirements, the student would be subject to deportation.

4

Support Paragraph 3

Since its introduction in 2001, legislators keep trying to get the Dream Act enacted, but it still remains in the first step in the legislative process—a process in which bills go to committees or "mini congresses" that deliberate, investigate, and revise the bill before it is brought up for general debate. The sad fact, though, is that the majority of bills never make it out of these committees. In addition, supporters of Comprehensive Immigration Reform (CIR) have been in favor of including the Dream Act as part of CIR, which could make the Dream Act subject to change yet again. And now, of course, there is an administration with strong views on immigration to deal with.

5

Closing Paragraph

Given these issues, it might be a long time before the bill becomes law. Sadly, time is the one thing that Maria and thousands of other undocumented students don't have. We need our Representatives and Senators to debate and approve the Dream Act now, thereby making Maria's dreams—and the dreams of thousands of students like her—a reality!

6

Used by permission of Renee Wielenga.

Creating an Opening Paragraph

The opening of your essay should capture the reader's interest, provide background information, and state your main claim. Here are three attention-grabbing strategies:

- **Start with a brief dramatic story.**

  Attending college, joining the military, creating a career path: these are dreams for most U.S. high school graduates. But for Maria Lopez, a senior at San Marshall High School who has lived in the U.S for seven years, her only legal next step is to return to Mexico.

- **Offer a surprising statistic.**

  A recent study estimates two acres of farmland and ranch land are lost to development every minute of every day.

- **Connect with the reader.**

  Birds motivate us to keep the world healthy for them, and they teach us what we have to accomplish in order to do this.

Developing the Middle Paragraphs

The middle paragraphs should develop your claim with strong support (background, supporting claims, and evidence).

- **Follow the pattern of arrangement you decided on for your supporting information.** It is common to present your most important reason first or last.
- **Include enough evidence to make your reasons clear or to explain your solutions.** Consider what the reader may already know about the topic and what they may need to know to understand your argument.
- **Consider possible objections.** Usually there is at least one main objection to concede or counter.

Creating the Closing Paragraph

The closing paragraph should restate the main claim, review the important support, and/or provide a final thought or make a call to action.

- Given these issues, it might be a long time before the bill becomes law. Sadly, time is the one thing that Maria and thousands of other undocumented students don't have. We need our Representatives and Senators to debate and approve the Dream Act now, thereby making Maria's dreams—and the dreams of thousands of students like her—a reality!

When you write your first draft, follow the advice given in this section. Refer to the essays in the chapter for additional ideas. Keep going until you get all of your ideas written.

10.5 Revising the Writing

Revision can begin with a peer review. Sharing your writing at various stages is important, especially when you review and revise a first draft. The feedback that you receive will help you improve and strengthen your essay. Here's an example of feedback for "Dream Act May Help Students Fight for Residency." Have at least one classmate or trusted friend read and react to your first draft. Have this person use these questions to help them respond to your essay.

Peer Review Sheet

Essay title: Dream Act May Help Students Fight for Residency

Writer: Renee Wielenga

Reviewer: Kim Bertrum

1. Which part of the essay works best—opening, middle, or closing? Why?

   Middle—it clearly explains the Dream Act.

2. Which part of the essay needs work—opening, middle, or closing? Why?

   Middle—you could have addressed one or two main objections.

3. Do the middle paragraphs support the writer's main claim? How so?

   Yes, the Dream Act provides a great solution to the problem.

4. Does the writer include strong evidence to support the claims? Are more details needed? Why or why not?

   You explain the Dream Act with clear explanations.

5. Does the writer build a convincing argument? Why or why not?

   You offer a reasonable solution to the problem.

Checking for Bias

Sometimes your strong feelings about a topic can result in argumentation that is not fair or balanced. As a result, watch for wording that shows **bias**—prejudice in favor of one side of an issue. Also, beware of words that may be overly emotional or personal rather than logical and thoughtful. The following passage demonstrates a biased, emotional argument.

> Clearly, marijuana needs to be legalized. Marijuana relieves stress and anxiety and may prevent Alzheimer's disease and glaucoma. It's obvious that marijuana is not any more addictive than alcohol and is less dangerous than other drugs.

This argument fails to address arguments about the risks of marijuana. In addition, words like "clearly" and "it's obvious that" appeal to the emotions.

Argumentation versus Persuasion

Remember that an academic argument should stick to the facts. You're writing to present an argument rather than to persuade readers, and there is a difference.

Argumentation	Persuasion
• Explains a point of view	• Tries to change beliefs
• Appeals to logical thinking	• Appeals to emotions
• Reveals balance (different perspectives of the topic)	• May be one-sided
	• More subjective (personal)

Revise your first draft by first making sure that the evidence throughout in your essay is convincing, unbiased, and factual. Also, use a checklist like the one in **Figure 10.2** to review your first draft for other important issues related to the development of your argument.

Figure 10.2 Revising Checklist

Ideas

☐ Do I focus on a debatable topic and make a provable claim about it?

☐ Do I effectively explain and support this claim?

☐ If necessary, do I counter or concede any objections?

Organization

☐ Does my essay include effective beginning, middle, and closing parts?

☐ Have I organized the supporting details in a logical way?

Voice

☐ Do I sound knowledgeable about and interested in the topic?

10.6 Editing the Writing

The main work during the editing step is to check your writing for clarity and accuracy. Clarity is essential in an argument essay; otherwise, a reader won't be able to follow your line of thinking. Three clarity problems to check for include vague or indefinite pronoun references, incomplete comparisons, and statements expressing multiple meanings.

Indefinite Pronoun Reference

An **indefinite pronoun reference** results when it is unclear in a sentence which word or phrase a pronoun refers to. There must always be a clear antecedent (usually a noun) that a pronoun replaces.

> **Ambiguous:** When Mike moved the lamp onto the wobbly chair, **it** fell on the floor. (*What fell on the floor—the lamp or chair?*)
>
> **Clear:** When Mike moved the lamp onto the wobbly chair, **the lamp** fell on the floor.
>
> ---
>
> **Ambiguous:** Monica reminded Misha that **she** needed to buy a new black dress for the party. (*Who needed to buy a black dress—Monica or Misha?*)
>
> **Clear:** Monica reminded Misha to buy a new black dress for the party.

Practice 10.2 Write *C* in the space before each sentence if it correctly expresses a clear idea. Write *I* in the blank if the sentence is incorrect and contains an indefinite or unclear pronoun reference.

1. As Brad drove his motorcycle into the garage, it shook. _____
2. After Scott finished the race, he drank two bottles of water. _____
3. Reverend Bell told his assistant that he needed to conduct the service. _____
4. Once the rain stopped, it turned into a nice day for the football game. _____
5. When Andrea placed the box of macaroni on the shelf, it tipped over. _____
6. As soon as Josie pulled her car up to the drive-in window, it made a strange rattling sound. _____
7. Todd turned off his computer after he completed his essay. _____
8. Whenever Chen talks with the pharmacist, she feels like she needs a translator. _____
9. While Jackson works at the coffee shop, he never forgets to be friendly with the customers. _____
10. Coach McCarthy reminded his quarterback that he volunteered to help with the fundraiser. _____

Incomplete Comparisons

Don't confuse the reader by leaving out a word or words that are necessary to complete a comparison. The two ideas, objects, or people being compared must be identified to ensure clarity.

> **Ambiguous:** The waiter said the clam chowder is tastier. (*The clam chowder is tastier than what?*)
> **Clear:** The waiter said the clam chowder is tastier than the tortilla soup.
> **Ambiguous:** Helium is lighter. (*Lighter than what?*)
> **Clear:** Helium is lighter than oxygen.

Sentences with Multiple Meanings

Also watch for sentences that have more than one possible meaning because of an unclear reference to something elsewhere in the sentence.

> **Ambiguous:** Jill decided to take her sister to a movie, which turned out to be a real bummer. (*It is unclear what was a real bummer—taking her sister to the movie or the movie itself.*)
> **Clear:** Jill decided to take her sister to a movie, but the film turned out to be a real bummer.

Practice 10.3   Write *C* in the space before each sentence if it correctly expresses a clear idea. Write *I* if the sentence incorrectly contains an incomplete comparison or if it suggests more than one meaning.

1. Going bowling is more fun. _____

2. I find pasta more satisfying than pizza. _____

3. Dao intended to wash the car when he finished studying, but he never did. _____

4. I can handle Melanie's personality better. _____

5. I get along better with Rosa than my sister does. _____

6. I couldn't believe that my mom bought a cat with all those allergy problems. _____

7. Most people feel more secure blending in with the crowd than standing out. _____

8. Mike brought his new car to the concert, which turned out to be a letdown. _____

9. Electric cars are more energy efficient. _____

10. After finishing her vocal check, the backup singer joined the lead performer. _____

Be sure to check your revised writing for any of these clarity problems. They can be easy to miss, so review your work carefully.

Editing an Essay

Becoming an effective editor takes practice. You must train yourself to look for different types of errors. Using an editing checklist (see **Figure 10.4**) can help you know what to look for. A checklist also helps you focus on one type of error at a time.

Figure 10.4 Editing Checklist

Words

☐ Have I used specific verbs and modifiers?

☐ Have I used more action verbs than "be" verbs (*is, are, was, were*)?

Sentences

☐ Have I varied the beginnings and lengths of sentences?

☐ Have I combined short, choppy sentences?

☐ Have I avoided fragments, run-ons, and comma splices?

☐ Have I avoided vague pronoun references, incomplete comparisons, and unclear wording?

Conventions

☐ Do I use correct verb forms (*he saw,* not *he seen*)?

☐ Do my subjects and verbs agree (*she speaks,* not *she speak*)?

☐ Have I used the right words (*their, there, they're*)?

☐ Have I capitalized first words and proper nouns and adjectives?

☐ Have I used commas after long introductory word groups?

☐ Have I punctuated dialogue correctly?

☐ Have I carefully checked my spelling?

Practice 10.4 The following essay contains agreement, comma, and capitalization errors. Use the given proofreading marks to correct the essay. *Hint:* The essay includes three subject-verb agreement errors, two comma errors, and five capitalization errors.

Ban Burmese Pythons

An invasive reptile are taking the southern tip of Florida by storm. Thousands of Burmese pythons—giant snakes native to warm Asian countries—are thriving in the tropic-like environment of everglades national park. Their presence in the park is a product of irresponsible pet owners, who intentionally release the snakes into the wild when they become too difficult to care for. As a result, florida lawmakers have passed a law making it illegal for individuals to own Burmese pythons. In order to protect native wildlife and treasured ecosystems of the southern United States this law should expand nationally.

Reports show some 144,000 pythons have been imported into the U.S., many of which end up in homes of irresponsible pet owners. "All of the Burmese pythons that we see in the park are a product of the international pet trade" said Skip Snow, a wildlife biologist at Everglades National Park. "Many pet owners don't fully understand the responsibility of taking care of a python." Often the python, which grows to between 10 and 20 feet, becomes too big and too expensive to be kept in a home. In the end, the owner releases the pet into the wild.

It is in the wild where Burmese pythons is causing havoc. The tropical environment of the Everglades provides perfect conditions for the pythons to breed and feed. With no natural competitor, the strong and stealthy python feeds at will on native everglades species. Scientists worry that the ecological effects could be devastating.

To be fair, there are no doubt thousands of responsible pet owners across the United States. But the drawbacks of owning Burmese pythons outweighs the benefits. If the United States wants to maintain its fragile southern ecosystem, it should take a hard look at making the importation of Burmese pythons illegal.

Proofreading Marks

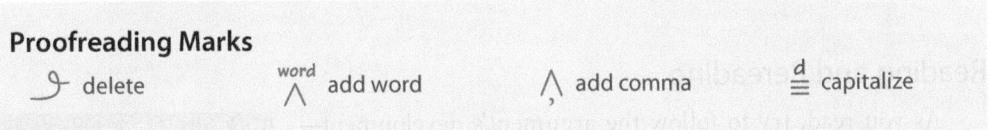

| ꝰ delete | word ∧ add word | ∧ add comma | d ≡ capitalize |

When you edit your revised essay, use the checklist in **Figure 10.4** as a guide. Keep going until you can check off each question. Also, have a classmate check your writing for errors. Then write a neat final copy of your argument essay.

Adding a Title

Make sure to add an attention-getting title. Here are three strategies to try:

- **Use a phrase from the essay:**
    - Denied an Opportunity
- **Make a dramatic pronouncement:**
    - A Necessary Protection
- **Use alliteration or another poetic technique:**
    - Ban Burmese Pythons

☑ Reading for Enrichment

You will be reading an online article entitled "The Problems of the Social Media Echo Chamber" from *Adweek*. As you read this essay, be sure to follow the steps in the reading process. The reading activities are followed by a variety of writing prompts.

About the Author

Vincent Gibson is a web designer and developer who founded Centric App, an app that matches a user's video content with similar videos from different social platforms based on location.

Prereading

Write freely for 5-10 minutes to consider how your social media habits influence your views on politics, culture, current events, and the world around you. Consider if you are getting a variety of perspectives on your social media or if you mostly engage with content that supports your existing beliefs and interests.

Before you read, answer the **STRAP** questions to identify the main features of the reading.

Subject: What is the specific topic of the reading?
Type: What form (*opinion article, narrative, news story*) does the reading take?
Role: What position (*web designer, professor*) does the writer assume?
Audience: Who is the intended audience (*social media users, students, scientists*)?
Purpose: What is the goal of the reading (*to argue* or *to entertain*)?

Reading and Rereading

As you read, try to follow the argument's development—main claim, supporting claims, and evidence. Also, try to identify the type of evidence that the writer uses most—observations, facts and statistics, explanations, etc. (See **Section 10.1**.) Reread any parts as needed.

The Reading Process

Prereading   Rereading

Reading   Reflecting

The Problems of the Social Media Echo Chamber

Where do you get your news and information around the world? By now, the 1
ideal dream of consuming a wide array of sources to understand a range of opinions
and cultures should have been fully realized.

So why does it feel like we are soaking up an ever-narrower range of 2 information? Why does it feel like every news story out there, and every response to it, perfectly matches our own **prejudices**?

Blame the Internet. More specifically, blame social media and the echo chambers that we have built inside them.

In the mid-1990s, the promise of the early Internet was to connect **divergent** communities from across the world—to surface the kinds of events and opinions that, though we may find challenging, would yield greater global understanding.

At the time, *The Hitchhiker's Guide to the Galaxy* author Douglas Adams wrote of his hope that this "**fourth wall**" of separation would come crashing down as we shared in online communities, forcing us mere "villagers" out to mingle in the whole wide world.

Bitterly, what is transpiring is the opposite. In Facebook, Twitter, and others, by connecting with our existing friends and by following our preferred information sources, we have only replicated our old villages. We have recreated our online communities in the image of our old worlds. . . .

Case in point: Having spent the majority of the **U.K.'s European Union referendum** campaign away from my homeland, my primary experience of the debate was **mediated** through my friends and the content they shared through Facebook. Such was the expression of support to remain that I had expected the outcome to be a walkover. So I was **flabbergasted**, on my return on results day, to find that the U.K. had voted the opposite way.

I had become just the latest victim of the big Facebook filter bubble. We surround ourselves with like-minded friends, they post the news content they feel **validates** their opinion and, **insidiously**, this becomes the lens through which we each view the world.

It didn't used to be this way. Once upon a time, we flipped through the pages of a newspaper or watched the nightly newscast specifically to discover what we didn't yet know about the world. But the past couple of years have seen a destructive inversion of this cycle, leading us only to learn what we choose—and, more often than not, what we know to justify our **preconception**.

Thanks to this social echo chamber, we are approaching a consequence at a dangerous **precipice**. How can we learn what is new in politics or culture when we

3

4

5

6

7

8

9

10

only choose to read news reports aligned with our existing views, or those shared by the friends whose world view matches our own?

Technology has created this problem. Now it is technology's duty to help.   *11*

Of course, social bubbles can be a good thing. When I endured a family   *12*
tragedy a couple of years back, for instance, it was much easier to post news and arrangements to my Facebook family network than to buy ads in the local newspaper.

The problem with technology today, however, is that **algorithms** amplify the   *13*
bubble—tracking systems identify where we go, analyze what we like, and simply serve us back more of the same. . . .

That's why, as the cure to the filter bubble problem, I am proposing a reverse   *14*
recommendation algorithm.

Imagine if, after reading consecutive posts about a presidential candidate,   *15*
your network purposely served you articles about his or her opponent instead. Wouldn't you get a rounder view of the whole presidential campaign?

This is the content equivalent of Amazon, where at the bottom of a product   *16*
page for running sneakers, you'll be served an inverse recommendation of a walking stick.

The world badly needs to develop ways of taking its inhabitants outside of   *17*
their comfort zones, to make good on the promise of the Internet to foster not enhanced tribal differences, but greater global understanding.

We need to train technology toward helping us challenge, not reinforce,   *18*
our own perceptions of the world daily. That could involve awarding points for exposure to **contrary** or alternative viewpoints, for example. After all, everyone likes discovering something new, something different—the tastemakers who introduce new material to a network are often the ones who walk away with most **social currency**.

The future was in sight once. Now we badly need to burst the bubble, knock   *19*
down the walls and link arms across the info waves.

Reprinted by permission of Vincent Gibson. Originally appeared online at *Adweek* on August 11, 2016

---

prejudices
personally held feelings or opinions formed without full knowledge, thought, or reason

divergent
far away; different

fourth wall
the invisible, imagined wall that separates users of the Internet

U.K.'s European Union referendum
the United Kingdom's vote to break away from the European Union

mediated
conveyed or filtered

flabbergasted
surprised

insidiously
to act in a misleading way

preconception
an idea or opinion formed without evidence

precipice
a tall cliff

algorithms
a computer code or program based on a step-by-step procedure for a targeted purpose

contrary
an opposite

social currency
the resources and abilities that come from offline or online networks and communities

Reflecting

Answer the comprehension and vocabulary questions about the reading.

1. What pattern of organization does the article follow?
   a. Chronological
   b. Comparison
   c. Problem-solution

2. What main claim does the author make?
   a. A solution is needed for the echo chamber created by social media that restricts users' world views to like-minded people, opinions, and preferred news sources.
   b. Social media bubbles can be a good thing.
   c. Using social media leads to greater global understanding because it breaks down communication barriers.

3. What solution does the author propose to minimize social-media echo chambers?
   a. A reverse recommendation algorithm
   b. Quitting social media
   c. A ban of social media

4. In what paragraph does the author make a concession to his argument?
   a. Paragraph 8
   b. Paragraph 12
   c. Paragraph 10

5. Study how the word *validates* is used in the reading, and then choose the most accurate definition of the word.
   Validates (paragraph 8)
   a. Doubts
   b. Confirms
   c. Reverses

Summarizing

Write a summary of "The Problems of the Social Media Echo Chamber."

Critical Thinking

- In paragraph 6, the author says social media "replicates our old villages." What does this phrase mean, and how does it support his argument?
- Did you find the author's argument convincing? What about his solution?
- Do your own social media habits support or oppose the author's argument? How so?
- What other solutions are there to the social media echo chamber?

Writing for Enrichment

Choose one of the following writing ideas, or decide upon an idea of your own related to the reading.

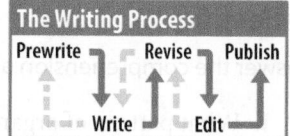

The Writing Process

1. Write a personal blog post or journal entry in which you explore the value (or lack thereof) of social media. Support your opinion with effective details.

2. Develop an argument about one specific social media app or website. Write an essay that develops a main claim and supports it with supporting details and evidence.

3. Write an argument essay that counters an argument made in one of the example essays in this chapter.

When planning . . .

- Choose a debatable topic and carry out your initial research.
- Establish a main claim for your essay. (See Section 10.1.)
- Gather reasons and evidence to support your claim.
- Decide on the best order for this information.

When writing . . .

- Develop opening, middle, and closing parts.
- Explain or develop each of your reasons with strong evidence.
- If necessary, consider key counterarguments. (See Section 10.1.)

When revising and editing . . .

- Predict key questions readers may have about your topic and claim, and make sure your essay answers them.
- Revise and edit your writing for content, style, and correctness. (See Sections 10.5 and 10.6 for checklists.)

Part 4:

Research

sollia, 2017 / Used under license from Shutterstock.com

Part 4: Research

pisaphotography, 2017 / Used under license from Shutterstock.com

Chapter

11

Understanding Research

Who actually conducts research? The simple answer is that everyone does. You may have reviewed reports about the latest smartphones before buying one. Or you might study different careers before choosing a college major. Or you may talk to experienced travelers before planning a trip. An academic research project is a similar process, though it follows guidelines and time lines established by your instructor and your field of study.

In this chapter, you will learn about a key aspect of the research process—using outside sources of information. The knowledge that you gain in this chapter will help you conduct effective research and write effective research reports.

Chapter Outline

- Understanding Sources of Information
- Evaluating Sources of Information
- Citing Sources of Information
- Avoiding Plagiarism
- Understanding Summarizing, Paraphrasing, and Quoting

11.1 Understanding Sources of Information

Sources of information fall into two general categories: primary sources and secondary sources.

Primary Sources

Primary sources are sources of facts that you collect through firsthand experiences. They involve you directly in the topic of your research. The following activities are examples that involve primary sources:

- Conducting interviews and surveys
- Doing experiments or other hands-on activities
- Observing events
- Attending presentations (art exhibits, museum displays, political speeches)
- Studying original documents (court records, letters, journals, diaries)

Secondary Sources

Secondary sources provide information that you collect indirectly, through the efforts and perspectives of other people. What follows is a list of secondary sources:

- Reference works
- Nonfiction books
- Periodicals (magazines and journals)
- Newspapers
- Websites
- Documentaries

Using Primary Sources

Primary sources are useful for gaining direct, firsthand information on a topic from sources close to the issue or question.

Conducting Interviews

During an interview you either (1) talk in person with an expert who knows about your topic, (2) communicate with that person in real time by phone or Internet connection, or (3) email questions you would like answered by the person.

> **Advantage:** Interviewing allows you to learn about your topic from an expert.
>
> **Disadvantage:** Interviewing requires more time than many other sorts of research, from contacting possible interviewees, to scheduling and conducting the interview, to recording and transcribing responses.

When conducting an interview, follow these guidelines:

1. **Schedule the interview**—in person, by phone, or online.
2. **Prepare a list of important questions.** Arrange them in a sensible order.
3. **Be polite** during the interview.
4. **Give background information** about yourself and your research.
5. **Listen carefully** to the person's answers and write them down or record them (with permission from the interviewee).
6. **Be prepared to reword a question** or to ask follow-up questions to get the information you need.
7. **Thank the person** for their help.
8. **Review your notes,** and contact the person to clarify anything you are unsure about.

Making Observations

Some topics can be studied by watching people, places, events, and things in action. Observations can help you formulate and test concepts, ideas, or theories related to the topic.

Advantage: Making observations allows you to experience your topic for yourself.

Disadvantage: Depending on the topic, it may be difficult to schedule or carry out an observation. Also, if you miss a detail, that moment cannot be recaptured.

When making an observation, follow these guidelines:

1. **Know what you want to accomplish**—your goal.
2. **Learn about your topic** before you observe it.
3. **Get permission to observe** if a location or an event isn't open to the public.
4. **Come prepared with the proper equipment**—pens, notebook, camera.
5. **Record sights and sounds** as you experience them.
6. **Review your notes** carefully to determine what you have learned.

Using Secondary Sources

Most of your research will deal with secondary sources. Information from secondary sources is one step removed from the origin. As such, it may offer quality information on your research topic based on expert perspectives and analysis by other people. Reference works, nonfiction books, periodical articles, and websites are the common types of secondary sources you will use.

Reference Works (Print and Digital)

Reference works are general sources of information, and they are available to you in print and online. Common reference books include encyclopedias, atlases, and almanacs.

Advantage: Most reference works serve as a trustworthy starting point for research.

Disadvantage: Reference works often contain only general information (two steps removed from primary sources), and they may not include the most recent knowledge on a subject. For some digital reference resources (*Wikipedia*, for instance), the quality and completeness of some entries may vary.

When using reference works, follow these guidelines:

1. **Learn about the structure of the reference.** Check the table of contents and index, and read the introductory material. Study help pages and tools. These will reveal how best to explore and document the work.

2. **Understand what the reference covers.** Also, think about what types of details it does not include.

3. **Use precise words in searches.** For example, the word "vegetarian" will lead to different information than the word "vegan" will.

4. **Take careful notes on your reading,** being sure to accurately record the information and details of how to document it.

5. **Refer to these notes during your further research** to remind yourself what you have learned and what you still need to find out.

6. **Look for clues to further research.** Reference works often provide citations and links to other secondary sources that will provide more depth on your topic.

Nonfiction Books

Nonfiction books traditionally have been a main source of information in college-level research projects. Your school's library likely gives you access not only to print books but also to ebooks through digital databases.

Advantage: Nonfiction books usually provide far more information about a topic than you will find in reference works.

Disadvantage: Books may not be as up-to-date as other sources. Also, not every author is a recognized authority in your field of study. Choose your books wisely.

When using nonfiction books, follow these guidelines:

1. **Look at the book's table of contents** to get an overall sense of the content.

2. **Use the reading process** to fully understand the text.

3. **Take careful notes,** using a proven strategy.

4. **Identify the source** of your notes (title and author) and the page numbers of the information.

5. **Use quotation marks** to enclose words and ideas taken directly from the text.

6. **Refer to the notes as a reminder** during your further research.

Periodicals (Print and Digital)

Periodicals are newspapers, magazines, and journals that are published on a regular basis (daily, weekly, monthly, or quarterly). Newspapers and news sites typically focus on the day's main news events. Magazines usually focus on general areas of interest. Journals usually address professional areas of study.

Advantage: Periodicals provide recent information on a topic.

Disadvantage: Information in periodicals may be as yet unproven or under debate. News stories, for example, may not be accurate and may even be fake news. Magazine articles may be written by people who are not true experts in the field, while journal articles may be written in a scholarly style that is challenging to understand.

When using periodicals, follow these guidelines:

1. **Learn about the periodical**—its purpose, structure, and features.
2. **Use the reading process** to fully understand the text.
3. **Take careful notes,** using a proven strategy.
4. **Identify the source of your notes**—the title and author of the article, page number, title of the periodical, volume number, and date.
5. **Use quotation marks to enclose** the exact words that you record.
6. **Refer to the notes as a reminder** of what you have learned and what research questions remain unanswered.

With so many periodicals available, it can be a challenge to find the most helpful articles. To get started, learn about the search tools your library offers.

Your library may subscribe to EBSCOhost, Lexis-Nexis, or another database service. Review the keyword search instructions for your service to find the best articles on your topic. When you locate promising articles, you may be able to print them, save them, or email them to yourself. If not, look for a print version. Check with your instructor or a librarian for help.

Websites

The Internet with its wealth of information will probably be one of the first places you turn to for beginning your research. Just make sure that it isn't the only place you turn to. Your instructors may, in fact, limit the number of Internet sources you can cite in your research.

Advantage: The Internet provides a vast amount of information that is easy to access.

Disadvantage: The information load can be overwhelming, some sites are unreliable sources, and it's easy to get distracted as you browse the Web.

When using the Internet for research, follow these guidelines:

1. **Check with a librarian** for special online searching options, such as the Library of Congress, EBSCOhost (a database of newspapers, magazines, and journals), and national and state government sites.
2. **Know the basics of Internet searching.** Check each site for its keyword guidelines.
3. **Review a number of choices** before deciding which ones to use. Finding good information takes time.
4. **Check the reliability** of sites that interest you.
5. **Take careful notes** or annotate copies of the information.
6. **Identify the key source of your information**—title of the article or Web page, author, name of the website, date of posting, and Web address.
7. **Refer to your notes often** as a reminder of what you have learned and what questions remain unanswered.

A Guide to Keyword Searching

The success of your Internet search depends on your understanding of search tools and the quality of the keywords you use. Although search sites are becoming more predictive of your intent, simple changes to a keyword can often provide very different results. (See Table 11.1.) Follow these guidelines for keyword searching:

1. Start by typing in your topic: *salmon, robotics.*
2. Add a word to call up pages containing any of the words: *wild salmon, home robotics.*
3. Enclose the phrase in quotation marks to call up just the pages containing that phrase: *"wild salmon."*
4. Use words such as *and* (+) or *not* (-) to narrow or focus your search: *salmon and harvesting* or *salmon not farmed.*
5. Experiment with word order to receive different results: *home robotics* versus *robotics home.*

Table 11.1 Boolean Operators: Special Search Functions

salmon **and** fishing	*and* indicates sites with both terms
salmon + fishing	+ indicates sites with both terms
salmon **not** fishing	*not* indicates sites with the first term but not the second
salmon – fishing	– indicates sites with the first term but not the second
salmon **or** fishing	*or* indicates sites with either term

11.2 Evaluating Sources of Information

When you conduct research, be sure that your sources are reliable and trustworthy. The following information will help you check sources for reliability.

Experts and Other Primary Sources

- Before deciding to interview an "expert," learn about the person. Does the interviewee have the education and experience to be an expert? Research the source's biography and other experts' opinions of the person. During an interview, consider the quality and depth of the person's responses.

Books and Other Print Materials

- When selecting print material, also learn about the author. Does the author have the proper background for the subject? Check the material's publisher and the date of publication to make sure that the information comes from a reputable source and is current. As you read, decide if the information seems fair and balanced and raises no questions about its reliability. Checking with other sources will help you do this.

Telecasts and Broadcasts

- When considering a TV special, radio program, or podcast, be aware that it may address a topic unfairly. Documentaries and straight news reports are generally more reliable than talk-radio conversations. Always consider the show's intended audience, its sponsors, and the particular broadcaster's approach to news and current events.

Websites

- Be sure that the author of a site (if identified) is respected in the field by learning what you can about the person's credentials (education, connection to the topic). Also check the type of site; government (.gov), education (.edu), and nonprofit (.org) sites often are more reliable than commercial (.com) sites. In addition, determine if the site presents current information that seems balanced and accurate. If you have questions about a site, check the information against other sources.

  The quality of a website's design is another clue for determining its reliability. A professional, error-free text with effective graphics is a good sign. Sites with poor design features, many grammatical errors, and broken links signal problems.

Insight   While wikis like *Wikipedia* can be a quick way to learn the basics of a topic and discover links to other sources, wiki entries are often incomplete or even subject to the original author's biases. For these reasons, they are not respected sources for a scholarly research paper.

11.3 Citing Sources of Information

You must give credit to the sources of ideas or words that you use in your academic essays and reports. Doing so avoids **plagiarism**, which is using the words and thoughts of others without crediting them in your writing.

Academic research uses a number of different styles for citing sources. For example, the **Modern Language Association (MLA) style** is generally used for research in the humanities (literature, philosophy, art history), and the **American Psychological Association (APA) style** is generally used for research in the social sciences (sociology, psychology, political science). Check with your instructor before choosing a citation style.

Insight *Plagiarism* is a serious offense that can damage your reputation. Penalties for plagiarism vary but can range from having a research paper rejected to losing financial aid to being dismissed from a university.

Table 11.2 shows the basic guidelines for using the MLA and APA styles for crediting sources in the text of a research report.

Table 11.2 MLA and APA Guidelines

Sources	MLA	APA
Work with one author	*Author last name and page number* (Waye 27)	*Author last name, year of publication, and page number* (Waye, 2008, p. 27)
Work with two authors	(Waye and Joniz 27)	(Waye & Joniz, 2008, p. 27)
Work with three or more authors	(Waye et al. 27)	(Waye et al., 2008, p. 27)
Author identified within the sentence	According to Mariah Waye, fishery expert, wild salmon need human help (27).	According to Mariah Waye (2008), fishery expert, wild salmon need human help (p. 27).
Work with no author specified	*First main word(s) of the title and page number* ("Salmon in Crisis" 27)	*First main word(s) of the title, date, and page number.* ("Salmon in Crisis," 2008, p. 27)
Work with no page number specified (as in a Web page)	*Author name only (or first main word[s] of title if no author is specified)* (Waye)	*Author name (or first main word[s] of title if no author is specified) and date* (Waye, 2008)

Using In-Text Citations

You can learn more about basic documentation by studying the following passages from a research report, demonstrating first the MLA style and then the APA style.

MLA Style

Source is cited in the sentence. → According to the Consumer Product Safety Commission, almost 25,000 children are treated in hospital emergency rooms each year as a result of shopping-cart injuries. New cart safety standards were implemented in 2004, but in the seven years that followed, the annual number of

Title only; this website names no author or page numbers → concussions in children jumped by 90 percent ("Shopping Cart Danger").

B. Potential Injuries

Shopping-cart injuries include cuts, bruises, fractures, internal injuries, and head injuries—even skull fractures. In fact, children have

Four authors, with page number → died as a result of shopping-cart falls (Smith et al. 161). For the sake of our customers, Jonesville Home Mart needs to take steps to ensure shopping-cart safety.

C. Solutions

A solution to this problem comes from a sister store in Anchorage,

Single author, with page number → which has made safety its motto (Clepper 47). Like this store, Jonesville . . .

APA Style

Online material with no page numbers specified → According to the Consumer Product Safety Commission (2009), almost 25,000 children are treated in hospital emergency rooms each year as a result of shopping-cart injuries. New cart safety standards were implemented in 2004, but in the seven years that followed, the annual number of concussions in children jumped by 90 percent ("Shopping Cart Danger," 2014).

B. Potential Injuries

Shopping-cart injuries include cuts, bruises, fractures, internal injuries, and head injuries—even skull fractures. In fact, children have

Four authors, with year and page number → died as a result of shopping-cart falls (Smith et al., 2010, p. 161). For the sake of our customers, Jonesville Home Mart needs to take steps to ensure shopping-cart safety.

C. Solutions

A solution to this problem comes from a sister store in Anchorage,

Single author, with year and page number → which has made safety its motto (Clepper, 2010, p. 47). Like this store, Jonesville . . .

Creating a Source List

At the end of your report, you must list your sources—either a **works-cited list** (MLA) or a **references list** (APA)—so that your reader can locate them. Table 11.3 shows the differences between the styles. In both the MLA and APA formats, any source listed must also be cited in your paper, and any source cited in your paper must appear in the source list. The exception, in APA format, is personal communication such as interviews and email, which should be cited in text but not included in the references list.

Whether your sources are books, magazine articles, podcasts, or websites, the citations should include all of the following elements that are available:

1. **Author name(s)**
2. **Title of the source** (e.g., a whole book, an essay or other text within a book, a periodical article, a Web page, a film, an episode of a TV program)
3. **Publication facts**
   - **MLA:** Include as much detail about the container or containers in which the source is found (e.g., a book, a magazine, a journal, a website, or a database), the contributor (e.g., editors), the version (e.g., second edition), a number (e.g., volume and issue numbers for journals), the publisher, the publication date, and the location (where the source can be found; for example, the page numbers of a periodical or the digital object identifier (DOI) or URL of a website).
   - **APA:** Include the date and the publisher, or appropriate Web information, including the DOI, if available.

Table 11.3 MLA and APA Source List Differences

	Author	Title	Publication Facts
MLA	Give the name as it appears on the title page, last name first.	Capitalize all important words.	Place the date after the publication information but before any location information (e.g., page numbers, DOI—digital object identifier, or URL).
	Waye, Mariah S. *Environmental Watch: Salmon in Danger.* Pudding Press, 2010.		
APA	Use initials for the first and middle names.	Capitalize only the first word in a title, the first word in a subtitle, and any proper nouns. Capitalize titles of periodicals normally.	Place the date in parentheses after the author's name.
	Waye, M. S. (2010). *Environmental watch: Salmon in danger.* Pudding Press.		

MLA Style

Works Cited

Magazine article — Clepper, Irene. "Safety First: Alaska Retailer Attracts Customers with Safe-and-Sound Seminars." *Playthings*, vol. 97, 2010, pp. 46-47.

Web article — Consumer Product Safety Commission. "Shopping Cart Injuries: Victims 5 years old and younger." *CPSC*, 25 July 2012, www.cpsc.gov/Media/Documents/Research--Statistics/Injury-Statistics/Public-Facilities-and-Products/Shopping-Cart-Injuries-Victims-5-years-old-and-younger.

Book — Shelov, Steven P., ed. *Caring for Your Baby and Young Child: Birth to Age 5*. Bantam Books, 2009.

Web article — "Shopping Cart Danger: 66 Kids Hurt Every Day, Study Finds." *NBC News*, 22 Jan. 2014, www.nbcnews.com/health/health-news/shopping-cart-danger-66-kids-hurt-every-day-study-finds-n14026.

Article, four authors — Smith, Gary A., et al. "Injuries to Children Related to Shopping Carts." *Pediatrics*, vol. 97, 2010, pp. 161-65.

APA Style (for the same sources)

References

Magazine article — Clepper, I. (2010). Safety first: Alaska retailer attracts customers with safe-and-sound seminars. *Playthings, 97,* 46-47.

Web article — Consumer Product Safety Commission. (2012). *Shopping cart injuries: Victims 5 years old and younger.* Retrieved September 22, 2014, from https://www.cpsc.gov/Media/Documents/Research--Statistics/Injury-Statistics/Public-Facilities-and-Products/Shopping-Cart-Injuries-Victims-5-years-old-and-younger

Book — Shelov, S. P. (Ed.). (2009). *Caring for your baby and young child: Birth to age 5.* Bantam Books.

Web article — *Shopping cart danger: 66 kids hurt every day, study finds.* (2014, January 22). NBC News. Retrieved September 22, 2014, from https://www.nbcnews.com/health/health-news/shopping-cart-danger-66-kids-hurt-every-day-study-finds-n14026

Article, four authors — Smith, G. A., Dietrich, A., Garcia, T., & Shields, B. (2010). Injuries to children related to shopping carts. *Pediatrics, 97,* 161-165.

11.4 Avoiding Plagiarism

The following article and explanations demonstrate different types of plagiarism. Use this information as a guide to check your own work and to avoid plagiarizing the sources you've used.

People in Need

On a chilly February afternoon, an old man stands on a city sidewalk and leans against a fence. In his hands a sign reads: "Will work for food. Please help!" Imagine, for a moment, the life this man leads. He probably spends his days alone on the street begging for handouts and his nights searching for shelter from the cold. He has no job, no friends, and nowhere to turn.

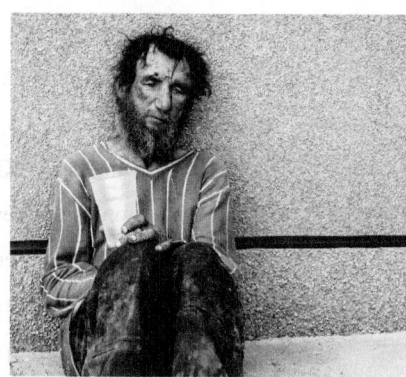

wrangler, 2014 / Used under license from Shutterstock.com

Most Americans would like to believe that cases like this are rare. However, the National Coalition for the Homeless estimates that as many as 3 million people in this country share this man's condition. Who are these people we call "the homeless," and what factors have contributed to their plight?

According to Pastor Joel Warren, the director of the Greater Mission Shelter in San Angela, most people experiencing homelessness are unemployed males, and from 40 to 60 percent have alcohol- or drug-related problems. Warren notes that the image of the typical person without permanent housing is changing. He says that the average age of a person experiencing homelessness has dropped from 55 to 30 in the last ten years. National studies have also shown that this population is changing.

A recent study by the United States Conference of Mayors found that one-third of people without permanent housing are families with small children, and 22 percent of this population have full- or part-time jobs. Statistics seem to show that more and more of the people experiencing homelessness are entire families who have simply become the victims of a bad economy.

Common Types of Plagiarism

The highlighted examples of plagiarism below are linked to the "People in Need" article from which the information was taken.

Copying Text Without Credit

Here the writer copies word-for-word from the original source without giving any credit.

It's not hard to imagine what life is like for a person experiencing homelessness. He probably spends his days alone on the street begging for handouts and his nights searching for shelter from the cold. He has no job, no friends, and nowhere to turn. Such a life is becoming all too familiar to many because of the poor economy.

Neglecting Quotation Marks

Here the writer credits the source but forgets to place quotation marks around exact words borrowed from it.

Many people have no real connection with a man experiencing homelessness like the one just described, and so they do not think much about this serious problem. In "People in Need," Anna Morales states that most Americans would like to believe that cases like this are rare. However, the National Coalition for the Homeless estimates that as many as 3 million people share this man's condition. Still, many of us seem to live in places far removed from people without permanent housing.

Paraphrasing Ideas Without Citing Them

Here the writer paraphrases information from a specific passage from an original article or book without identifying the source.

The economy has changed the profile of the population of people experiencing homelessness. Studies indicate that families with young children now make up more than 30 percent of this population. In addition, more and more people without permanent housing have part-time or full-time jobs.

Insight In addition to citing sources properly, it is important to use language free of bias. Avoid use of any language that demeans or discriminates, and strive to use accurate, inclusive language at all times. To do this, describe people and groups with an appropriate level of specificity and be sensitive to labels. See apastyle.apa.org for more information.

11.5 Summarizing, Paraphrasing, and Quoting

Summarizing, paraphrasing, and quoting are three main ways of incorporating sources in your writing.

Summarizing

A **summary** condenses a source to its most basic ideas while retaining their original order. It is usually no more than one-third the length of the original material. In a research paper, you might spend a few paragraphs summarizing a major resource. Review the example summary of this chapter:

> Kemper et al. say that everyone does research, whether comparing cell phones, evaluating college careers, planning a trip, or writing an academic research paper. Guidelines are provided to help you use sources in your research paper.
>
> Research resources can be either primary or secondary. Primary sources include interviews and personal observations. Using these requires careful planning but gives you direct access to information. Secondary sources include reference works, books, periodicals, and websites. Using these can save time, but they may be limited by someone else's purpose and understanding. You are responsible for evaluating the sources for accuracy and completeness.
>
> You must also cite your sources to avoid plagiarizing, which can damage your reputation and college career. Most college papers use either MLA or APA style. Working sources into your paper involves accurately summarizing, paraphrasing, and quoting (285–298).

Paraphrasing

A **paraphrase** restates an idea from a source in your own words. This both demonstrates your understanding of the material and restates the content to complement the voice of your paper and the flow of your ideas. Review the sample paraphrase of the previous sentences:

> Paraphrasing rephrases a source's thought in language you would normally use, to show your understanding and to suit your paper's voice and structure (Kemper et al. 298).

Quoting

Quotations add authority to your work by integrating the words of experts. But too many quotations can make a paper seem to be a patchwork of other people's ideas. Working a quotation into your writing smoothly may require replacing or leaving out some words. Take care that the results represent the original source accurately. Review an example quotation from this paragraph:

> Avoid having your paper seem a "patchwork of other people's ideas" from too many quotations (Kemper et al. 298).

Practice 11.1 Read the following excerpt and complete the bulleted activities. In each case, use MLA documentation style to give credit for the material you have borrowed.

- ■ Write a summary of the entire selection.
- ■ Choose one of the three paragraphs and write a paraphrase of it.
- ■ Write a personal response in which you incorporate a quotation from the selection.

This excerpt comes from a college textbook on health. It is part of a larger section dealing with proper use of prescription drugs.

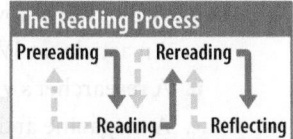

About the Author

Dianne Hales is an award-winning freelance journalist with writing credits in numerous national periodicals and more than a dozen published nonfiction books.

Drug Interactions

OTC [over the counter] and prescription drugs can interact in a variety of ways. For example, mixing some cold medications with tranquilizers can cause drowsiness and coordination problems, thus making driving dangerous. Moreover, what you eat or drink can impair or completely wipe out the effectiveness of drugs or lead to unexpected effects on the body. For instance, aspirin takes five to ten times as long to be absorbed when taken with food or shortly after a meal than when taken on an empty stomach. If **tetracyclines** encounter calcium in the stomach, they bind together and cancel each other out.

1

To avoid potentially dangerous interactions, check the label(s) for any instructions on how or when to take a medication, such as "with a meal." If the directions say that you should take a drug on an empty stomach, take it at least one hour before eating or two or three hours after eating. Don't drink a hot beverage with a medication; the temperature may interfere with the effectiveness of the drug.

2

Whenever you take a drug, be especially careful of your intake of alcohol, which can change the rate of metabolism and the effects of many different drugs. Because it dilates the blood vessels, alcohol can add to the dizziness sometimes caused by drugs for high blood pressure, angina, or depression. Also, its irritating effects on the stomach can worsen stomach upset from aspirin, ibuprofen, and other anti-inflammatory drugs.

3

From Hales, *An Invitation to Health*, 7E. © 2012 Cengage Learning

---

tetracyclines
a type of antibiotic

☑ Reviewing the Chapter

Chapter Review Quiz

Answer the questions about what you've learned in this chapter.

1. Which of the following is a primary source?
   a. An article on *Wikipedia* about the Chicago Bulls
   b. A researcher's visit to and observation of a rodeo
   c. A magazine article about bull riding

2. Which of the following is a secondary source?
   a. An email to a researcher from a city planner answering questions about condo development
   b. A city council meeting in which transportation expansion is debated
   c. A nonfiction book about megacities

3. Which of the following resources is typically good for basic information, but not for in-depth information about a topic?
   a. A journal article
   b. A reference work entry
   c. A nonfiction book

4. Which of the following is an advantage of Internet searching?
   a. Easy access to vast amounts of information
   b. Information overload
   c. Source unreliability

5. When evaluating sources for reliability, which of the following is *not* a key issue?
   a. The author or publisher's reputation and credentials
   b. The fairness and balance of the discussion
   c. The city where the source was published

6. Citing sources of information typically involves which two types of information?
   a. In-text citations within the paper and a source list at the end
   b. In-text citations within the paper and footnotes at the bottom of each page
   c. A source list at the beginning and numbered endnotes on the last page

7. Which of the following is plagiarism if it appears in a paper?
   a. Using the direct words of a source without quotation marks, but including an in-text citation
   b. Referencing a source without page numbers simply by its author
   c. Using many direct statements from sources within quotation marks, along with an in-text citation for each

12

Research Report

Everyone has at least one favorite pastime or interest. You may, for example, enjoy hair design and like learning and talking about the latest styles. Or you may follow the NASCAR circuit and enjoy keeping up with the latest standings and discussing them with friends. Then again, you may be attracted to music, movies, gaming, or working out. Your choices are endless.

Writing a research report is a similar experience: A topic interests you, and after learning enough about it, you share what you have learned. While the research described in the first paragraph may seem like pure enjoyment, you put effort into that learning. A research report rewards that same effort with a deeper understanding of the world around you.

In this chapter, you will read and react to a research report and then write one of your own. In the process, you will learn about a number of important strategies that will help you with research writing in all of your classes.

Chapter Outline

- Understanding a Research Assignment
- Learning Reading Strategies
- Reading and Reacting to a Research Report
- Planning a Research Report
- Writing a Research Report
- Revising and Editing a Research Report

12.1 Understanding a Research Assignment

When instructors ask you to write a research report, they are asking you to do two main things: (1) become knowledgeable about a topic and (2) share this information in a clear, organized paper.

A research report is a carefully planned form of informational writing, usually at least three double-spaced pages long. It cites information from reference works, books, periodicals, websites, interviews, or observations following MLA, APA, or another recognized documentation style. It may also include headings and graphics—charts, diagrams, maps, or photographs. Each instructor will have specific guidelines for researching your topic and compiling your report.

The Internet serves as an easy first source of information, giving you access to an unlimited number of resources almost immediately. Unfortunately, all of this information can overwhelm you and not all of it is reliable. Effective research requires the ability to narrow your choices by recognizing the difference between quality and questionable sources of information and then choosing those that best apply to your specific purpose. (See Chapter 11 for additional research tips.)

Since a research report is an extended writing assignment, it requires careful planning and patience. During the first part of the process, you need to learn as much as you can about your topic. During the second part, you need to plan and write your report. Finally, you need to leave enough time to carefully revise and edit your writing. Your instructor may provide a timetable for accomplishing your work; if not, you'll need to establish your own timetable for meeting your deadline.

Research Report Versus Research Paper

In a **research report**, you collect, organize, and compile information about a topic. You share important facts and details from multiple reliable sources in order to enhance or expand upon your own ideas.

In a **research paper**, you go further. You do the same amount of research, but you analyze the topic more deeply, perhaps even developing an argument about the topic in which you clarify your own thinking and take a position in a debate. In short, a research report shares information, and a research paper develops a more complex understanding or defends a point of view. You will write both reports and papers in your field of study during your college career.

Insight   Report writing is common not only in school but also in the workplace. Depending on your job, you may be asked to write an annual report, a marketing report, a budget report, or a safety report. These all require careful planning, research, and clear writing.

12.2 Learning Reading Strategies

Using an Organized List

The purpose of reading a report is to learn about a particular topic. Using an organized list is one strategy that will help you keep track of all the supporting information. Figure 12.1 shows how this simple strategy works.

Understanding the Writer's Approach

Research reports, always full of information, require careful reading. When reading a report, it may be helpful to understand the writer's basic approach. Often a writer presents information objectively, letting the facts and details speak for themselves. Sometimes a writer takes a subjective approach, including personal thoughts and feelings throughout. Objective reports are written in the third person (*he, she, it,* and *they*), subjective reports in the first person (*I, me,* and *we*). These two passages show the difference:

Figure 12.1 Organized List

Organized List

Report topic/thesis:

1. Main idea or topic sentence of the first middle paragraph
   + (Key supporting points)
   +
   +

2. Main idea or topic sentence of the second middle paragraph
   +
   +
   +

3. Main idea or topic sentence of the third middle paragraph

TIP: If needed, add another level of detail under the (+) key supporting points introduced by another symbol (-).

Objective: Squatters often live by simple, straightforward rules. They know that rule number one is keep the lights off to avoid being noticed. Rule number two is don't bother people when they are sleeping. Rule number three involves . . .

Subjective: I chose to investigate a funeral home to cure myself of the grim-reaper syndrome. When I walked inside Vander Furniture Store/Funeral Home, I half expected to see a well-dressed, evil individual standing by a counter, sharpening his sickle. . . .

Insight Writers who are especially involved in their research sometimes include subjective personal thoughts and feelings in their reports. Some such reports may seem more like personal stories. However, both the subjective and the objective report have their place and value.

12.3 Reading and Reacting to a Research Report

Read the following report that explores a new form of agriculture called vertical farming. The report follows MLA documentation style. Use the reading process to help you fully appreciate and understand the text and how it incorporates sources of information.

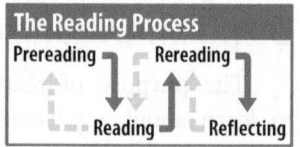

The Reading Process

Prereading · Rereading · Reading · Reflecting

Steifle 1

Maurice Steifle

Dr. Dakota Hinton

Life Sciences 101

19 February 2017

The title is centered.

Agriculture Must Grow Up

The opening paragraph includes a thesis statement.

Imagine living in the middle of New York City, right next to a farm. This farm is located in a skyscraper made of stacked greenhouses. And you can shop there for fresh fruits and vegetables. Does this sound unrealistic? It isn't. It's a real possibility, considering recent developments in agriculture. Vertical farms may be a main source of fresh food for city dwellers in the future.

An MLA paper is double spaced throughout.

A key spokesperson for vertical farming is Dickson Despommier, a professor at Columbia University in New York City. At *Verticalfarm.com*, he talks about new agricultural techniques. By 2050, 80 percent of all people will live in cities, and the world's population will have increased by 3 billion. To feed everyone will require a lot of new farmland. A logical solution is to farm vertically in urban areas, right where the food is needed. In his book *The Vertical Farm*, the professor proposes stacked greenhouses for growing food (Despommier 3-9).

Middle paragraphs give details to support the thesis statement.

1

2

Steifle 2

The *Economist* reports that vertical farming makes good
sense. First of all, vertical farms need no soil. Crops are grown
hydroponically, in a solution of essential minerals dissolved in water.
The roots of plants absorb nutrients directly from this liquid. Second,
since crops are grown in a controlled environment, few pesticides
or herbicides are needed. That's good news for the environment.
Third, everything is recycled, so vertical farming uses far less water
and nutrients than traditional farms use. Finally, vertical farms will
provide food to local areas, which saves on transportation costs
("Does It Really Stack Up?").

3

Two key technologies already exist for vertical farming—
greenhouses and hydroponics. *The Economist* mentions a number of
experiments already in place. For example, the South Pole Growth
Chamber is a semi-automated hydroponic facility that produces food
for scientists and technicians working in Antarctica. The Science
Barge in New York has also been growing food hydroponically ("Does
It Really Stack Up?"). Another example is Plantlab, a company in the
Netherlands that has grown strawberries, corn, and beans on three
floors, all underground (Kretschmer and Kollenberg).

4

Closer to home, Joe Heineman and Johanna Hearron-Heineman
have been growing butter lettuce on two floors of an old building in
Racine, Wisconsin. As the *Milwaukee Journal Sentinel* reports, the
couple uses treated wastewater from tilapia fish tanks to grow the
lettuce. In this building, they hope to produce the same amount of
lettuce that would take 40 acres of traditional farmland to grow. The

5

Text cues
indicate
where
borrowed
ideas begin.

In-text
citations
show the
sources of
borrowed
ideas.

Steifle 3

couple also wants to grow a half-million pounds of tomatoes in a
rooftop greenhouse (Herzog).

The idea of vertical farming on a grand scale, however, still   6
needs work. There are no stacked greenhouses yet, as Despommier
has envisioned them. As a matter of fact, environmental scientists
and engineers have serious questions about the efficiency of
vertical farming.

The exact words of a source are placed in quotation marks.

The Economist explains one main concern: "Light has to be   7
very tightly controlled to get uniform production of very high-
quality food," says British engineer Peter Head. Often this means
using expensive artificial light. Dr. Ted Caplow, a pioneer in rooftop
greenhouses, believes vertical farming will work only if it uses natural
light ("Does It Really Stack Up?"). Vertical farms also need power for
heating and cooling. In Racine, the Heinemans say that lighting and
temperature control are expensive. It costs 40 cents worth of electricity
for every head of lettuce, which sells for $1.50. Joe Heineman hopes
to cut this cost in half (Herzog). As it is, the electric bill for vertical
farming could wipe out the savings in transportation costs.

The Economist mentions ideas for addressing these concerns. In   8
single-story structures, for example, movable trays can give plants the
best exposure to natural and artificial light. The magazine also shares
Dr. Caplow's idea for farming in existing multistory buildings: "plants
growing around edges of the building, sandwiched between two glass
layers and rotating on a conveyor." Another idea is rooftop gardens,
which get the best natural light, as Peter Head explains. Members
of the Science Barge project have started a business to create a huge

Steifle 4

commercial rooftop farm in Queens, NY. Powered by solar panels, it will produce 30 tons of vegetables per year ("Does It Really Stack Up?").

The conclusion revisits the thesis statement.

Whether urban farming ultimately follows the Despommier model or takes some other form, it looks like it will become an important part of the urban landscape. What the pioneers in the field learn today may lead to multilevel, integrated systems that can feed large cities in a cost-effective way. Greenhouses may one day reach into the sky.

Steifle 5

Works Cited

A separate page lists works cited in the report.

Despommier, Dickson. *The Vertical Farm: Feeding the World in the 21st Century.* St. Martins, 2010.

---. "The Problem." *Verticalfarm.com*, verticalfarm.com.

"Does It Really Stack Up?" *The Economist*, 11 Dec. 2010, pp. 15-16.

Herzog, Karen. "Urban Farm in Racine Is No Fish Tale." *Milwaukee Journal Sentinel*, 15 July 2010, p. B3.

Sources are formatted with hanging indentation (all lines after the first are indented).

Kretschmer, Fabian, and Malte E. Kollenberg, "Can Urban Agriculture Feed a Hungry World?" *Spiegel Online*, 22 July 2011, spiegel.de/international/zeitgeist/vertical-farming-can-urban-agriculture-feed-a-hungry-world-a-775754.html.

Practice 12.1 Answer the comprehension and vocabulary questions about the reading.

1. What is the main purpose of this report on vertical farming?
   a. To entertain readers with stories about high-tech farming methods
   b. To inform readers about the possibilities of vertical farming in the future
   c. To persuade readers to invest in vertical farms

2. Which of the following is the best definition of *vertical farming*?
   a. A series of stacked greenhouses used for growing food
   b. Average people who live in apartments growing food on their balconies
   c. Techniques that allow farmers to grow crops on steep hillsides or mountain slopes

3. Which of the following sentences from the first paragraph is the thesis?
   a. Does this sound unrealistic? It isn't.
   b. Vertical farms may be a main source of fresh food for city dwellers in the future.
   c. Imagine living in the middle of New York City, right next to a farm.

4. In the second paragraph, why does the writer refer to Dickson Despommier?
   a. Despommier has created his own vertical farm.
   b. Despommier is a journalist who has researched and written stories about the agriculture industry.
   c. Despommier is a professor who has written an important book on vertical farming and established a website on the topic.

5. What does it mean to grow food *hydroponically*?
   a. Using electricity to stimulate the growth of plants within rich compost
   b. Growing plants in mineral-rich water rather than in soil
   c. Growing plants in planter beds on roof tops

6. Which of the following is *not* a reason that vertical farming makes good sense?
   a. Vertical farming uses carefully controlled lighting and temperature.
   b. Vertical farming uses no soil, as well as less herbicide, pesticide, and water than traditional farming.
   c. Vertical farming in cities would cut transportation costs for food.

7. In paragraphs 4-5, the writer lists several examples of farming experiments taken from three different sources. What do these examples add to the discussion of vertical farming?
   a. A sense that vertical farming is becoming a real possibility in many places around the world
   b. A sense that vertical farming faces some serious technological challenges
   c. A sense that vertical farming is being resisted by society, especially traditional farmers

12.4 Planning a Research Report

A research report requires a lot of planning, which takes time. You won't write an effective report if you wait until the last minute to start your work. Be sure to use the writing process to do your best work.

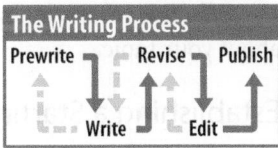

Scheduling Your Work

Follow the schedule or timetable that your instructor provides. If you must make your own schedule, use the timetable in **Figure 12.2** as a guide. It gives you approximately three weeks to complete the assignment, but you may adjust the schedule as necessary.

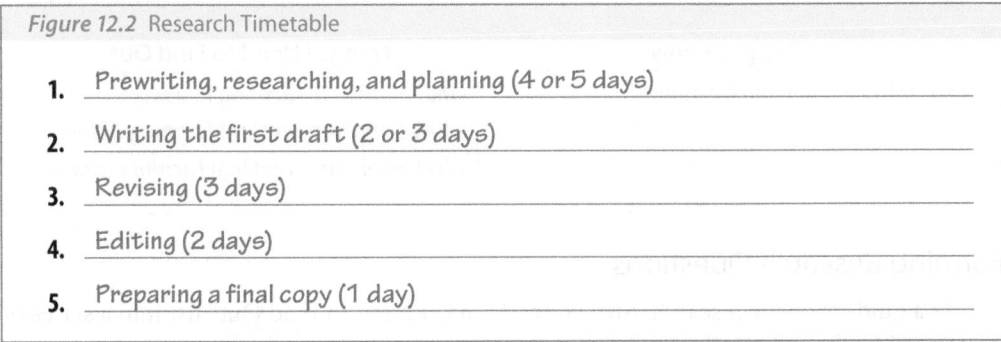

Figure 12.2 Research Timetable

1. Prewriting, researching, and planning (4 or 5 days)
2. Writing the first draft (2 or 3 days)
3. Revising (3 days)
4. Editing (2 days)
5. Preparing a final copy (1 day)

Planning a research paper, like any other project, involves predicting how long each step will take. You should also allow extra time for unforeseen problems.

To begin, mark your due date on the calendar. Then work backward, estimating the time needed for each step. If possible, also include a few days away from the paper between writing and revising to let yourself see it with fresh eyes. As you work, keep checking your schedule. If a step is running long, you will have to adjust later dates to compensate. If a step runs shorter than expected, you can do added research or more extended revising and editing.

Selecting a Topic

Write your report about a new trend or development in technology, culture, science, health, careers, or another topic that fits your instructor's guidelines.

Be sure that . . .

- the topic is well suited to your interests.
- the topic is neither too general nor too specific. (*Alternative energy sources* is too general; *biking to school* may be too specific.)
- you can find enough information about the topic.
- you have enough time to research and write about this topic.

Researching Your Topic

Effective research begins with questions that will guide you as you gather information about your topic.

Establishing a Starting Point

You can establish a starting point for your research by identifying what you already know about the topic and what you need to learn about it. Create a research chart like the one in Figure 12.3 to help you list what you know and what you need to find out.

Figure 12.3 Research Chart

Topic: Vertical Farming

Things I Know	Things I Need to Find Out
examples of vertical farming	where vertical farming is used
	what benefits vertical farming offers
	what problems vertical farming faces

Forming Research Questions

As a guide for your research, turn your "Things I Need to Find Out" list into a series of questions like the ones in Figure 12.4.

Figure 12.4 Research Questions

Where are vertical farms?
What are some benefits of vertical farming?
What are some problems or obstacles facing vertical farming?

Identifying Your Sources

Once you have formed a series of questions, you can begin your research to try to answer them. Always follow your instructor's guidelines for the number and types of resources to consult. Whether you refer to reference works, books, periodicals, or websites, determine first that your sources are current and reliable.

You can fill in a chart like the one in Figure 12.5 with sources of information that seem promising for your research. (You may or may not use all of the different types listed.) Include enough information—title, author, key page numbers, location, publisher—so that you can easily find or refer to each source. This list is often called a **preliminary bibliography**, because it functions as an early list of resources that you may need to include in your source list at the end of your actual paper.

Figure 12.5 Source List

Websites	
Articles (from reference works)	
Books	
People to interview	
Places to visit	

Taking Notes

As you read and learn about your topic, take notes on key points and record important quotations. No matter what form your notes take—notebook, electronic file—follow these guidelines.

- **Write your research questions at the top** of your notes.
- **Take notes on key information** that answers each question.
- **Use your own words,** except for direct quotations or special information.
- **Write the source and the page number** (if appropriate) of the information you record.

Sample Notes

③

Where is vertical farming being used?

- a modified farm in Racine (parts of two floors in an old building)
- Joe Heineman and Johanna Hearron-Heineman grow butter
  lettuce and raise tilapia.
- use treated fish water to nourish the lettuce (hydroponics)
- Joe: "We're a green business." "Water is a scarce resource, and
  we use a tenth of what soil-based farms use."

Karen Herzog, "Urban Farm in Racine Is No Fish Tale."
Milwaukee Journal Sentinel. July 15, 2010. B3.

Focusing Your Research

After gathering information, you are ready to form a thesis statement and organize your notes before you begin writing your report.

Writing a Thesis Statement

A thesis statement identifies the main idea of your report. It also determines the best way to organize the supporting information. This formula will help you write your thesis statement:

Topic		Main Idea About Topic		Thesis Statement
Vertical farming	+	main source of food for future cities	=	Vertical farms could be a main source of fresh food for city dwellers in the future.

Organizing Your Notes for Writing

Next, organize your notes into groups that deal with each main supporting point. The information in the vertical farming report was grouped into the following categories.

- spokesperson
- history
- advantages
- early experiments
- disadvantages
- alternatives

Creating an Outline

An outline serves as a blueprint for your report. It identifies the main ideas and details in the order that you want to include them in the body of your report. Outlines can be general or detailed, depending on your personal choice and your instructor's guidelines.

List your main ideas (categories) using Roman numerals (I, II, III), key supporting points using capital letters (A, B, C), and further details using numbers (1, 2, 3). Figure 12.6 shows the first part of an outline for the vertical farming report you read.

Figure 12.6 Research Report Outline

I. A key spokesperson—Dickson Despommier, a professor at Columbia (NY)

    A. Talks about the future of agriculture

        1. By 2050, 80% of people living in cities

        2. Three billion increase in world's population

        3. Will need a lot of new farmland

    B. Vertical farming a logical solution

        1. Hydroponics—no soil needed

        2. Controlled environment—fewer pesticides

12.5 Writing a Research Report

Writing your first draft allows you to connect all of your information and thoughts about the topic. You can improve your writing later during the revising and editing steps. At this stage, you should focus on organizing your ideas and information within the relevant paragraphs.

Creating an Opening Paragraph

Your opening paragraph should (1) gain the reader's interest, (2) introduce your topic, and (3) state your thesis. Here are three strategies for gaining the reader's interest:

- **Create an inviting image or mental picture:**

  Imagine living in the middle of New York City, right next to a farm. This farm is located in a skyscraper made of stacked greenhouses.

- **Make a dramatic statement:**

  By 2050, 80 percent of all people will live in cities, and the world's population will have increased by 3 billion (Despommier 3–9).

- **Ask an important question:**

  In the future, how will it be possible to feed our rapidly increasing world's population?

Developing the Middle Paragraphs

Your middle paragraphs must explain and develop your thesis. Use your outline and notes as a guide for writing these paragraphs. Here are a few additional tips:

- **Turn each main idea in your outline**—Roman numerals I, II, III—into a topic sentence.

  Main idea: Vertical farming is sensible.

  Topic sentence: *The Economist* reports that vertical farming makes good sense.

- **Develop each paragraph with the details under the main points** (A, B, C) in your outline and related details in your notes.
- **If a paragraph seems too long, separate the information into two paragraphs.**
- **Use your own words as much as possible,** and always give credit for borrowed information and ideas, whether they be summaries, paraphrases, or direct quotations from sources.
- **Be objective** unless your instructor allows you to include personal thoughts and feelings.

Integrating Quotations

Research reports may contain quotations to support but not replace the writer's own ideas. Remember, quotations are the exact words of a speaker or source. They must be set off with quotation marks. Here are a few strategies for integrating them, using examples from the report you read earlier:

- **Use quotations to back up a main point.**

    The magazine also shares Dr. Caplow's idea for farming in existing multistory buildings: "plants growing around the edges of the building, sandwiched between two glass layers and rotating on a conveyor." Another idea is rooftop gardens, which get the best natural light, as Peter Head explains.

- **Use quotations to add the thoughts of an expert.**

    The Economist explains one main concern: "Light has to be very tightly controlled to get uniform production of very high-quality food," says British engineer Peter Head. Often this means using expensive artificial light.

Writing a Closing Paragraph

The final paragraph should re-emphasize the main idea and leave the reader with a clear understanding of the importance of your topic. Here are three strategies for an effective ending. You can try out different combinations of the strategies to close out your own research report.

- **Restate and expand on the main point in your report:**

    Whether urban farming ultimately follows the Despommier model or takes some other form, it looks like it will become an important part of the urban landscape.

- **Emphasize the value or importance of the topic:**

    What the pioneers in the field learn today may lead to multilevel, integrated systems that can feed large cities in a cost-effective way.

- **Reconnect with the opening:**

    Greenhouses may one day reach into the sky.

12.6 Revising and Editing a Research Report

Make sure to leave plenty of time to revise and edit your report so you can strengthen your ideas, correct your citations, and submit a clean copy of your report to your instructor.

Revising

Revising the first draft involves adding, deleting, rearranging, and reworking parts of your report. Revision can begin with a peer review, where you share your draft with a trusted classmate or peer for feedback. Besides asking a classmate to review your report, you need to carry out a careful review of your own. These reminders will help you improve the ideas, organization, voice, and coherence of your writing.

Ideas

- **Read your report from start to finish.** This will give you an overall sense of your writing.
- **If you had a peer review your work, compare your first impressions against your classmate's comments.** How are they similar? Different?

Organization

- **Consider your beginning.** Does it gain the reader's attention, introduce your topic, and state your thesis (the main idea of your report)?
- **Review your middle paragraphs.** Do they support or explain your thesis, and are they arranged in a logical order?
- **Consider your closing.** Does it provide important final ideas about your topic?

Voice and Coherence

- **Check your writing for voice.** Do you sound informed and interested in your topic?
- **Consider your reporting style.** Do you, for the most part, use your own words in your report?
- **Check for proper citation.** Have you followed an accepted documentation style to give credit to your sources? When you use exact quotations from a source, do you use quotation marks and a proper citation? When you paraphrase specific ideas from a source, do you include a citation?
- **Consider the flow of your ideas.** Does your draft read smoothly from start to finish?
- **Review your works-cited or references page.** Does it list the sources you have cited in your report following the proper documentation style?

Editing

After you finish revising, editing is the next step. When editing, you check your writing for style and correctness. These guidelines will help:

Sentences

- **Consider their readability.** Do your sentences read smoothly from one to the next? If not, are there opportunities to combine sentences or add transition words between key ideas?
- **Check them for variety.** Do your sentences start in different ways? Do they vary in length?
- **Consider their correctness.** Watch for fragments, run-ons, and comma splices. (See Chapter 16 for more help.)

Word Choice

- **Consider your nouns.** For the most part, do you use specific nouns like *Science Barge* and *Columbia University*?
- **Check your verbs.** Do you avoid the "be" verbs *(is, are, was,* and *were)* in most of your sentences, choosing active verbs like *imagine* and *absorb*?

Conventions

- **Check for correct verb forms.** For example, use *he saw,* not *he seen; she brought,* not *she brung.*
- **Consider subject-verb agreement.** For example, use *she speaks,* not *she speak* and *they travel,* not *they travels.*
- **Check for commonly misused words.** For example, use *their, there, they're; your, you're;* and *it's, its* correctly.
- **Look for capitalization problems.** Capitalize the first words of sentences and quotations as well as specific names.
- **Check for punctuation problems.** Use correct end punctuation after sentences, commas in compound sentences, and apostrophes to show possession, for example.
- **Carefully check citations.** Follow the correct documentation style, including proper capitalization and punctuation, when citing sources in your report (within the text and at the end). Make sure you know what documentation style your instructor wants you to follow. Check online for the most updated guidelines for the citation style.

Editing a Report

Practice 12.2 Fix the capitalization errors, agreement errors, and misused words (*their, there, they're*) in the following excerpt from a research report that follows MLA style. Mark changes with the correction symbols shown. *Hint:* There are two capitalization errors, three subject-verb agreement errors, and three misused words.

Wolves in Wisconsin

The gray wolf is one of the most controversial animal species in North America. in no state is this more evident than in Wisconsin. A great number of gray wolves roamed the northern woods of this state from the time of the retreating glaciers to the 1950s, when the wolf population all but disappeared. Today, however, gray wolves is back in Wisconsin. There return is an ecological triumph, but it also brings up old concerns. Hunters and farmers worry about the impact of wolves on deer populations and livestock, and state environmental officials says the wolf population is too large to manage. Decisions concerning these key issues will determine the future of gray wolves in Wisconsin ("Wolves").

Evidence of gray wolves (*Canis lupus*) in Wisconsin traces back 10,000 years. The wolves thrived in the thick forest habitat of northern Wisconsin, where retreating glaciers formed many lakes and streams. by the 1800s, their were believed to be between 3,000 and 5,000 wolves living in the state (Wydeven). Around this same time, many European settlers arrived in the area. Mostly hunters and farmers, they feared that the wolves would diminish the deer population and endanger their livestock. Consequently, Wisconsin passed bounty laws, which paid hunters up to $20 for every wolf killed ("Wolves"). Hundreds of wolves was killed, and the survivors took refuge in surrounding states. By 1960, they're were no gray wolves in Wisconsin ("Wolves").

Correction Marks

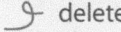 delete

$\overset{word}{\wedge}$ capitalize

$\overset{d}{\underline{\underline{\ }}}$ add word

☑ Reviewing the Chapter

Chapter Review Quiz

Answer the questions about what you've learned in this chapter.

1. What is the main purpose of a research report?
    a. To persuade
    b. To entertain
    c. To inform

2. Which statement best describes how a research paper is different from a research report?
    a. A research paper shares the writer's personal feelings about the topic.
    b. A research paper analyzes the topic deeply and may also take a position on it.
    c. A research paper is twice as long as a research report.

3. What does the phrase "documentation guidelines" mean?
    a. The rules and procedures that students should follow to submit their research reports to their instructors
    b. The note-taking system that students must follow when doing research
    c. The rules to follow for giving credit for material borrowed from other sources within a report

4. In report writing, what are citations?
    a. Penalties that the instructor assigns to the grade for errors made
    b. In-text details that identify the sources referred to in the report
    c. Visuals and other graphics (tables, pie charts) incorporated into the report

5. When you are working on a research report, what are research questions?
    a. The questions about the topic that you want to answer through your research
    b. The questions that you need to ask a librarian if you get stuck
    c. The questions you should ask your instructor before you get started on your project

6. Which of the following strategies is a good approach for opening a research report?
    a. Supply lots of background information.
    b. Talk about how you went about doing the research for your report.
    c. Engage the reader with a dramatic statement.

Part 5:

Sentence Workshops

Part 5: Sentence Workshops

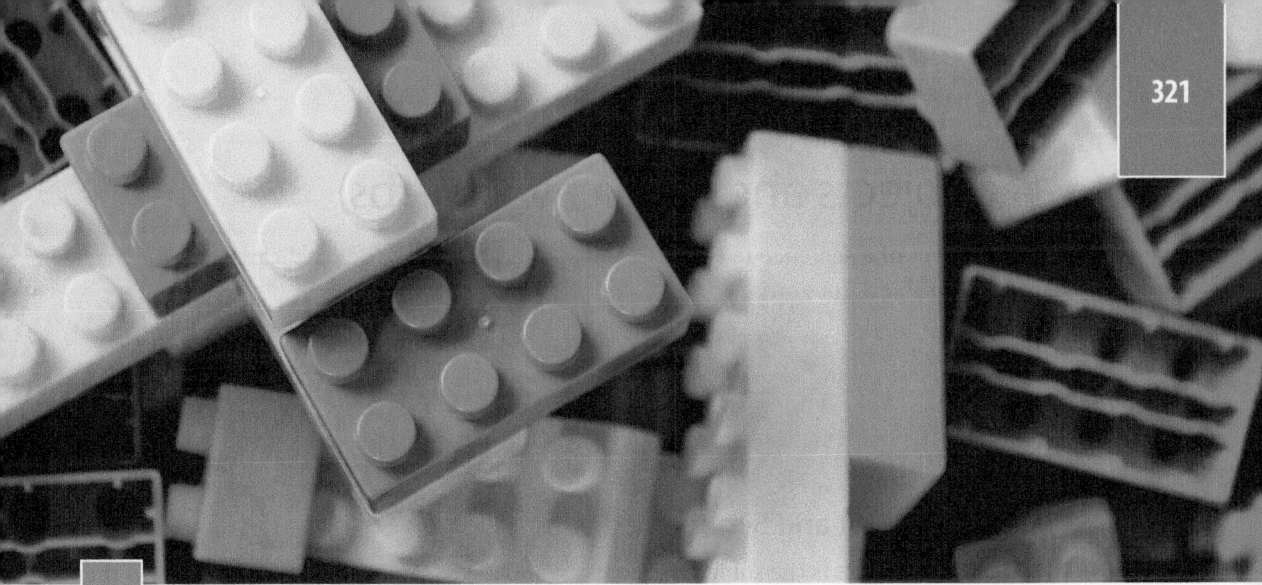

hxdbzxy, 2017 / Used under license from Shutterstock.com

13

Sentence Basics

Sentences are built from some very simple parts—nouns, verbs, and modifiers. Every sentence has, at its base, the pairing of a noun and a verb, or a few of them. The other words in the sentence merely modify the noun and verb.

These are sentence basics—the building blocks of thought. With these blocks, you can build tiny towers or magnificent mansions. It all comes down to understanding how to put the pieces together and deciding what you want to create.

Chapter Outline

- Subjects and Predicates (Verbs)
- Special Types of Subjects
- Special Types of Predicates
- Adjectives
- Adverbs
- Prepositional Phrases
- Clauses

13.1 Subjects and Predicates (Verbs)

The **subject** of a sentence tells what the sentence is about. The **predicate** of a sentence tells what the subject does or is.

Dogs bark.

Subject: what the   Predicate: what
sentence is about   the subject does

► Simple Subject and Simple Predicate

The **simple subject** is the subject without any modifiers, and the **simple predicate** is the verb and any helping verbs without modifiers or objects.

The black and white schnauzer was barking all day long.

simple subject   simple predicate

► Complete Subject and Complete Predicate

The **complete subject** is the subject with modifiers, and the **complete predicate** is the verb with modifiers and objects. **Modifiers** add information to the subject and predicate.

The black and white schnauzer was barking all day long.

complete subject   complete predicate

In this example, the words "black and white" modify, or give more information about, the schnauzer. The words "all day long" give more information about the simple predicate.

► Implied Subject

In commands, the subject *you* is implied. Commands are the only type of sentence in English that can have an **implied subject**.

(You)   Stop barking!

implied subject   complete predicate

► Inverted Order

Most often in English, the subject comes before the predicate. However, in questions and sentences that begin with *here* or *there*, the subject comes after the predicate.

subject   subject
Why are you so loud?   Here is a biscuit.

predicate   predicate

13.2 Special Types of Subjects

As you work with subjects, watch for these special types.

▶ Compound Subjects

A **compound subject** is two or more subjects connected by *and* or *or*.

My <u>sister</u> and <u>I</u> swim well. <u>Terri, Josh,</u> or <u>I</u> will dive.
      compound subject   compound subject

▶ Infinitives as Subjects

An **infinitive** can function as a subject. An infinitive is a verb form that begins with *to* and may be followed by objects or modifiers.

<u>To become a park ranger</u> is my dream.
     infinitive subject with modifiers

▶ Gerunds as Subjects

A **gerund** can function as a subject. A gerund is a verb form that ends in *ing* and may be followed by objects or modifiers.

<u>Hiking</u> builds strong calves.   <u>Hiking the Appalachian trail</u> is amazing.
gerund subject   gerund subject with modifiers

▶ Noun Clauses as Subjects

A **noun clause** can function as a subject. The clause itself has a subject and a verb but cannot stand alone as a sentence. Noun clauses are introduced by words like *what, that, when, why, how, whatever, whoever,* or *whichever.*

<u>Whoever hikes the trail</u> should bring replacement boots.
     noun clause subject

<u>Whatever you need</u> must be carried on your back.
     noun clause subject

Insight   Note that each of these special subjects functions as a noun. A sentence is still, at root, the connection between a noun and a verb.

Practice 13.1 For the following sentences, identify the underlined word or words as the simple subject, complete subject, simple predicate, or complete predicate.

1. For thousands of years, humans <u>bred</u> dogs.
   - a. Simple subject
   - b. Complete subject
   - c. Simple predicate
   - d. Complete predicate

2. <u>All dog breeds</u> descended from wolf ancestors.
   - a. Simple subject
   - b. Complete subject
   - c. Simple predicate
   - d. Complete predicate

3. At the end of the Ice Age, humans <u>lived nomadically with their dogs</u>.
   - a. Simple subject
   - b. Complete subject
   - c. Simple predicate
   - d. Complete predicate

4. Ever since that time, <u>dogs</u> have enjoyed going for walks.
   - a. Simple subject
   - b. Complete subject
   - c. Simple predicate
   - d. Complete predicate

5. Why <u>are</u> dogs so popular in Ireland?
   - a. Simple subject
   - b. Complete subject
   - c. Simple predicate
   - d. Complete predicate

Practice 13.2 For the following sentences, identify the underlined subject as a compound subject, infinitive, gerund, or noun clause.

1. <u>You and I</u> should go hiking sometime.
   - a. Compound subject
   - b. Infinitive
   - c. Gerund
   - d. Noun clause

2. <u>To reach the peak of Mount Rainier</u> would be amazing.
   - a. Compound subject
   - b. Infinitive
   - c. Gerund
   - d. Noun clause

3. <u>Whoever wants to go</u> should train with a mountaineer.
   - a. Compound subject
   - b. Infinitive
   - c. Gerund
   - d. Noun clause

4. <u>Hiking the Rockies at high altitudes</u> is challenging.
   - a. Compound subject
   - b. Infinitive
   - c. Gerund
   - d. Noun clause

5. <u>Whenever the snow arrives</u> is the time to descend.
   - a. Compound subject
   - b. Infinitive
   - c. Gerund
   - d. Noun clause

13.3 Special Types of Predicates

As you work with predicates, watch for these special types.

▶ Compound Predicates

A **compound predicate** consists of two or more verbs joined by *and* or *or*.

I <u>watched</u> and <u>laughed</u>. My cat <u>stalks, pounces, or tumbles</u>.
      compound predicate   compound predicate

▶ Predicates with Direct Objects

A **direct object** follows a transitive verb and tells what or who receives the action of the verb. A **transitive verb** is an action verb that transfers action to a direct object.

I pointed the <u>laser</u>. My cat saw the <u>spot</u>. He batted <u>it</u> and nipped the <u>ground</u>.
     direct object   direct object   direct object   direct object

▶ Predicates with Indirect Objects

An **indirect object** comes between a transitive verb and a direct object and tells to whom or for whom an action was done.

I gave <u>him</u> a rest. My cat shot <u>me</u> a puzzled look.
   indirect object   indirect object

▶ Passive Predicates (Verbs)

When a verb is **passive**, the subject of the sentence is being acted upon rather than acting. Often, the actor is the object of the **preposition** in a phrase that starts with *by*. To make the sentence **active**, rewrite it, turning the object of the preposition into the subject.

Passive

<u>My cat</u> <u>was exhausted</u> by the <u>game</u>.
subject   passive verb   object of the preposition

Active

The <u>game</u> <u>exhausted</u> <u>my cat</u>.
    subject   active verb   direct object

Practice 13.3 For the following sentences, identify the underlined word or words as a compound predicate, direct object, or indirect object.

1. Our pet rabbits <u>hopped and thumped</u>.
   a. Compound predicate
   b. Direct object
   c. Indirect object

2. The lop-ear leaped the <u>gate</u>.
   a. Compound predicate
   b. Direct object
   c. Indirect object

3. I gave <u>her</u> a carrot.
   a. Compound predicate
   b. Direct object
   c. Indirect object

4. She <u>crouched or nibbled</u>.
   a. Compound predicate
   b. Direct object
   c. Indirect object

5. Then she gave <u>my brother</u> a suspicious glance.
   a. Compound predicate
   b. Direct object
   c. Indirect object

Practice 13.4 Identify the predicates in the following sentences as active or passive.

1. My cat was mesmerized by the laser.
   a. Active
   b. Passive

2. The light danced in his paws.
   a. Active
   b. Passive

3. The light was chased up and down the hallway by my cat.
   a. Active
   b. Passive

4. The kittens are fed by my sister.
   a. Active
   b. Passive

5. They view my sister as a human vending machine.
   a. Active
   b. Passive

13.4 Adjectives

To modify a subject (noun), use an adjective. A word, phrase, or clause can act as an adjective. Adjectives answer these basic questions: *which? what kind of? how many? how much?*

To modify the noun athletes, ask . . .

Which athletes? ⟶	college athletes
What kind of athletes? ⟶	female athletes
How many athletes? ⟶	few athletes

few female college athletes

▶ ## Adjective Phrases and Clauses

A **phrase** is a group of words that lacks a subject or predicate or both. A **clause** is a group of words that has a subject and a predicate but does not form a complete sentence.

To modify the noun athletes, ask . . .

Which athletes? ⟶	athletes who are taking at least 12 credit hours
What kind of athletes? ⟶	athletes with a 3.0 average

The administration will approve loans for athletes with a 3.0 average who are taking at least 12 credit hours.

13.5 Adverbs

To modify a verb, use an adverb. A word, phrase, or clause can act as an adverb. Adverbs answer these basic questions: *how? when? where? why? how long? how often?*

To modify the verb dance, ask . . .

How did they dance? ⟶	danced happily
When did they dance? ⟶	danced yesterday
Where did they dance? ⟶	danced there
How often did they dance? ⟶	danced often

Yesterday, the bride and groom danced happily and often there in the ballroom.

▶ Adverb Phrases and Clauses

Below are some examples of phrases and clauses acting as adverbs to modify verbs.

To modify the verb dance, ask . . .

How did they dance? ⟶ danced with great joy

When did they dance? ⟶ danced from the first song

Where did they dance? ⟶ danced all around the room

Why did they dance? ⟶ danced to celebrate their wedding

How often did they dance? ⟶ danced until the last song

From the first song until the last song, the couple danced all around the room with great joy to celebrate their wedding.

Insight   Read the last sentence aloud. Though it may look imposing on the page, it sounds natural, probably because adverbs are a common part of our speech. Experiment with these modifiers in your writing as well.

Practice 13.5   Identify the underlined words as adjectives or adverbs.

1. Yesterday, the team won its <u>third</u> Division 1 <u>soccer</u> championship.
   a. Adjectives   b. Adverbs

2. <u>From the opening whistle</u>, the players played with <u>pride</u> and <u>passion</u>.
   a. Adjectives   b. Adverbs

3. Jill and Shaunda, in particular, handled the ball <u>skillfully</u> and <u>effectively</u>.
   a. Adjectives   b. Adverbs

4. Shaunda, <u>who is an all-league player</u>, kicked an <u>amazing opening</u> goal.
   a. Adjectives   b. Adverbs

5. <u>Early in the second half</u>, the opposing team tied the game <u>with a penalty kick</u>.
   a. Adjectives   b. Adverbs

6. <u>In the final minute</u>, Shaunda passed the ball <u>between a defender's legs</u> to Jill, who deflected it <u>into the corner of the net</u>.
   a. Adjectives   b. Adverbs

7. For the <u>third</u> year in a row, the team went home with a <u>gleaming gold</u> trophy.
   a. Adjectives   b. Adverbs

13.6 Prepositional Phrases

One of the simplest and most versatile types of phrases in English is the **prepositional phrase**. A prepositional phrase can function as an adjective or an adverb.

▶ Building Prepositional Phrases

A prepositional phrase is a preposition followed by an object (a noun or pronoun) and any modifiers.

Preposition	+	Object	=	Prepositional Phrase
at		noon		at noon
in		an hour		in an hour
beside		the green clock		beside the green clock
in front of		my aunt's vinyl purse		in front of my aunt's vinyl purse

As you can see, a propositional phrase can be just two words long or many words long. As you can also see, some prepositions are themselves made up of more than one word. Table 13.1 shows a list of common prepositions.

Table 13.1 Prepositions

aboard	back of	except for	near to	round
about	because of	excepting	notwithstanding	save
above	before	for	of	since
according to	behind	from	off	subsequent to
across	below	from among	on	through
across from	beneath	from between	on account of	throughout
after	beside	from under	on behalf of	'til
against	besides	in	onto	to
along	between	in addition to	on top of	together with
alongside	beyond	in behalf of	opposite	toward
alongside of	but	in front of	out	under
along with	by	in place of	out of	underneath
amid	by means of	in regard to	outside	until
among	concerning	inside	outside of	unto
apart from	considering	inside of	over	up
around	despite	in spite of	over to	upon
as far as	down	instead of	owing to	up to
aside from	down from	into	past	with
at	during	like	prior to	within
away from	except	near	regarding	without

Insight A preposition is pre-positioned before the other words it introduces to form a phrase. Other languages have post-positional words that follow their objects.

13.7 Clauses

A clause is a group of words with a subject and a predicate. If a clause can stand on its own as a sentence, it is an **independent clause**. If it cannot, it is a **dependent clause**.

▶ Independent Clause

An independent clause has a subject and a predicate and expresses a complete thought. It is the same as a simple sentence.

Clouds piled up in the stormy sky.

▶ Dependent Clause

A dependent clause has a subject and a predicate but does not express a complete thought. Instead, it is used as an adverb clause, an adjective clause, or a noun clause.

- An **adverb clause** begins with a subordinating conjunction (see Table 13.2) and functions as an adverb. To form a complete sentence, it must be connected to an independent clause.

Table 13.2 Subordinating Conjunctions

after	because	in order that	though	where
although	before	provided that	unless	whereas
as	even though	since	until	while
as if	given that	so that	when	
as long as	if	that	whenever	

Even though the forecast said clear skies, the storms rolled in.
adverb clause (dependent)

- An **adjective clause** begins with a relative pronoun (*which, that, who*) and functions as an adjective, so it must be connected to an independent clause to be complete.

I don't like a meteorologist who often gets the forecast wrong.
adjective clause (dependent)

- A noun clause begins with words like those in Table 13.3 and functions as a noun. It is used as a subject or an object in a sentence.

Table 13.3 Subordinating Conjunctions

how	what	whoever	whomever
that	whatever	whom	why

I wish he had known that the afternoon would bring rain and hail.
noun clause (dependent)

Practice 13.6 For each sentence, identify the function of the underlined word or words.

1. I wonder <u>why weather is so unpredictable</u>.
   a. Prepositional phrase
   b. Adverb clause
   c. Adjective clause
   d. Noun clause

2. Storms still surprise meteorologists <u>who have years of experience</u>.
   a. Prepositional phrase
   b. Adverb clause
   c. Adjective clause
   d. Noun clause

3. When lightning streaks <u>across the sky</u>, people must pause many outdoor activities.
   a. Prepositional phrase
   b. Adverb clause
   c. Adjective clause
   d. Noun clause

4. <u>Until we can track all factors</u>, we can't predict weather perfectly.
   a. Prepositional phrase
   b. Adverb clause
   c. Adjective clause
   d. Noun clause

5. <u>Whoever gives a forecast</u> is making a guess.
   a. Prepositional phrase
   b. Adverb clause
   c. Adjective clause
   d. Noun clause

6. <u>Since weather is so uncertain</u>, predictions include percentages.
   a. Prepositional phrase
   b. Adverb clause
   c. Adjective clause
   d. Noun clause

7. Giving an accurate percentage is <u>among the chief concerns</u> of meteorologists.
   a. Prepositional phrase
   b. Adverb clause
   c. Adjective clause
   d. Noun clause

8. A 50 percent chance of rain means <u>that a 50 percent chance of fair weather also exists</u>.
   a. Prepositional phrase
   b. Adverb clause
   c. Adjective clause
   d. Noun clause

9. <u>When air crosses a large lake</u>, it picks up moisture that often turns into rain or snow.
   a. Prepositional phrase
   b. Adverb clause
   c. Adjective clause
   d. Noun clause

10. <u>In addition to cold winters</u>, Buffalo gets whatever snow Lake Erie dishes up.
   a. Prepositional phrase
   b. Adverb clause
   c. Adjective clause
   d. Noun clause

Real-World Application

Practice 13.7 Underline the dependent clauses in the following email. *Hint:* There are six in the email.

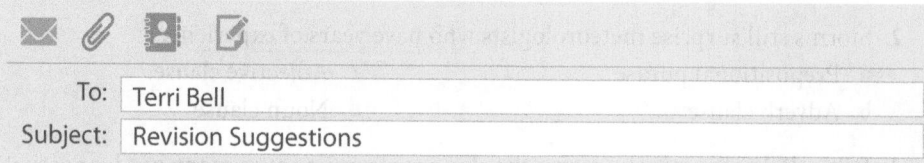

To: Terri Bell

Subject: Revision Suggestions

Hi, Terri:

I enjoyed your article, "Taking On the New *BattleTown 2*," which you submitted for publication on MMORPNews2.com. We like your article but request a few revisions before we send contracts.

This is a quick rundown of our revision suggestions:

1. The opening could be more gripping. The title works well to grab the reader's interest, but the opening feels flat. Perhaps you could provide a glimpse of new features of game play or even give a scenario that was not possible in *BattleTown 1*.

2. A direct quotation from Todd Allen would strengthen the center section. Though you allude to your interview on many occasions, Todd never speaks for himself, and he is a definite name in the industry.

3. Can you get permission to use the visuals? AssemblyArts would love the free publicity, but you need written permission to include the screenshots.

If you could make these changes, we would be very interested in publishing your article. Once I see the revised piece, I can send a contract for you to sign.

Thanks,

Richard Prince

Robsonphoto, 2017 / Used under license from Shutterstock.com

Simple, Compound, and Complex Sentences

Most leaves have a central stem with veins extending from it. Sometimes this structure forms a simple oval, but at other times, two or more ovals connect to form a compound leaf. And the shape of some leaves is complex, as if a number of leaves were fused together.

Sentences are similar. All have a subject and a predicate, and some stop at this simple structure. In other cases, two or more sentences combine to make a compound sentence. And when a sentence has one or more dependent clauses fused to it, the sentence becomes complex.

This chapter shows how to create simple, compound, and complex sentences. As with leaves, variety makes sentences beautiful.

Chapter Outline

- Simple Sentences
- Simple Sentences with Compound Subjects
- Simple Sentences with Compound Predicates
- Compound Sentences
- Complex Sentences
- Complex Sentences with Relative Clauses

14.1   Simple Sentences

A **simple sentence** consists of a subject and a predicate. The subject is a noun or pronoun that names what the sentence is about. The predicate is verb that tells what the subject does or is.

$$\underbrace{\text{My roommate}}_{\text{Subject}} \; \underbrace{\text{plays.}}_{\text{Predicate}}$$

▶ Modifiers

Other words can be used to modify the subject. Words that modify the subject answer the adjective questions: *which? what kind of? how many? how much?*

> My college roommate plays. *(Which roommate?)*

> Three people play the tuba. *(How many people play the tuba?)*

Other words can also modify the verb. These words and phrases answer the adverb questions: *how? when? where? why? to what degree? how often?*

> My college roommate plays in the pep band. *(Where does my roommate play?)*

> She practices every night of the week. *(How often does she practice?)*

▶ Direct and Indirect Objects

The verb might also be followed by a noun or pronoun that receives the action of the verb. Such a word is called the **direct object**, and it answers the question *what?* or *whom?*

> My college roommate plays the tuba. *(What does my roommate play?)*

Another noun or pronoun could come between the verb and the direct object, telling *to whom* or *for whom* an action is done. Such a word is the **indirect object**.

> The college gives him one credit per semester for playing.
> *(The college gives one credit to whom?)*

14.2 Simple Sentences with Compound Subjects

A simple sentence can have a compound subject (two or more subjects).

▶ Two Subjects

To write a simple sentence with two subjects, join them using *and* or *or*.

One Subject: Lee worked on the Rube Goldberg machine.

Two Subjects: Lee and Jerome will add the lever arm to tip the bucket.
Lee or Jerome will add the lever arm to tip the bucket.

One Subject: Ms. Claymore will attach the flywheel.

Two Subjects: Ms. Claymore and her aide will attach the flywheel.
Either Ms. Claymore or her aide will attach the flywheel.

▶ Three or More Subjects

To write a simple sentence with three or more subjects, create a series. Use commas between all subjects, and place *and* or *or* before the last subject.

Three Subjects: Jerome, Lee, and Sandra are finishing the machine soon.

Five Subjects: Jerome, Lee, Sandra, Ms. Claymore, and her aide will enter the machine in a contest.

When a compound subject is joined by *and*, the subject is plural and requires a plural verb. When a compound subject is joined by *or*, the verb should agree with the last subject.

Ms. Claymore and her aide need to submit the entry form.

Ms. Claymore or her aide needs to submit the entry form.

Ms. Claymore or her aides need to submit the entry form.

Insight A compound subject does not make the sentence compound. As long as all of the subjects connect to the same predicate, the thought is still a simple sentence.

14.3 Simple Sentences with Compound Predicates

A simple sentence can have a compound predicate (two or more verbs).

▶ Two Verbs

To create a compound predicate, join two verbs using *and* or *or*.

> **One Verb:** The band rocked.
> **Two Verbs:** The band rocked and danced.

Remember that the predicate includes not just a verb but also words that modify or complete the verb.

> **One Verb plus Other Words:** The band played their hit single.
> <u>played their hit single</u>
> predicate

> **Two Verbs plus Other Words:** The band played their hit single and covered other songs.
> <u>played their hit single and covered other songs</u>
> compound predicate

▶ Three or More Verbs

To create a compound predicate with three or more verbs, use a series. Put commas between all the verbs, and place *and* or *or* before the last verb.

> **Three Verbs:** The singer crooned, wailed, and roared.
> **Five Verbs:** The fans clapped, screamed, danced,
>   cheered, and swayed.

If each verb also includes modifiers or completing words (direct and indirect objects), place the commas after each complete predicate.

> The crowd members got to their feet, waved their hands back and forth, **and** sang along with the band.

Insight   Remember that the predicate tells what the subject is doing or being. As long as both predicates connect to the same subject, the sentence is still a simple sentence.

Practice 14.1 Answer the questions about simple sentences.

1. What is the subject of a sentence?
   a. A verb that tells what happens in the sentence
   b. A noun or pronoun that names what the sentence is about
   c. Words that answer adjective questions: *which? what kind of? how many? how much?*

2. What word(s) functions as the direct object in the following sentence? The golden retriever chased a bunny.
   a. Golden retriever
   b. Chased
   c. Bunny

3. Which of the following sentences includes an indirect object?
   a. Budget cutbacks reduced class choices.
   b. Four classes were canceled.
   c. Recent budget cuts have given students fewer class choices.

4. Which of the following sentences includes a compound subject?
   a. Jerome enjoys creating new smartphone apps.
   b. Jerome and Sandra collaborate on the project.
   c. She submitted their app to a competition.

5. How can you connect three or more subjects in a simple sentence?
   a. Use commas between all subjects, and place *and* or *or* before the last subject.
   b. Write all the subjects consecutively with no punctuation, and place *and* or *or* before the last subject.
   c. Use periods between all the subjects.

6. Which sentence's verb agrees with its compound subject?
   a. Jerome, Sandra, and Lee makes a good team.
   b. Jerome, Sandra, and Lee make a good team.
   c. Jerome, Sandra, or Lee make a good team.

7. Which sentence's verb does *not* agree with its compound subject?
   a. Mechanics and technicians need plenty of training to recognize car problems.
   b. The mechanic or the technician checks my car for problems.
   c. The mechanic or the technician check my car for problems.

8. Which sentence includes a compound predicate?
   a. The first-responders and news crews surveyed the damage.
   b. The reporters walked through the crowd and looked for witnesses.
   c. The first-responders asked the reporters to back away.

14.4 Compound Sentences

A **compound sentence** is made by joining simple sentences with a **coordinating conjunction** (connecting word): *and, but, or, nor, for, so,* or *yet.*

▶ Compound of Two Sentences

Most compound sentences connect two simple sentences, which are also called independent clauses. Connect the sentences with a comma and a coordinating conjunction.

> **Two Sentences:** We ordered pizza. I got just one piece.

> **Compound Sentence:** We ordered pizza, but I got just one piece.

▶ Compound of Three or More Sentences

You can also join three or more short sentences to form a compound sentence.

> **Three Sentences:** Tim likes cheese. Jan likes veggie. I like pepperoni.

> **Compound Sentence:** Tim likes cheese, Jan likes veggie, and I like pepperoni.

Simple sentences can also be joined with semicolons. Authors sometimes use this approach to describe a long, involved process or a flurry of activity.

> Tim ate the cheese pizza; Jan ate the veggie pizza; Ray showed up and ate the pepperoni pizza; I got back in time for the last slice.

NOTE: A compound sentence is made of two or more complete sentences. Each part must have its own subject and verb.

Insight Coordinating conjunctions provide information about how the parts of a compound sentence are related. The word *and* indicates that the second clause provides additional information. The words *but, or, nor,* and *yet* create a contrast. The words *for* and *so* indicate that one clause is the cause of the other.

14.5 Complex Sentences

A **complex sentence** joins an independent clause to one or more dependent clauses. The independent clause can stand alone as a sentence, but a dependent clause cannot. (Remember that a clause is a group of words with a subject and verb. See **Section 13.7**.)

▶ Using a Subordinating Conjunction

You can create a complex sentence by placing a **subordinating conjunction** before the clause that is less important. **Table 14.1** shows common subordinating conjunctions:

Table 14.1 Common Subordinating Conjunctions

after	before	so that	when
although	even though	that	where
as	if	though	whereas
as if	in order that	till	while
as long as	provided that	'til	
because	since	until	

The subordinating conjunction shows that one clause depends on the other to make sense.

Two Simple Sentences: We played flawless offense. We won the football game.

Complex Sentence: Because we played flawless offense, we won the football game.
<u>dependent clause</u>

We won the football game because we played flawless offense.
<u>dependent clause</u>

NOTE: The subordinating conjunction goes at the beginning of the less important clause, but the two clauses could go in either order. When the dependent clause comes first, it is set off by a comma.

▶ Compound-Complex Sentences

You can create a **compound-complex sentence** by placing a subordinating conjunction before a simple sentence and connecting it to a compound sentence.

Simple Sentence: I threw two touchdowns.

Compound Sentence: Jake kicked the extra points, and we took the lead.

Compound-Complex: After I threw two touchdowns, Jake kicked the extra points, and we took the lead.

14.6 Complex Sentences with Relative Clauses

In a complex sentence, one clause depends on the other. You've seen how a dependent clause can start with a subordinating conjunction. Another type of dependent clause starts with a relative pronoun.

A **relative clause** is a group of words that begins with a **relative pronoun** (*that*, *which*, *who*, *whom*) and includes a verb and any words that modify or complete the verb.

> **Relative Clauses:** that leads into the garden
> which usually leans against the shed
> who planted the scallions
> whom I asked to help me weed

Each relative clause example has a subject and a verb, but not one of the clauses is a complete sentence. They all need to be connected to an independent clause.

> **Complex Sentences:** I followed the path that leads into the garden.
> I looked for the shovel, which usually leans against the shed.
> We have many onions thanks to a friend who planted the scallions.
> I worked with Tina, whom I asked to help me weed.

▶ *That* and *Which*

The pronoun *that* at the beginning of a clause signals information that is necessary to the sentence. The pronoun *which* signals information that is not necessary, so the clause is set off with a comma.

> **That:** The scallions that we planted this spring taste strong. (The clause is needed to understand which scallions taste strong.)
>
> **Which:** I love scallions, which I eat raw or fried. (The clause adds information that is not needed to understand the sentence.)

▶ *Who* and *Whom*

The pronoun *who* is used as the subject when it introduces a clause, and *whom* is used either as a direct object of a clause it introduces or as an object of a preposition. Remember, the object is a noun phrase that receives the action of a verb.

> **Who:** I helped the woman who was harvesting scallions. (*Who* is the subject of the clause.)
>
> **Whom:** The woman whom I helped shared her produce. (*Whom* is the direct object of the verb *helped*.)
>
> The woman whom I talked to is a good neighbor. (*Whom* is the object of the preposition *to*.)

Practice 14.2 Answer the questions about compound and complex sentences.

1. What is a compound sentence?
   a. A complicated sentence with lots of words
   b. A simple sentence joined by a dependent clause
   c. Two or more simple sentences combined by a comma and coordinating conjunction or by a semicolon

2. Which of the following compound sentences is correct?
   a. I want to see the new *Star Wars* movie tonight but I have to work the night shift.
   b. I want to see the new *Star Wars* movie tonight, but I have to work the night shift.
   c. I want to see the new *Star Wars* movie tonight but, I have to work the night shift.

3. Which of the following coordinating conjunctions would be a good choice to create a contrast between two simple sentences?
   a. And
   b. For
   c. But

4. Which of the following can stand alone as a sentence?
   a. Independent clause
   b. Dependent clause

5. Identify the dependent clause in the following complex sentence.
   When I find the time, I'm going to clean the inside of my refrigerator.
   a. When I find the time
   b. I'm going to clean the inside of my refrigerator

6. Which of the following sentences is a compound-complex sentence?
   a. I'll miss the ball game, for I'll need a few days of rest to recover.
   b. Because I caught the flu, I'll miss the ball game.
   c. Because I caught the flu, I'll miss the ball game, for I'll need a few days of rest to recover.

7. Which of these complex sentences includes a relative clause?
   a. After class got out, I hustled to the metro station.
   b. I needed to catch the 3:30 train, which would get me to my job interview on time.
   c. I had to sprint because the station is on the north end of campus.

8. Which of the clauses in italics signals information that is necessary to the meaning of the sentence?
   a. The concert, *which we had looked forward to for weeks*, was canceled.
   b. The concert *that was cancelled* was supposed to be the show of the year.

Real-World Application

 Complete the email by selecting the correct coordinating conjunction, subordinating conjunction, or relative pronoun in parentheses.

To: Melvin Lindau

Subject: Production Meeting Summary

Dear Mr. Lindau:

You asked about the Monday production meeting, (which, that) I will summarize here. The production staff met with the writers, (whom, who) explained their new project. The project will focus on twenty-first-century skills. The writers presented two chapters, (which, that) will become a prototype.

We're excited to publish this project, (but, for) it will require a lot of hard work. The new project needs to be visual, appealing to students and teachers, (but, and) designed to make text accessible. The writing has an open quality but still feels academic. The book should be available for sale in the fall, (and, yet) a teacher's edition will follow.

The designers are beginning work on a prototype, (while, when) the writers continue to create chapters.

I hope this answers your questions.

Sincerely,

Amy Lentz

Anna Jurkovska, 2017 / Used under license from Shutterstock.com

Chapter

15

Agreement

When two people agree, they can work together. They have the same goals and outlook, and they can become a team.

Subjects and verbs are much the same. If the subject is plural, the verb needs to be plural as well, or they can't work together. Pronouns also need to agree in number with their antecedents, which are the nouns the pronouns replace. Without agreement, these words fight each other, and instead of conveying ideas, they disrupt communication.

This chapter focuses on the agreement between subjects and verbs and between pronouns and antecedents. It also tackles other pronoun problems. After you work through the exercises here, you'll find it easier to write sentences that agree.

Chapter Outline

- Subject-Verb Agreement
- Agreement with Compound Subjects
- Agreement with *I* and *You*
- Agreement with Indefinite Pronouns
- Pronoun-Antecedent Agreement
- Other Pronoun Problems

15.1 Subject-Verb Agreement

A verb must agree in number with the subject of the sentence. If the subject is singular, the verb must be singular. If the subject is plural, the verb must be plural.

singular subject + **singular verb** = **agreement**

The gymnast jumps.

plural subject + **plural verb** = **agreement**

The gymnasts jump.

Plural subjects often end in *s*, but plural verbs usually do not. Also note that only present-tense verbs and certain *be* verbs have separate singular and plural forms. Table 15.1 shows the singular and plural forms of common present- and past-tense verbs.

Table 15.1 Singular and Plural Forms of Common Verbs

Present:	Singular	Plural		Past:	Singular	Plural
	walks	walk			walked	walked
	sees	see			saw	saw
	eats	eat			ate	ate
	is/am	are			was	were

- To make most verbs singular, add just an *s*.

  run—runs   write—writes   stay—stays

- The verbs *do* and *go* are made singular by adding an *es*.

  do—does   go—goes

- When a verb ends in *ch*, *sh*, *x*, or *z*, make it singular by adding *es*.

  latch—latches   wish—wishes   fix—fixes   buzz—buzzes

- When a verb ends in a consonant followed by a *y*, change the y to *i* and add *es*.

  try—tries   fly—flies   cry—cries   quantify—quantifies

15.2 Agreement with Compound Subjects

Sentences with compound subjects have special agreement rules.

- When a sentence has two or more subjects joined by *and*, the verb should be plural.

  plural subject + **plural verb** = **agreement**

  Mani and Sutu march.

■ When a sentence has two or more subjects joined by *or* or *nor*, the verb should agree with the last subject.

singular subject + **singular verb** = **agreement**

Either Mani or Sutu eats.

The sentence has two subjects joined by *or*. The second subject (*Sutu*) is singular, so a singular verb (*eats*) is needed for the sentence to agree.

plural subject + **plural verbs** = **agreement**

Neither the rhino nor the elephants eat or sleep by each other.

The sentence has two subjects joined by *nor*. The second subject (*elephants*) is plural, so plural verbs (*eat, sleep*) are needed for the sentence to agree.

Practice 15.1 To create agreement in the following sentences, select the correct verb form in parentheses.

1. Succeeding as a philosophy major (require, requires) deep and creative thinking.

2. A philosopher (try, tries) to find philosophical work.

3. Employers rarely (wish, wishes) to hire philosophers.

4. But philosophers often (think, thinks) outside the box.

5. My roommate (study, studies) philosophy.

6. He also (needs, need) to study the want ads for jobs.

7. He (say, says) employers need thinkers.

8. That idea (makes, make) sense to me.

9. Neither my roommate nor my brother (play, plays) an instrument.

10. I (trick, tricks) them into going to the symphony with me.

11. The band and the director (entertains, entertain) the crowd.

12. The music or the marching (puts, put) the crowd in a frenzy.

13. The trumpeter or flute players (receives, receive) plenty of applause.

14. Harmony and tempo (produce, produces) beautiful music.

15. Either Todd or Lewis (plan, plans) to join the band.

15.3   Agreement with *I* and *You*

The pronouns *I* and *you* usually take plural verbs, even though they are singular.

plural verbs

Correct: I go to Great America and ride roller coasters. You do, too.

singular verbs

Incorrect: I goes to Great America and rides roller coasters. You does, too.

The pronoun *I* takes the singular verbs *am* and *was*. **Do not** use *I* with *be* or *is*.

Correct: I am excited. I was nervous.
            I am eager to ride the roller coaster.

Incorrect: I are excited. I were nervous.
             I is eager to ride the roller coaster.

Table 15.2 shows when to use *am*, *is*, *are*, *was*, and *were*.

Table 15.2 Using *am*, *is*, *are*, *was*, and *were*

Present:	Singular	Plural	Past:	Singular	Plural
	I *am*	we *are*		I *was*	we *were*
	you *are*	you *are*		you *were*	you *were*
	he *is* she *is* it *is*	they *are*		he *was* she *was* it *was*	they *were*

15.4   Agreement with Indefinite Pronouns

An **indefinite pronoun** is intentionally vague. Instead of referring to a specific person, place, or thing, an indefinite pronoun refers to something general or unknown.

▶ Singular Indefinite Pronouns

Singular indefinite pronouns (see Table 15.3) take singular verbs:

Someone cooks every night.

No one gets out of kitchen duty.

Everyone benefits from the chore schedule.

Table 15.3 Singular Indefinite Pronouns

someone	somebody	something
anyone	anybody	anything
no one	nobody	nothing
everyone	everybody	everything
one	each	either / neither

Note that indefinite pronouns that end in *one, body,* or *thing* are singular, just as these words themselves are singular. Just as you would write "That thing is missing," you would write "Something is missing."

Using *one, each, either,* and *neither* as subjects can be tricky because these words are often followed by a prepositional phrase that contains a plural object. The verb must still be singular.

One <u>of my friends</u> is a great cook.
prepositional phrase

Each <u>of us</u> wants to cook as well as he does.
prepositional phrase

Remember, a compound subject joined with *or* needs a verb that matches the last subject.

No one or nothing keeps him from making a wonderful meal.

Other indefinite pronouns are plural, and some indefinite pronouns can be singular *or* plural depending on how they are used.

▶ Plural Indefinite Pronouns

Plural indefinite pronouns take plural verbs (see **Table 15.4**).

Many of us follow classical music.

Several are big fans.

Few musicians are greater than Mozart.

Table 15.4 Plural Indefinite Pronouns

both	many
few	several

▶ Singular or Plural Indefinite Pronouns

Some indefinite pronouns are singular or plural (see **Table 15.5**). If the object of the prepositional phrase following the pronoun is singular, the pronoun takes a singular verb; if the object is plural, the pronoun takes a plural verb.

Table 15.5 Singular or Plural Indefinite Pronouns

all	most
any	none
half	some
part	

NOTE: The *object* of the prepositional phrase is the noun that follows the preposition. It is needed to complete the phrase's meaning.

Most of the song thrills us.

indefinite   singular   singular
pronoun   object   verb

Most of the songs thrill us.

indefinite   plural   plural
pronoun   object   verb

Notice the shift in meaning, depending on the prepositional phrase. "Most of the song" means that one song is mostly thrilling. "Most of the songs" means that all but a few of several songs are thrilling. Here's another example:

Half of the concert features Mozart.

Half of the concerts feature Mozart.

In the first sentence, half of one concert features Mozart's compositions. In the second sentence, half of several concerts feature Mozart's music. Here's a final example:

Some of class was devoted to studying Mozart's music.

Some of the classes were devoted to studying Mozart's music.

In the first sentence, some of one class was devoted to studying Mozart's music. In the second sentence, some of multiple classes were devoted to studying Mozart's music.

Practice 15.2 Correct any agreement errors you find by crossing out the verb and writing the correct verb. *Hint:* There are 13 agreement errors in the reading.

I is starting a class in astronomy, and I wonders if I can borrow your

telescope. You rarely uses it anymore, and I needs it to be able to look at the moons

of Jupiter. My professor says that even a moderate-size telescope will show the

moons. She have instructions for finding Jupiter. I knows how to use the telescope,

but if you is afraid I would break it, you could set it up for me.

I has a yard away from city lights, and I has lawn chairs and blankets we

could use. If you agrees to come out and set up the telescope, I'll gets us snacks.

What do you think? I hopes I'm not asking too much and that you are willing

to help. I is just excited to see Jupiter's moons; you might like to see them, too.

Practice 15.3   In the following sentences, select the correct form of the verb in parentheses.

1. Everyone (complete, completes) an application.

2. Somebody (has, have) to get the job.

3. Each of the jobs (is, are) available.

4. Neither of the applicants (is, are) qualified.

5. Either of the prospects (hope, hopes) to be trained.

6. Nobody (want, wants) to go home empty-handed.

7. Everybody (has, have) bills to pay.

8. All of the songs (is, are) dramatic.

9. Everyone (like, likes) Tchaikovsky.

10. One of my friends (listen, listens) to classical radio.

11. Several (listen, listens) to Internet radio.

12. Half of the album (feature, features) symphonies.

15.5 Pronoun-Antecedent Agreement

A pronoun must agree in person, number, and gender with its **antecedent** (see **Table 15.6**). The antecedent is the noun that the pronoun refers to or replaces.

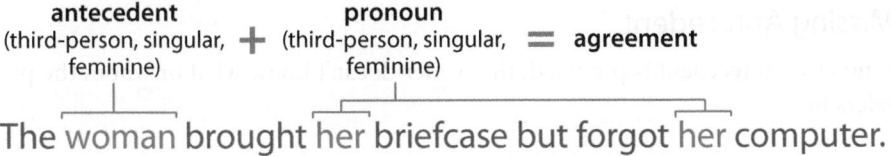

Table 15.6 Pronoun-Antecedent Agreement

	Singular	Plural
First Person:	I, me, my, mine	we, us, our, ours
Second Person:	you, your, yours	you, your, yours
Third Person:		
masculine	he, him, his	they, them, their, theirs
feminine	she, her, hers	they, them, their, theirs
neuter	it, its	they, them, their, theirs

▶ Two or More Antecedents

When two or more antecedents are joined by *and*, the pronoun should be plural.

> Kali and Teri want to fill their baskets with eggs.

When two or more singular antecedents are joined by *or* or *nor*, the pronoun or pronouns should be singular.

> Either Alice or Dave planned the hunt, so she or he hid the eggs.
> Neither Kali nor Teri filled her basket with eggs.
> Either Alice or Dave will search for her or his favorite hiding spots next year.

NOTE: Avoid sexism when choosing a pronoun to replace a general noun. Don't assume the pronoun refers to only males or only females. To avoid gender binaries, do not use the singular "his or her." Instead, rewrite the sentence with a plural subject or use *they/their/them* as a third-person singular pronoun.

> **Sexist:** Each child should bring his basket.
> **Corrected with plural construction:** Children should bring their baskets.
> **Corrected with singular *they*:** Each child should bring their basket, so they can fill it with eggs.

15.6 Other Pronoun Problems

▶ Missing Antecedent

If no clear antecedent is provided, the reader doesn't know what or whom the pronoun refers to.

> **Confusing:** In Illinois, they claim Lincoln as their own.
>   (To whom does the pronoun "they" refer?)
> **Clear:** In Illinois, the citizens claim Lincoln as their own.

▶ Vague Pronoun

If the pronoun could refer to two or more words, the passage can be unclear and confusing.

> **Unclear:** Sheila told her daughter to use her new tennis racket.
>   (To whom does the pronoun "her" refer, Sheila or her daughter?)
> **Clumsy:** Sheila told her daughter to use Sheila's new tennis racket.
> **Clear:** Sheila loaned her new tennis racket to her daughter.

Incorrect Case

Pronouns have three cases. That means they can be used in three ways—as subjects, objects, or possessives. Table 15.7 outlines which pronouns to use in each case. One common error is using an object pronoun as a subject.

Table 15.7 Cases of Personal Pronouns

Subject	Object	Possessive
I	me	my, mine
we	us	our, ours
you	you	your, yours
he	him	his
she	her	her, hers
it	it	its
they	them	their, theirs

Incorrect: Them are funny videos.
Him and I laughed hard.

Correct: They are funny videos.
He and I laughed hard.

Also, remember to use *my* before the thing possessed and *mine* afterward: *my cat*, but *that cat is mine*. Do the same with *our/ours*, *your/yours*, *her/hers*, and *their/theirs*.

Double Subject

If a pronoun is used right after the subject, an error called a double subject occurs.

Incorrect: Your father, he is good at poker.
Correct: Your father is good at poker.

Practice 15.4 Select the pronoun(s) in parentheses that agrees with its underlined antecedent(s).

1. Shandra and Shelli will bring (their, her) lawn chairs to the fireworks display.

2. Either John or Grace will play (they, their) favorite patriotic songs.

3. John plays trombone and will bring (its, his) instrument.

4. All participants should bring (his, their) own flag.

5. Linda will sing (its, her) rendition of the national anthem.

6. Each portable table will need (its, their) legs locked in place.

Practice 15.5 Choose the sentence that avoids a pronoun problem.

1. a. Him and I worked on the project in class.
   b. He and I worked on the project in class.

2. a. Before we climbed in the tent with our air mattress, it collapsed.
   b. Before we climbed in the tent with our air mattress, the tent collapsed.

3. a. Trina and Lois bought frozen custard.
   b. Trina and Lois, they bought frozen custard.

Real-World Application

 **Practice 15.6** In the following email, correct the agreement errors and any other pronoun problems. *Hint:* There are 10 total errors in the email.

To: Jean Leuinski

Subject: Thank You for Your Recommendation

Hi, Ms. Leuinski:

Thank your for recommending me for the position of research analyst at Bismark Laboratories. During the interview last Monday, Dr. Jason Lemark said that she had received your letter and had talked with you by phone. On both occasions, him noted, you described mine work as "well researched, meticulous, and professional." I deeply appreciates your comments and you trust.

The outcome of the application process could not be more positive. Dr. Lemark are offering me not just one job, but two! The first position is the one that I applied for in Bismark's San Diego office. The second position have more responsibility and higher pay, but they is in the company's Houston office.

Thanks again for your strong recommendation, Ms. Leuinski! Your positive words clearly affected the decision made by Dr. Lemark and the Research and Development Department. You has my deepest gratitude.

Best wishes,

Rodell

Robsonphoto, 2017 / Used under license from Shutterstock.com

16

Sentence Problems

Cars are great when they go, but when they break down, they're a huge headache. After a look under the hood, a bit of scrabbling beneath the thing, maybe a push, maybe a jack, and probably a tow truck, there's probably going to be a big bill.

Sentences also are great until they break down. But you don't need to be stuck with the confusing mess for long. This chapter outlines a few common sentence problems and explains how to fix them.

Chapter Outline

- Common Fragments
- Tricky Fragments
- Comma Splices
- Run-On Sentences
- Rambling Sentences
- Dangling and Misplaced Modifiers
- Shifts in Sentence Construction

16.1 Common Fragments

In everyday speech and informal writing, sentence fragments are occasionally used. In academic conversations and formal writing, fragments should be avoided because they are too easily misunderstood.

► Missing Parts

A sentence requires a subject and a verb. If one or the other or both are missing, the sentence is a fragment. Such fragments can be fixed by supplying the missing part.

Fragment: Went to the concert.

Fragment + Subject: We went to the concert.

Fragment: Everyone from Westville Community College.

Fragment + Verb: Everyone from Westville Community College may participate.

Fragment: In the interest of student safety.

Fragment + Subject and Verb: The president acted in the interest of student safety.

► Incomplete Thoughts

A sentence also must express a complete thought. Some fragments have a subject and a verb but do not express a complete thought. These fragments can be corrected by providing words that complete the thought.

Fragment: The concert will include.

Completing Thought: The concert will include an amazing light show.

Fragment: If we arrive in time.

Completing Thought: If we arrive in time, we'll get front-row seats.

Fragment: That opened the concert.

Completing Thought: I liked the bluegrass band that opened the concert.

16.2 Tricky Fragments

Some fragments are more difficult to find and correct. They creep into our writing because they are often part of the way we talk.

► Absolute Phrases

An **absolute phrase** may look like a sentence, but it isn't. An absolute phrase can be made into a sentence by adding a **helping verb** or by connecting the phrase to a complete sentence.

**Absolute Phrase
(Fragment):** Our legs trembling from the hike.

**Absolute Phrase +
Helping Verb:** Our legs were trembling from the hike.

**Absolute Phrase +
Complete Sentence:** We collapsed on the couch, our legs trembling from the hike.

► Informal Fragments

Fragments that are commonly used in speech should be eliminated from formal writing. Avoid the following types of fragments unless you are writing dialogue.

Interjections: Hey! Yeah!

Exclamations: What a nuisance! How fun!

Greetings: Hi, everybody. Good afternoon.

Questions: How come? Why not? What?

Answers: About three or four. As soon as possible.

Sentences that begin with *here* or *there* have a **delayed subject**, which appears after the verb. Other sentences (commands) have an implied subject (*you*). Such sentences are not fragments.

Delayed Subject: Here are some crazy fans wearing wild hats.

Implied Subject: Tackle him! Bring him down!

Practice 16.1 Review the choices that follow. Some are fragments. Choose the one that forms a complete sentence.

1. a. The reason most magazines fail.
   b. Not publishing long enough to be able to sell advertisers on their concept.
   c. All magazines are vulnerable to changing economic and technology trends.

2. a. Several strategies for reducing fire-related harm to forests.
   b. One way is to allow some controlled fires on public lands.
   c. Clearing away small fire-prone trees and underbrush under careful controls.

3. a. A broad expanse of the river turned blood red.
   b. In the middle distance the red hue.
   c. That glowed like a flame in the unobstructed reflection of the sun.

4. a. With supporting fatherhood and stable family life.
   b. Nobody can disagree.
   c. Not necessarily the presence of a nuclear family.

5. a. Our boisterous behavior announcing our approach.
   b. The owner's gaze tracking us from the front porch.
   c. His dogs were barking loudly from the backyard.

6. a. He decided to spend his life figuring out how humans could benefit from ecological principles.
   b. Rested on a hillside and started to put together what he had learned and seen.
   c. One night while hitchhiking in Africa.

7. a. Did you know that Neanderthals ate mainly?
   b. Did you know that Cro-Magnon and Neanderthal tribes at times lived side by side?
   c. Did you know that although Neanderthal tribes used spears and stone tools?

Practice 16.2 Underline the fragments in the following paragraph. *Hint:* There are six total fragments.

Some classes ask you to learn lots of facts. Art-history classes, for example. Require strong memorization skills. I panicked this one time. When a semester's worth of art-history notes went missing. Yikes! My test was the next day, and I had lost my notes. Without those notes was done for. Then there was a phone call. My friend had found them. Soggy but intact.

16.3 Comma Splices

Comma splices occur when two sentences are connected with only a comma. A comma splice can be fixed by adding a coordinating conjunction (*and, but, or, nor, for, so,* or *yet*) or a subordinating conjunction (*while, after, when, before, because, although*). The two sentences can also be joined by a semicolon (;) or separated by a period.

Comma Splice: The Eiffel Tower was a main attraction at the Paris Exposition, the Ferris wheel was its equivalent at the Chicago Exposition.

Corrected by adding a coordinating conjunction:	The Eiffel Tower was a main attraction at the Paris Exposition, and the Ferris wheel was its equivalent at the Chicago Exposition.
Corrected by adding a subordinating conjunction:	While the Eiffel Tower was a main attraction at the Paris Exposition, the Ferris wheel was its equivalent at the Chicago Exposition.
Corrected by replacing the comma with a semicolon:	The Eiffel Tower was a main attraction at the Paris Exposition; the Ferris wheel was its equivalent at the Chicago Exposition.

Comma Splice: An engineer named George Washington Gale Ferris planned the first Ferris wheel, many people thought he was crazy.

Corrected by adding a coordinating conjunction:	An engineer named George Washington Gale Ferris planned the first Ferris wheel, but many people thought he was crazy.
Corrected by adding a subordinating conjunction:	When an engineer named George Washington Gale Ferris planned the first Ferris wheel, many people thought he was crazy.
Corrected by replacing the comma with a period:	An engineer named George Washington Gale Ferris planned the first Ferris wheel. Many people thought he was crazy.

Insight A comma without a conjunction is not strong enough to join two sentences. A semicolon can join two related sentences, or a period can separate them.

16.4   Run-On Sentences

A **run-on sentence** occurs when two sentences are joined without punctuation or a connecting word. A run-on can be corrected by adding a comma and a conjunction or by inserting a semicolon or period between the two sentences.

Run-On: Horace Wilson taught in Tokyo in 1872 he introduced the Japanese to baseball.

Corrected by adding a comma and coordinating conjunction:	Horace Wilson taught in Tokyo in 1872, and he introduced the Japanese to baseball.
Corrected by adding a subordinating conjunction and a comma:	While Horace Wilson taught in Tokyo in 1872, he introduced the Japanese to baseball.
Corrected by inserting a semicolon:	Horace Wilson taught in Tokyo in 1872; he introduced the Japanese to baseball.

Run-On: The first team in Japan was formed in 1878 no one knew how popular the sport would become.

Corrected by adding a comma and coordinating conjunction:	The first team in Japan was formed in 1878, yet no one knew how popular the sport would become.
Corrected by adding a subordinating conjunction:	The first team in Japan was formed in 1878 although no one knew how popular the sport would become.
Corrected by inserting a period:	The first team in Japan was formed in 1878. No one knew how popular the sport would become.

Here's an additional way to correct a run-on sentence: Turn one of the sentences into a phrase or series of phrases; then combine it with the other sentence.

The first team in Japan was formed in 1878 without a thought about how popular the sport would become.

Practice 16.3 ▶ Decide whether each sentence is a comma splice or a complete sentence.

1. We set out for a morning hike, it was raining.

   a. Comma splice   **b.** Complete sentence

2. When the weather cleared by the afternoon, we hit the trail.

   a. Comma splice   **b.** Complete sentence

3. Both Jill and I were expecting wonderful scenery; we were not disappointed.

   a. Comma splice   **b.** Complete sentence

4. The view of the valley was spectacular, it was like a portrait.

   a. Comma splice   **b.** Complete sentence

5. We snacked on granola bars and apples, and we enjoyed the view.

   a. Comma splice   **b.** Complete sentence

6. Then we strapped on our backpacks, the final leg of the hike awaited us.

   a. Comma splice   **b.** Complete sentence

Practice 16.4 ▶ Decide whether each sentence is a run-on or a complete sentence.

1. In 1767 English scientist Joseph Priestley discovered a way to infuse water with carbon dioxide this invention led to carbonated water.

   a. Run-on sentence   **b.** Complete sentence

2. Carbonated water is one of the main components of soft drinks; it gives soft drinks the fizz and bubbles we enjoy.

   a. Run-on sentence   **b.** Complete sentence

3. The first soft drinks in America were dispensed out of soda fountains they were most often found at drug stores and ice-cream parlors.

   a. Run-on sentence   **b.** Complete sentence

4. Interestingly, soda was sold at drug stores because it promised healing properties.

   a. Run-on sentence   **b.** Complete sentence

5. The first carbonated-drink bottles could not keep bubbles from escaping, so it was more popular to buy a soda from a soda fountain.

   a. Run-on sentence   **b.** Complete sentence

6. Most of the formulas for American soft drinks were invented by pharmacists the idea was to create nonalcoholic alternatives to traditional medicines.

   a. Run-on sentence   **b.** Complete sentence

16.5 Rambling Sentences

A **rambling sentence** occurs when many separate ideas are connected by one *and, but,* or *so* after another. The result is an unfocused sentence that goes on and on. To correct a rambling sentence, break it into smaller units, adding and cutting words as needed.

Rambling: When we signed up for the two-on-two tournament, I had no thoughts about winning, but then my brother started talking about spending his prize money and he asked me how I would spend the share so we were counting on winning when we really had little chance and as it turned out, we lost in the second round.

Corrected: When we signed up for the two-on-two tournament, I had no thoughts about winning. Then my brother started talking about spending the prize money. He even asked me how I would spend my share. Soon we were counting on winning when we really had little chance. As it turned out, we lost in the second round.

16.6 Dangling and Misplaced Modifiers

▶ **Dangling Modifiers**

A modifier is a word, phrase, or clause that functions as an adjective or adverb. When the reader cannot find the word that is being described by the modifier, the modifier is called a **dangling modifier**. This error can be corrected by inserting the missing word or rewriting the sentence.

Dangling Modifier: After putting some raw chicken in the bowl, my cat began to purr. *(The cat could put chicken in the bowl?)*

Corrected: After I put some raw chicken in the bowl, my cat began to purr.

Dangling Modifier: Trying to gobble the food quickly, the bowl got tipped over. *(The bowl was trying to gobble the food?)*

Corrected: Trying to gobble the food quickly, the cat tipped over the bowl.

▶ **Misplaced Modifiers**

When a modifier is placed beside a word that it does not modify, the modifier is misplaced. This often results in an amusing or illogical statement. The reader must ask,

"Who or what is actually being described?" The **misplaced modifier** can be corrected by moving it next to the word that it modifies.

Misplaced Modifier: My cat was diagnosed by the vet with fleas.
(The vet has fleas?)

Corrected: The vet diagnosed my cat with fleas.

Misplaced Modifier: The vet gave a pill to my cat that tastes like fish.
(The cat tastes like fish?)

Corrected: The vet gave my cat a pill that tastes like fish.

Avoid placing any adverb modifiers between a verb and its direct object.

Misplaced: I will throw quickly the ball.

Corrected: I will quickly throw the ball.

Also, do not separate two-word verbs with an adverb modifier.

Misplaced: Please take immediately out the trash.

Corrected: Please immediately take out the trash.

Practice 16.5 Choose the sentence that does *not* include a misplaced or dangling modifier.

1. a. I bought a hound dog for my brother named Rover.
   b. I bought a hound dog named Rover for my brother.

2. a. The doctor diagnosed me with scoliosis and referred me to a specialist.
   b. The doctor diagnosed me and referred me to a specialist with scoliosis.

3. a. The coroner reported that the man was murdered.
   b. The man was reported murdered by the coroner.

4. a. Please present the recommendation that is attached to Mrs. Burble.
   b. Please present the attached recommendation to Mrs. Burble.

5. a. Jack drove me in a Chevy to our home.
   b. Jack drove me to our home in a Chevy.

6. a. I couldn't believe my brother would hire a disco DJ who hates disco.
   b. I couldn't believe my brother, who hates disco, would hire a disco DJ.

7. a. Give quickly the report to your boss.
   b. Quickly give the report to your boss.

8. a. We will immediately provide an explanation.
   b. We will provide immediately an explanation.

16.7 Shifts in Sentence Construction

▶ Shift in Person

A **shift in person** is an error that occurs when first, second, and third person are improperly mixed in a sentence.

> **Shift in Person:** If you exercise and eat right, an individual can lose weight.
> (The sentence improperly shifts from second person—*you*—to third person—*individual*.)
>
> **Corrected:** If you exercise and eat right, you can lose weight.

▶ Shift in Tense

A **shift in tense** is an error that occurs when more than one verb tense is improperly used in a sentence.

> **Shift in Tense:** He tried every other option before he agrees to do it my way.
> (The sentence improperly shifts from past tense—*tried*—to present tense—*agrees*.)
>
> **Corrected:** He tried every other option before he agreed to do it my way.

▶ Shift in Voice

A **shift in voice** is an error that occurs when active voice and passive voice are mixed in a sentence.

> **Shift in Voice:** When she fixes the radiator, other repairs may be suggested.
> (The sentence improperly shifts from active voice—*fixes*—to passive voice—*may be suggested*.)
>
> **Corrected:** When she fixes the radiator, she may suggest other repairs.

Practice 16.6 Choose the sentence that does *not* include an improper shift in construction.

1. a. You should be ready for each class in a person's schedule.
   b. You should be ready for each class in your schedule.

2. a. I work for my brother most days and attend classes at night.
   b. I work for my brother most days and classes are attended by me at night.

3. **a.** When you give me a review, can he also give me a raise?
   b. When you give me a review, can you also give me a raise?

4. **a.** As we walked to school, last night's football game was discussed by us.
   b. As we walked to school, we discussed last night's football game.

5. **a.** David exercises daily and eats well.
   b. David exercises daily and ate well.

6. **a.** Marianne goes running each morning and usually friends are met.
   b. Marianne goes running each morning and usually meets friends.

7. **a.** After you choose an exercise routine, a person should stick to it.
   b. After you choose an exercise routine, you should stick to it.

8. **a.** Lamar swam every morning and does ten laps.
   b. Lamar swam every morning and did ten laps.

9. **a.** The personal trainer made a schedule for me, and a diet was suggested by her.
   b. The personal trainer made a schedule for me and suggested a diet.

10. **a.** As you search for your essay, you may also find your keys.
   b. As you search for your essay, your keys may also be found.

Practice 16.7 Underline any sentences that include improper shifts in construction. *Hint:* The paragraph includes four sentences with improper shifts.

Some people are early adopters, which means they adopt technology when it is new. Other people are technophobes because you are afraid of technology, period. I am not an early adopter or a technophobe, but I have to see the value in technology before I use it. Technology has to be cheap, intuitive, reliable, and truly helpful before I start using it. I let others work out the bugs and pay the high prices before a piece of technology is adopted by me. But when I decide it is time to get a new gadget or program, you buy it and use it until it is worn out. Then I look for something else that is even cheaper and more intuitive, reliable, and helpful, which is then bought by me.

Real-World Application

Practice 16.8 Underline the sentence fragments in the following business memo. *Hint:* There are five fragments.

Slovik Manufacturing

Date: August 8, 2017
To: Jerome James, Personnel Director
From: Ike Harris, Graphic Arts Director
Subject: Promotion of Mona Veal from Intern to Full-time Graphic Artist

For the past five months, Mona Veal as an intern in our Marketing Department. I recommend that she be offered a position as a full-time designer. Are the two main reasons behind this recommendation.

1. Mona has shown the traits that Slovik Manufacturing values in a graphic designer. Creative, dependable, and easy to work with.

2. Presently, we have two full-time graphic designers and one intern. While this group has worked well. The full-time designers have averaged 3.5 hours of overtime per week. Given this fact, our new contract with Lee-Stamp Industries will require more help, including at least one additional designer.

If you approve this recommendation. Please initial below and return this memo.

Yes, I approve the recommendation to offer Mona Veal a full-time position.

———————

Attachment: Evaluation report of Mona Veal

cc: Elizabeth Zoe
     Mark Moon

Practice 16.9 In the following email, correct any run-on sentences by inserting a period and, if necessary, capitalizing the new sentence. Correct any comma splices by inserting the coordinating conjunction *and* to form a compound sentence. Use the correction marks to make your changes. *Hint:* There are three run-ons and two comma splices in the email.

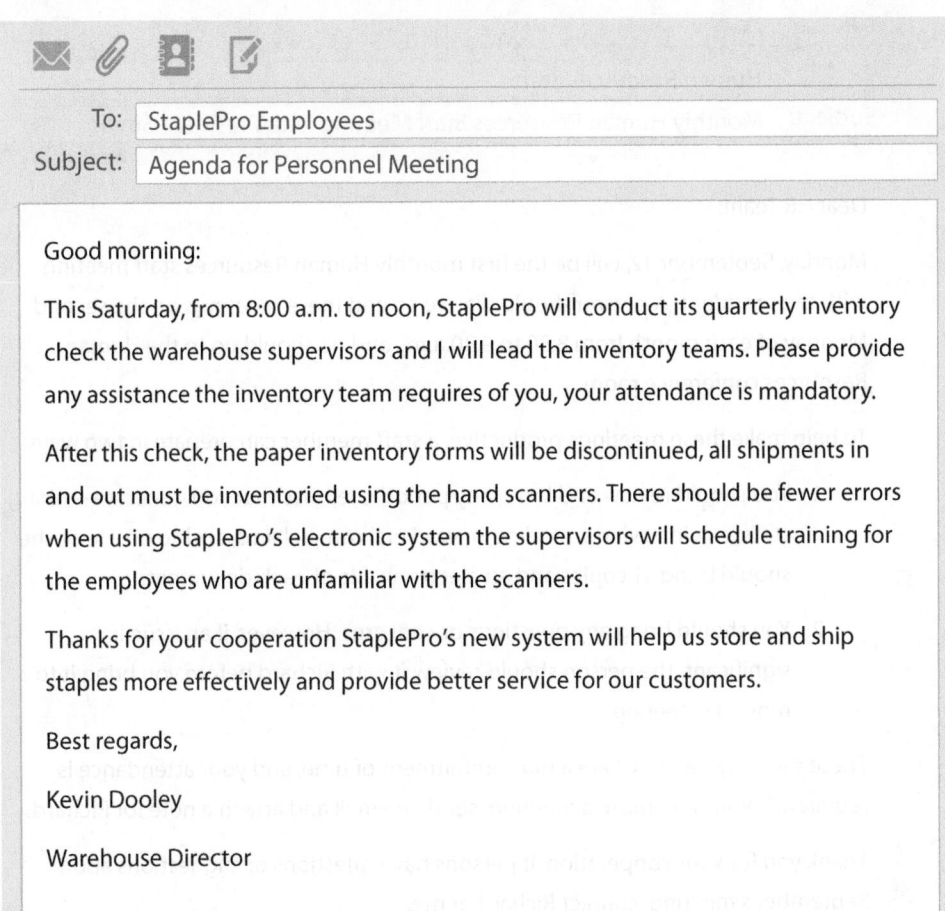

To: StaplePro Employees

Subject: Agenda for Personnel Meeting

Good morning:

This Saturday, from 8:00 a.m. to noon, StaplePro will conduct its quarterly inventory check the warehouse supervisors and I will lead the inventory teams. Please provide any assistance the inventory team requires of you, your attendance is mandatory.

After this check, the paper inventory forms will be discontinued, all shipments in and out must be inventoried using the hand scanners. There should be fewer errors when using StaplePro's electronic system the supervisors will schedule training for the employees who are unfamiliar with the scanners.

Thanks for your cooperation StaplePro's new system will help us store and ship staples more effectively and provide better service for our customers.

Best regards,

Kevin Dooley

Warehouse Director

Correction Marks

d̲̲ capitalize   ^word add word   ⊙ add period

Practice 16.10 In the following email, fix any shifts in person so that the entire email uses the second-person (you) consistently. One example is provided for you. *Hint:* There are five other shifts to cross out and fix.

To: Human Resources Staff

Subject: Monthly Human Resources Staff Meeting with President Smith

Dear HR Team:

Monday, September 12, will be the first monthly Human Resources staff meeting with the president. ~~A person~~ ^{You} should plan to attend these meetings on the second Monday of each month from 8:30 to 9:30 a.m., and he should go to the Human Resources conference room.

To help make these meetings productive, a staff member can prepare in two ways:

1. You should review and bring any periodic reports that you generate—hiring stats, exit interviews, medical or workers' comp claims, and so on. He or she should bring 11 copies and an electronic file of each document.

2. You should bring any questions or concerns. However, if an issue is significant, the person should review it with Richard before you bring it to a monthly meeting.

These monthly meetings are a big commitment of time, and your attendance is required. If you can't make a meeting, send an email and attach a note for Richard.

Thank you for your cooperation. If persons have questions or suggestions about September's meeting, contact Richard or me.

Thanks,
Julia

Part 6:

Word Workshops

Part 6: Word Workshops

Kevin Key, 2017 / Used under license from Shutterstock.com

17

Nouns

Astrophysicists tell us that the universe is made up of two things—matter and energy. Matter is the stuff, and energy is the movement or heat of the stuff.

Grammarians tell us that thoughts are made up of two things—nouns and verbs. Nouns name the stuff, and verbs capture the energy. In that way, the sentence reflects the universe itself. You can't express a complete thought unless you are talking about matter and energy. Each sentence, then, is the basic particle of thought.

This chapter focuses on nouns, which describe not just things you can see—such as people, places, or objects—but also things you can't see—such as love, justice, and democracy.

Chapter Outline

- Classes of Nouns
- Number of Nouns
- Count and Noncount Nouns
- Articles with Nouns
- Other Noun Markers

17.1 Classes of Nouns

All nouns are either *common* or *proper*. They can also be *collective, concrete,* or *abstract*.

▶ Common or Proper

A **common noun** names a general person, place, thing, or idea and is not capitalized. A **proper noun** names a specific person, place, thing, or idea and is capitalized. Table 17.1 shows common and proper nouns.

Table 17.1 Common and Proper Nouns

	Common Nouns	Proper Nouns
Person:	politician	John F. Kennedy
Place:	park	Yellowstone
Thing:	marker	Sharpie
Idea:	religion	Hinduism

▶ Collective

A **collective noun** names a group or unit of people, animals, or things: *team, class, family, committee, herd*.

▶ Concrete or Abstract

A **concrete noun** can be seen, heard, smelled, tasted, or touched. An **abstract noun** (a condition, an idea, or a feeling) cannot be sensed. Table 17.2 demonstrates each type.

Table 17.2 Concrete and Abstract Nouns

Concrete Nouns	Abstract Nouns
judge	impartiality
brain	mind
heart	courage
train	transportation

17.2 Number of Nouns

The **number** of a noun indicates whether it is singular (one) or plural (more than one). Table 17.3 shows singular and plural nouns.

Table 17.3 Singular and Plural Nouns

Singular Nouns	Plural Nouns
sister	sisters
church	churches
child	children
tooth	teeth

NOTE: Form the plural of most nouns by adding *s*. For nouns ending in *ch, s, sh, x* or *z*, add *es*. Also note that some nouns take a special spelling in the plural form.

17.3 Count and Noncount Nouns

Some nouns name things that can be counted, and other nouns name things that cannot be counted. Different rules apply to each type.

▶ Count Nouns

A **count noun** names something that can be counted—*pens, people, votes, cats*. It can be singular or plural and be preceded by a number or an article (*a, an,* or *the*): *two* pens, *a* room, *an* apple, *the* iguanas. Table 17.4 shows singular and plural count nouns.

Table 17.4 Count Nouns

Singular	Plural
apple	apples
iguana	iguanas
thought	thoughts
room	rooms

Insight Many native English speakers, although unaware of count and noncount nouns, naturally use these nouns correctly. Listen to how these speakers use count and noncount nouns.

▶ Noncount Nouns

A **noncount noun** names something that cannot be counted. It is used in singular form and can be preceded by *the*, but rarely by *a* or *an*.

This semester, I'm taking mathematics and biology as well as Spanish.

Table 17.5 lists noncount nouns by category.

Table 17.5 Noncount Nouns

Substance	Foods	Activities	Science	Languages	Abstractions
wood	water	reading	oxygen	Spanish	justice
cloth	milk	boating	weather	English	harm
ice	wine	smoking	heat	Mandarin	publicity
plastic	sugar	dancing	sunshine	Farsi	advice
wool	rice	swimming	electricity	Greek	happiness
steel	meat	soccer	lightning	Latin	health
aluminum	cheese	hockey	biology	French	joy
metal	flour	photography	history	Japanese	love
leather	pasta	writing	mathematics	Afrikaans	anger

▶ Two-Way Nouns

Two-way nouns can function as either count or noncount nouns.

Please set a glass in front of each place mat. (count noun)

The display case was made of tempered glass. (noncount noun)

Practice 17.1 Complete the following noun activities.

1. Choose the proper noun(s) in the following sentence.

   William Faulkner wrote about the death of the Old South.

   a. William Faulkner
   b. death
   c. Old South
   d. both *a* and *c*

2. Choose the common noun(s) in the following sentence.

   The Unvanquished tells about the aftermath of the Civil War.

   a. *The Unvanquished*
   b. aftermath
   c. Civil War
   d. both *a* and *c*

3. Choose the collective noun in the following sentence.

   He chronicles the end of the genteel class in the South.

   a. He
   b. end
   c. class
   d. South

4. Choose the concrete noun(s) in the following sentence.

   The character Quentin Compson appears often in his writing.

   a. character
   b. Quentin Compson
   c. writing
   d. all of the above

5. Choose the abstract noun(s) in the following sentence.

   Faulkner is known for dark humor and unwavering honesty.

   a. Faulkner
   b. humor
   c. honesty
   d. both *b* and *c*

6. Choose the plural noun(s) in the following sentence.

   Faulkner's novels are set in Yoknapatawpha County, a fictional Mississippi county.

   a. novels
   b. Yoknapatawpha County
   c. Mississippi county
   d. both *b* and *c*

7. Identify the following set of nouns as count or noncount nouns.

   bowling   health   Japanese   poetry   rain   health

   a. count nouns
   b. noncount nouns

8. Choose the count nouns in the following list.

   window   aluminum   lawyer   holiday   rain   English

   a. window, lawyer, holiday
   b. aluminum, rain, English

17.4 Articles with Nouns

Articles show whether a noun refers to a specific thing or to a general thing. Articles are either definite or indefinite.

▶ Definite Article

The **definite article** is the word *the*. It signals that the noun refers to one specific person, place, thing, or idea.

> Look at the rainbow.
> (*Look at a specific rainbow.*)

NOTE: *The* can be used with most nouns, but usually not with proper nouns.

> **Incorrect:** The Joe looked at the rainbow.
> **Correct:** Joe looked at the rainbow.

Insight If your native language does not use articles, pay close attention to the way native English speakers use *the* when referring to a specific thing.

▶ Indefinite Articles

The **indefinite articles** are the words *a* and *an*. They signal that the noun refers to a general person, place, thing, or idea. The word *a* is used before nouns that begin with consonant sounds, and the word *an* is used before nouns that begin with vowel sounds.

> I enjoy seeing a rainbow.
> (*The speaker is talking about any rainbow, as indicated by "a rainbow."*)

> It was an experience I'll never forget.
> (*"Experience" is a general idea and begins with a vowel sound.*)

NOTE: Use *the* rather than *a* or *an* with noncount nouns or plural count nouns.

> **Incorrect:** I love a sunshine.
> **Correct:** I love the sunshine.

NOTE: If a word begins with an *h* that is pronounced, use *a*. If the *h* is silent, use *an*.

> **Incorrect:** I stared for a hour.
> **Correct:** I stared for an hour.

17.5 Other Noun Markers

▶ Possessives

A **possessive** is the possessive case of a noun or pronoun showing ownership of another noun. Possessives are formed by adding an apostrophe and an *s* to singular nouns and an apostrophe to plural nouns. Table 17.6 lists possessive pronouns.

- **Paul's** car is in the shop, but **Taylor's** is fixed.
- **Florida's** coast is beautiful.
- The **Smiths'** porch has screens.
- That is **my** pen. This pen is **mine**.
- It's **your** choice. The choice is **yours**.

Table 17.6 Possessive Pronouns

	Singular		Plural	
	Before Noun	**After Noun**	**Before Noun**	**After Noun**
First Person	my	mine	our	ours
Second Person	your	yours	your	yours
Third Person	his	his	their	theirs
	her	hers	their	theirs
	its	its	their	theirs

▶ Indefinite Adjectives

An **indefinite adjective** marks a general noun. Some indefinite adjectives mark count nouns and others mark noncount nouns.

> **Each** person brought food. **Much** food was set out. **Some** ants found **some** food.

Table 17.7 shows how to use indefinite adjectives.

Table 17.7 Indefinite Adjectives

With Count Nouns			With Noncount Nouns			With Count or Noncount		
each	either	several	much	little	less	all	any	more
few	many	neither				most	enough	some

▶ Demonstrative Adjectives

A **demonstrative adjective** marks a specific noun. The words *this* and *that* (singular) or *these* and *those* (plural) demonstrate exactly which one is meant.

> **These** pickles are from **that** jar.   **This** taste comes from **those** spices.

▶ Quantifiers

A **quantifier** tells *how many* or *how much* of something. Table 17.8 shows examples.

Table 17.8 Quantifiers

With Count Nouns		With Noncount Nouns		With Count or Noncount	
each	nine	a bag of	a little	no	a lot of	most
several	every	a bowl of	much	not any	lots of	all
a number of	many	a piece of	a great deal of	some	plenty of	
both	a few					

Practice 17.2 ▸ Choose the correct article in parentheses to complete the following paragraph.

Climate scientists see a shift in (a, an, the) weather. With rising levels of carbon dioxide in (a, an, the) environment, the atmosphere is trapping (a, an, the) heat of the sun. More heat in the air means more heat in the oceans. If (a, the) ocean gets warmer, the storms it creates are more intense. (A, An) hurricane could advance to (a, an) higher category, with stronger winds and more lightning. Kerry Emanuel, (a, an) hurricane expert at the Massachusetts Institute of Technology, developed (a, an) approach to measure (a, an, the) total energy expended by tropical cyclones over their lifetimes. In 2005, he showed that Atlantic hurricanes were about 60 percent more powerful than they were in the 1970s. (A, An, The) Earth is already (a, an, the) stormy world, but with (a, an) rise in global temperatures, (a, an, the) weather could become even more extreme.

Practice 17.3 ▸ Identify the appropriate noun marker in parentheses to complete each sentence.

1. I brought one of (my, mine) favorite recipes, and you brought one of (your, yours).

2. Is this (her, hers) recipe, or is it (their, theirs)?

3. How (many, much) sugar should I add to the batter?

4. I can't believe the recipe does not use (any, each) flour.

5. Next, we should make (this, these) casserole.

6. Your face tells me you don't like (that, those) idea.

7. After making the dough, we had (several, a little) butter left over.

8. We liked (a number of, much) the recipes.

9. The best pie of all was (her, hers).

10. Let's make sure they have a copy in (their, theirs) recipe files.

 Real-World Application

Choose the correct article and noun markers in the following email.

To: Design and Printing Staff

Subject: Internship Program for College Students

Hi, Team:

Could you use (a, an, the) assistant—(a, an, the) intern who is ready to work hard?

The head of the Graphic Arts Department at Northwestern College has asked us if we'd be interested in developing internships for third-year students in (a, an, the) college's four-year graphic-arts program.

Internships could be (an, the) solution to our current staff shortage. Interns would do the following:

- work on tasks that you assign.
- improve (their, theirs) professional experience by working with you.
- give us an opportunity to work with potential employees.

Please consider working with (a, an, the) student intern during the fall semester. If you are interested, let me know before January 28.

Thanks for considering (this, these) invitation to help future members of (the, an) graphic arts profession.

Melissa

Rawpixel.com, 2017 / Used under license from Shutterstock.com

18

Pronouns

"Clothes make the man" is an old saying. But is it true? Well, not quite. Just because a suit is standing on a mannequin in the window doesn't mean that a living, breathing, and thinking person is in the room. The clothes are just temporary stand-ins.

Pronouns, similarly, are stand-ins for nouns. They aren't nouns, but they suggest nouns or refer back to them. That's why it's especially important for the pronoun to clearly connect to whatever it is replacing.

This chapter will help you make sure your pronoun stand-ins work well.

Chapter Outline

- Personal Pronouns
- Pronoun-Antecedent Agreement
- Indefinite Pronouns
- Relative Pronouns
- Other Pronoun Types

18.1 Personal Pronouns

A **pronoun** takes the place of a noun or another pronoun. **Personal pronouns** indicate whether the person is speaking (first person), is being spoken to (second person), or is being spoken about (third person). **Table 18.1** lists the personal pronouns.

Table 18.1 Personal Pronouns

Person	Singular			Plural		
	Nom.	Obj.	Poss.	Nom.	Obj.	Poss.
First *(speaking)*	I	me	my/mine	we	us	our/ours
Second *(spoken to)*	you	you	your/yours	you	you	your/yours
Third *(spoken about)*						
masculine	he	him	his	they	them	their/theirs
feminine	she	her	her/hers	they	them	their/theirs
neuter	it	it	its	they	them	their/theirs

Nom. = nominative case / **Obj.** = objective case / **Poss.** = possessive case

► Case of Pronouns

The case of a pronoun indicates how it can be used.

- **Nominative pronouns** are used as subjects or as subject complements. Subject complements follow linking verbs (*am, is, are, was, were, be, being,* or *been*) and refer to the subject. The subject complement in the example follows the linking verb "was" and refers to the subject "it."

  He ate the pie. It was he.
  subject   subject   subject complement

- **Objective pronouns** are used as direct objects, indirect objects, or objects of prepositions.

  The police officer warned us about them.
                        direct object   object of the preposition

Insight To decide whether to use *I* or *me* with compound subjects, read the sentence aloud without the second subject; the sentence should make sense with the pronoun—*I* or *me*—alone.
My roommate and *me* went to the library. (Incorrect)
My roommate and *I* went to the library. (Correct: Take out "my roommate and"; the sentence still makes sense.)

- **Possessive pronouns** show ownership.

  Her lawn looks much greener than mine.
  possessive   possessive

▶ **Gender**

Pronouns can be masculine, feminine, or neuter.

He showed her how to fix it.
masculine   feminine   neuter

18.2 Pronoun-Antecedent Agreement

The antecedent is the word that a pronoun refers to or replaces. A pronoun and its antecedent agree when they have the same person, number, and gender.

Colleen thought she would need a lift, but her car started.

Antecedent   Third-person: singular feminine

▶ **Agreement in Person**

A pronoun needs to match its antecedent in person (first, second, or third).

third person   second person

Incorrect: If people keep going, you can usually reach the goal.

Correct: If you keep going, you can usually reach the goal.

Correct: If people keep going, they can usually reach the goal.

▶ **Agreement in Number**

A pronoun needs to match its antecedent in number (singular or plural).

plural   singular

Incorrect: Lifeguards must buy his own uniform.

Correct: Lifeguards must buy their own uniforms.

Correct: Each lifeguard must buy their own uniform.

▶ **Agreement in Gender**

A pronoun needs to match its antecedent in gender (masculine, feminine, or neuter).

feminine   masculine

Incorrect: Mrs. Miller will present his speech.

Correct: Mrs. Miller will present her speech.

Practice 18.1 Select the correct personal pronoun in parentheses.

1. (I, Me, My) love to hang out at the corner coffee shop.

2. (I, Me, My) friends and I go there on Saturday morning.

3. One friend, Zach, is making a film, and (he, him, his) asked Susan and me to be in it.

4. The coffee shop owners agreed to let (we, us, our) film there.

5. We read over the lines, and other patrons listened to (we, us, our).

6. The camera rolled, and Rachel and (I, me, my) started reading our lines.

7. Unfortunately, we forgot (we, us, our) lines a few times.

8. A couple of times, Rachel and (I, me, my) had to stop because the owners were laughing, and that made (we, us, our) laugh, too.

9. Eventually, (she, her, hers) and I finished the scene in flawless fashion.

Practice 18.2 Select the pronoun that agrees with the underlined antecedent in person, number, and gender.

1. When you go to the multiplex, (you, a person) have a lot of movies to choose from.

2. We must buy (your, our) own tickets and snacks.

3. If viewers arrive early enough, (you, they) can see a triple feature.

4. People may be overwhelmed by how many movies (you, they) can see.

5. The moviegoers choose which movies (you, they) may want to see.

6. Snack-counter attendants serve treats, and (she, they) also clean up messes.

7. Movie critics give (his, their) opinions about different films.

8. If a critic gives away the ending, (you, they) will ruin the movie for viewers.

9. When viewers love a movie, (he, they) often tell others about it.

10. The multiplex is impressive; (she, it) looks like a palace on the hill.

18.3 Indefinite Pronouns

An indefinite pronoun does not have an antecedent, and it does not refer to a specific person, place, thing, or idea. These pronouns pose unique issues with agreement.

► Singular Indefinite Pronouns

The indefinite pronouns in **Table 18.2** are singular. When used as subjects, they require a singular verb (see **Section 19.2**). As antecedents, they must be matched to singular pronouns.

Table 18.2 Personal Pronouns

each	anyone	somebody	everything
either	someone	everybody	nothing
neither	everyone	nobody	
another	no one	anything	
one	anybody	something	

Nobody on our camping trip expects to see Bigfoot.
singular subject   singular verb

NOTE: When a singular pronoun refers to a person of any gender, do not use the singular "his or her." Instead, use *they/their/them* as a third-person singular pronoun.

Someone used their own money to buy a Bigfoot detector at a novelty shop.
singular antecedent   singular *they* pronoun

► Plural Indefinite Pronouns

The indefinite pronouns in **Table 18.3** are plural. As subjects, they require a plural verb (see **Section 19.2**), and as antecedents, they require a plural pronoun.

Table 18.3 Plural Indefinite Pronouns

both	several
few	many

A few of the campers hear thumps in the night.
plural subject   plural verb

Several of my friends swear they can see eyes glowing eight feet off the ground.
plural antecedent   plural pronoun

► Singular or Plural Indefinite Pronouns

The indefinite pronouns in Table 18.4 can be singular or plural, depending on the object of the preposition in the phrase that follows them.

Table 18.4 Singular or Plural Indefinite Pronouns

all	most	some
any	none	

plural object   singular object

Most of us are too frightened to sleep.   Most of the night is over anyway.
plural subject   plural verb   singular subject   singular verb

18.4   Relative Pronouns

A **relative pronoun** *(who, whom, which, whose, whoever, whomever, that)* introduces a dependent clause. (The dependent clauses in the examples that follow are indicated by **bold** type.)

> I would like to meet the person who **discovered dark matter**.

■ **Who/Whoever** and **Whom/Whomever**—These pronouns refer to people. *Who* and *whoever* are used as subjects, while *whom* and *whomever* are used as objects.

> The astronomer who **imagined invisible matter** amazes me. The astronomer, whom **I was honored to meet**, is Vera Rubin.

■ **That** and **Which**—These pronouns usually refer to things. Clauses beginning with *that* are not set off with commas, while those that begin with *which* are set off with commas.

> I saw a show that **explained dark matter**. The show, which **is called *Into the Wormhole***, is on the Science Channel.

■ **Whose**—This pronoun indicates ownership or connection.

> Morgan Freeman, whose **voice is soothing**, hosts the show.

18.5   Other Pronoun Types

Other types of pronouns have specific uses in your writing.

■ An **interrogative pronoun** asks a question *(who, whose, whom, which, what)*.

> What shall we call our band? Who will be in it?

■ A **demonstrative pronoun** points to a specific thing *(this, that, these, those)*.

> That is a great name! This will get attention.

■ A **reflexive pronoun** reflects back to the subject of a sentence *(myself, ourselves, yourself, yourselves, himself, herself, itself, themselves)*.

> We gave ourselves credit for thinking of an awesome name.

■ An **intensive pronoun** emphasizes the noun or pronoun it refers to *(myself, ourselves, yourself, yourselves, himself, herself, itself, themselves)*.

> I myself suggested the name Psycho Drummer.

■ A **reciprocal pronoun** refers to the individuals within a plural antecedent *(each other, one another)*.

> The band members always support one another.

Practice 18.3 Select the correct verb for each underlined indefinite pronoun.

1. <u>Everyone</u> (need, needs) to set up their own tent.

2. <u>Anyone</u> who (want, wants) to be dry (puts, put) up a rain fly.

3. <u>Nothing</u> (is, are) more miserable than lying in a wet sleeping bag.

4. <u>Several</u> (has, have) gone hiking to look for Bigfoot.

5. <u>One</u> of the Bigfoot hunters (remind, reminds) the others to take their cameras.

6. <u>Most</u> of the hunters (is, are) also going to carry big sticks.

7. <u>None</u> of the campers (is, are) planning to hike after dark.

8. <u>None</u> of the food (is, are) left out to attract animals or Bigfoot.

Practice 18.4 For each sentence, select the correct relative pronoun.

1. Vera Rubin, (who, whom) first discovered dark matter, wasn't seeking fame.

2. In the 1960s, she avoided black holes, (that, which) were a hot topic.

3. Instead, Rubin focused on the rotation of spiral galaxies, (that, which) few other people studied.

4. She expected stars (that, which) were on the outside of galaxies would move faster than stars (that, which) were near the center.

5. Instead, Rubin discovered that all of the galaxy's stars, (that, which) are in many different positions within the galaxy, move at the same speed.

6. Other astrophysicists (who, whom) did not believe Rubin did similar observations and calculations and confirmed her findings.

Practice 18.5 Write the type of each underlined pronoun: *interrogative, demonstrative, reflexive, intensive,* or *reciprocal.*

1. <u>That</u> is why this band needs a road crew. _____

2. <u>What</u> are we supposed to do without power cords? _____

3. I <u>myself</u> would not mind playing unplugged. _____

4. You need to remind <u>yourself</u> that we don't have acoustic guitars. _____

5. As a band, we should help <u>one another</u> solve this problem. _____

🌐 Real-World Application

Practice 18.6 Select the correct pronoun from those listed within parentheses.

Psycho Drummer
12185 W. 22nd Avenue, Elkhorn, WI 53100 Ph: 262.555.7188

July 30, 2017

Ms. Marcia Schwamps, Manager
Piedog Studios
350 South Jackson Street
Elkhorn, WI 53100

Dear Ms. Schwamps:

One of your recording technicians says that you are looking for session musicians (who, whom) could play instruments for other artists. My bandmate Jerome and (me, I) would like to offer (our, ours) services.

Jerome and (me, I) are the power duo (who, whom) is called Psycho Drummer, a name that refers to Jerome (himself, hisself). He is a master percussionist, and (he, him) has trained (himself, hisself) in many styles, from heavy metal to rock, pop, jazz, blues, and even classical.

I am the guitarist in Psycho Drummer. I play electric and acoustic guitars as well as electric bass, and I, too, have taught (me, myself) to perform different styles of music.

Attached, you will find (our, ours) résumés, a list of recent gigs (us, we) have played, and a review of (us, we) from the *Walworth County Week*.

Please consider Jerome and (I, me) for work as session musicians at Piedog Studios. We look forward to hearing from (you, yous) and would very much appreciate an interview/audition.

Sincerely,

Terrance 'Tear-It-Up' Clark

Terrance "Tear-It-Up" Clark
Guitarist

Chapter **19**

Verbs

You've probably heard that a shark has to keep swimming or it suffocates. That's not entirely true. Yes, sharks breathe by moving water across their gills, but they can also lie on the bottom and push water through their gills or let currents do the work. Still, most sharks stay on the move, and when a shark is still, it has to work harder to breathe.

Verbs are similar in that some are active whereas others seem to be still. Most verbs are action words, describing what is happening. However, some verbs describe states of being—much like sharks sitting on the bottom, breathing. Either way, though, the verb gives life to the sentence. This chapter takes you into the compelling world of verbs.

Chapter Outline

- Classes of Verbs
- Number and Person
- Voice
- Basic Tenses
- Progressive-Tense Verbs
- Perfect-Tense Verbs
- Verbals
- Verbals as Objects

19.1 Classes of Verbs

Verbs show action or express a state of being.

▶ Action Verbs

Verbs that show action are called **action verbs**. Some action verbs are **transitive**, which means that they transfer action to a direct object.

> Trina hurled the softball. (The verb *hurled* transfers action to the direct object *softball*.)

Others are **intransitive** and do not transfer action to a direct object.

> Trina pitches. (The verb *pitches* does not transfer action to a direct object.)

▶ Linking Verbs

Verbs that link the subject to a noun, a pronoun, or an adjective are **linking verbs**. They express a state of being.

> Trina is a pitcher. (The linking verb *is* connects *Trina* to the noun *pitcher*.)
>
> She seems unbeatable. (The linking verb *seems* connects *She* to the adjective *unbeatable*.)

Table 19.1 lists common linking verbs.

Table 19.1 Linking Verbs					
is	was	being	seem	look	sound
am	were	been	grow	smell	appear
are	be	become	feel	taste	remain

▶ Helping Verbs

A helping (or auxiliary) verb works with an action or a linking verb to form a certain tense, mood, or voice.

> Trina has pitched two shut-out games, and today she may be pitching her third. (The helping verbs *has* and *may be* work with the main verbs *pitched* and *pitching* to form special tenses.)

Table 19.2 lists common helping verbs.

Table 19.2 Helping Verbs

am	have	are	is	be	may
been	might	being	must	can	shall
could	should	did	was	do	were
does	will	had	would	has	

19.2 Number and Person

Verbs reflect number (singular or plural) and person (first, second, or third person).

▶ Number

The **number** of the verb indicates whether the subject is singular or plural.

> **Singular:** A Civil War re-enactment involves infantry, cavalry, and artillery units.
> **Plural:** Actors stage amazing battle scenes from the war.

NOTE: As shown in the examples, third-person present-tense singular verbs end in *s*; third-person present-tense plural verbs do not.

▶ Person

The **person** of a verb indicates whether the subject is speaking, being spoken to, or being spoken about. **Table 19.3** shows the number and person of *be* verbs.

Table 19.3 *Be* Verbs (Number and Person)

	Singular	Plural
First Person:	(I) am	(we) are
Second Person:	(you) are	(you) are
Third Person:	(he, she, it) is	(they) are

NOTE: The pronoun *I* takes a special form of the *be* verb—*am*—in present tense and is paired with *was* in past tense.

> **Incorrect:** I is eager to see the cannons fire.
> **Correct:** I am eager to see the cannons fire.

> **Incorrect:** I were not at the re-enactment last year.
> **Correct:** I was not at the re-enactment last year.

NOTE: No matter its use, *you* takes the plural form of the *be* verb.

> **Incorrect:** You is in for a treat when the battle begins.
> **Correct:** You are in for a treat when the battle begins.

> **Incorrect:** You was here early this morning.
> **Correct:** You were here early this morning.

Practice 19.1 Identify the correct class of the underlined verbs.

1. I <u>love</u> fast-pitch softball, but I rarely <u>pitch</u>.
   - a. Action
   - b. Linking
   - c. Helping

2. I play first base; it <u>is</u> a pressure-filled position.
   - a. Action
   - b. Linking
   - c. Helping

3. Runners charge first base, and I <u>must</u> tag them out.
   - a. Action
   - b. Linking
   - c. Helping

4. If a runner <u>steals</u>, the pitcher and second baseperson <u>work</u> with me.
   - a. Action
   - b. Linking
   - c. Helping

5. We <u>can</u> catch the runner in a "pickle" and tag her out.
   - a. Action
   - b. Linking
   - c. Helping

6. If we miss the tag, the runner can <u>remain</u> on base.
   - a. Action
   - b. Linking
   - c. Helping

Practice 19.2 For the following sentences, select the verb in parentheses that agrees with the sentence's subject in number and person.

1. We (is, are) at a Civil War re-enactment.

2. It (is, are) a gathering of Union and Confederate regiments.

3. I (am, are) wearing a gray uniform of the Confederacy.

4. You (am, are) in a uniform of Union blue.

5. I (jump, jumps) the first time a cannon goes off.

6. The guns (blow, blows) huge white smoke rings; the rings (whirl, whirls) into the air.

7. The cavalry regiments (charge, charges), and they (battle, battles) with sabers.

8. In the fray, one cavalry officer (fall, falls) from his horse.

9. We (is, are) acting as infantry soldiers. We (line, lines) up in two rows to send out volleys of bullets.

10. After the battle, President Lincoln (deliver, delivers) a solemn address.

11. I (is, am) humbled by his sincere words.

12. Let us all (take, took) his words to heart.

19.3 Voice

The voice of the verb indicates whether the subject is acting or being acted upon.

▶ Active Voice and Passive Voice

In **active voice**, the subject is acting. In **passive voice**, the subject is being acted upon.

> **Active:** The cast sang the song "Our State Fair."
>
> **Passive:** The song "Our State Fair" was sung by the cast.

Table 19.4 gives examples of active and passive voice.

Table 19.4 Active Voice and Passive Voice

	Active Voice		Passive Voice	
	Singular	**Plural**	**Singular**	**Plural**
Present Tense	I see you see he/she/it sees	we see you see they see	I am seen you are seen he/she/it is seen	we are seen you are seen they are seen
Past Tense	I saw you saw he saw	we saw you saw they saw	I was seen you were seen it was seen	we were seen you were seen they were seen
Future Tense	I will see you will see he will see	we will see you will see they will see	I will be seen you will be seen it will be seen	we will be seen you will be seen they will be seen
Present Perfect Tense	I have seen you have seen he has seen	we have seen you have seen they have seen	I have been seen you have been seen it has been seen	we have been seen you have been seen they have been seen
Past Perfect Tense	I had seen you had seen he had seen	we had seen you had seen they had seen	I had been seen you had been seen it had been seen	we had been seen you had been seen they had been seen
Future Perfect Tense	I will have seen you will have seen he will have seen	we will have seen you will have seen they will have seen	I will have been seen you will have been seen it will have been seen	we will have been seen you will have been seen they will have been seen

Active voice is preferred for most writing because it is direct and energetic.

> **Active:** The crowd gave the cast a standing ovation.
>
> **Passive:** The cast was given a standing ovation by the crowd.

Passive voice is preferred when the focus is on the receiver of the action or when the subject is unknown.

> **Passive:** A donation was left at the ticket office.
>
> **Active:** Someone left a donation at the ticket office.

19.4 Basic Tenses

Basic verb tenses tell whether action happens in the present, future, or past.

- **Present-tense verbs** express action that is happening now or routinely: *help, look, try.*

  Musicians gather at the Marlboro Music Festival.

- **Future-tense verbs** express action that will happen later: *will help, will look, will try.*

  The festival will launch the careers of many young stars.

- **Past-tense verbs** express action that already happened: *helped, looked, tried.*

  My friend attended the Marlboro Music Festival last year.

▶ Irregular Verbs

Most verbs form the past tense by adding *ed*, but irregular verbs form the past tense by changing the verb itself. **Table 19.5** shows the past tense of irregular verbs.

Table 19.5 Present and Past Tense of Irregular Verbs

Pres.	Past Part.	Pres.	Past Part.	Pres.	Past Part.
am, are	was, were	find	found	see	saw
become	became	fly	flew	shake	shook
begin	began	forget	forgot	shine	shone
blow	blew	freeze	froze	shrink	shrank
break	broke	get	got	sing	sang
bring	brought	give	gave	sink	sank
buy	bought	go	went	sit	sat
can	could	grow	grew	sleep	slept
catch	caught	hang	hung	speak	spoke
choose	chose	have	had	stand	stood
come	came	hear	heard	steal	stole
dig	dug	hide	hid	swim	swam
do	did	keep	kept	swing	swung
draw	drew	know	knew	take	took
drink	drank	lead	led	teach	taught
drive	drove	pay	paid	tear	tore
eat	ate	ride	rode	think	thought
fall	fell	ring	rang	throw	threw
feel	felt	rise	rose	wear	wore
fight	fought	run	ran	write	wrote

▶ Present Tense in Academic Writing

Use present-tense verbs to discuss fictional events in literature.

In the short story, the young pianist dreams of going to Marlboro.

Also use present-tense verbs (*writes, reports, asserts,* and so on) when quoting or summarizing material from periodicals.

The New York Times says that the performances at Marlboro are usually extraordinary.

Practice 19.3 Rewrite the following sentences, changing passive verbs to active verbs. Think about who or what is performing the action and make that the subject. The first one is done for you.

1. *State Fair* was put on by the community theater group.

   The community theater group put on <u>*State Fair.*</u>

2. The Frake family is featured in the musical.

   _____

3. Many songs were sung by the cast.

   _____

4. Pickles and mincemeat are rated by judges at the fair.

   _____

5. Mrs. Frake's mincemeat is spiked with too much brandy.

   _____

Practice 19.4 Select the present-tense form of the verb in parentheses.

1. Young musicians (come, came) to the Marlboro Music Festival by special invitation.

2. Seasoned professionals (treat, treated) them like colleagues, not students.

3. Musicians (worked, work) side by side for weeks before performing.

4. The town of Marlboro, Vermont, (had, has) only 987 citizens.

5. Many visitors (travel, traveled) to the city each summer.

Practice 19.5 Select the past-tense form of the verb in parentheses.

1. Jillian (swings, swung) from rope to rope during the obstacle race.

2. She almost (slipped, slips) on a wet rock along the forest trail.

3. She (runs, ran) alongside her friend and training partner.

4. Approaching the final obstacle, they (give, gave) each other a reassuring glance.

5. Holding hands, they triumphantly (jump, jumped) across the finish line.

19.5 Progressive-Tense Verbs

The basic tenses tell when action takes place—past, present, or future. The progressive tenses indicate that action is ongoing.

- **Progressive tenses** are formed by using a helping verb along with the *ing* form of the main verb. Each uses a helping verb in the appropriate basic tense—either past, present, or future.

> For thousands of years, most humans were working in agriculture. (past progressive)
>
> Currently in the West, most humans are working in nonagricultural jobs. (present progressive)
>
> In the future, people will be working in unimaginable occupations. (future progressive)

	Forming Progressive Tense				
Past:	was/were	+	main verb	+	ing
Present:	am/is/are	+	main verb	+	ing
Future:	will be	+	main verb	+	ing

Insight   **Avoid** using the progressive tense with . . .

- Verbs that express thoughts, attitudes, and desires: *know, understand, want, prefer*
- Verbs that describe appearances: *seem, resemble*
- Verbs that indicate possession: *belong, have, own, possess*

> **Incorrect:** I am knowing your name.
>
> **Correct:** I know your name.

> **Incorrect:** Stan was owning a new car.
>
> **Correct:** Stan owned a new car.

19.6 Perfect-Tense Verbs

The perfect tenses tell that action is finished, not ongoing, whether in the past, present, or future.

■ **Perfect tenses** are formed by using a helping verb along with the past-tense form of the main verb. Each uses a helping verb in the appropriate basic tense—either past, present, or future.

By the end of my first year on the job, I had learned the basic sales procedures. (past perfect)

This year, I have learned new technology skills. (present perfect)

By this time next year, I will have learned how to be an effective salesperson. (future perfect)

	Forming Perfect Tense		
Past:	had	+	past-tense main verb
Present:	has/have	+	past-tense main verb
Future:	will have	+	past-tense main verb

▶ Perfect Tense with Irregular Verbs

To form the perfect tenses with irregular verbs, use the past participle instead of the past-tense form. Table 19.6 shows the past participles of common irregular verbs.

Table 19.6 Present Tense and Past Participles of Irregular Verbs

Pres.	Past Part.	Pres.	Past Part.	Pres.	Past Part.
am, are	been	fly	flown	see	seen
become	become	forget	forgotten	shake	shaken
begin	begun	freeze	frozen	shine	shone
blow	blown	get	gotten	show	shown
break	broken	give	given	shrink	shrunk
bring	brought	go	gone	sing	sung
buy	bought	grow	grown	sink	sunk
catch	caught	hang	hung	sit	sat
choose	chosen	have	had	sleep	slept
come	come	hear	heard	speak	spoken
dig	dug	hide	hidden	stand	stood
do	done	keep	kept	steal	stolen
draw	drawn	know	known	swim	swum
drink	drunk	lead	led	swing	swung
drive	driven	pay	paid	take	taken
eat	eaten	prove	proven	teach	taught
fall	fallen	ride	ridden	tear	torn
feel	felt	ring	rung	throw	thrown
fight	fought	rise	risen	wear	worn
find	found	run	run	write	written

Practice 19.6   Select the type of progressive-tense verb demonstrated in each sentence.

1. Agribusiness will be making food production more efficient in the future.
    a. Present progressive
    b. Past progressive
    c. Future progressive

2. The products and services in greatest demand were producing the greatest wealth.
    a. Present progressive
    b. Past progressive
    c. Future progressive

3. The new agribusiness will be providing a boost to the local economy.
    a. Present progressive
    b. Past progressive
    c. Future progressive

4. Agribusinesses are providing various products and services.
    a. Present progressive
    b. Past progressive
    c. Future progressive

Practice 19.7   Select the type of perfect-tense verb demonstrated in each sentence.

1. I have worked hard and have listened carefully.
    a. Present perfect
    b. Past perfect
    c. Future perfect

2. The employees will have gained their positions by being qualified, and they will have kept them by being helpful.
    a. Present perfect
    b. Past perfect
    c. Future perfect

3. Your colleagues had depended on you, and you had delivered the reports on time.
    a. Present perfect
    b. Past perfect
    c. Future perfect

19.7 Verbals

A **verbal** is formed from a verb but functions as a noun, an adjective, or an adverb. Each type of verbal—gerund, participle, and infinitive—can appear alone or can begin a **verbal phrase**.

▶ Gerund

A gerund is formed from a verb ending in *ing*, and it functions as a noun.

> Kayaking **is a fun type of exercise.** (subject)
>
> I love kayaking. (direct object)

A **gerund phrase** begins with a gerund and includes any objects and modifiers.

> Running rapids in a kayak **is exhilarating.** (subject)
>
> I enjoy paddling a kayak through white water. (direct object)

▶ Participle

A **participle** is formed from a verb ending in *ing* or *ed*, and it functions as an adjective.

> I was exhilarated **by the experience.** (adjective modifying *I*)
>
> That was an exhilarating **ride!** (adjective modifying *ride*)

A **participial phrase** begins with a participle and includes any objects and modifiers.

> Shocking my parents, **I said I wanted to go again.** (adjective modifying *I*)

▶ Infinitive

An infinitive is formed from *to* and a present-tense verb, and it functions as a noun, an adjective, or an adverb.

> To kayak in rough waters **is dangerous.** (noun)
>
> I will schedule more time to kayak. (adjective modifying *time*)
>
> My whole family is eager to kayak. (adverb modifying *eager*)

An **infinitive phrase** begins with an infinitive and includes any objects or modifiers.

> I want to kayak the Colorado River through the Grand Canyon. (noun phrase)

19.8 Verbals as Objects

Though both infinitives and gerunds can function as direct objects, some verbs take infinitives but not gerunds, and others take gerunds but not infinitives.

► Gerunds as Objects

Verbs that tell something real or true use gerunds as direct objects. Table 19.7 lists verbs that are followed by gerunds.

Table 19.7 Verbs Followed by Gerunds

admit	miss	discuss	regret	imagine
deny	recommend	finish	consider	recall
enjoy	avoid	quit	dislike	

> **Incorrect:** I miss to walk along the beach.
> **Correct:** I miss walking along the beach.
> **Incorrect:** I regret to cut our vacation short.
> **Correct:** I regret cutting our vacation short.

► Infinitives as Objects

Verbs that tell something you hope for or intend use infinitives as direct objects. Table 19.8 lists verbs that are followed by infinitives.

Table 19.8 Verbs Followed by Infinitives

agree	volunteer	promise	need	fail	hesitate
demand	appear	want	refuse	offer	plan
hope	deserve	attempt	wish	seem	tend
prepare	intend	endeavor	consent	decide	

> **Incorrect:** We plan going back to the lake.
> **Correct:** We plan to go back to the lake.
>
> **Incorrect:** We intend saving money for the trip.
> **Correct:** We intend to save money for the trip.

► Gerunds or Infinitives as Objects

Some verbs use other gerunds or infinitives as direct objects. Table 19.9 lists verbs that can be followed by either gerunds or infinitives.

Table 19.9 Verbs Followed by Gerunds or Infinitives

begin	love	stop	like	start
hate	remember	continue	prefer	try

> **Correct:** I love walking by the ocean.
> **Correct:** I love to walk by the ocean.

Practice 19.8 Select whether the underlined verbal or verbal phrase is a *gerund, participle,* or an *infinitive.*

1. <u>Rock climbing</u> is an extreme sport.
   a. Gerund   b. Participle   c. Infinitive

2. I'd like <u>to climb El Capitan</u> one day.
   a. Gerund   b. Participle   c. Infinitive

3. <u>Rappelling down a cliff</u> in Arizona, I almost slipped.
   a. Gerund   b. Participle   c. Infinitive

4. <u>Catching myself</u>, I checked my lines and carabiners.
   a. Gerund   b. Participle   c. Infinitive

5. <u>To fall while climbing</u> could be fatal.
   a. Gerund   b. Participle   c. Infinitive

6. I keep my equipment in top shape <u>to avoid a mishap</u>.
   a. Gerund   b. Participle   c. Infinitive

7. When rock climbing, remember <u>to breathe deeply</u>.
   a. Gerund   b. Participle   c. Infinitive

8. <u>Reaching the summit</u> feels amazing.
   a. Gerund   b. Participle   c. Infinitive

Practice 19.9 For the following sentences, select the appropriate verbal in parentheses.

1. I imagine (walking, to walk) along the Pacific Coast.

2. We want (seeing, to see) whales or dolphins when we are there.

3. I hope (getting, to get) some beautiful shots of the ocean.

4. We should avoid (getting, to get) sunburned when we are on the beach.

5. I enjoy (getting, to get) sand between my toes.

6. Maybe a surfer will offer (showing, to show) me how to surf.

7. We deserve (going, to go) on vacation more often.

8. Later, we will regret not (taking, to take) the time for ourselves.

9. I have never regretted (taking, to take) a vacation.

10. I wish (having, to have) a vacation right now.

🌐 Real-World Application

Review the following business letter. Select the correct form of the verb or verbal in the parentheses. Remember that verbs must agree with their subjects in number and person.

Guiverra's Computer Training
2204 East Chase Dr. Miami, FL 33166

March 22, 2017

Mr. Gavin Farnsworth
Miami Computer Enterprises
1202 South Benton
Miami, FL 33166-1217

Dear Mr. Farnsworth:

I (has, have) reviewed your letter of March 15. In response to your proposal, I (is, am) happy to offer my consulting services to Miami Computer Enterprises customers.

This arrangement will benefit all parties involved. Together, we will be able (to offer, offering) your clients "one-stop shopping" for all (its, their) computer needs—hardware, software, training, and support. And I will be able to work with your established customer base without having (generating, to generate) my own.

Therefore, I (accept, accepts) your proposed rate of $45 per hour as indicated in the amended agreement. Please note that the bold items on the outline (indicate, indicates) additions to the original proposal. I simply added the items (cover, covered) in your letter.

Please let me know of any specific information or documentation that you (need, needs) to see on my invoices. I anticipate (to have, having) a productive partnership in which we will serve each other and your clients.

Yours sincerely,

Juanita Guiverra

Juanita Guiverra

Chapter 20

Adjectives and Adverbs

The purpose of makeup is to accentuate the beauty that is already in your face. The focus should be on you, not on the mascara, lipstick, foundation, or blush you use.

In the same way, the real beauty of a sentence lies in the nouns and verbs. Adjectives and adverbs can modify those words, adding fine points to the message, but modifiers should never overwhelm a sentence. Use them sparingly to make your meaning clear. This chapter will show you how to get the most out of adjectives and adverbs.

Chapter Outline

- Adjective Basics
- Adjective Order
- Adverb Basics
- Adverb Placement

20.1 Adjective Basics

An **adjective** is a word that modifies a noun or pronoun. Even articles such as *a, an,* and *the* are adjectives, indicating whether you mean a general or specific thing. Adjectives answer these basic questions: *which? what kind of? how many? how much?*

Adjectives often appear before the words they modify.

> I saw a beautiful gray tabby cat.

A **predicate adjective** appears after the noun it modifies and is linked to the word by a linking verb.

> The cat was beautiful and gray.

Proper adjectives are formed from proper nouns and are capitalized.

> I also saw a Persian cat.

► Forms of Adjectives

Adjectives have three forms: positive, comparative, and superlative.

- **Positive adjectives** describe a noun or pronoun without making a comparison.

  > Fred is a graceful cat.

- **Comparative adjectives** compare two nouns or pronouns.

  > Fred is more graceful than our dog, Barney.

- **Superlative adjectives** compare three or more nouns or pronouns.

  > He is the most graceful cat you will ever see.

NOTE: Create the comparative form of most one- or two-syllable words by adding *er*, and create the superlative form by adding *est*. For words of three syllables or more, use *more* (or *less*) to create comparatives and *most* (or *least*) to create superlatives. The adjectives *good* and *bad* have special comparative and superlative forms. Table 20.1 shows examples of the forms.

Table 20.1 Forms of Adjectives

Positive	Comparative	Superlative
big	bigger	biggest
happy	happier	happiest
wonderful	more wonderful	most wonderful

Positive	Comparative	Superlative
good	better	best
bad	worse	worst

20.2 Adjective Order

Adjectives describe in different ways. Some adjectives refer to time; some refer to shape, size, color, and other features. English uses a specific order for adjectives when several of them appear before a noun. **Table 20.2** shows the correct order of different adjectives.

Table 20.2 Adjective Order

Begin with . . .

1. articles	a, an, the
demonstrative adjectives	that, this, these, those
possessives	my, our, her, their, Kayla's

Then position adjectives that tell . . .

2. time	first, second, next, last
3. how many	three, few, some, many
4. value	important, prized, fine
5. size	giant, puny, hulking
6. shape	spiky, blocky, square
7. condition	clean, tattered, repaired
8. age	old, new, classic
9. color	blue, scarlet, salmon
10. nationality	French, Chinese, Cuban
11. religion	Baptist, Buddhist, Hindu
12. material	cloth, stone, wood, bronze

> **Insight** Even though there is an accepted order for multiple adjectives, avoid stacking too many modifiers in front of a noun.

Finally place . . .

13. nouns used as adjectives	baby [seat], shoe [lace]

Example:

I visited that ruined ancient stone temple.

(1 + 7 + 8 + 12 + noun)

▶ Adjective Phrases and Clauses

There are many single-word adjectives to choose from when you write, but several kinds of phrases (prepositional, participial, infinitive) and **adjective clauses** also modify nouns and pronouns.

I enjoy the restaurant at the corner of 5th Avenue and Erie Street. (adjective phrase)

I'm impressed by chefs who take creative risks. (adjective clause)

Practice 20.1 Cross out and correct the adjective errors in the following sentences. The first one has been done for you. Note: Some sentences can be corrected by crossing out a word and not replacing it.

1. The shelter had a Siamese cat with the ~~most dark~~ *darkest* eyes I've ever seen.

2. Some people say dogs are more tamer than cats.

3. But cats have a more great place in some people's hearts.

4. Cats were probably first attracted to human civilizations during the most early days of the agricultural revolution.

5. Cats that were the most best mousers were welcomed by humans.

6. In time, cuter and more cuddly cats became pets.

7. Even now, a barn cat that is not used to human touch can be wilder than a dog.

Practice 20.2 Select the correct order of adjectives to fill in each blank and complete each sentence.

1. I lost _____button.
   a. square blue that
   b. that blue square
   c. that square blue

2. A tailor made _____kilt.
   a. my new Scottish
   b. my Scottish new
   c. new Scottish my

3. Go buy a _____beads.
   a. brand-new plastic few
   b. few brand-new plastic
   c. few plastic brand-new

4. This is _____tack.
   a. a brass worthless
   b. a worthless brass
   c. worthless a brass

5. The museum holds _____masks.
   a. Kenyan classic many
   b. many Kenyan classic
   c. many classic Kenyan

6. We'll need _____stands.
   a. seven identical music
   b. identical seven music
   c. seven music identical

20.3 Adverb Basics

An **adverb** modifies a verb (or verbal), an adjective, an adverb, or a whole sentence. An adverb answers these basic questions: *how? when? where? why? to what degree? how often? how long?*

> Insight Intensifying adverbs such as *very* and *really* should be used sparingly. Also, in academic writing, it is better to use a precise, vivid verb than to prop up an imprecise verb with an adverb.

Sheri leaped fearlessly.
(*Fearlessly* modifies the verb *leaped*.)

Sheri leaped quite readily.
(*Quite* modifies the adverb *readily*, which modifies the verb *leaped*.)

Obviously she wants to fly.
(*Obviously* modifies the whole sentence.)

NOTE: Most adverbs end in *ly*. Some can be written with or without the *ly*, but when in doubt, use the *ly* form.

loud ⟶ loudly   tight ⟶ tightly   deep ⟶ deeply

▶ Forms of Adverbs

Adverbs have three forms: positive, comparative, and superlative.

- **Positive adverbs** describe without comparing.

    Sheri leaped high and fearlessly.

- **Comparative adverbs** (*-er, more,* or *less*) compare two actions.

    She leaped higher and more fearlessly than I did.

- **Superlative adverbs** (*-est, most,* or *least*) compare three or more actions. (Superlative adverbs are usually preceded by the definitive article *the*.)

    She leaped the highest and the most fearlessly of any of us.

NOTE: Some adverbs have special comparative or superlative forms.

well ⟶ better ⟶ best   badly ⟶ worse ⟶ worst

20.4 Adverb Placement

Adverbs should be placed in a way that makes the meaning of the sentence.

- *How* **Adverbs:** These can appear in several places but not between a verb and a direct object.

  Correct: Steadily we hiked the trail.
  Correct: We steadily hiked the trail.
  Correct: We hiked the trail steadily.
  Incorrect: We hiked steadily the trail.

- *When* **Adverbs:** Place these at the beginning or end of the sentence.

  We hiked to base camp yesterday. Today we'll reach the peak.

- *Where* **Adverbs:** Place these after the verb they modify but not between the verb and the direct object. (**NOTE:** Prepositional phrases often function as *where* adverbs.)

  Correct: The trail wound uphill and passed through rock-slide debris.
  Correct: We avoided falling rocks along the way.
  Incorrect: We avoided along the way falling rocks.

- **Adverbs of *Degree*:** Place these right before the adverb or adjective they modify.

  I very definitely learned the value of good hiking boots. They were really helpful.

- *How Often* **Adverbs:** Place these right before an action verb (between the verb and its helping verb if it has one).

  I often remember that wonderful hike.
  I will never forget the sights I saw.

▶ Adverb Phrases and Clauses

There are many single-word adverbs to choose from when you write, but certain phrases (prepositional and infinitive) and **adverb clauses** also serve this purpose.

Slowly and carefully, check each line of code. (adverb phrase)

Before you submit the report, make certain to double-check your data. (adverb clause)

NOTE: Adverb clauses are dependent clauses, meaning they must connect to an independent clause to form a complete sentence. (See Section 13.7.)

Practice 20.3 For the following sentences, select the correct form of the adverb in parentheses: *positive, comparative,* or *superlative.*

1. My friend eats (quickly, more quickly, the most quickly).

2. She eats (quickly, more quickly, the most quickly) than I do.

3. She eats (quickly, more quickly, the most quickly) of all our friends.

4. Compared to his classmates, my brother eats (reluctantly, more reluctantly, the most reluctantly).

5. He eats (reluctantly, more reluctantly, the most reluctantly) than I do.

6. And I eat (reluctantly, more reluctantly, the most reluctantly) too.

7. I eat (slowly, more slowly, the most slowly) than I used to.

8. Of all my family members, I eat (slowly, more slowly, the most slowly).

9. I suppose the three of us all eat (oddly, more oddly, the most oddly) than most.

10. Do you eat (oddly, more oddly, the most oddly)?

Practice 20.4 Choose the sentence that places the underlined adverb correctly.

1. **a.** In order to scare off bears, we <u>occasionally</u> made noise.
  b. In order to scare off bears, we made <u>occasionally</u> noise.

2. **a.** Bears avoid <u>usually</u> contact with human beings.
  b. Bears <u>usually</u> avoid contact with human beings.

3. **a.** A bear that is surprised or cornered by people will turn <u>often</u> to attack.
  b. A bear that is surprised or cornered by people will <u>often</u> turn to attack.

4. **a.** A mother bear with cubs is <u>very</u> likely to attack.
  b. A mother bear with cubs is likely <u>very</u> to attack.

5. **a.** If a bear approaches, playing dead may <u>sometimes</u> work.
  b. If a bear approaches, playing dead <u>sometimes</u> may work.

6. **a.** Climbing a tree won't <u>usually</u> work.
  b. Climbing a tree <u>usually</u> won't work.

7. **a.** Black bears climb <u>often</u> trees.
  b. Black bears <u>often</u> climb trees.

8. **a.** Grizzly bears <u>usually</u> knock the tree down.
  b. Grizzly bears knock <u>usually</u> the tree down.

 Real-World Application

Practice 20.5 In the following document, choose the correct adjective or adverb in parentheses.

January 6, 2017

Mrs. Judy Bednar
38115 North Bayfield Drive
Eugene, OR 97401

Dear Ms. Bednar:

It's time for a birthday party! You've thought of everything—balloons, decorations, cake. . . . But what about (awesomely, awesome) entertainment? How many kids are coming, and how much time do you have to keep them entertained?

Fear not. At Clowning Around, we work (ambitious, ambitiously) to make every birthday the (memorably, most memorable) it can be. For young kids, we offer (colorfully, colorful) balloon animals, amazing magic tricks, and goofy backyard games. For older kids, we have wild water games and (impressive, impressively) magic illusions. And for kids of all ages, we (proudly, proud) have the funniest clowns, the bravest superheroes, and the most (amazingly, amazing) impressionists.

That's right. You can throw a (terrific, terrifically) party for your loved one without worrying about the entertainment—and without paying a lot either. Give us a call at Clowning Around, and we'll (sure, surely) make your party next an event to remember.

Let's talk soon!

Dave Jenkins

Dave Jenkins
CEO, Clowning Around

Business Images, 2017 / Used under license from Shutterstock.com

21

Conjunctions and Prepositions

A family is a network of relationships. Some people have an equal relationship, like wives and husbands or brothers and sisters. Some people have unequal relationships, like mothers and daughters or fathers and sons. And the very young or very old are often dependent on middle-aged family members.

Ideas also have relationships, and conjunctions and prepositions show those relationships. When two ideas are equal, a coordinating conjunction connects them. When two ideas are not equal, a subordinating conjunction makes one idea depend on the other. Prepositions create special relationships between nouns and other words.

Conjunctions and prepositions help you connect ideas and build whole families of thought.

Chapter Outline

- Coordinating and Correlative Conjunctions
- Subordinating Conjunctions
- Common Prepositions
- *By, At, On,* and *In*

21.1 Coordinating and Correlative Conjunctions

A **conjunction** is a word or word group that joins parts of a sentence—words, phrases, or clauses.

▶ Coordinating Conjunctions

A coordinating conjunction joins grammatically equal parts—a word to a word, a phrase to a phrase, or a clause to a clause. (A clause is a word group that has a subject and a predicate.) Table 21.1 lists coordinating conjunctions.

Table 21.1 Coordinating Conjunctions						
and	but	or	nor	for	so	yet

- **Equal importance:** A coordinating conjunction shows that the two things joined are of equal importance.

    Rachel and Lydia enjoy arts and crafts.
    (*And* joins equal words.)

    They have knitted sweaters and pieced quilts.
    (*And* joins the phrases *knitted sweaters* and *pieced quilts*.)

    I tried to knit a sweater, but the thing unraveled.
    (*But* joins the two clauses, with a comma after the first.)

- **Items in a series:** A coordinating conjunction can join more than two equal parts.

    Rachel, Lydia, and I will take a class on making mosaics.
    (*And* joins *Rachel*, *Lydia*, and *I*, three parts of a compound subject. A comma follows each word except the last.)

    We will take the class, design a mosaic, and complete it together.
    (*And* joins three parts of a compound verb.)

▶ Correlative Conjunctions

Correlative conjunctions consist of a coordinating conjunction and another word or words. They connect related ideas that work together: word to word, phrase to phrase, or clause to clause. Table 21.2 lists correlative conjunctions.

Table 21.2 Correlative Conjunctions				
either/or	neither/nor	whether/or	both/and	not only/but also

- **Stressing equality:** Correlative conjunctions stress the equality of parts.

    Both Rachel and Lydia love crafts. They not only knit but also crochet.
    (*Both/and* stresses equal subjects; *not only/but also* stresses equal verbs.)

21.2 Subordinating Conjunctions

A subordinating conjunction is a word or word group that connects two clauses of different importance. **Table 21.3** lists subordinating conjunctions.

Table 21.3 Subordinating Conjunctions

after	whenever	unless	that	since
as long as	although	where	until	though
if	because	as	whereas	when
so that	in order that	before	as if	while
till	than	provided that	even though	

- **Subordinate clause:** The subordinating conjunction comes at the beginning of the less-important subordinate clause, which does not form a complete thought. The **subordinate clause** can come before or after the more important clause (the independent clause).

  Summer is too hot to cook inside. I often barbecue.
  (two clauses)

  Because summer is too hot to cook inside, I often barbecue.
  (*Because* introduces the subordinate clause, which is followed by a comma.)

  I often barbecue because summer is too hot to cook inside.
  (If the subordinate clause comes second, a comma usually isn't needed.)

- **Special relationship:** A subordinating conjunction shows a special relationship between ideas. **Table 21.4** shows the type of relationship that subordinating conjunctions indicate.

Table 21.4 Subordinating Conjunctions and Relationship

Time	after, as, before, since, till, until, when, whenever, while
Cause	as, as long as, because, if, in order that, provided that, since, so that, that
Contrast	although, as if, even though, though, unless, whereas, while

Whenever the temperature climbs, I cook on the grill. (time)

I grill because I don't want to heat up the house. (cause)

Even though it is hot outside, I feel cool in the shade as I cook. (contrast)

Practice 21.1 For the following sentences, select the best coordinating conjunction.

1. I would like to learn knitting (but, for, or) crocheting.

2. Lydia, Rachel, (and, nor, yet) I enjoy making cloth with our hands.

3. We have different talents, (or, so, for) we teach each other what we know.

4. Lydia is best at knitting, (nor, but, for) I am best at tatting.

5. Rachel is our weaver, (but, yet, so) she is the loom master.

6. Each week, Lydia, Rachel, (and, but, or) I meet to share our work.

7. We want to broaden our skills, (and, or, yet) it's hard to learn something new.

8. I like yoga, Rachel likes Pilates, (and, nor, so) Lydia likes spin cycling.

9. Come join us one day, (and, for, so) we love to teach beginners.

10. We'll show you our work, (but, nor, so) you'll need to decide what you want to learn.

Practice 21.2 For the following sentences, select the best subordinating conjunction.

1. (Because, After, Although) I marinated the chicken, I put it on the grill.

2. I like grilling chicken (even though, as long as, since) steak is my favorite food.

3. Grilling bratwurst is tough (because, whereas, until) the grease causes big flames.

4. (Because, Before, While) of trichinosis, pork should not be pink inside, so you need to cook it all the way through.

5. Some people use barbecue sauce, (provided that, since, whereas) I prefer marinades.

6. I use a gas grill (since, although, while) it is fast and convenient.

7. Purists use charcoal (as if, because, whenever) it creates a nice flavor.

8. (Provided that, As if, So that) you have plenty of time available, you can smoke your meat.

9. Smoking can cause meats to dry out (unless, since, so that) you cook them "low and slow," meaning for a long time at low temperatures.

21.3 Common Prepositions

A preposition is a word or word group that creates a relationship between a noun or pronoun and another word. Table 21.5 shows common prepositions.

Table 21.5 Common Prepositions

aboard	back of	except for	near to	round
about	because of	excepting	notwithstanding	save
above	before	for	of	since
according to	behind	from	off	subsequent to
across	below	from among	on	through
across from	beneath	from between	on account of	throughout
after	beside	from under	on behalf of	'til *or* till
against	besides	in	onto	to
along	between	in addition to	on top of	together with
alongside	beyond	in behalf of	opposite	toward
alongside of	but	in front of	out	under
along with	by	in place of	out of	underneath
amid	by means of	in regard to	outside	until
among	concerning	inside	outside of	unto
apart from	considering	inside of	over	up
around	despite	in spite of	over to	upon
as far as	down	instead of	owing to	up to
aside from	down from	into	past	with
at	during	like	prior to	within
away from	except	near	regarding	without

► Prepositional Phrases

A prepositional phrase starts with a preposition and includes an object of the preposition (a noun or pronoun) and any modifiers. A prepositional phrase functions as an adjective or adverb.

> **The Basset hound flopped** on his side on the rug.
> (*On his side* and *on the rug* modify the verb *flopped.*)

> **He slept** on the rug in the middle of the hallway.
> (*On the rug* modifies *slept; in the middle* modifies *rug;* and *of the hallway* modifies *middle.*)

Insight   A prepositional phrase can be used to break up a string of adjectives. Instead of writing "the old blue-awninged store," you can write "the old store with the blue awning."

21.4 *By, At, On,* and *In*

Prepositions often show the physical position of things—above, below, beside, around, and so on. Four specific prepositions not only show position but also have other uses in English.

▶ Uses for *By, At, On,* and *In*

I traveled
in a boat
on the Seine
by the roadway
in Paris
at dusk
on May 30.

Rostislav Glinsky, 2017 / Used under license from Shutterstock.com

- **By** means "beside" or "up to" a certain place or time.

    by the creek, by the garage

    by noon, by August 16

- **At** refers to a specific place or time.

    at the edge, at the coffee shop

    at 6:45 p.m., at midnight

- **On** refers to a surface, a day or date, or an electronic medium.

    on the table, on the T-shirt

    on July 22, on Wednesday

    on the computer, on your smartphone

- **In** refers to an enclosed space; a geographical location; a certain amount of time, a month, or a year; or a print medium.

    in the hall, in the bathroom

    in Madison, in France

    in a minute, in December, in 2017

    in the magazine, in the book

Practice 21.3 In the following sentences, underline the prepositional phrases. The first one has been done for you.

1. Yesterday, I ran <u>around the block</u> and <u>up the dirt road</u>.

2. Another runner across the street waved at me.

3. I was so distracted that I tripped over a crack in the sidewalk.

4. Soon, though, I raced along my route again.

5. Birds chirped at me from tree branches.

Practice 21.4 In the following sentences, circle the word that each underlined prepositional phrase modifies.

1. Dogs barked <u>from their backyards</u>.

2. Clouds gathered <u>in the sky</u>.

3. Rain drops fell, making splotches <u>on the road</u>.

4. <u>By the time</u> I got home, the shower had stopped.

5. My shoes were soaked and caked <u>with mud</u>.

Practice 21.5 For each sentence, select the correct preposition.

1. The guests arrived (by, on, in) 7:30 p.m., so we could eat (at, on, in) 8:00 p.m.

2. Put your suitcase (at, in) the trunk or (by, at, on) the rooftop luggage rack.

3. I looked for the new album in a music store, but could find it only (by, at, on) an online streaming service.

4. We waited (at, on, in) the lobby for a half-hour, but Jerry didn't show up or even call (by, at, on, in) his cell phone.

5. Three people standing (by, in) the corner saw a traffic accident (by, on) the intersection of 45th and Monroe.

6. Pranksters may post apocalypse hoaxes (by, at, on, in) the Internet.

7. Let's meet (on, at, in) the classroom.

8. Place your order form (by, at, on, in) the postage-paid envelope, write your return address (by, at, on, in) the envelope, and post it.

🌐 Real-World Application

Practice 21.6 Correct the following email by inserting missing coordinating or subordinating conjunctions (see Tables 21.1 and 21.3) and replacing any incorrect prepositions with correct ones. *Hint:* The email is missing four coordinating conjunctions and one subordinating conjunction. It also includes four incorrect prepositions.

✉ 📎 📇 📝

To: dkraitsman@delafordandco.com

Subject: Completed Photo Log

Attach: Photolog.doc

Dear Deirdra:

Attached, please find the photo log shows all photos in the website. Some photos are from Getty Images, others are from Shutterstock, a few are from AP Images. All photos have been downloaded have the right resolution.

I hope you are pleased with the log, it includes permissions details, the resolution, and a description of each photo. You can contact me in this email address if you have any comments about my work.

I am available for more work starting in December 12. I could compile another photo log, I could also do the permissions work on these photos. I do writing and editing as well.

Please let me know in December 11 if you would like me to continue with this project.

Thanks,

Roger Haverson

Photo Editor

Part 7:

- Punctuation
and
Mechanics
Workshops

Part 7: Punctuation and Mechanics Workshops

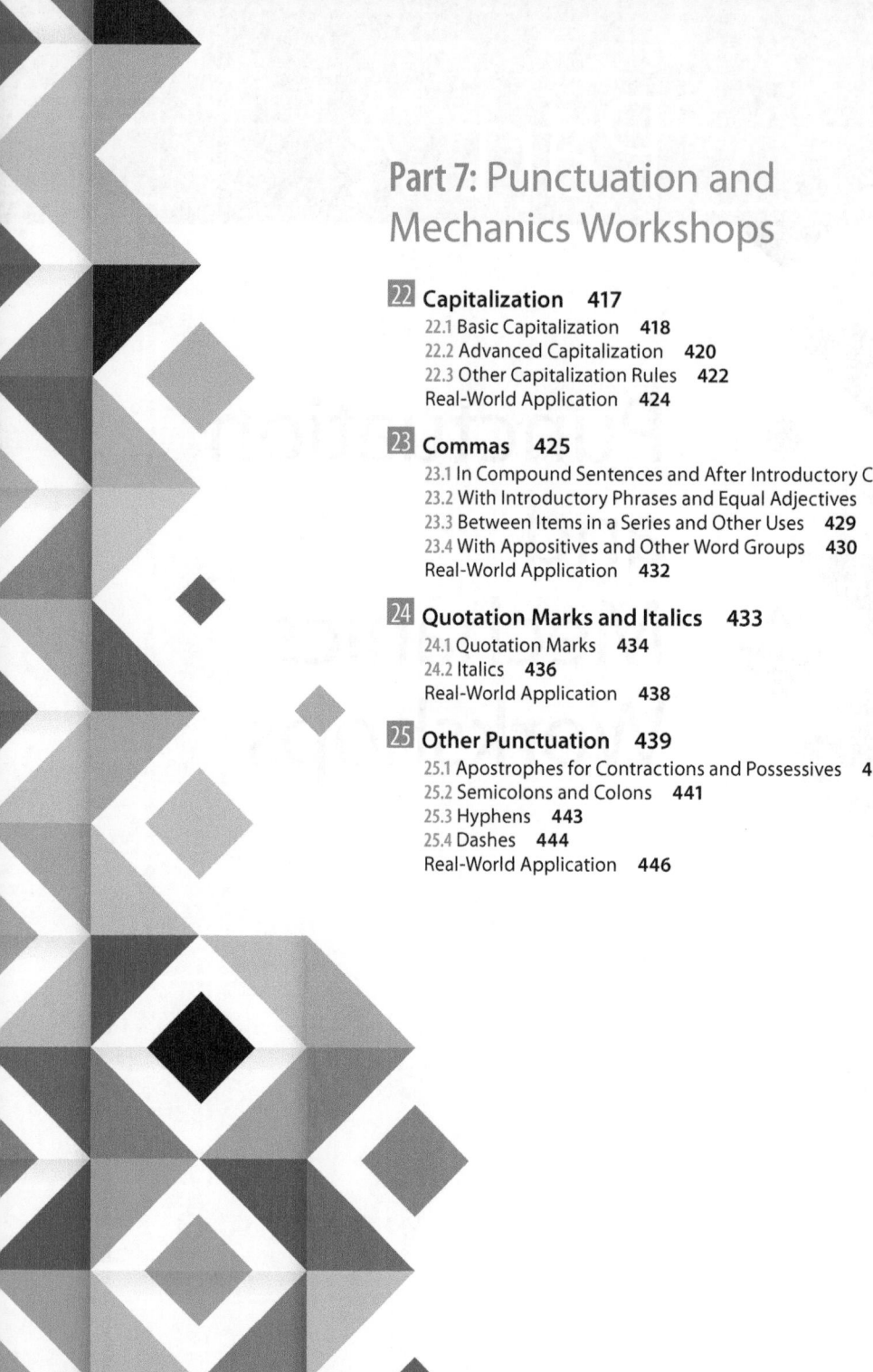

Doug Lemke, 2017 / Used under license from Shutterstock.com

Chapter

22

Capitalization

Why is the word *mom* capitalized in "Did Mom call?" and not in "Did my mom call?" This is just one of the quirks when it comes to proper capitalization in our language. As you review this chapter, you will find others.

One of the best ways to learn about the unexpected changes in capitalization is to become a reader and writer yourself. Combine regular reading and writing with the practice in this chapter and you will be well on your way to mastering correct capitalization. You can also use this chapter as a reference whenever you have questions about capitalization.

Chapter Outline

- Basic Capitalization
- Advanced Capitalization
- Other Capitalization Rules

22.1 Basic Capitalization

▶ First Words

Capitalize the first word in every sentence and the first word in a direct quotation that is a full sentence.

> **P**rofessional sports have become far too important in the United States.
>
> Yvonne asked, "**W**hy do baseball players spit all of the time?"

▶ Proper Nouns and Adjectives

Capitalize all proper nouns (names of specific persons, places, things, and ideas) and all proper adjectives (adjectives derived from proper nouns). Table 22.1 lists examples.

Table 22.1 Proper Nouns and Adjectives

Days of the week	Saturday, Sunday, Tuesday
Months	March, August, December
Holidays, holy days	Christmas, Hanukkah, President's Day
Periods, events in history	the Renaissance, Middle Ages
Special events	Tate Memorial Dedication Ceremony
Political parties, organizations	Republican Party, Habitat for Humanity
Religions, Supreme Beings, holy books	Buddhism, Allah, the Holy Bible
Official documents	Bill of Rights
Trade names	Frisbee disc, Heinz ketchup
Formal epithets	Alexander the Great
Official titles	Vice President Pence, Senator Davis
Official state nicknames	the Garden State, the Beaver State
Planets, heavenly bodies	Earth, Mars, the Milky Way
Continents	Asia, Australia, Europe
Countries	France, Brazil, Japan, Pakistan
States, provinces	Montana, Nebraska, Alberta, Ontario
Cities, towns, villages	Portland, Brookfield, Broad Ripple
Streets, roads, highways	Rodeo Drive, Route 66, Interstate 55
Nationalities and ethnic groups	African, Navajo, Serbs
Sections of the U.S. and the world	the West Coast, the Middle East
Languages	Spanish, English, Hindi
Landforms and bodies of water	Appalachian Mountains, Lake Erie
Public areas	Central Park, Yosemite National Park

NOTE: Words that indicate sections of the country are proper nouns and should be capitalized; words that simply indicate directions are not proper nouns.

> I drove **southwest** on my way to the **M**idwest.

Practice 22.1 Choose the sentence in which capital letters are used correctly.

1. a. Louis Armstrong helped make jazz music popular in America and europe.
   b. Louis Armstrong helped make Jazz music popular in america and europe.
   c. Louis Armstrong helped make jazz music popular in America and Europe.

2. a. The American south—particularly new orleans, louisiana—is credited as the birthplace of jazz music.
   b. The American South—particularly New Orleans, Louisiana—is credited as the birthplace of jazz music.
   c. The American south—particularly New Orleans, Louisiana—is credited as the birthplace of jazz music.

3. a. Armstrong grew up in new orleans in a neighborhood called the "Battleground."
   b. Armstrong grew up in New Orleans in a neighborhood called the "Battleground."
   c. Armstrong grew up in New Orleans in a neighborhood called the "battleground."

4. a. He was sent to Reform School because he fired a gun in the air on New Year's Eve.
   b. he was sent to reform school because he fired a gun in the air on New Year's eve.
   c. He was sent to reform school because he fired a gun in the air on New Year's Eve.

5. a. Upon his release, He visited music halls like Funky Butt Hall to hear King Oliver.
   b. Upon his release, he visited music halls like Funky Butt Hall to hear King Oliver.
   c. Upon his release, he visited music halls like funky butt hall to hear King Oliver.

6. a. Oliver gave Armstrong his first real cornet, and he played with Oliver's band in Storyville, a district in New Orleans.
   b. Oliver gave Armstrong his first real cornet, and he played with Oliver's band in storyville, a district in New orleans.
   c. Oliver gave Armstrong his first real cornet, and he played with oliver's band in storyville, a district in New Orleans.

7. a. He also played with the Allen Brass Band on the Strekfus line of riverboats.
   b. He also played with the Allen Brass Band on the strekfus line of Riverboats.
   c. He also played with the allen brass band on the Strekfus line of riverboats.

8. a. He really made a name for himself in the land of lincoln at Chicago Jazz Clubs.
   b. He really made a name for himself in the land of lincoln at Chicago jazz clubs.
   c. He really made a name for himself in the Land of Lincoln at Chicago jazz clubs.

22.2 Advanced Capitalization

▶ **Sentences in Parentheses**

Capitalize the first word in a sentence that is enclosed in parentheses if that sentence is not within another complete sentence.

> I need to learn more about the health care system in Canada. (**My** friend just married a guy from Toronto.)

NOTE: Do *not* capitalize the first word in a sentence that is enclosed in parentheses and is located in the middle of another sentence.

> Missy's husband (his name is Andre) works in a family business.

▶ **Sentences Following Colons**

Capitalize a complete sentence that follows a colon when that sentence is a formal statement, a quotation, or a sentence that you want to emphasize.

> Seldom have I heard such encouraging words: **The** economy is on the rebound.

▶ **Words Used as Names**

Capitalize words such as *father, mother, uncle, senator,* and *professor* only when they are parts of titles that include a personal name or when they are substitutes for proper nouns (especially in direct address).

> Hello, **Representative** Baldwin. (*Representative* is part of the name.)
>
> It's good to meet you, **Representative**. (*Representative* is a substitute for the name.)
>
> Our **representative** is a member of two important committees.

> Who was the volleyball **coach** last year?
>
> We had **Coach Snyder** for two years.
>
> I met **Coach** in the athletic office.

To test whether a word is being substituted for a proper noun, simply read the sentence with a proper noun in place of the word. If the proper noun fits in the sentence, the word being tested should be capitalized. Usually the word is not capitalized if it follows a possessive, such as *my, his, our,* or *your.*

> Did **Mom** (Mary) pick up the dry cleaning? (*Mary* works in the sentence.)
>
> Did your **mom** (Mary) pick up the dry cleaning? (*Mary* does not work in the sentence; the word *mom* follows *your.*)

Practice 22.2 Choose the sentence in which capital letters are used correctly.

1. a. Golda Meir is a former prime minister of israel.
  b. Golda Meir is a former prime minister of Israel.
  c. Golda Meir is a former Prime Minister of Israel.

2. a. Meir once said this about gender: "Whether women are better than men I cannot say—but I can say they are certainly no worse."
  b. Meir once said this about gender: "whether women are better than men I cannot say—but I can say they are certainly no worse."
  c. Meir once said this about gender: "Whether Women are better than men I cannot say—but I can say they are certainly no worse."

3. a. My dad is planning for his retirement. (what will he do with his free time?)
  b. My Dad is planning for his retirement. (What will he do with his free time?)
  c. My dad is planning for his retirement. (What will he do with his free time?)

4. a. I chatted with coach after practice; he's the best coach I've ever had.
  b. I chatted with Coach after practice; he's the best Coach I've ever had.
  c. I chatted with Coach after practice; he's the best coach I've ever had.

5. a. My Mechanic made a bad day worse: He told me that my car needed new tires.
  b. My mechanic made a bad day worse: He told me that my car needed new tires.
  c. My mechanic made a bad day worse: he told me that my car needed new tires.

6. a. Whenever Mom talks about politics, she eventually criticizes our local congressman.
  b. Whenever Mom talks about politics, she eventually criticizes our local Congressman.
  c. Whenever mom talks about politics, she eventually criticizes our local Congressman.

7. a. At the town hall meeting, my Dad asked senator Ryan about health care.
  b. At the town hall meeting, my dad asked Senator Ryan about health care.
  c. At the town hall meeting, my dad asked senator Ryan about health care.

8. a. My friend Bryan (He's the loud one) is actually quite skilled at accounting.
  b. My friend Bryan (he's the loud one) is actually quite skilled at accounting.
  c. My friend Bryan (he's the loud one) is actually quite skilled at Accounting.

22.3 Other Capitalization Rules

▶ Titles

Capitalize the first word of a title, the last word, and every word in between except articles (*a*, *an*, *the*), short prepositions, *to* in an infinitive, and coordinating conjunctions. Follow this rule for titles of books, newspapers, magazines, poems, plays, songs, articles, films, works of art, and stories.

> *The Dark Knight* (movie)   *The Sound and the Fury* (novel)
>
> "What a Wonderful World" (song)   "Death Penalty's False Promise" (essay)

▶ Titles of Courses

Words such as *history* and *science* are proper nouns when they are included in the titles of specific courses; they are common nouns when they name a field of study.

> I'm glad **Introduction to Politics** fits my schedule. (title of a specific course)
>
> Judy Kenner advises anyone interested in **politics**. (a field of study)

NOTE: Always capitalize *English*, even if it is used as a common noun.

▶ Organizations

Capitalize the name of an organization or a team and its members.

> **Habitat for Humanity**   **Libertarian Party**
>
> **The Bill & Melinda Gates Foundation**   **Chicago Cubs**

▶ Abbreviations

Capitalize abbreviations of titles and organizations.

> **MD   PhD   NAACP   CE   BCE   GPA**

▶ Web Terms

The words *Internet* and *World Wide Web* are capitalized because they are considered proper nouns. When your writing includes a Web address (URL), capitalize any letters that the site's owner does (in print or on the site itself).

> When doing research on the **Internet**, be sure to record each site's **Web** address (URL) and each contact's **email** address. One popular research site is **Google.com**.

Practice 22.3 ▷ Choose the answer that includes *all* the words that should be capitalized in the following sentences.

1. To me, *a midsummer night's dream* is one of Shakespeare's best plays.
   a. *A, Midsummer, Night's, Dream*
   b. *Midsummer, Night's, Dream*
   c. *A, Midsummer, Night's, Dream,* Plays

2. The San Francisco giants used to play in Candlestick park.
   a. Park
   b. Giants
   c. Giants, Park

3. I hope my grade in contemporary history 301 will improve my gpa.
   a. Contemporary, History
   b. GPA
   c. Contemporary, History, GPA

4. You can find a treasure trove of information on the web thanks to sites like google.
   a. Google
   b. Web, Google
   c. Web, Sites, Google

5. I participated in a fundraising event for the american cancer society.
   a. American
   b. American, Cancer
   c. American, Cancer, Society

6. Javier Lopez, an old friend from the neighborhood, earned a phd in history.
   a. PhD
   b. PhD, History
   c. PhD, History, Neighborhood

7. Perhaps the least known of The beatles is George Harrison; I love his song "here comes the sun."
   a. Beatles
   b. Beatles, Here, Comes, Sun
   c. Here, Comes, Sun

8. Anna Quindlen's article "uncle sam and aunt samantha" first appeared in *newsweek.*
   a. *Newsweek*
   b. Uncle, Sam, Aunt, Samantha, *Newsweek*
   c. Uncle, Sam, Aunt, Samantha

Real-World Application

 Review the sample email. Then place capitalization marks (☰) under any letters that should be capitalized. *Hint:* There are 13 words that need to be capitalized.

To: Professor Ellen Thielen

Subject: Thank You for Your Recommendation

Dear professor thielen,

Thank you for recommending me for the internship at cohill Laboratories. During my interview last monday, Dr. Keenan said that he had received your letter and had talked with you by phone. Apparently you said this: "clearly Raul has demonstrated thorough lab techniques." I appreciate this description of my work.

The outcome of the application and interviewing process could not have gone any better; this morning dr. Keenan offered me the position. I will be working with chemists at Farwell science center, one of Cohill's newest labs.

I am so glad that I had you for biochemistry 101. You made that course interesting, and I learned so much. Dr. Keenan also was impressed that I had taken analytical chemistry 101 and 203, taught by professor Williams.

Thanks again, professor, for all your help. I can't wait to start the internship. (you can expect to hear from me about my work.)

Sincerely,

Raul Samuelson

Pressmaster, 2017 / Used under license from Shutterstock.com

Chapter

23

Commas

When you speak, you communicate with much more than words. You pause, raise or lower your pitch, change your tone or volume, and use facial expressions and body language to get your point across.

When you write, you can forget about pitch or volume, facial expressions or body language. You're left with the tone of your words and with the pauses that you put in them. Commas give you one way to create soft pauses. They help to show which words belong together, which should be separated, and which create parallel constructions. In other words, commas help you clarify your message.

In this chapter you will learn about the conventional use of commas. Understanding correct comma usage is an important step in becoming a college-level writer.

Chapter Outline

- In Compound Sentences and After Introductory Clauses
- With Introductory Phrases and Equal Adjectives
- Between Items in a Series and Other Uses
- With Appositives and Other Word Groups

23.1 In Compound Sentences and After Introductory Clauses

The following principles will guide the use of commas in your writing.

▶ In Compound Sentences

Use a comma before the coordinating conjunction (*and, but, or, nor, for, yet, so*) in a compound sentence.

> Heath Ledger completed his brilliant portrayal as the Joker in *The Dark Knight,* **but** he died before the film was released.

NOTE: Do not confuse a compound verb with a compound sentence. Compound verbs should not be separated by commas.

> Ledger's Joker became instantly iconic and won him the Oscar for best supporting actor. *(compound verb)*

> His death resulted from the abuse of prescription drugs, but it was ruled an accident. *(compound sentence)*

▶ After Introductory Clauses

Use a comma after most introductory clauses.

> **Although Charlemagne was a great patron of learning,** he never learned to write properly. *(adverb dependent clause)*

When the adverb clause follows the independent clause and is not essential to the meaning of the sentence, use a comma. This comma use generally applies to clauses beginning with *even though, although, while,* or some other conjunction expressing a contrast.

> Charlemagne never learned to write properly, **even though he continued to practice**.

NOTE: A comma is not used if the adverb clause following the independent clause is needed for clarity.

> Charlemagne continued to practice **because he wanted to write well**.

23.2 With Introductory Phrases and Equal Adjectives

► After Introductory Phrases

Use a comma after introductory phrases.

> **In spite of his friend's prodding,** Jared decided to stay home and study.

A comma is usually omitted if the phrase follows an independent clause.

> Jared decided to stay home and study **in spite of his friend's prodding.**

You may omit a comma after a short (four or fewer words) introductory phrase unless it is needed to ensure clarity.

> **At 10:32 p.m.** he quit studying and went to sleep.

► To Separate Adjectives

Use commas to separate adjectives that equally modify the same noun. Notice in the following examples that no comma separates the last adjective from the noun.

> You should exercise regularly and follow a **sensible, healthful** diet.

> A good diet is one that includes lots of **high-protein, low-fat** foods.

► To Determine Equal Modifiers

To determine whether adjectives modify a noun equally, use these two tests.

1. Reverse the order of the adjectives; if the sentence is clear, the adjectives modify equally. (In the following example, *hot* and *crowded* can be switched, but *short* and *coffee* cannot.)

> Matt was tired of working in the **hot, crowded** lab and decided to take a **short coffee** break.

2. Insert *and* between the adjectives; if the sentence reads well, use a comma when *and* is omitted. (The word *and* can be inserted between *hot* and *crowded*, but *and* does not make sense between *short* and *coffee*.)

Practice 23.1 For each selection, choose the sentence that uses commas correctly. (Some selections will not need commas.)

1. a. Creativity is his best quality but, leadership is not far behind.
   b. Creativity is his best quality, but leadership is not far behind.
   c. Creativity is his best quality but leadership is not far behind.

2. a. To train for the triathlon, Brent altered his diet.
   b. To train for the triathlon, Brent, altered his diet.
   c. To train for the triathlon Brent altered his diet.

3. a. Although, the appetizer was delicious my entrée was bland.
   b. Although the appetizer was delicious my entrée was bland.
   c. Although the appetizer was delicious, my entrée was bland.

4. a. Should I finish my essay a day early or should I go to my friend's house party?
   b. Should I finish my essay a day early or, should I go to my friend's house party?
   c. Should I finish my essay a day early, or should I go to my friend's house party?

5. a. I checked my social media as I waited for the dentist appointment.
   b. I checked my social media, as I waited for the dentist appointment.
   c. I checked my social media as I waited, for the dentist appointment.

6. a. Catherine had questions about her class schedule so she set up an appointment with her academic adviser.
   b. Catherine had questions about her class schedule, so she set up an appointment with her academic adviser.
   c. Catherine, had questions about her class schedule, so she set up an appointment with her academic adviser.

7. a. There's nothing like the warm emerald water off the Florida Gulf Coast.
   b. There's nothing like the warm, emerald water off the Florida Gulf Coast.
   c. There's nothing like the warm emerald water off the Florida, Gulf Coast.

8. a. My grumpy economics instructor is one of a kind.
   b. My grumpy, economics instructor is one of a kind.
   c. My grumpy economics, instructor is one of a kind.

9. a. In accordance with the academic code plagiarism is deemed a major offense.
   b. In accordance with the academic code, plagiarism is deemed a major offense.
   c. In accordance with the academic, code plagiarism is deemed a major offense.

23.3 Between Items in a Series and Other Uses

▶ Between Items in a Series

Use commas to separate individual words, phrases, or clauses in a series. A series contains at least three items.

> Many college students must balance studying with **taking care of a family, working, getting exercise, and finding time to relax.**

Do not use commas when all the items are connected with *or, nor,* or *and.*

> Hmm . . . should I study **or** do laundry **or** go out?

▶ To Set Off Transitional Expressions

Use a comma to set off **conjunctive adverbs** and transitional phrases.

> Handwriting is not, **as a matter of fact,** easy to improve upon later in life; **however,** you can improve your handwriting if you are determined enough.

If a transitional expression blends smoothly with the rest of the sentence, the transition does not need to be set off.

> If you are **in fact** coming, I'll see you there.

▶ To Set Off Dialogue

Use commas to set off the exact words of the speaker from the rest of the sentence.

> **"Never be afraid to ask for help,"** advised Ms. Kane.

> **"With the evidence that we now have,"** Professor Thom said, **"many scientists believe there could be life on Mars."**

Do not use a comma before an indirect quotation.

> Professor Thom said **that his astronomy class is full.**

▶ To Enclose Explanatory Words

Use commas to enclose an explanatory phrase that interrupts the flow of the sentence, providing extra information.

> Time management, **according to many professionals,** is an important skill that should be taught in college.

23.4 With Appositives and Other Word Groups

▶ To Set Off Some Appositives

Use commas to set off a specific kind of explanatory word or phrase called an **appositive**. An appositive identifies or renames a preceding noun or pronoun.

> Albert Einstein, **the famous mathematician and physicist,** developed the theory of relativity.

Do not use commas if the appositive is important to the basic meaning of the sentence.

> The famous physicist **Albert Einstein** developed the theory of relativity.

▶ With Some Clauses and Phrases

Use commas to enclose phrases or clauses that add information that is not necessary to the basic meaning of the sentence. For example, if the clause or phrase (in **boldface**) were left out of the following two examples, the meaning of the sentences would remain clear. Therefore, commas are used to set off the information.

> The locker rooms in Swain Hall, **which were painted and updated last summer,** give professors a place to shower. *(unnecessary clause)*
>
> Work-study programs, **offered on many campuses,** give students the opportunity to earn tuition money. *(unnecessary phrase)*

Do not use commas to set off necessary clauses and phrases—which add information that readers need to understand the sentence.

> Only the professors **who run at noon** use the locker rooms. *(necessary clause)*

▶ Using "That" or "Which"

Use *that* to introduce necessary clauses; use *which* to introduce unnecessary clauses.

> Campus jobs **that are funded by the university** are awarded to students only. *(necessary clause)*
>
> The cafeteria, **which is run by an independent contractor,** can hire non-students. *(unnecessary clause)*

Practice 23.2   For each selection, choose the sentence that uses commas correctly. (Some selections will not need commas.)

1. a. While in Boston, I visited Fenway Park, Bunker Hill, and Old North Church.
   b. While in Boston, I visited Fenway Park Bunker Hill, and Old North Church.
   c. While in Boston, I visited Fenway Park, Bunker Hill and Old North Church.

2. a. Avocados, the key ingredient of guacamole are a good source of fiber.
   b. Avocados, the key ingredient of guacamole, are a good source of fiber.
   c. Avocados the key ingredient of guacamole are a good source of fiber.

3. a. "Though my car's navigational system is certainly convenient," said Emilie "it sometimes gets me more lost than driving without it."
   b. "Though my car's navigational system is certainly convenient," said Emilie, "it sometimes gets me more lost than driving without it."
   c. "Though my car's navigational system is certainly convenient" said Emilie "it sometimes gets me more lost than driving without it."

4. a. The concert hall which is on the corner of Meridian Avenue and 1st Street is expected to revitalize the downtown district.
   b. The concert hall, which is on the corner of Meridian Avenue and 1st Street is expected to revitalize the downtown district.
   c. The concert hall, which is on the corner of Meridian Avenue and 1st Street, is expected to revitalize the downtown district.

5. a. Thomas as you may have noticed, is eager to share his knowledge of astronomy.
   b. Thomas, as you may have noticed is eager to share his knowledge of astronomy.
   c. Thomas, as you may have noticed, is eager to share his knowledge of astronomy.

6. a. Regarding transportation, you could use the subway, cabs or ride-share services.
   b. Regarding transportation, you could use the subway, cabs, or ride-share services.
   c. Regarding transportation, you could use the subway cabs or ride-share services.

7. a. Many people think of Rosa Parks as the first African American to refuse to give up a bus seat in the segregated South; however Claudette Colvin, a fifteen-year old schoolgirl was arrested for the same act in Birmingham nine months earlier.
   b. Many people think of Rosa Parks as the first African American to refuse to give up a bus seat in the segregated South; however, Claudette Colvin a fifteen-year old schoolgirl was arrested for the same act in Birmingham nine months earlier.
   c. Many people think of Rosa Parks as the first African American to refuse to give up a bus seat in the segregated South; however, Claudette Colvin, a fifteen-year old schoolgirl, was arrested for the same act in Birmingham nine months earlier.

Real-World Application

 Insert commas where they are needed in the following email message. *Hint:* There are six missing commas.

✉   ✐   ▣   ▧

To: Michael_Green@shieldmarketing.com

Subject: Revised Agenda for Quarterly Update

Hi, Michael:

I've attached the agenda for the quarterly update with the marketing team. Daniel Gilchrest the senior marketing coordinator will moderate the meeting but I want you to familiarize yourself with the material. Here are some highlights of the new agenda:

1. The advertising allowance for Gillette, Hillsboro Farms and Justice Inc. has increased by 5 percent.

2. The penetrated market which accounts for actual users of products declined in the health-care sector.

3. We will shift the focus of marketing efforts to meet the digital and social media demands of today's market.

Please review the agenda by the end of the day.

Thanks,

Tru Sha

Marketing Associate

Andrey Bayda, 2017 / Used under license from Shutterstock.com

24

Quotation Marks and Italics

Times Square in New York City is plastered with billboards five stories high and jammed with marquees that flash in the night. They advertise plays and movies, books and magazines, albums and TV shows—all in spotlights or neon trying to make people take notice.

In writing, there are no spotlights. There is no neon. Instead of writing the names of plays, movies, books, short stories, or articles in giant, flashing letters, writers set them off with italics or quotation marks. This chapter will show you how to correctly punctuate titles as well as significant words, letters, and numbers.

Chapter Outline

- Quotation Marks
- Italics

24.1 Quotation Marks

► To Punctuate Titles of Smaller Works

Use quotation marks to enclose the titles of smaller works, including speeches, short stories, songs, poems, episodes of audio or video programs, chapters or sections of books, unpublished works, one-act plays, and articles from magazines, journals, newspapers, or encyclopedias.

Speech: "Ain't I a Woman?"   **Book chapter:** "The Second Eve"

Song: "Thriller"   **Television episode:**
                                                   "The Empty Child"
Short story: "The Tell-Tale Heart"

Magazine article: "The Falling Man"   **Encyclopedia article:** "Autobahn"

► Placement of Punctuation

When quoted words end in a period or comma, always place the period or comma inside the quotation marks.

"When you leave the kitchen," Tim said, "turn out the light."

When a quotation is followed by a semicolon or colon, always place the semicolon or colon outside the quotation marks.

I finally read "The Celebrated Jumping Frog of Calaveras County"; it is a hoot!

You won't forget this character from "A Good Man Is Hard to Find": the Misfit.

If an exclamation point or a question mark is part of the quotation, place it inside the quotation marks. Otherwise, place it outside.

Shawndra asked Mark, "Would you like to go to the movies?"

Did Mark actually say, "No thanks"?

► For Special Words

Quotation marks can be used (1) to show that a word is being referred to as the word itself; (2) to indicate that it is jargon, slang, or a coined term; (3) to show that it is used in an ironic or sarcastic sense; or for (4) quoting other people's words, such as a definition.

(1) & (4)   The word "chuffed" is British slang for "very excited."

(2)   I'm "chuffed" about my new computer.

(3)   I'm "chuffed" about my root canal.

Practice 24.1   Choose the sentence that uses quotation marks correctly.

1. a. Benjamin loves The Cask of Amontillado, a short story by "Edgar Allan Poe."
   b. Benjamin loves "The Cask of Amontillado," a short story by Edgar Allan Poe.
   c. Benjamin loves "The Cask of Amontillado", a short story by Edgar Allan Poe.

2. a. "After class, please hand in your midterm papers, said the instructor.
   b. "After class, please hand in your midterm papers", said the instructor.
   c. "After class, please hand in your midterm papers," said the instructor.

3. a. What does the word "hypertrophy" mean?
   b. What does the word hypertrophy "mean"?
   c. What does the "word hypertrophy" mean?

4. a. Ta-Nehisi Coates wrote the article "My President Was Black".
   b. Ta-Nehisi Coates wrote the article "My President Was Black."
   c. Ta-Nehisi Coates wrote the "article My President Was Black".

5. a. "Let's meet at the coffee house", Lisa told Jennie. "It will be good to study in a new environment".
   b. "Let's meet at the coffee house, Lisa told Jennie. "It will be good to study in a new environment."
   c. "Let's meet at the coffee house," Lisa told Jennie. "It will be good to study in a new environment."

6. a. Was she thinking, "That's a better option than cooking?
   b. Was she thinking, "That's a better option than cooking"?
   c. Was she thinking, "That's a better option than cooking?"

7. a. Gloria was "shocked when her habitually late friend was late for another show.
   b. Gloria was "shocked" when her habitually late friend was late for another show.
   c. "Gloria was shocked when her habitually late friend was late for another show".

8. a. The first part of the book "Fever" by Mary Beth Keane is called Habeas Corpus.
   b. The first part of the book *Fever* by Mary Beth Keane is called "Habeas Corpus."
   c. The first part of the book *Fever* by Mary Beth Keane is called "Habeas Corpus".

9. a. Check out the *Hardcore History* podcast for an episode called "Shield of the West"; it features a fascinating analysis of the Greek and Persian wars.
   b. Check out the *Hardcore History* podcast for an episode called "Shield of the West;" it features a fascinating analysis of the Greek and Persian wars.
   c. Check out the *Hardcore History* podcast for an episode called "Shield of the West; it features a fascinating analysis of the Greek and Persian wars.

24.2 Italics

▶ To Identify Titles of Larger Works

Use italics to indicate the titles of larger works, including newspapers, magazines, journals, pamphlets, books, full-length plays, films, podcasts, radio and television programs, movies, music albums, ballets, operas, software programs, and legal cases, as well as the names of ships, trains, aircraft, and spacecraft.

Magazine: *The Week*	**Newspaper:** *Chicago Tribune*
Play: *Cat on a Hot Tin Roof*	**Journal:** *Nature*
Movie: *Casablanca*	**Television program:** *Doctor Who*
Book: *Death's Disciples*	**Podcast:** *Revisionist History*

▶ For a Word, Letter, or Number Referred to as Itself

Use italics or quotation marks (either is correct) to show that a word, letter, or number is being referred to as itself. If a definition follows a word used in this way, place that definition in quotation marks.

> The word *courage* comes from the French word *cour*, which means "heart."
> In the handwritten note, I couldn't distinguish an *N* from an *M*.

Quotation marks can also be used to indicate words that refer themselves. However, it is important that you maintain a consistent style in whatever piece you are writing. In general, italics are preferable for digital writing, while quotation marks work better for handwritten work.

▶ For Foreign Words

Use italics to indicate a word that is being borrowed from a foreign language.

> The phrase *et cetera* is a Latin phrase meaning "and so forth."

▶ For Technical Terms

Use italics to introduce a technical term for the first time in a piece of writing. After that, the term may be used without italics.

Particle physicists finally discerned the elusive *Higgs boson* particle in 2012. The Higgs boson is a subatomic particle thought to provide mass to all other particles.

If a technical term is being used within an organization or a field of study where it is common, it may be used without italics even the first time in a piece of writing.

Practice 24.2 Select whether the word or words in parentheses should be written in italics or put inside quotation marks.

1. (*Eastward*, "Eastward") is the title of the first chapter of the book (*Blue Highways*, "Blue Highways") by William Least Heat-Moon.

2. The Academy-Award winning movie (*Moonlight*, "Moonlight") stars Mahershala Ali.

3. The dance (*paso doble*, "paso doble") means (*double step*, "double step") in Spanish.

4. In 1945, the air bomber (*Enola Gay*, "Enola Gay") dropped the first atomic bomb, a weapon predicted in the 1914 novel (*The World Set Free*, "The World Set Free") by H. G. Wells.

5. She always has a real (*joie de vivre*, "joie de vivre") about her. That foreign phrase means (*a great happiness or enjoyment of life*, "a great happiness or enjoyment of life") in French.

6. In one context, the words *profane* and (*profanity*, "profanity") do not refer to swearing but simply to things that are not divine.

7. The television show (*Project Runway*, "Project Runway") pits fashion designers against each other. The episode (*Even Designers Get the Blues*, "Even Designers Get the Blues") features contestants creating a runway look based on denim fabric.

8. My dream is to see (*Hamilton*, "Hamilton") on Broadway. (*Cabinet Battle #1*, "Cabinet Battle #1") is my favorite song from the performance.

9. Stephen King's short story (*The Body*, "The Body") was made into a movie.

10. Do you know what it means to be (*bummed out*, "bummed out") about something?

 Real-World Application

Practice 24.3 Insert any missing quotation marks and underline any words that should be italicized in the following email.

✉ 📎 🗐 ☑

To: Will McMartin

Subject: McDermott Author Bio

Hi, Will:

Here is the author bio you requested from me to be published in my next book, War Child:

John Metrameme has published over a dozen novels, most recently the historical epic Sons of Thunder and the romp Daddy Zeus. He also has written articles for The Atlantic and The New Yorker, and his short story Me and the Mudman won the Rubel Prize. Metrameme is perhaps best known for his novel Darling Buds of May.

In his spare time, Metrameme enjoys volunteering at his community theater. He often leads the lessons during children's acting classes. Metrameme has also starred in two plays. He played Kit Gill in No Way to Treat a Lady and Jonathan in Arsenic and Old Lace.

Please let me know if you need anything more from me.

Thanks,

John

Mila Supinskaya, 2017 / Used under license from Shutterstock.com

Chapter 25

Other Punctuation

Work is important, of course. Progress. Motion. Getting somewhere. Yet sometimes it's important to pause and take a breath. Breaks allow you to work even more effectively afterward.

Written materials need pauses and breaks, too. A break doesn't have to be a full stop (a period); maybe something softer will do. Semicolons, colons, and dashes can give the reader just the right break to be refreshed and to set out again. This chapter covers these three punctuation marks as well as apostrophes and hyphens.

Chapter Outline

- Apostrophes for Contractions and Possessives
- Semicolons and Colons
- Hyphens
- Dashes

25.1 Apostrophes for Contractions and Possessives

Apostrophes are used primarily to show that a letter or number has been left out or that a noun is possessive.

Contractions

Use an apostrophe to form a **contraction**. A contraction is a word formed by joining two words, leaving out one or more letters and using an apostrophe in their place.

do not—don't	he would—he'd	would have—would've
(*o* is left out)	(*woul* is left out)	(*ha* is left out)

► Missing Characters

Use an apostrophe to signal when one or more characters are left out.

class of '16	rock 'n' roll	good mornin'
(*20* is left out)	(*a* and *d* are left out)	(*g* is left out)

Possessives

Form possessives of singular nouns by adding an apostrophe and an *s*. The word before the apostrophe is the owner.

Sharla's pen	the man's coat	*The Pilgrim's Progress*

► Singular Noun Ending in *s* (One Syllable)

Form the possessive by adding an apostrophe and an *s*.

the boss's idea	the lass's purse	the bass's teeth

► Singular Noun Ending in *s* (Two or More Syllables)

Form the possessive by adding an apostrophe and an *s*—or by adding only an apostrophe.

Kansas's plains	*or*	Kansas' plains

► Plural Noun Ending in *s*

Form the possessive by adding an apostrophe.

the bosses' idea	the Smiths' home	the girls' ball

► Plural Noun Not Ending in *s*

Form the possessive by adding an apostrophe and an *s*.

the children's toys	the women's room

Insight Pronoun possessives *do not use* apostrophes: *its, whose, hers, his, ours.*

25.2 Semicolons and Colons

Semicolon

A **semicolon** (;) can be called a soft period. Use the semicolon to join two sentences that are closely related.

> The mosquitoes have returned; it must be August in Wisconsin.

▶ Before a Conjunctive Adverb

Often, the second sentence will begin with a conjunctive adverb (*also, besides, however, instead, meanwhile, therefore*), which signals the relationship between the sentences. Place a semicolon before the conjunctive adverb, and place a comma after it.

> The outdoor mosquito treatment was rated for six weeks; however, it lasted only four.

▶ In a Series

Use a semicolon to separate items in a series if any of the items already include commas.

> Before the party, I'll cut the grass and treat the lawn; buy a bug zapper, citronella candles, and bug spray; and get ready to swat and scratch.

Colon

Use a **colon** (:) to introduce an example or a list.

> Here's one mosquito treatment: napalm.
>
> I have an irrational fear of three animals: snakes, spiders, and mosquitos!

▶ After Salutations

In business documents, use a colon after a **salutation**, the formal greeting.

> Dear Ms. Alvarez: To: Tawnya Smith

▶ Times and Ratios

Use a colon to separate hours, minutes, and seconds. Also use a colon between the numbers in a ratio.

> 8:23 a.m.   4:15 p.m.   14:32:46   The mosquito-person ratio is 5:1.

Practice 25.1 Complete each sentence by choosing the word in the parentheses that correctly uses apostrophes. Some correct answers will not include apostrophes.

1. I'm going to (Jeremys', Jeremy's) house.

2. Have you heard if (its, it's) supposed to rain tomorrow?

3. Poor service spoiled (her, her's) opinion of the (restaurants, restaurant's) food.

4. (Texas, Texas's) reputation is summed up by (its, it's) nickname: The Lone Star State.

5. Were you more impressed by Bruno (Mars', Mars) singing or dancing?

6. A contractor assessed the (houses, house's) structure for (flaws, flaw's).

7. Sarah scanned the movie (theaters, theater's) aisles for her missing car (keys, key's).

8. These (politician's, politicians') economic policies (dont, don't) seem realistic to me.

9. The (women's, womens') locker room is at the end of the hallway.

10. You won't believe (whats, what's) on the (classes, class's) reading list.

Practice 25.2 Choose the sentence that uses semicolons or colons correctly.

1. a. These three animals cause the most human deaths; mosquitos, snakes, and dogs.
   b. These three animals cause the most human deaths: mosquitos, snakes, and dogs.

2. a. Mosquitoes in America are a nuisance; however, in many places they are deadly.
   b. Mosquitoes in America are a nuisance: however, in many places they are deadly.

3. a. Mosquitoes in Africa and South America carry malaria; the disease infects millions of people.
   b. Mosquitoes in Africa and South America carry malaria: the disease infects millions of people.

4. a. Each year, mosquito-borne illnesses affect 700 million victims; sadly, many of them die.
   b. Each year, mosquito-borne illnesses affect 700 million victims: sadly, many of them die.

5. a. Mosquitoes in Egypt can carry another deadly disease; yellow fever.
   b. Mosquitoes in Egypt can carry another deadly disease: yellow fever.

6. a. Mosquitoes breed in stagnant water; they need only a small amount.
   b. Mosquitoes breed in stagnant water: they need only a small amount.

25.3 Hyphens

A **hyphen** (-) joins words and letters to form various kinds of compounds.

▶ Compound Nouns

Use hyphens to create **compound nouns**.

city-state   act-check   one-liner   mother-in-law

▶ Compound Adjectives

Use hyphens to create **compound adjectives** that appear before the noun. If the adjective appears after the noun, it usually is not hyphenated.

peer-reviewed article   an article that was peer reviewed

Don't hyphenate a compound made from an -ly adverb and an adjective or a compound that ends with a single letter.

newly acquired songs   grade B plywood

▶ Compound Numbers

Use hyphens in **compound numbers** from twenty-one to ninety-nine and in fractions.

twenty-two   fifty-fifty   three-quarters   seven thirty-seconds

▶ With Letters

Use a hyphen to join a letter to a word that follows it.

L-bracket   U-shaped   T-shirt   O-ring   G-rated   X-ray

▶ With Common Elements

Use hyphens to show that two or more words share a common element included in only the final term.

We offer low-, middle-, and high-coverage plans.

25.4 Dashes

Unlike the hyphen, the **dash** (—) with no spacing before or after does more to separate words than to join them.

► For Emphasis

Use a dash instead of a colon if you want to emphasize a word, phrase, clause, or series.

> Donuts—they're not just for cops anymore.
>
> There's only one thing better than a donut—two donuts.
>
> I like all kinds of donuts—fritters, crullers, and cake donuts.

► To Set Off a Series

Use a dash to set off a series of items.

> Elephant ears, Danish, funnel cakes—they just aren't as cool as donuts.
>
> They have many similarities—batter, frosting, and sugar—but where's the hole?

► With Nonessential Elements

Use a dash to set off explanations, examples, and definitions, especially when these elements already include commas.

> The hole—which is where the "dough nut" got its name originally—is a key component.

► To Show Interrupted Speech

Use a dash to show that a speaker has been interrupted or has started and stopped while speaking.

> "I'd like a—um—how about a fritter?"
>
> "You want an apple—"
>
> "Yes, an apple fritter. Well—make it two."

Insight In most academic writing, use dashes sparingly. If they are overused, they lose their effect.

Practice 25.3 Choose the sentence that uses hyphens and dashes correctly.

1. a. My father—in—law is an attorney—at—law.
   b. My father-in-law is an attorney-at-law.
   c. My father in law is an attorney-at-law.

2. a. I've set a new short—term goal-resurfacing the blacktop by the end of the week.
   b. I've set a new short term goal—resurfacing the blacktop by the end of the week.
   c. I've set a new short-term goal—resurfacing the blacktop by the end of the week.

3. a. The sales-tax percentage is at an all-time high.
   b. The sales-tax percentage is at an all—time high.
   c. The sales tax percentage is at an all-time high.

4. a. A quickly-emerging trend is driverless vehicles—spooky!
   b. A quickly emerging trend is driverless vehicles—spooky!
   c. A quickly emerging trend is driverless vehicles-spooky!

5. a. Could I have-um-what's this week's five dollar special, again?
   b. Could I have—um—what's this week's five dollar special, again?
   c. Could I have—um—what's this week's five-dollar special, again?

6. a. The major pre-WWI alliance was known as the Triple Entente—a pact between Russia, Great Britain, and France.
   b. The major pre-WWI alliance was known as the Triple Entente-a pact between Russia, Great Britain, and France.
   c. The major pre WWI alliance was known as the Triple Entente—a pact between Russia, Great Britain, and France.

7. a. He guessed the diner's tabletop was three-eighths inch thick.
   b. He guessed the diner's tabletop was three—eighths inch thick.
   c. He guessed the diner's tabletop was three-eighths-inch thick.

8. a. Fozzy's—at the corner of Pine St. and 6th Ave. makes the best sandwiches.
   b. Fozzy's—at the corner of Pine St. and 6th Ave.—makes the best sandwiches.
   c. Fozzy's-at the corner of Pine St. and 6th Ave.-makes the best sandwiches.

9. a. Which do you prefer-a glazed donut or a long john?
   b. Which do you prefer a glazed-donut or a long-john?
   c. Which do you prefer—a glazed donut or a long john?

10. a. The double-decker BLT sandwich includes low fat spicy mayo.
    b. The double-decker BLT sandwich includes low-fat spicy mayo.
    c. The double—decker BLT sandwich includes low—fat spicy mayo.

🌐 Real-World Application

Insert the missing colons, hyphens, and apostrophes in the following business letter. *Hint:* There are seven total errors: five missing apostrophes, one missing colon, and one missing hyphen.

Redland State Bank

October 13, 2017

Phillip Jones
2398 10th Ave.
Westchester, NY 10959

Dear Mr. Jones

This letters a response to your inquiry about financing your low income housing project. I enjoyed discussing your project and appreciated your honesty about your current loan.

As of today, weve decided to accept your proposal. Enclosed is Redland State Banks commitment letter. Please take time to read the agreements terms.

If there is any part you do not understand, please do not hesitate to call or email; wed be happy to answer any questions. As always, we look forward to serving you.

Sincerely,

Melinda Erson

Melinda Erson
Loan Officer

Enclosure: Commitment Letter

Part 8:

Readings for Writers

Part 8: Readings for Writers

Mikael Damkier, 2017 / Used under license from Shutterstock.com

Chapter

26

Anthology

In *The Philosophy of Literary Form*, Kenneth Burke describes all of history as an unending conversation. It is a conversation that has been going on long before anyone you know arrived, and one that will continue long after you are gone. But right now, you can listen until you get a sense of its direction and then add your own part to that conversation.

Your college career and education are also part of that unending conversation. With each new class you take, you arrive uncertain of exactly what will be said, you listen for awhile, and then you respond. Much of that "listening" will be in the form of reading. Much of your "speaking" will be in the form of writing.

The essays in this anthology provide another opportunity to listen to someone speak about a topic and then give your own response. Before you read each selection, use the **STRAP** strategy to identify the main parts of the text.

Chapter Outline

Frannyanne, 2017 / Used under license from Shutterstock.com

This essay suggests that employability might not be the best reason for choosing a field of study. Pay careful attention to the author's reasons for this claim.

About the Author

Scott Keyes is a 2009 graduate of Stanford University. He majored in political science. Today, he is the owner of Scott's Cheap Flights, a successful Internet start-up company.

Stop Asking Me My Major

One of my best friends from high school, Andrew, changed majors during his first semester at college. He and I had been fascinated by politics for years, sharing every news story we could find and participating in the Internet activism that was exploding into a new political force. Even though he was still passionate about politics, that was no longer enough. "I have to get practical," he messaged me one day, "and think about getting a job after graduation. I mean, it's like my mom keeps asking me: What can you do with a degree in political science anyway?" 1

I heard the same question from my friend Jesse when students across campus were agonizing about which major was right for them. He wasn't quite sure what he wanted to study, but every time a field sparked his interest, his father would pepper him with questions about what jobs were available for people in that discipline. Before long, Jesse's dad had convinced him that the only way he could get a job and be successful after college was to major in pre-med. 2

My friends' experiences were not **atypical**. 3

Choosing a major is one of the most difficult things students face in college. There are two main factors that most students consider when making this decision. First is their desire to study what interests them. Second is the fear that a particular major will render them penniless after graduation and result in that dreaded postcollege possibility: moving back in with their parents. 4

All too often, the concern about a major's practical prospects are pushed   *5*
upon students by well-intentioned parents. If our goal is to cultivate students who
are happy and successful, both in college as well as in the job market, I have this
piece of advice for parents: Stop asking, "What can you do with a degree in (fill
in the blank)?" You're doing your children no favors by asking them to focus on
the job prospects of different academic disciplines, rather than studying what
interests them.

It is my experience, both through picking a major myself and witnessing   *6*
many others enduring the process, that there are three reasons why parents
(and everyone else) should be encouraging students to focus on what they enjoy
studying most, rather than questioning what jobs are supposedly available for
different academic concentrations.

The first is psychological. For his first two years of college, Jesse followed   *7*
his dad's wishes and remained a pre-med student. The only problem was that he
hated it. With no passion for the subject, his grades slipped, hindering his chances
of getting into medical school. As a result his employability, the supposed reason
he was studying medicine in the first place, suffered.

The second reason to stop asking students what they can do with a major is   *8*
that it **perpetuates** the false notion that certain majors don't prepare students
for the workplace. The belief that technical majors such as computer science are
more likely to lead to a job than a major such as sociology or English is certainly
understandable. It's also questionable. "The problem," as my friend José explained
to me, "is that even as a computer-science major, what I learned in the classroom
was outdated by the time I hit the job market." He thought instead that the main
benefit of his education, rather than learning specific skills, was gaining a better
way of thinking about the challenges he faced. "What's more," he told me, "no
amount of education could match the specific on-the-job training I've received
working different positions."

Finally, it is **counterproductive** to demand that students justify their choice   *9*
of study with potential job prospects because that ignores the lesson we were all
taught in kindergarten (and shouldn't ignore the closer we get to employment):
You can grow up to be whatever you want to be. The jobs people work at often fall
within the realm of their studies, but they don't have to. One need look no further
than some of the most prominent figures in our society to see illustrations. The

TV chef Julia Child studied English in college. Author Michael Lewis, whose best sellers focus on sports and the financial industry, majored in art history. Matt Groening, creator of *The Simpsons*, got his degree in philosophy, as did the former Hewlett Packard chief executive Carly Fiorina. Jeff Immelt, chief executive of General Electric, focused on mathematics. Indeed, with the Department of Labor estimating that on average people switch careers (not just jobs) two or three times in their lives, relying on a college major as career preparation is misguided.

I'm not saying any applicant can get any job. Job seekers still need marketable   10
skills if they hope to be hired. However, in a rapidly changing economy, which majors lead to what jobs is not so clear cut. Many employers look for applicants from a diverse background—including my friend who has a degree in biochemistry but was just hired at an investment consulting firm.

That doesn't mean that majors no longer matter. It is still an important   11
decision, and students are right to seek outside counsel when figuring out what they want to study. But questioning how a particular major will affect their employability is not necessarily the best approach. Although parents' intentions may be pure—after all, who doesn't want to see their children succeed after graduation?—that question can hold tremendous power over **impressionable** freshmen. Far too many of my classmates let it steer them away from what they enjoyed studying to a major they believed would help them get a job after graduation.

One of those friends was Andrew. He opted against pursuing a degree in   12
political science, choosing instead to study finance because "that's where the jobs are." Following graduation, Andrew landed at a consulting firm. I recently learned with little surprise that he hates his job and has no passion for the work.

Jesse, on the other hand, realized that if he stayed on the pre-med track, he   13
would burn out before ever getting his degree. During his junior year he changed tracks and began to study engineering. Not only did Jesse's grades improve markedly, but his enthusiasm for the subject recently earned him a **lucrative** job offer and admission to a top engineering master's program.

Andrew and Jesse both got jobs. But who do you think feels more successful?   14

First appeared in *The Chronicle of Higher Education*, January 10, 2010. Reprinted by permission of the author.

---

perpetuates continues	**impressionable** easily influenced
counterproductive to act against an aim or goal	**lucrative** producing profit

Reflecting

Answer the comprehension and vocabulary questions about the reading.

1. What main claim (idea) does the author make in this essay?
   a. Choosing a major is one of the most difficult things students face in college.
   b. To cultivate happy and successful students, both in college as well as in the job market, stop asking, "What can you do with a degree in (fill in the blank)?"
   c. Parents don't understand how to help their children pick the right college major.

2. What reason does *not* support the author's main idea?
   a. Parents don't have the best interests in mind for their children.
   b. Not all jobs fall within the realm of a specific field of study.
   c. Student choice allows them to choose a major they are passionate about.

3. What is the main purpose of this essay?
   a. To explain
   b. To persuade
   c. To entertain

4. Study how the word *atypical* is used in the reading, and then choose the most accurate definition of the word.
   Atypical (paragraph 3)
   a. Standard
   b. Normal
   c. Unusual

Summarizing

Write a summary of "Stop Asking Me My Major."

Critical Thinking

- Do you agree with the author? Why or why not?
- What advice would you give a friend who is choosing a major?
- What claims could be made to counter or oppose the author's argument? Are those claims convincing enough to weaken his argument?
- How do you react to the claim that on-the-job training is more valuable than theories learned in the classroom?
- How would you describe the author's writing voice? Is it appropriate for his topic and writing purpose?

In this first-person narrative, the author shares details about her relationship with her mentally ill brother. The article first appeared in *Salon* online magazine in March 2011.

About the Author

Ashley Womble is the author of *The Cahoots*, a memoir about loving a person suffering from mental illness.

The Homeless Brother I Cannot Save

Like any New Yorker, I was no stranger to homeless people. I passed by them *1* on my way to the shiny glass tower where I worked for a glossy women's magazine: the older lady perched atop a milk crate in the subway station, the man curled up in a dirty sleeping bag and clutching a stuffed animal. They were unfortunate ornaments of the city, unlucky in ways I never really considered.

Until one hot summer day in 2009 when my little brother Jay left his key on *2* the coffee table and walked out of his house in West Texas to live on the streets. In the days that followed, I spent hours on the phone with detectives, social workers, and even the FBI, frantically trying to track him down. A friend designed a "Missing" poster using the most recent picture I had of him; he was wearing a hoodie and a Modest Mouse T-shirt, a can of beer in his hand and a deer-in-headlights expression on his face. I created a Facebook group and contacted old acquaintances still living in our hometown of Lubbock, begging everyone I even remotely knew to help me find him. No luck. If it had been me, a pretty young white woman, chances are my face would have been all over the news—but the sudden disappearance of a 20-year-old guy with paranoid schizophrenia didn't exactly warrant an Amber Alert.

In the year and a half that mental illness had **ravaged** my brother's mind, *3* I'd learned to lower my expectations of what his life would be like. The smart kid who followed politics in elementary school probably wouldn't become a lawyer after all. Instead of going to college after high school, Jay became obsessed with 9/11 conspiracy theories. What began as merely **eccentric** curdled into something **manic** and disturbing: He believed the planners of 9/11 were a group of people called "the **Cahoots**" who had created a 24-hour television network to monitor his actions and control his thoughts. Eventually, his story expanded until the Cahoots became one branch of the New World Order, a government whose purpose was to overturn Christianity, and he had been appointed by God to stop it.

This made it hard for him to act normal, even in public. He'd lost his job   4
busing tables after yelling "Stop the filming and hand over the tapes" to everyone dining in the restaurant. Having friends or even a coherent conversation wouldn't be possible unless he took the **antipsychotic** medication he'd been prescribed while he was in the mental hospital. A legal adult, he was allowed to refuse treatment, and he did. Otherwise the Cahoots would win.

I counted each day he'd been missing until they became weeks, until the   5
number was so high I wondered if he was even still alive. That number was about the only thing I continued to keep track of. Dirty clothes and dishes piled up at home, I missed deadlines at work, and I got out of bed only if it was absolutely necessary. I cried often, but especially during thunderstorms, a reminder that wherever my brother was, he was unprotected. Eventually it became clear that I was losing it, too. So I did what my brother wouldn't allow himself to do: I started taking a pill that helped usher away my anxiety and depression.

Weeks after Jay disappeared, police in Maryland found him talking to a   6
spider and had him hospitalized. He stayed for 72 hours. Then he went missing again.

September 11, 2009, was one of those drizzling mornings when I thought of   7
my brother. There was the usual undertone of **reverent** sadness in the city, but for me, the date was a reminder of all that had gone wrong inside Jay's mind. And on that day my phone finally rang.

"Hello." Jay's Southern drawl was unmistakable. I sat straight up in my desk   8
chair at work wondering what I should do. Record the call? Take notes?

"Where are you?" I asked, as images of him sitting in a jail cell or stranded   9
alone in an alley flashed in my head.

"Manhattan," he said. My heart filled with hope. Then he asked me if I'd gone   10 to the witchcraft celebration at the World Trade Center, where the Sorcerers had ordered the wind and the rain to destroy the ceremony. Once again, I just felt like a helpless stranger.

I asked nervously if I could buy him dinner. To my surprise, he agreed. Twenty minutes later I met him near Penn Station; he was hunched under an awning next to a big blue tarp that covered his backpack and the **paisley** duffel he'd once borrowed. His pale skin had tanned and hair covered his face. He was staring at people as they walked by, but he didn't see me until I said his name. Standing face-to-face with him, I could see that he had lost a lot of weight.   11

His cheekbones jutted out from his once-full face. If I had seen his picture I would have gasped. Instead, I just held out my arms.   12

Zagat has no recommendations for where to take your homeless brother to dinner. We settled on the Mexican chain Chevys and sat in a booth near the back. He told me about hitchhiking to New York and sleeping in Central Park until the cops kicked him out. He grinned as he talked about sleeping on the steps of a downtown school, his smile still as charming as it had been when he was 7.   13

"Do you consider yourself homeless?" I asked.   14

"Oh, yes!" he answered proudly.   15

I wondered if the constant motion of wandering from town to town helped quiet the voices he heard. If it was his own kind of medication and, if so, could I really tell him that was the wrong way to live?   16

Earlier in the year I'd bribed him with a trip to visit me on the condition that he took his meds. Now he was sitting in front of me, and as much as I wanted to let him stay in my apartment, I knew I couldn't let him (my therapist discouraged it and my roommate rightly put her foot down). I approached the topic cautiously, my voice shaking as I asked, "Do you know why you can't stay with me?" His voice small and shamed, he answered, "Because I won't take my medication." He had always denied that he had schizophrenia, but his admission gave me hope that maybe some day that would change.   17

I tried to quiet my own inner voice, which told me Jay needed to be in the hospital where a team of psychiatrists could experiment with medications that would fix his mind. I could do some things for my brother: I could give him a little money for cigarettes. I could buy him a new backpack, a sleeping bag, good walking shoes. But the more I pushed him to get help, the more my own sanity escaped me.   18

So I let him go. He went to New Jersey. Florida. Louisiana. To a place where 19 he told me from a pay phone he wouldn't call anymore because he didn't want me to know his whereabouts. I can only imagine what he looks like after a year on the streets: His hair must be long, skin tan and hardened, and his rail-thin body caked in dirt. He probably doesn't look much different from the homeless people I pass by on the streets of New York City. Seeing them makes my heart ache, makes me think about those they may have left behind, people who long to dust them off and put them on the right path but who know, in the end, it's not their choice.

Reprinted by permission of Ashley Womble. Originally appeared at *Salon* online, July 28, 2010.

schizophrenia
a type of mental disorder that creates fragmentation of thought, emotion, and perception

eccentric
irregular, odd

manic
deranged excitement

cahoots
conspiring together

antipsychotic
a medication for mental conditions that involve perception of reality

reverent
deeply respectful

paisley
an intricately feathered design, originally based on a pine-cone design from India

Zagat
a restaurant ranking service

Reflecting

Answer the comprehension and vocabulary questions about the reading.

1. Which of these inferences can you make from this essay?
   a. Mental illness can be life-altering without proper medication.
   b. Anyone with a mental illness will experience homelessness.
   c. Mental illness can be controlled by loving family members.

2. What is the main idea of paragraph 5?
   a. That the author's dishes were piling up and she was losing focus at work because of her missing brother
   b. That the author realized her missing brother was triggering her own depression and she needed to seek help
   c. That her brother went missing for a very long time

3. What conclusion does the author make at the end of the essay?
   a. That she will do whatever she can to find her brother and make him take his medicine

    b. That as much as she tries, she cannot make her brother take the right path, for only he can make the final choice about his medication and lifestyle

    c. That her brother is a lot like the people experiencing homelessness she sees in New York City

4. Does the writer use an academic or personal voice?

    a. Academic voice

    b. Personal voice

5. What types of supporting details does the author use?

    a. Personal anecdotes and reflections

    b. Facts and statistics

    c. Descriptions and dialogue

    d. Both *a* and *c*

6. Study how the word *ravaged* is used in the reading, and then choose the most accurate definition of the word.
   Ravaged (paragraph 3)

    a. Calmed

    b. Improved

    c. Consumed

Summarizing

Write a summary of "The Homeless Brother I Cannot Save."

Critical Thinking

- How has this essay affected your thinking about homelessness and mental illness? Explain.

- How is this selection as much about the author as it is about her brother? Explain.

- Would this selection have been as affecting if it was written in a formal academic voice? Why or why not?

- Is homelessness a personal problem, a social problem, or both? How so?

- In what ways are homelessness and mental health related?

Daniel Prudek, 2017 / Used under license from Shutterstock.com

In this article, Joseph Angier describes the feats of a man who can withstand remarkably cold temperatures.

About the Author

Joseph Angier is a writer and Emmy-award winning television producer. He's produced everything from breaking news to long-form documentary series. In addition to his time at ABC News, Angier has worked for PBS, Fox, NBC, and more.

Iceman on Everest: "It Was Easy"

It's a bitterly cold winter day and students on the University of Minnesota campus are bundled up, hurrying to their next class. Wim Hof, dressed in shorts, sandals, and nothing else, appeared from the doorway of a school building. 1

He's known as "The Ice Man." 2

Scientists can't really explain it, but the 48-year-old Dutchman is able to withstand, and even thrive, in temperatures that could be **fatal** to the average person. 3

From the Arctic Circle to Mount Everest

It's an ability he discovered in himself as a young man 20 years ago. 4

"I had a stroll like this in the park with somebody and I saw the ice and I thought, what would happen if I go in there. I was really attracted to it. I went in, got rid of my clothes. Thirty seconds I was in," Hof said. 5

"Tremendous good feeling when I came out and since then, I repeated it every day." 6

It was the moment that Hof knew that his body was different somehow: He was able to withstand fatally freezing temperatures. 7

Hof began a lifelong **quest** to see just how far his abilities would take him. In January of 1999, he traveled 100 miles north of the Arctic Circle to run a 8 half-marathon in his bare feet. Three years later, dressed only in a swimsuit, he dove under the ice at the North Pole and earned a Guinness World Record for the longest amount of time swimming under the ice: 80 meters, almost twice the length of an Olympic-sized pool.

When he didn't experience frostbite or hypothermia, the body's usual reactions to extreme cold, his extraordinary ability started to get the attention of doctors who specialize in extreme medicine. *9*

Dr. Ken Kamler, author of *Surviving the Extremes*, has treated dozens of people who tried to climb Mount Everest, and instead nearly died from the frigid temperatures. He couldn't believe it when he got word of a Dutchman making the ascent with no protection other than a pair of shorts. *10*

"People are always looking for new firsts on Everest. It's been climbed so many times now, people climb it without oxygen, they . . . they climb it with all different kinds of handicaps. But no one has come close to climbing Everest in those kinds of conditions," Dr. Kamler said. "It's . . . it's almost inconceivable." *11*

Hof made the expedition in shorts. *12*

"It was quite easy," Hof said. "I was in a snowstorm before, say, on the fifteen, sixteen thousand feet up 'til eighteen thousand feet." *13*

"I know my body, I know my mind, I know what I can do," Hof said. And he says he can withstand heat as well as cold. *14*

Nearly Naked, Surrounded by Ice

Dr. Kamler met Hof for the first time at the Rubin Museum in New York, where Hof was set to break another Guinness World Record, this time for remaining nearly naked in ice poured up to his neck. *15*

Hof came out of the museum, stripped to his swim trunks and climbed in a 5-foot tall plexiglass container filled with ice. Once he got in, they poured more ice into the container until it reached his chin. *16*

All the while, Dr. Ken Kamler monitored Hof from outside the tank. *17*

Normally, when a person is exposed to freezing temperatures for a prolonged period of time, the body goes into survival mode, as its liquids begin to freeze. *18*

Frostbite sets in, and in order to save the major organs, the body sacrifices blood flow to the extremities, cutting circulation from the fingers, toes, ears and nose to keep the blood flowing to the organs necessary for survival. *19*

If not treated immediately, the damage to these extremities is **irreversible**. *20*

The other danger is hypothermia, an abnormally low body temperature.

At about 90 degrees, body functions start shutting down, and once that starts, *21* you could be dead within minutes.

But Hof stayed in his tomb of ice for one hour and 12 minutes. Then, the ice *22* was poured out of the tank, and Hof emerged, his skin still pink.

"He's not moving, he's not generating heat, he's not dressed for it, and he's *23* immersed in ice water. And water will transmit heat 30 times faster than air. It literally sucks the life right out of you. And yet, despite all those negative factors, Wim Hof was very calm, very comfortable the entire time that he was immersed in that water," Kamler said.

It was a new entry for the Guinness World Records, but really, no one else out *24* there seems able to compete with him. He just keeps breaking his own records.

Response to Cold "Completely Obliterated"

At the hypothermia lab at the University of Minnesota in Duluth, scientists *25* who've studied the cold for years say they've never seen anything like it.

Dr. Robert Pozos and Dr. Larry Wittmers, director of the lab, hooked up Hof *26* to heart rate and core temperature monitors to evaluate his body's response after being submerged in an extremely cold water tank.

A normal response might include intense pain, cardiovascular stress and *27* mounting hysteria, but with Hof, it's a much different story.

As he went into the tank, Dr. Wittmers explained, "What you're seeing *28* basically is a situation in which the usual response to a shock or a cold was completely obliterated. There was no—none of the usual response you would see. And those responses that you see in most individuals that are exposed to that type of situation are uncontrollable."

From inside the tank, Hof said, "I feel the cold is a noble force, as they always *29* say, and for me, right now, these readings are important but this is what I do every day in the winter, because I like it."

Since there's nothing abnormal about his body, all doctors can tell is that *30* Hof's secret must lie in the wiring of his brain.

"It's very easy to speculate that the same mind control that you use to control *31* your heart when you're scared also can be called upon to control the other organs in the body. And maybe that's how Wim Hof does this," said Kamler. "That's . . . it's speculation, but it sort of makes sense, and a lot of scientists are working very hard to try to figure this out now."

One answer might lie in an ancient Himalayan meditation called "Tummo," 32
which is thought to generate heat. Hof began practicing the ritual years ago.

"Legends abound of practitioners of Tummo sitting out on the ice naked 33
except for wet sheets that they have draped around them, and as they meditate,
the sheets dry and the ice melts around them, even though it's freezing
temperature," Kamler said.

The Mystery of Swimmer Lynne Cox

If there's one ice-lover who has baffled scientists as much as Hof, it's 34
American swimmer Lynne Cox.

At 15, Cox swam the English Channel in 14 hours, a Guinness World Record. 35
She has also written two books about her adventures: *Grayson* and *Swimming to
Antarctica*.

Like Hof, Lynne soon discovered that she had an almost super-human ability 36
to survive in frigid water. In 1987, she became the first person to swim across the
Bering Strait, from Alaska to what was then the Soviet Union, in 38-degree water.

And in 2002, she set a new goal: to swim a mile through the massive icebergs 37
of the Antarctic.

Like Hof, Cox prepares herself by somehow using her mind to control her 38
body's temperature.

"I went into the cabin and sat down and focused and breathed and thought 39
about how I was gonna enter the water, how I was gonna do the swim. I sort
of . . . I went through a mental rehearsal of it all. And that preparation, my body
knew that I was going to jump into very cold water," Cox said. "Before I went in
the water, one of the doctors took my core temperature, my internal temperature,
and found it was 102.2."

The water was 32 degrees and hovering near the freezing point. 40

Without a wet suit or a dry suit, in wind gusting 35 knots, Cox used metal 41
steps to enter the water.

"As I came down, it was like stepping on ice trays," she said. 42

She began swimming between the icebergs. 43

"That was amazing to be able to physically do it," she said. 44

But how do they do it? Kamler said the answer lies deep in the brain. "It's 45
a mystery that we have not yet come close to solving, although we do have

tantalizing clues," he said. "It tells us that there's enormous potential within the brain that is going untapped. And if we can study them more, and study people like them more, maybe we can unleash that potential for the rest of us."

fatal
deadly

expedition
a journey made for a specific purpose

hypothermia
a condition that results from an extremely low body temperature

frostbite
injury to the body, most often hands and feet, resulting from long exposure to extreme cold

inconceivable
not believable

Reflecting

Answer the comprehension and vocabulary questions about the reading.

1. What type of text is this?
   a. An argument text with some narrative elements
   b. An expository text with some narrative elements
   c. An expository text with some argument elements

2. Why is Wim Hof called "The Iceman"?
   a. He has broken many Guinness World Records for icefishing.
   b. He is able to withstand cold temperatures for periods that would be deadly to the average person.
   c. He is known for keeping his cool while driving on dangerous Alaskan roads as an ice-road trucker.

3. What opening strategy does the author use to introduce the topic?
   a. He uses an anecdote, a brief illustrative story.
   b. He uses a bold statement to grab attention.
   c. He uses a little-known fact that may surprise readers.

4. What makes Dr. Kamler a good source to include in this text?
   a. He is a doctor.
   b. He's written a book on surviving extreme conditions.
   c. He's treated many patients with serious injuries from exposure to cold conditions.
   d. All of the above.

5. Study how the word *quest* is used in the reading, and then choose the most accurate definition of the word.
   Quest (paragraph 8)
   a. Question
   b. Pursuit
   c. Stroll

6. Study how the word *irreversible* is used in the reading, and then choose the most accurate definition of the word.
   Irreversible (paragraph 20)
   a. Not able to be changed
   b. Able to be changed
   c. Easily changed

Summarizing

Write a summary of "Iceman on Everest: 'It Was Easy.'"

Critical Thinking

- How would you describe Hof's attitude toward his condition? Does he embrace it or attempt to conceal it? What would your attitude be toward having the same condition?
- Besides breaking records, what practical benefits might there be to having the ability to withstand cold temperatures for as long as Hof?
- Why is it important that the author includes details about how the average person's body reacts to cold temperatures? (See paragraphs 18–21.) What effect do those details have on your reading or understanding of the article's topic?
- Do you have any questions about the topic that were not answered by the piece? What are they, and where might you find the answers?
- Even though the reading focuses on Wim Hof, the author also includes details about Lynne Cox. What is significant about Cox? Why do you think the author included her in the article?

This narrative from author Nicholas Best's book entitled *The Greatest Day in History* describes the hours immediately following the conclusion of World War I. The fighting officially stopped at the eleventh hour on the eleventh day of the eleventh month. We celebrate Armistice Day, which coincides with Veterans Day, on November 11.

About the Author

Nicholas Best is an English author who grew up in Kenya. An alumnus of Trinity College, Dublin, he served in the Grenadier Guards and worked in London as a journalist before becoming a full-time author.

The Greatest Day in History

For most people at the front, the prevailing mood was one of distinct **anticlimax** as 11 o'clock passed and the firing died away all along the line. For as long as anyone could remember, there had always been firing somewhere within earshot, but now there wasn't any more. The quiet seemed unnatural after all the noise, almost a **contradiction** in terms. It took a great deal of getting used to.

Brigadier Richard Foot, an artilleryman supporting the Guards battalions at Maubeuge, had fired off the last of his surplus ammunition before 7 a.m. and then went to visit a couple of wounded soldiers at an advanced operating station. He spoke for millions as he returned later to his unit:

"It was a strange feeling to ride back to the battery in the quiet that followed 11 o'clock. One had got used to the background noise of shellfire, which could often be heard as far away as the south coast of England. Near the front, it seemed a continuous orchestration of deep and echoing sound, punctuated by the sharper rat-tat-tat of rifle or machine-gun fire. The landscape was different too; no observation balloons to be seen, no plumes of smoke from shell bursts or burning buildings, no aeroplanes glinting in the sky. After three and a half years of front-line service, broken only by short spells of leave or hospital, peace seemed a very strange and new experience."

Just outside Perquise, some German officers came forward in the silence to show the Royal Welch Fusiliers where the road was mined. They were followed by a hunchback with an accordion who played the "Marseillaise" in triumph as the Fusiliers marched into his village. The **refugees** were already beginning to return, wending their way home again now that there was no more shooting. Army chaplain Harry Blackburne watched some of them near Mons: [4]

"The roads filled with civilians hurrying back to their homes which they had been forced to leave by the Germans, all of them struggling along the muddy roads, pushing their handcarts and barrows. It is like it was during the retreat from Mons: old women, pinched and ill, absolutely deadbeat. Our **lorries** pick up as many as they can, and our soldiers push along the wheelbarrows for the older ones who can hardly walk. More often than not, on arrival at their homes they find no home—it has been battered to pieces by shellfire: "It doesn't matter," they say, "we have tasted liberty." [5]

In Mons itself, the inhabitants were determined to have a party for their liberators, even though many of the Canadians were so exhausted that they lay fast asleep in the street. The Canadians weren't due to make their official entry into the town until half past three, when they would march in with bands playing and colors flying, but the party had already begun and the inhabitants weren't about to stop now. The **reprisals** were beginning too. The Belgians wanted to get at the Germans captured in the fighting and take their revenge for four years of occupations. It needed all the Canadians' **tact** to stop the Belgians falling on their German prisoners and tearing them limb from limb. [6]

Not far from Mons, men of the Royal Marine Light Infantry were lying in a line along a railway bank as the fighting came to an end. A battalion of the Manchester Regiment had lined up along the same bank during the retreat from Mons in 1914. After the shooting stopped, marine Hubert Trotman and a few others got up and strolled down to the wood in the nearby valley. They stumbled across some skeletons from 1914, men of the Manchesters still lying there from the beginning of the war. "Lying there with their boots on, very still, no helmets, no rusty rifles or equipment, just their boots." The sight was one that the marines never forget. [7]

Everywhere, there was a feeling of disbelief that the war was actually over, a   *8*
sense that it was all just a dream that wasn't really happening. US Private Arthur
Jensen was one of many who said, "Don't worry, it'll soon start up again," when
the firing stopped at eleven. British rifleman Aubrey Smith at Erquennes echoed
his sentiments:

"To think there would be no more shells, no more bombs, no more **gas**, no   *9*
more cold nights to be spent on **picket** through fear of lighting a fire. Of all the
incredible announcements that had ever been made to us, this left us the most
staggered. It must be only a dream! Surely we should hear the distant sound of
guns in a minute or so, which would prove we had been deluded! We strained
our ears for distant gunfire . . . Silence! Only the sound of church bells in other
villages proclaiming the event. . . .

"Twice during the afternoon our hearts sank to our feet at the sound of a   *10*
distant report like the firing of a big gun, but word came along presently that it
was either blasting or else the exploding of some German mines under the roads!
Everyone, troops and civilians, had knocked off work for the day, and we were
welcomed into the cottages, where the good folks made cups of coffee out of the
scanty supplies they had, and told us many tales of suffering and hardships.
We palled up with a peasant and his family in a small cottage near our field,
and we listened to stories which were a replica of those we had heard during the
past week."

All along the line, French and Belgian civilians produced food that they had   *11*
been hiding for this special day. The Germans had been through their houses so
often that they had very little left beyond a bottle or two of wine buried in the
garden and a few choice items that they had somehow managed to conceal. They
happily produced what they had and thrust it on the soldiers, not realizing that
the troops on the Allied side were perfectly well fed and had no need of anything
to eat. It had been so long since civilians behind the German lines had eaten
properly that they had forgotten what it was like to have a full stomach. Food was
their greatest gift, the most valuable present they had to offer to their liberators.
They gave it willingly, delighted to do what they could to mark the occasion.
At Maubeuge, one elderly Frenchman was so pleased at the day's events that he
dressed up in his old uniform from the Franco-Prussian war in celebration.

Among the Americans, Harry Truman had been as glad as anyone to see an   *12*
end to the war. Like everyone else, however, he found it distinctly unsettling when
the guns ceased to roar at eleven:

"It was so quiet it made me feel as if I'd been suddenly deprived of my ability   *13*
to hear. The men at the guns, the captain, the lieutenants, the sergeants and
corporals looked at each other for some time and then a great cheer arose all along
the line. We could hear the men in the infantry a thousand metres in front raising
holy hell. The French battery behind our position were dancing, shouting and
waving bottles of wine. . . ."

Truman's men promptly joined in, drinking all the red wine they could   *14*
find and more **cognac** than they could hold. The sun came out at midday and
the party continued throughout the afternoon into the evening. Rockets were
fired and **Very lights** soared as the men of the 129th Field Artillery celebrated
the release from tension. Above them, Lieutenant Broaddus of Battery F watched
unhappily from his balloon. He had been sent up earlier to direct the last of
the artillery fire. The war had stopped while he was up there and everyone had
forgotten about him in his excitement. It was two hours before they remembered
him again and hauled him down.

Elsewhere, Americans wandered out into no-man's-land, looking for   *15*
souvenirs to take home now that the fighting was done. There was a market
for souvenirs behind the lines, a brisk trade among base soldiers who had not
themselves been anywhere near the action. Pistols, helmets, bayonets, anything
good would fetch a price. Sometimes the souvenir hunters strayed too close to
the Germans in the trenches opposite. Feldwebel Georg Bucher and his fellow
lice-ridden scarecrows had emerged cautiously from their holes in the early
afternoon, scarcely able to believe that their heads wouldn't be blown off as soon
as they raised them above the **parapet**. They watched warily as the men they had
machine-gunned that morning, who had dropped gas on them in return, now
hunted for trophies a few yards away:

"We were squatting with **incredulous** eyes in front of the parapet. The   *16*
Americans were wandering around in no-man's land, but there wasn't much they
could find, for the shellfire had played havoc there. Some of them came within
twenty yards of us. How angrily and **contemptuously** they looked at us! They
didn't seem pleased that we still had hand grenades hanging from our belts and
rifles in our hands. . . .

"Some of us tried to make friends with the enemy, but to no avail. The   17
Americans were too bitter from the events of the previous day, which wasn't
surprising. They had attacked three times and been beaten back with heavy losses.

"It was indeed a strange sensation to be sitting openly in front of the trench.   18
The reality was hard to believe; we were conscious of a vague fear that it might all
turn out to be a dream."

It was no dream. The war was really over and the fighting really had stopped.   19
Whoever was in charge of the nightmare had finally come to their senses, and not
a moment too soon.

contradiction
contrary or opposite

lorries
British word for "trucks"

reprisal
the act of retaliation

tact
upstanding character

gas
in this case, mustard gas, a blistering agent that when inhaled destroys the lungs

picket
a soldier or party of soldiers assigned a particular duty

cognac
a French brandy liquor

Very lights
colored flares fired from a special pistol, for illumination at night or for signalling

parapet
a low protective wall

incredulous
not willing to believe

contemptuously
with extreme dislike

Reflecting

Answer the comprehension and vocabulary questions about the reading.

1. What sensation from November 11 was referenced the most by the soldiers interviewed in this piece?
   a. The sound of silence
   b. The smell of food
   c. The feeling of homesickness

2. What was so significant about the food French and Belgium civilians offered their liberators?
   a. The food had special meaning, for it was hidden and saved for this occasion, even as the civilians went hungry.
   b. The food was very expensive, and the civilians wanted to impress their liberators.
   c. The food offered the civilians a chance to show off their skillful cooking, so as to show the war had not defeated them.

3. In paragraph 14, the author develops the paragraph's main idea with a series of major and minor details. Read the following major detail from the paragraph. Then identify a minor detail that completes the idea.

> There was a market for souvenirs behind the lines, a brisk trade among base soldiers who had not themselves been anywhere near the action.

   a. [The Germans] watched warily as the men they had machine-gunned that morning, who had dropped gas on them in return, now hunted for trophies.

   b. Sometimes the souvenir hunters strayed too close to the Germans in the trenches opposite.

   c. Pistols, helmets, bayonets, anything good would fetch a price.

4. How would you describe the author's voice in selection?

   a. Academic (semiformal)

   b. Personal (informal)

   c. Satiric (humorous)

5. Study how the word *anticlimax* is used in the reading, and then choose the most accurate definition of the word.
Anticlimax (paragraph 1)

   a. Lacking excitement

   b. Exaggerated excitement

   c. Intense

6. Study how the word *refugees* is used in the reading, and then choose the most accurate definition of the word.
Refugees (paragraph 4)

   a. Prisoners of war

   b. Soldiers who survive a war

   c. People who flee their homelands for safety

Summarizing

Write a summary of "The Greatest Day in History."

Critical Thinking

- Why does the author quote soldiers from different sides of the war—British, American, and German?
- Some texts and films glorify war. Does this reading fit into this category? Why or why not?
- In paragraph 5, the civilians state they have "tasted liberty," so they were eager to get home. What does it mean to "taste liberty"?
- What is your own attitude about military service and war? How does it affect your feelings about this selection?

In this article from *The Conversation* website, Susan Lawler outlines an interesting solution for feeding our overcrowded planet.

About the Author

Susan Lawler is the head of the Department of Environmental Management & Ecology at La Trobe University in Australia.

Eating Insects: Good for You, Good for the Environment

The Food and Agriculture Organization of the United Nations released a report in May 2013 called "Edible Insects: Future prospects for food and feed security" and since then news outlets have been looking for images of people eating bugs.

Even I was on our local TV news this week commenting on the issue. The reporter who rang to seek my input asked if I would be willing to eat a live bug for the camera. I politely declined, not just because I am a vegetarian, and not because I am squeamish. As I told the reporter and camera man, if I were to eat an animal, it would most certainly be a bug.

Indeed, I probably eat bugs all the time. As explained by an insect food producer, most of us eat a quarter of a kilogram of insects by accident each year. Insects find their way into our foodstuffs no matter how hard we try to keep them out. Interestingly, if you eat **organic**, your rate of insect consumption is much higher.

So even though I have avoided eating animal flesh (including fish) for over 30 years, I nevertheless engage in **entomophagy**. And so do billions of people all over the world.

It is not true that the eating of insects is something that humans resort to only when they are starving. Many cultures cherish the flavors and texture of insects.

Right here in Australia, **indigenous** people traveled to the alps each summer to feast on the bounty provided by the annual influx of bogong moths.

Which, you might say, is fine for them but not likely to convince me to fry up some moths (hint: remove the wings by scorching). So what are the arguments for entomophagy, and why on earth does the United Nations want us to do this apparently disgusting thing?   6

Eating insects is efficient, good for the environment, improves animal welfare, and reduces the risk of diseases in humans. Let's go through the arguments presented in the FAO report.   7

Efficient feed conversion. The amount of feed you need to provide to get animal based food varies greatly depending on the species. Predatory fish are expensive to raise in aquaculture because they need to be fed fish. Herbivores are more efficient, but it still takes 10 kilograms of food to produce 1 kilogram of cow, only half of which can actually be eaten. By contrast, 10 kilograms of feed will produce up to 9 kilograms of insects, of which over 95% can be eaten. If we want to find a way to produce more protein with less, insects are the way to go.   8

Food inputs from waste. Now let's talk about what kind of food we give our livestock. If we have to catch fish to feed our aquaculture fish we are still dependent on wild caught protein. If we grow grain to feed our cattle, we still have to use land and fertilizer and water. But if we choose to raise insects we can feed them our waste products. Think about it, flies grow on manure. Other insects could grow on agricultural waste products high in **cellulose**. This **transcends** efficiency. Growing insects for food could actually clean up the mess made by growing other food.   9

Less greenhouse gases. Cattle produce so many greenhouse gases that a kilogram of beef has an impact similar to driving 250 kilometers in a car. The only insects that even produce methane as a waste product are cockroaches, termites, and scarab beetles. Getting our protein from insects would significantly reduce greenhouse gas emissions.   10

Water savings. Agriculture consumes 70% of water worldwide, and the production of animal protein requires 100 times more water than protein from grain. This includes the water used to grow the grain to feed the animal, also known as "virtual water." By this method of calculation, 1 kg of chicken requires 3500 liters of water and 1 kg of beef requires between 22,000 and 43,000 liters of water. Insects need far less, and can be grown throughout the drought.   11

Animal welfare. All of our concerns about live animal exports and **battery farm** hens are based on the need to reduce animal suffering. High density of   12 livestock is necessary for commercial food production but is undesirable from an animal welfare point of view. Insects, on the other hand, are naturally **gregarious**. Many of them prefer to live in high densities and killing them humanely is possible and easy. No more nightmare film clips from **abattoirs**.

Reduced risk of disease. Think about the infections that move from animals 13 to people and have frightened all of us: swine flu, bird flu, mad cow disease. These infections are called zoonotics, and they spread because we are similar enough to our livestock to be able to catch their diseases. Insects have a much lower risk of passing disease on to us.

In fact, it is difficult to find many disadvantages to eating insects. We don't 14 even have to get over our **aversion** to biting into a crunchy morsel with too many legs. Factories are already growing insects to produce protein powders which can be used to supplement foods we already enjoy.

The only downside I could find is that eating fresh insects collected in the 15 wild puts you at risk of consuming **pesticides**. Which is one of the reasons I did not want to eat a bug for the camera—we did not have any insects from a trusted source.

The other reason is the backlash that could result from the disgust factor. Yes, 16 it would make good TV viewing, because it is shocking and kind of gross. But if we really want people to eat more bugs (and we do!) then I don't think we want to give the impression that we will have to start picking crickets up off the lawn and popping them in our mouths.

No, we are much more sophisticated than that. Insect protein will be 17 produced by reputable growers who will care for their charges and ensure a high quality product. Make no mistake, this is a growth industry.

In future, entomophagy will be something we do by design, instead of by 18 accident.

From *The Conversation* at theconversation.com

---

organic
food grown without the use of pesticides or other fertilizers

entomophagy
the practice of eating inspects, especially by people

indigenous
native to a country

cellulose
a carbohydrate and major component of plant cell walls

transcends
goes beyond; exceeds

battery farm
A housing system used for animal production methods and a major concern of animal rights activists

gregarious
fond of living in packs

abattoirs
slaughterhouses

pesticides
chemicals for destroying plant, fungal, or animal pests

Reflecting

Answer the comprehension and vocabulary questions about the reading.

1. What is the main claim (idea) made in the United Nations report?
   a. Insects will always find their way into our foodstuffs.
   b. Eating insects is efficient, good for the environment, improves animal welfare, and reduces the risk of diseases in humans.
   c. It is not true that the eating of insects is something that humans resort to only when they are starving.

2. What is *not* a reason identified by the report for treating insects as a food source?
   a. Insects as a food source reduce the risk of disease.
   b. Insects are easy to prepare for cooking.
   c. Insects are an efficient source for food conversion.

3. What is the main idea of paragraph 10?
   a. Cattle produce so many greenhouse gases that a kilogram of beef has an impact similar to driving 250 kilometers in a car.
   b. The only insects that even produce methane as a waste product are cockroaches, termites, and scarab beetles.
   c. Getting our protein from insects would significantly reduce greenhouse gas emissions.

4. In what paragraph does the author address a counterargument? (See Section 10.1.)
   a. Paragraph 15
   b. Paragraph 9
   c. Paragraph 11

5. Study how the word *aversion* is used in the reading, and then choose the most accurate definition of the word.
   Aversion (paragraph 14)
   a. Strong dislike
   b. Affection

Summarizing

Write a summary of "Eating Insects: Good for You, Good for the Environment."

Critical Thinking

- Does the writer make a convincing argument in favor of eating insects? What is the most convincing part? What is the least convincing part?
- What would have to happen to make eating insects more socially acceptable?
- How would you describe the author's writing voice? Is it strictly academic? Strictly personal? Or a mixture of both?

In this article from the National Education Association, Cindy Long discusses the challenges facing undocumented students on their path to higher education.

About the Author

Cindy Long is a Washington, D.C. based writer who covers education and social issues.

Undocumented Students Walk the "Trail of Dreams"

Felipe Matos, 24, teaches English to young students in Miami. When he asked 1
his class one day who had been told that they would never make it to college, every hand went up. The students were only in first grade, and Matos was appalled that they were already so discouraged about their futures, but he wasn't surprised. The students were also mostly **undocumented** immigrants, brought to the United States by their parents.

Matos understands their circumstances. He's also undocumented. 2

Born to a single mother in the slums of Brazil, he was sent to the United 3
States at age 14 so that he could have a chance at a better life. He worked hard, and graduated fourth in his high school class of 500. With dreams of becoming a teacher, he was accepted at top universities, but was **barred** from receiving financial aid and couldn't afford to go.

Instead, he attends Miami Dade Community College, where he studies 4
economics and is ranked one of the top 20 college students in the United States for academic excellence. Still, he's unable to enter the classroom because of his immigration status.

"My dream is to become a teacher in an inner city high school, so that I can 5
tell students going through the same thing that they can succeed in life, that they

are not worthless, but that they are worth a million," he says. "We can't keep denying young people their dreams."

It was for the dreams of the estimated 65,000 undocumented immigrants who graduate from high school each year, but are unable to go to college, that Matos walked 1,500 miles from Miami to Washington, D.C. 6

He's one of four college students, including Gaby Pacheco, Carlos Roa, and Juan Rodríguez, who left Miami on January 1 in a march they call the "Trail of Dreams." 7

Brought here as children, the United States is the only country they call home. Even though they have the same dreams as other American children, and have excelled in school, they live in the shadows of society, unable to work and put their years of schooling to use. 8

Gaby Pacheco, 25, came to the United States from Ecuador when she was seven, and was considered a "gifted student" by her American teachers. She now has three education degrees from Miami Dade College, and dreams of one day becoming a special education teacher, using music therapy as a communication tool to teach autistic children and adults. 9

She says she marched 1,500 miles from Florida to Washington so she could say to President Obama, "We just want a chance." 10

Just days after Arizona passed a law allowing the police to stop suspected illegal immigrants and demand proof of citizenship, hundreds of immigrant rights **advocates** joined the four Miami students—as well as five other immigrant students who marched 250 miles from New York City—at the White House on May 1 for the "March for America" rally, asking President Obama to live up to his campaign promise of passing comprehensive immigration reform. 11

Waving American flags and signs that said "We are ALL Arizona" and "Education, Not Deportation," participants in the rally heard the Trail of Dreamers speak about the importance of the DREAM Act—a bill now before Congress that would help immigrants brought here as children, and who have grown up in the United States, gain permanent status after six years by going to college or joining the military. 12

Students from around the country joined in the rally, including a busload of DREAM Act supporters from Harrisonburg, Virginia, organized in their hometown by special education teacher Sandy Mercer. 13

Mercer collaborates in English classes, focusing on reading and writing, often with ELL students. The stories written by her undocumented students convinced her that they deserve a chance to earn legal residency in the country they call home. 14

"I support the DREAM Act because as an educator for over 30 years, I understand what happens when students lose hope," Mercer says. "I am not willing to stand by and do nothing and allow the spark I see in these students to fade." 15

Many of her undocumented students have trusted her with their stories, and she has worked tirelessly to help them pursue their educations, including a young man whose parents fled with him and his brother from Guatemala after a gang "tagged" their house, a signal that they planned to kill the two brothers for not agreeing to join the gang. 16

Now an Honors Society Student, this young man hopes to study astronomy and one day work at NASA, but he never thought it was possible for him to attend college. 17

"These students have more courage in their little fingers than I will ever have. It takes courage to keep working when one sees little hope for a future," Mercer says. "These are bilingual, talented, motivated, hard-working, family-loving young people in whom our schools and communities have invested so much." 18

Mercer has told her students about the few scholarships that don't have residency requirements, and that they can attend the local community college, although they must pay out-of-state tuition. She's networked with other Virginia teachers who've helped their students go on to college, and has worked with local financial aid officers to brainstorm ways for students to get money for tuition since they're not eligible for federal loans or grants. 19

She and her colleagues also continually try to raise funds through members of the community willing to sponsor the students' education. But she's most committed to working for passage of the DREAM Act. 20

"Anyone who works with students recognizes this legislation needs to be passed now," she says. 21

Long, Cindy, "Undocumented Students Walk the Trail of Dreams." Published at nea.org. May 2010. Copyright National Education Association.

---

undocumented
not having the official documents needed to live or work in a country legally

"Trail of Dreams"
a play on the "Trails of Tears," the forced march of Native Americans from eastern states such as Georgia and Florida to the Oklahoma Territory

advocates
people arguing for or supporting a cause

residency
in this case, being a resident of a state

Reflecting

Answer the comprehension and vocabulary questions about the reading.

1. What is the main idea of the article?
   a. Undocumented students desire to go to college, and the DREAM Act is the best path to that dream.
   b. Laws disallow undocumented students to go to U.S. colleges.
   c. Undocumented students feel discouraged and wish to drop out of school.

2. Is the main idea directly stated or implied?
   a. Directly stated
   b. Implied

3. Paragraph 3 includes background details about Felipe Matos. What pattern is used to organize the details?
   a. Logical
   b. Chronological (time)
   c. Cause-effect

4. Study how the word *barred* is used in the reading, and then choose the most accurate definition of the word.
   Barred (paragraph 3)
   a. Accepted
   b. Denied
   c. Jailed

Summarizing

Write a summary of "Undocumented Students Walk the 'Trail of Dreams.'"

Critical Thinking

- How has this article confirmed or changed your attitude about undocumented students?
- This article was written in 2010. How has the debate over undocumented students evolved since then? Are undocumented students any closer to attending college?
- In paragraph 18, undocumented students are described as "courageous." Why are they courageous?
- Why is immigration a common theme in the United States, past and present?

In this article, Sanela Osmanovic and Loretta Peccinoni explore the bonding effect of video game play between young and aging generations.

About the Authors

Sanela Osmanovic is a doctoral candidate in communication studies at Louisiana State University. **Loretta Pecchioni** is an associate professor of communication studies at Louisiana State University.

Family Matters: How Video Games Help Successful Aging

Sitting quietly in the corner, we watch a daily family ritual: in the living room **awash** with soft afternoon light, a six-year-old boy is sitting on the floor, controller in hand, eyes firmly on the television screen. His fingers expertly guide the colorful character in *Skylanders*, from time to time glancing over his shoulder and grinning at the figure on the sofa, his 68-year-old grandmother.

Perched on the edge of the seat, she follows his game dutifully, exclaiming and clapping when he finishes a task or meets a challenge, responding with enthusiasm and praise to his frequent **inquiries**: "Did you see me, Gram?" Every day after school, the two of them do this. Sometimes he plays with friends, but still asks his grandmother to watch. Sometimes he sits calmly on the sofa by her, and they play *Minecraft* together. Well, he plays; she watches.

Such a scenario has become common in households across America, with older family members **partaking** in the gaming activities of the younger generation—and not just watching them play. From 1999 to 2015, the share of American gamers older than 50 increased from 9 to 27 percent. They enjoy the challenge, the fun and especially the social side of playing video games. A major draw is that gaming can be a way to spend time together with others, including their children and grandchildren.

Our research shows that members of all generations—young and old—view family togetherness as a benefit, and many play video games with that as a specific purpose. They enjoy the games, they enjoy playing, but what they really enjoy is the interaction, which helps to create connections among family members. Better yet, these connections can improve mental and physical well-being and improve relationships, which are all keys to maintaining a high quality of life as people age. *4*

Changing families need to remain connected

America's population is aging, and the world's population of people over 65 is growing quickly: according to the National Institute on Aging, by 2030 one billion people will be 65 or older. Rising life expectancy combined with declining birth rates makes older adults an increasingly large fraction of the world's population, changing the relationships and the structure of family. *5*

Three and even four generations are now likely to share significant parts of their lives, whether living together or separately. As the numbers of grandparents and great-grandparents increase, it becomes more important to form and maintain strong bonds among older and younger adults in families. As newly independent **adolescents** become involved in the unforgiving whirlpool of romantic, academic and social activities, family ties take a back seat. The frequency and intensity of family connections weaken, especially with grandparents. *6*

One way to maintain the important **intergenerational** relationships within families is through shared activities. Spending time in ways that appeal to both sides of the age spectrum also creates closeness to further strengthen connections. Video games are one important way to achieve this. *7*

Playing for togetherness

Through many conversations with families like the one at the start of this story, we found that older adults who regularly play video games with their relatives find the experience enjoyable, fun and, most importantly, bonding. Mainly partaking in casual, social games, they relish the informal daily contact and the common ground gaming creates between them and their children and grandchildren. *8*

"Time together, and something that is just ours, that just the two of us do," one 63-year-old told us, explaining why she plays video games with her granddaughter. "It is like a secret language when we talk about it in front of the rest of the family, something that ties us. I feel like I have been more a part of my *9* granddaughter's life now that we get to do something closer to her generation."

Younger adults, in turn, play video games with older family members mainly   10
as a means of maintaining or deepening their relationships. In most cases, they
carefully select the games based on their family member's **perceived** interests and
abilities. When playing with friends, they typically focus on games with higher
levels of control **complexity** or story involvement, such as *Call of Duty* or *World
of Warcraft*. But when playing with older adults they select "exergames" such
as *Dance Dance Revolution* or app games such as *Words with Friends*, meeting
the perceived necessity for simple controls, as well as outcomes beyond mere
enjoyment, such as physical or mental exercise.

They use the gaming to spend time together, to connect and to talk   11
about both simple and complex topics in a setting they find comfortable and
comforting. "Playing helps me talk to my dad more, because I don't have the
luxury of going home every week," one 19-year-old man told us. "So, playing
online games together helps me in continuation of the bond I have with my dad."

Regardless of age, the ability to stay connected through gaming is the most   12
prominent motive for playing. For the young, playing simple, casual games that do
not necessarily excite them is still a good way to feel the comfort of family. For the
old, working through frustrations of learning to use new technologies is a small
price to pay to actively participate in the lives of their children and grandchildren.
The results are happiness and enjoyment stemming from the bonding, the
conversations, the feelings of being closer to loved ones and even maintaining
relationships across distances.

Originally published by *The Conversation* on May 16, 2016 at www.theconversation.com

awash	**adolescents**	**perceived**
filled	young people	noticeable
partaking	**intergenerational**	**complexity**
sharing; taking part in	between generations	difficulty

Reflecting

Answer the comprehension and vocabulary questions about the reading.

1. What is the main idea of the article?
   a. Playing video games improves the health of aging people.
   b. Playing video games is becoming an activity for building and maintaining bonds
   between young and old family members.

c. Older generations of people are playing more video games than they did in the past.

2. What major detail from the reading directly supports the main idea?
   a. Regardless of age, the ability to stay connected through gaming is the most prominent motive for playing.
   b. When playing with friends, [young people] typically focus on games with higher levels of control complexity or story involvement, such as *Call of Duty*.
   c. Rising life expectancy combined with declining birth rates makes older adults an increasingly large fraction of the world's population, changing the relationships and the structure of family.

3. What is the author's main purpose with this text?
   a. To entertain
   b. To explain
   c. To persuade

4. How would you describe the writing voice in the reading?
   a. Academic
   b. Personal
   c. Satiric

5. Study how the key term *inquiries* is used in the reading, and then choose the most accurate definition of the word.
   Inquiries (paragraph 2)
   a. Ideas
   b. Answers
   c. Questions

Summarizing

Write a summary of "Family Matters: How Video Games Help Successful Aging."

Critical Thinking

- Video game play among youth tends to be viewed in a negative light by media and health professionals. What common negative stereotypes are associated with video games, and how does this article confirm or counteract those stereotypes?
- In paragraphs 5 and 6, the authors offer statistics on America's aging population and changing family dynamics. What is the purpose of these paragraphs? How do they support the article's main idea?
- What other shared activities could strengthen the connection between intergenerational family members?

Rawpixel.com, 2017 / Used under license from Shutterstock.com

In this article from *Scientific American*, Katherine W. Phillips explains why being around people who are different from us leads to greater creativity, focus, and productivity.

About the Author

Katherine W. Phillips is a Professor of Leadership and Ethics and senior vice dean at Columbia Business School.

How Diversity Makes Us Smarter

The first thing to acknowledge about diversity is that it can be difficult. In the U.S., where the dialogue of **inclusion** is relatively advanced, even the mention of the word "diversity" can lead to anxiety and conflict. Supreme Court justices disagree on the **virtues** of diversity and the means for achieving it. Corporations spend billions of dollars to attract and manage diversity both internally and externally, yet they still face discrimination lawsuits, and the leadership ranks of the business world remain predominantly white and male.

It is reasonable to ask what good diversity does us. Diversity of expertise **confers** benefits that are obvious—you would not think of building a new car without engineers, designers, and quality-control experts—but what about social diversity? What good comes from diversity of race, ethnicity, gender and sexual orientation? Research has shown that social diversity in a group can cause discomfort, rougher interactions, a lack of trust, greater perceived interpersonal conflict, lower communication, less cohesion, more concern about disrespect, and other problems. So what is the upside?

The fact is that if you want to build teams or organizations capable of innovating, you need diversity. Diversity enhances creativity. It encourages the search for **novel** information and perspectives, leading to better decision making

1

2

3

and problem solving. Diversity can improve the bottom line of companies and lead to **unfettered** discoveries and breakthrough innovations. Even simply being exposed to diversity can change the way you think. This is not just wishful thinking: it is the conclusion I draw from decades of research from organizational scientists, psychologists, economist, and demographers.

The key to understanding the positive influences of diversity is the concept   4
of informational diversity. When people are brought together to solve problems in groups, they bring different information, opinions and perspectives. This makes obvious sense when we talk about diversity of disciplinary backgrounds— think of the **interdisciplinary** team building a car (engineers, designers, and quality-control experts). The same logic applies to social diversity. People who are different from one another in race, gender, and other dimensions bring unique information and experiences to bear on the task at hand. A male and female engineer might have different perspectives—and that is a good thing.

In 2006 Margaret Neale of Stanford University, Gregory Northcraft of   5
the University of Illinois at Urbana-Champaign, and I set out to examine the impact of racial diversity on small decision-making groups in an experiment where sharing information was a requirement for success. Our subjects were undergraduate students taking business courses at the University of Illinois. We put together three-person groups—some consisting of all white members, others with two whites and one nonwhite member—and had them perform a murder mystery exercise. We made sure that all group members shared a common set of information, but we also gave each member important clues that only they knew.

To find out who committed the murder, the group members would have   6
to share all the information they collectively possessed during discussion. The groups with the racial diversity significantly outperformed the groups with no racial diversity. Being with similar others leads us to think we all hold the same information and share the same perspective. This perspective, which stopped the all-white groups from effectively processing the information, is what hinders creativity and innovation.

Other researchers have found similar results. In 2004 Anthony Lising   7
Antonio, a professor at the Stanford Graduate College of Education, collaborated with five colleagues from the University of California, Los Angeles, and other institutions to examine the influence of racial and opinion composition in small

group discussions. More than 350 students from three universities participated in the study. Group members were asked to discuss a **prevailing** social issue (either child labor practices or the death penalty) for 15 minutes. The researchers wrote **dissenting** perspectives and had both black and white members deliver them to their groups.

When a black person presented a dissenting perspective to a group of whites, the perspective was perceived as more novel and led to broader thinking and consideration of alternatives than when a white person introduced that same dissenting perspective. The lesson: when we hear dissent from someone who is different from us, it provokes more thought than when it comes from someone who looks like us.   *8*

The effect is not limited to race. For example, last year professors of management Denise Lewin Loyd of the University of Illinois, Robert B. Lount, Jr., of Ohio State University, and I asked 186 people whether they identified as a Democrat or a Republican, then had them read a murder mystery and decide who they thought committed the crime. Next, we asked the subjects to prepare for a meeting with another group member by writing an essay communicating their perspective. More important, in all cases, we told the participants that their partner disagreed with their opinion but that they would need to come to an agreement with the other person. Everyone was told to prepare to convince their meeting partner to come around to their side; half of the subjects, however, were told to prepare to make their case to a member of the opposing political party, and half were told to make their case to a member of their own party.   *9*

The result: Democrats who were told that a fellow Democrat disagreed with them prepared less well for the discussion than Democrats who were told that a Republican disagreed with them. Republicans showed the same pattern. When disagreement comes from a socially different person, we are prompted to work harder. Diversity jolts us into **cognitive** action in ways that **homogeneity** simply does not.   *10*

For this reason, diversity appears to lead to higher-quality scientific research. This year Richard Freeman, an economics professor at Harvard University and director of the Science and Engineering Workforce Project at the National Bureau of Economic Research, along with Wei Huang, a Harvard economics Ph.D. candidate, examined the ethnic identity of the authors of 1.5 million scientific papers written between 1985 and 2008 using a **comprehensive** database of   *11* published research. They found that papers written by diverse groups receive more citations and have higher impact factors than papers written by people from the same ethnic group. Moreover, they found that stronger papers were associated with a greater number of author addresses; geographical diversity, and a larger number of references, is a reflection of more intellectual diversity.

Diversity is not only about bringing different perspectives to the table. 12 Simply adding social diversity to a group makes people believe that differences of perspective might exist among them and that belief makes people change their behavior.

inclusion
the act of including a variety of people, opinions, and lifestyles

confers
carries forward

novel
a new kind of something

unfettered
freeing

interdisciplinary
combining or including two or more fields of study or expertise

prevailing
current and well known

dissenting
a differing opinion

cognitive
involving the brain; intellect

comprehensive
all-encompassing

Reflecting

Answer the comprehension and vocabulary questions about the reading.

1. What is the main idea of this reading?
   a. Supreme Court justices disagree on the virtues of diversity and the means for achieving it.
   b. Despite increased attention and dollars spent recruiting diverse workers, American businesses still have a diversity problem.
   c. Greater diversity within teams and organizations boosts innovation, creativity, decision making, and problem solving.

2. What best describes the concept of informational diversity (see paragraph 4)?
   a. When people are brought together to solve problems in groups, they bring different information, opinions, and perspectives.
   b. When lots of sources of information are available, organizations get a fuller picture of the issue at hand.
   c. When a person considers a topic from a number of points of view, they can approach it with a clear-headed and objective point of view.

3. What is the conclusion of the author's study on the connection between a group's racial makeup and solving a murder mystery game?
   a. Racially diverse groups performed the same as groups with no racial diversity.

    b. Racially diverse groups outperformed the groups with no racial diversity.

    c. Racially diverse groups performed worse than the groups with no racial diversity.

4. What main pattern of organization does the article follow?

    a. Chronological

    b. Logical

    c. Comparison

5. What type of voice does the author use?

    a. Academic

    b. Personal

    c. Satiric

6. Study how the word *virtues* is used in the reading, and then choose the most accurate definition of the word.
Virtues (paragraph 1)

    a. Advantages

    b. Truth

    c. Reality

7. Study how the word *homogeneity* is used in the reading, and then choose the most accurate definition of the word.
Homogeneity (paragraph 10)

    a. Sameness

    b. Difference

    c. Intellect

Summarizing

Write a summary of "How Diversity Makes Us Smarter."

Critical Thinking

- Have you had experience working with a socially diverse group of people? Did your group experience connect with the author's conclusions about diversity? How so?
- The author opens the essay by acknowledging that diversity "can be difficult." Do you agree? What real-world examples support your answer?
- What types of obstacles may arise when working with socially diverse teammates? How could you avoid or overcome such obstacles?
- Is the author's writing voice appropriate for the topic and writing situation? Explain your answer.

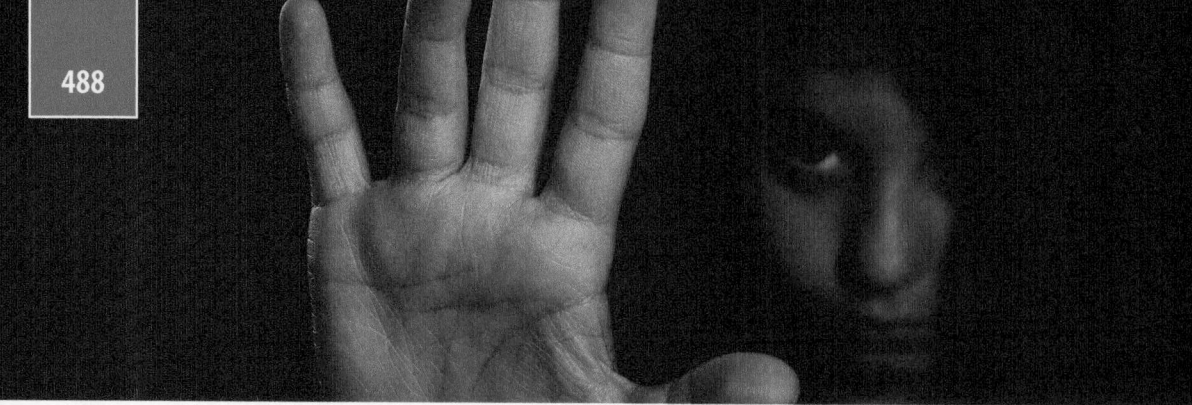

In this essay, which first appeared in *Newsweek*, journalist Jessica Bennett raises a number of difficult questions about bullying and how it should be addressed.

About the Author

Jessica Bennett is a writer at *The New York Times* and author of *Feminist Fight Club: A Survival Manual for a Sexist Workplace.* She writes about gender issues, pop culture, and social trends.

Phoebe Prince: Should School Bullying Be a Crime?

It started with rumors, a love triangle, and a dirty look in a high-school bathroom. Soon jokes about an "Irish slut" cropped up on Facebook, and a girl's face was scribbled out of a class photo hanging up at school. One day, in the cafeteria, another girl marched in, pointed at her, and shouted "stay away from other people's men." A week later, as the girl walked home, a car full of students crept close. One kid hurled a crumpled soda can out the window, followed closely by shrieks of "whore!"

If your children had behaved like this, how would you want them punished? Certainly a proper grounding would be in order; computer privileges revoked. Detention, yes—maybe even suspension. Or what about 10 years in jail? Now what if we told you that the girl had gone home after the soda-can incident and killed herself—discovered by her little sister, hanging in a stairwell. Now which punishment fits the crime?

This is the **conundrum** of Phoebe Prince, the 15-year-old South Hadley, Mass., girl the media have already determined was "bullied to death"—her alleged "mean girl" tormentors charged with felony crimes. Bullied to death is the crime of the moment, the blanket explanation slapped on suicide cases from Texas to

California, where two 13-year-olds recently killed themselves, bullied for being gay. The most twisted example yet came last week, when Tyler Clementi, an 18-year-old New Jersey college student, threw himself off the George Washington Bridge after his roommate and a friend allegedly streamed a Webcam video of his **tryst** with a man.

Cases like these are being invoked as potent symbols for why, in the digital age, schools need bullying policies and states need legislation. But do they? Is the notion of being bullied to death valid? No one would deny that Clementi's roommate did the unconscionable; the alleged crime is all the more disturbing because of the specter of antigay bias. Yet he couldn't have known how badly the stunt would end. (He and his friend now face up to five years in prison for privacy invasion; there is also talk of additional bias charges.) In the case of Prince, the answer of who's to blame might change if you knew that she had tried to kill herself before the **epithets**, was on medication for depression, and was struggling with her parents' separation. So where is the line now between behavior that's bad and behavior that's criminal? Does the definition of old-school bullying need to be rewritten for the new-media age?

In effect, it already has been. Forty-five states now have anti-bullying laws; in Massachusetts, which has one of the strictest, anti-bullying programs are mandated in schools, and criminal punishment is outlined in the text for even the youngest offenders. It's a good-will effort, to be sure—prevention programs have been shown to reduce school bullying by as much as 50 percent. With 1 in 5 students bullied each year—and an appalling 9 in 10 gay and lesbian students— that's good news: kids who are bullied are five times more likely to be depressed, and nearly 160,000 of them skip school each day, fearful of their peers. Bullies themselves don't fare well, either: one study, of middle-school boys, found that 60 percent of those deemed "bullies" would be convicted of at least one crime by the time they reached 24.

But forget, for the moment, the dozens of articles that have called bullying a "**pandemic.**" Forget the talk-show specials, the headlines, the Florida dad who rushed onto a school bus to scare his 13-year-old daughter's bullies straight. School bullying can be devastating, but social scientists say it is no more extreme, nor more prevalent, than it was a half century ago. (And it's even gotten better over the past decade, says Dan Olweus, a leading bullying expert.) Today's world of cyberbullying is different, yes—far-reaching, more visually potent, and harder

4

5

6

to wash away than comments scrawled on a bathroom wall. All of which can make it harder to combat. But it still happens a third less than traditional bullying. And those "mean girls" we keep hearing about? Turns out, boys are still twice as likely to bully as girls.

The reality may be that while the incidence of bullying has remained relatively the same, it's our reaction to it that's changed: the helicopter parents who want to protect their kids from every stick and stone, the cable-news commentators who whip them into a frenzy, the insta-**vigilantism** of the Internet. When it comes down to it, bullying is not just a social ill; it's a "**cottage industry**," says Suffolk Law School's David Yamada—complete with commentators and prevention experts and a new breed of legal scholars, all preparing to take on an enemy that's always been there. None of this is to say that bullying is not a serious problem (it is), or that tackling it is not important. But like a stereo with the volume turned too high, all the noise distorts the facts, making it nearly impossible to judge when a case is somehow criminal, or merely cruel.

In Phoebe Prince's case, it's hard to make sense of the punishment without first understanding the crime. Court records indicate that Phoebe's problems at South Hadley High School began around November of last year, when the freshman became involved with two senior boys—Austin Renaud and Sean Mulveyhill, the school's star football player—both of whom had girlfriends. According to their **indictments**, the boys, their girlfriends, and students Ashley Longe and Sharon Velasquez engaged in what the DA described as a "nearly three-month campaign" of verbal assault and physical threats against Phoebe. What appear to be the worst of their crimes involves repeated taunts of "whore" and "Irish slut"; threats to "beat Phoebe up"; and, on the day of her death, the soda-can incident, which left Phoebe in tears. When Phoebe got home that afternoon, she texted a friend: "I can't do it anymore." At 4:30 pm, her sister found her body, hanging from the scarf she'd given her for Christmas.

Phoebe's death, understandably, sent normally quiet South Hadley into a spiral of shame and blame. The school principal opened an internal investigation, but allowed the then-unidentified bullies to remain in class. A community member sympathetic to Phoebe's story went to *The Boston Globe*, which published a column chastising school officials for allowing the "untouchable mean girls"

7

8

9

to remain in school, "defiant, unscathed." A Facebook group with the headline "Expel the three girls who caused Phoebe Prince to commit suicide" suddenly had thousands of fans. School officials took to the press—defending how they could have let the bullying go on, asserting they had only learned of the problem the week before Phoebe's death. "I'm not naive [enough] to think we'll have zero bullying . . . but this was a complex tragedy," the principal of South Hadley High School, Dan Smith, tells *Newsweek*.

Enter District Attorney Elizabeth Scheibel, whose profile on the National District Attorneys Association webite, until recently, detailed how, as a child, she beat up a schoolyard bully who was picking on her brother. On March 29, Scheibel released the names of the six students she would indict on felony charges, whose "relentless activity," she said, was "designed to humiliate [Phoebe] and make it impossible for her to remain at school." Since there is no law in Massachusetts explicitly making bullying a crime, Scheibel charged two of them with stalking, two with criminal harassment, and five with civil-rights violations resulting in bodily injury, alleging that Phoebe's ability to get an education had been made impossible. She also charged both of the boys with **statutory rape**, for allegedly having sex with Phoebe while she was underage—an offense punishable by up to three years in jail. The civil-rights violation carries a maximum of 10 years. (All six defendants have pleaded not guilty.)

The law (and the media) may assess the world in black or white, but the players in the case don't fall into neat categories. Quiet and pretty, Phoebe had moved only recently from Ireland to South Hadley, a working-class town full of wood-paneled homes, manicured lawns and a vibrant Irish-American community where Phoebe's family fit right in. She would ultimately suffer a terrible tragedy, but court filings, uncovered by Emily Bazelon, of *Slate Magazine*, have since revealed that Phoebe had her own demons, too. She struggled with depression, self-mutilation, had been prescribed Seroquel (a medication used to treat bipolar disorder, among other psychiatric conditions), and had attempted suicide once before. Bazelon also reported that Phoebe—like nearly a third of kids who are victimized by bullies, studies show—had also played the role of bully, calling another girl a "paki whore" while she was still in Ireland, enrolled in a private school. By the same token, each of the students charged with bullying Phoebe were in good academic standing, says South Hadley's superintendent, Gus Sayer.

Does that in any way excuse their behavior? Not at all—and each has been out of school since March, suspended, indefinitely, until their case is resolved in court. (Their trials are expected early next year.) But it goes to show there's more to this story than the headlines might imply. "These are not the troubled kids we sometimes deal with," Sayer tells *Newsweek*. "These are nice kids, regular kids. They come from nice families. They were headed to college. And now, in addition to losing Phoebe, we're losing [them] too."

Phoebe's father, Jeremy Prince, has said he would ask the court for leniency   12
if the teens confess and apologize. Yet even if they are acquitted, it's clear their lives are forever altered—their names and faces now international symbols of teen **callousness**. None completed school last year; Mulveyhill has already lost a football scholarship to college. Angeles Chanon, the mother of Sharon Velasquez, says her daughter is studying for her GED, but heartbroken that she can't return to class—and since there aren't any other public high schools in South Hadley (and schools in Massachusetts can deny entrance based on a felony charge) her options are slim. In the meantime, Sharon is haunted by the tragedy of Phoebe's death. It's hard for her to turn on the television without seeing Phoebe's smiling face (or her own) staring back at her; reporters camp out in the parking lot outside her mother's housing complex, peering into windows at all hours. Sharon sits at home most days, reading, listening to music—but scared to leave the house alone. Her family has received death threats, prank calls, and a rock thrown through a second-story window—along with a stream of nasty unsigned letters delivered to their door. Some call for Sharon to be "raped and killed"; others hurl insults and racial slurs. "I don't know if I can even describe what my family has been through," says Sharon's mother, who agreed to speak exclusively to *Newsweek*, in the presence of her lawyer. "The cameras in our faces, the harassment, the letters—I'd come home and people would be in the parking lot waiting for me."

The irony, of course, is that it all sounds a bit like the kind of torment Phoebe   13
allegedly endured—particularly when it comes to the anonymous vigilantes who've taken to the Web to **chastise** the teens, publishing their phone numbers and addresses to the public, along with violent rape imagery and calls for their deaths. "It's painful to watch what [these kids] have had to go through," says Colin Keefe, the attorney for Velasquez. Indeed, if these students are bullies, according to the law, what does that make the rest of us? Massachusetts's anti-bullying

statute defines bullying as repeated behavior that, among other things, "causes emotional harm" or "creates a hostile environment" at school. If it were applied to the real world, wouldn't most of us be bullies? It's easy to see how the blossoming field of bullying law could ultimately criminalize the kind of behavior we engage in every day—not just in schoolyards, but in workplaces, in politics, at home. And what do you do when the bullies get bullied? "You're not going to prevent a lot of this stuff," says former New York prosecutor Sam Goldberg, a Boston criminal attorney. "It may seem harsh, but to some degree, you're going to have to tell your kid, 'Sometimes people say mean things.'"

What most bullying experts and legal scholars agree on is that prosecution— 14 in the Prince case, anyway—may be the worst possible scenario. There is longstanding research to show that law is not a deterrent to kids who respond emotionally to their surroundings; ultimately, labeling a group of raucous teens as "criminals" will only make it harder for them to engage with society when they return. Certainly, there is behavior that should be treated as a crime— the story of Clementi, the young Rutgers student who jumped off the bridge, is particularly hard to stomach. But many kids "just mess up," says Sameer Hinduja, a criminologist at Florida Atlantic University, and the codirector of the Cyberbullying Research Center. "They react emotionally, and most of them express a lot of remorse. I think most kids deserve another chance."

conundrum
a difficult, puzzling question

tryst
a private, romantic meeting of lovers

epithets
adjectives describing an innate quality, often a negative one

pandemic
a wide-spread disease

vigilantism
when individuals take the law into their own hands, typically for vengeance

cottage industry
a business based in the home

indictments
formal criminal charges

statutory rape
for an adult to have sexual intercourse with a minor

callousness
lack of sensitivity

Reflecting

Answer the comprehension and vocabulary questions about the reading.

1. What is the main idea of the reading?
   a. All bullies whose actions lead someone else to commit bodily harm or live with extreme mental anguish should face prosecution for their crimes.

b. As the country moves toward harsher penalties for bullying, the proper punishment for bullies is more unclear than ever, for every situation is unique and prosecution brings its own unintended consequences.

c. Tougher penalties for bullying lowers rates of school bullying, protects victims, and improves school culture.

2. Is this idea directly stated or implied?
   a. Directly stated
   b. Implied

3. What main pattern of organization does the writer follow?
   a. Chronological
   b. Classification
   c. Logical

4. What is the main idea of paragraph 7?
   a. The frenzy of anti-bullying efforts is leading to a rush to judgement rather than a careful exploration of each case.
   b. Helicopter parents are partially to blame for the increased severity of punishment for bullying.
   c. Anti-bullying efforts exaggerate the problem of bullying, and we should accept bullying as a normal part of adolescence.

5. Study how the word *chastise* is used in the reading, and then choose the most accurate definition of the word.
   Chastise (paragraph 13)
   a. Poke fun of
   b. Cheer
   c. Criticize harshly

Summarizing

Write a summary of "Phoebe Prince: Should School Bullying Be a Crime?"

Critical Thinking

- Why was Phoebe's case a "complex tragedy"? Give two reasons.
- In paragraph 12 you learn about Sharon Velasquez. What is significant about her experience?
- What is the main idea of paragraph 14? Do you agree with the conclusion? Explain.
- Who and/or what is to blame for school bullying?
- In your opinion, what should or should not be done to prevent bullying in school?

In this essay, journalist Kris Frieswick reveals surprising links between an entrepreneurial director of a rehabilitation program and the ex-convicts being rehabilitated.

About the Author

An award-winning journalist, **Kris Frieswick** is senior editor at *Inc.* She has also been published in *The Wall Street Journal*, the *Economist*, *The Boston Globe Magazine*, *Departures*, and *Hemispheres*.

Ex-Cons Relaunching Lives as Entrepreneurs

Catherine Rohr stands at the front of a drab, fluorescent-lit classroom in Midtown Manhattan. Her 27 students, who sit crammed into chair-desks, are ex-cons whose crimes include narcotics trafficking and murder. Rohr, 35, is dressed conservatively in long black pants, a button-down white shirt, fitted jacket, and high heels. Beneath her razor-straight bangs, Rohr's kohl-rimmed eyes zero in on a man in the back of the room, leaning against the wall.

"Are you sleeping back there?" she barks.

"No," says the man. "I'm just not feeling that well."

"From now on, no one in the back row can rest their heads against the wall," she orders. "It looks like you're not paying attention."

These men are the inaugural class of Defy Ventures, a yearlong, M.B.A.-style program that Rohr created to teach former inmates how to start their own companies. For months, they have been meeting here for 14 to 16 hours a week to learn about things such as cash flow, balance sheets, intellectual property, accounting, and taxes. There are workshops on how to behave in professional settings, how to speak in public, and how to be a better parent. These men are also learning how to create business plans. In June, they will compete in a business-plan competition. The winners will split $100,000 in **seed funding**.

Rohr has an interesting theory about criminals. She says that many of the   6
qualities that made these men good at being bad guys (until they got caught,
of course) are the same qualities that make effective entrepreneurs. Some of
the men in this class had up to 40 employees under management. Though
their merchandise was illegal narcotics and not, say, office supplies, these men
developed certain business skills—the ability to motivate a team, identify new
markets, manage risk, and inspire loyalty and hard work. Rohr's goal is to help
these students apply their abilities to legal endeavors.

Rohr continues today's lesson, evaluating the company names proposed by   7
each student. "What's the name of your business?" she asks, pointing to one of the
students.

"Mine's is . . . "   8

"What did you say?" Rohr pounces. She's a stickler for proper speech. He   9
stops and takes a deep breath.

"Mine is . . . " he carefully **enunciates**. Rohr smiles slightly as the man   10
continues.

In this room of former criminals, Rohr may be the most intimidating figure.   11
She runs the show. It's not just because these men respect her, though they clearly
do, but because part of the deal of being in this room is doing what Rohr tells
them to do. In exchange, they get a once-in-a-lifetime opportunity. And for that,
they are willing to sit up straight, put their personal lives on hold, and study hard.

This program is the type of second chance that none of these men ever   12
thought they would get. It's also a second chance for Rohr, who not very long ago
had her own—very public—fall from grace.

At age 25, Rohr found God. She and her husband, Steve, a lawyer, began   13
attending a church in the Bay Area. She worked as an associate at Summit
Partners, a venture capital firm in Palo Alto. At church, Rohr was introduced
to the concept of tithing, giving away 10 percent of her income to the church or
charity. Donating felt really good. So good that she resolved to make $1 million a
year by age 30, just so she could give away 95 percent of it.

A couple of years later, after landing a job in New York City at American   14
Securities Capital Partners, a private equity firm, Rohr took a trip to several
prisons in Texas as part of a Christian outreach program. It was there that Rohr
first made the connection between criminals and entrepreneurs. These men

exhibited many of the same qualities she looked for when she met with founders as an investor.

In 2004, Rohr launched the Prison Entrepreneurship Program, or PEP, in Houston to teach inmates basic business skills. After several months of running the program remotely, Rohr left her job and moved to Texas to focus all her efforts on PEP. She and her husband spent nearly every penny they had, including her entire **401(k)**, on the program. She and volunteer executives taught classes about marketing, finance, and how to act professionally. And it was all topped with a thick frosting of religion—both because it fueled Rohr's passion and because religion is an unspoken requirement for any prison rehabilitation program in Texas.   15

Rohr believed God had called her to this ministry. And what she was able to accomplish in a short time struck many as miraculous. In five years, about 500 students graduated from the program. About 60 of them started businesses when they left prison. More important, the **recidivism** rate of graduates—at the time, around 10 percent—was much lower than the US average of 40 percent. Rohr and her program received several honors for public service, including awards from Texas Governor Rick Perry and President George W. Bush.   16

But everything came crashing down in 2009, when Rohr admitted to her staff of volunteers that she had had inappropriate relationships with four graduates of her prison program. "I felt like I'd been punched in the gut," says Bert Smith, one of those volunteers. After someone sent an anonymous letter to the Texas Department of Criminal Justice, which has strict policies against volunteers becoming personally involved with inmates, the department launched an investigation. Rohr says that none of the relationships started until after the prisoners were out of jail. But the department barred her from ever entering the Texas prison system again, citing security concerns. It also threatened to kick PEP out of the prison system if Rohr was involved in the program in any way. Devastated, she resigned.   17

The troubles, says Rohr, started a year earlier, when her husband asked for a divorce after nine years of marriage. In retrospect, the divorce wasn't so unexpected, she says. As the program grew, Rohr traveled frequently, visiting prisons and raising money for the program. She slept four hours a night and was rarely home. "I didn't have good boundaries in terms of working a certain   18 number of hours and then I'll be home and be a wife," says Rohr. "I wasn't living sustainably."

After the divorce, she felt ashamed. "Instead of reaching out for help, I chose   19
to be on my own," Rohr says. "And in that aloneness, I didn't make the best decisions." Rohr won't discuss specifics but claims that not all four relationships were "what people thought."

The media, which had frequently celebrated Rohr's efforts to **reform** prisoners,   20
pounced on the story of her downfall. The scandal became news as far away as China. "Prisons Ban Founder for 'Improper Relationships,'" read the headline in the *Austin American-Statesman*. That particular story attracted more than 60 online comments, most of them negative. "Let me guess, the greater the crime committed by the ex-convict, the dirtier the sex?" wrote one commenter. Others claimed to have knowledge of more than four affairs. "I was just bawling my eyes out," says Rohr. "They wrote untrue things—all sorts of uninformed comments. I didn't want to live anymore. I thought that I would live my whole life covered in shame."

Before the scandal, Rohr often spoke at churches and conferences about the   21
prison program. She would always ask the crowd, "What would it be like if you were known for the worst thing that you ever did in your life?" Now, she was in that very situation.

At the lowest point of her life, something unexpected happened that helped   22
Rohr pick herself back up. "I got over a thousand emails from people of love and support," she says, still looking surprised by it nearly three years later. "They were saying, 'What are you doing next?' and 'Thank you for your honesty.' Some came back with confessions of their own."

It was far too soon, the pain still too fresh, for her to realize what these   23
messages were telling her about the way this failure would transform her life. But those notes of encouragement gave her the strength to reach out to friends for support. With their help, she put the contents of her apartment in storage and got out of Texas. She traveled for six months, staying with friends. "I went through a period of questioning my calling, or that I could be worth anything or do anything good for the world ever again," she says. "But at the same time, I had this sense that I was born to lead. I needed to get my crap together so I could be an effective leader."

Rohr decided she had had enough sitting around. She dyed her auburn hair   24
back to its naturally darker shade and moved back to New York City, hoping that the city's energy would help jolt her back to life. She entertained a job offer from

a VC firm before finally giving in to what her heart was telling her to create: a new nonprofit. She would create a version of PEP that operated outside the prison system. (PEP is still going strong in Texas. "We came very close to having the doors locked," says Bert Smith, who is now CEO of the program. "There were a number of people who were convinced that without Catherine Rohr, PEP would fail. I'm happy to say that it didn't.")

Defy Ventures has raised more than $1.5 million in donations and pledges   25
from VC firms, hedge funds, businesses, and private foundations. Last fall, Rohr began accepting applications for the first class. After requesting referrals from the New York parole and probation departments and about 25 prisoner rehabilitation programs, Defy received more than 180 applications from former inmates interested in the free classes. Rohr looked for candidates who had high school diplomas or GEDs, who owned up to their crimes, and who were motivated to change their lives.

Today, when Rohr stands before a classroom of ex-cons and future   26
entrepreneurs, everyone understands that the group shares a common story of failure—separated by degrees, of course. A few weeks after the program began, she told them all about what happened in Texas. "I was very hesitant to step foot in the classroom again," says Rohr. "I was concerned about how would these guys look at me. But I've never felt that. They are so respectful. I think that I'm able to be a better leader now that, in a way, we have a shared experience. I know what it feels like to let people down."

Here in the classroom, student Marlon Llin, who served 10 years for   27
conspiracy to sell narcotics, stands at the blackboard. Llin, 37, is trying to figure out how much he should charge for the various services he provides through his new company, Mylo's Repairs. Kene Turner, an instructor from the Network for Teaching Entrepreneurship and one of Defy's course leaders, is teaching the men about pricing. Turner asks Llin what he charges to remodel a bathroom. Llin says $150 to $200, and the customer pays for the materials. As the class watches, Turner shows Llin all the things he will have to pay for out of that fee, including insurance, gas for his truck, office supplies, and taxes. As it turns out, Llin isn't making nearly as much as he thought he was. "You're undercharging," says Turner.

Llin—and every other man in the room—has a visible "aha" moment. "I   28
never thought about it that way before," says Llin. "I get it," adds another man in the back. They had been used to thinking like men living paycheck to paycheck,

worried only about how much they needed to make per hour to survive and feed their families. Now they are seeing what it means to think like entrepreneurs.

At its core, the true purpose of Defy is to change the way these men think about themselves and their lives, says Rohr. One of her techniques is something she calls the Ten Bear Hugs. Every class starts with group hugs. It's a strange sight, watching these men, many of whom have done decades of hard time, warmly embrace one another and everyone else in the room. "Initially, we didn't like it," says Jeff Ewell, who was incarcerated for a little less than a year for conspiracy to sell firearms. He is creating an online music exchange that would let artists buy instrumental tracks directly from producers. "But now we have to get told, 'Sit down, stop hugging each other; we've got to get stuff done.'" Rohr's goal is to break down the walls these men have had up around themselves for much of their lives. 29

Fabian Ruiz spent more than half his life with corrections officers who, he says, "don't even look at inmates as people." At 16, Ruiz killed the man who shot his older brother. While awaiting trial on Rikers Island in New York City, he attempted to escape and was recaptured. He was tried as an adult and sentenced to 20 years to life. He spent the next 21 years in a series of maximum-security prisons in New York State. He was released about a year ago at the age of 37. 30

Ruiz learned about Defy from a friend. His brown eyes dance when he talks about his start-up, Infor-Nation. It will sell printouts of Web pages to inmates of New York's prison system, who are blocked from using the Internet. Ruiz thinks his business has huge market potential. He really wants to win the business-plan competition—all the students do. The winners not only get the prize money, but they will also get to participate in Defy's six-month incubator program, helped by a team of entrepreneurs-in-residence and volunteer accountants, lawyers, and other mentors. 31

But the benefits of this program go well beyond prize money, says Ewell. Defy has helped him open up to other people, he says. "I've always been the type of person to attack everything alone," says Ewell. "The one thing we never learned to do was trust in another individual." But he developed a powerful bond with his fellow classmates. "We kind of became a brotherhood," he says. 32

To succeed, these men must learn to reject failure, which isn't always easy. Failure can have its own comforts, says Rohr. "When Jesus would go up to a leper 33 or a blind person and ask, 'Do you want to be healed?' it always seemed to me such an idiotic question," she says. "Of course you want to be healed. But a leper was taken care of. If you're not a leper anymore, you have to provide for yourself. You have all these different expectations if you're no longer the blind man. That's how it is with our guys, too. And not all of them want to see."

In fact, almost half the class has quit—Rohr started with 50 students. Some   34
left because they got jobs they couldn't pass up. Others just couldn't hack the workload. Those who have stayed hope that maybe they won't be known for the worst thing they ever did. Maybe they will be known for building something great. The same goes for Rohr, who hopes to eventually expand Defy Ventures to other cities around the country. "I've spent my whole life talking about grace and second chances," she says, "and I have now been the recipient of it."

kohl
a black powder used for eye makeup, especially popular in Eastern countries

M.B.A.
Masters of Business Administration

seed funding
an early investment in a new company

401(k)
a type of employee savings plan for retirement

recidivism
a pattern of repeat criminal behavior

VC firm
a business that invests "venture capital" (VC) money into a business with a potential for long-term growth

hedge funds
high-risk, high-returns partnerships of investors

Reflecting

Answer the comprehension and vocabulary questions about the reading.

1. Besides entrepreneurship, what broad theme (big idea) does this reading focus on?
a. Guilt
b. Redemption
c. Failure

2. What is the primary purpose of this essay?
a. To inform
b. To persuade
c. To entertain

3. What is the purpose of the "Ten Bear Hugs" described in paragraph 29?
   a. To break down the hardened attitude of the participants in the program
   b. To brainstorm unique names for the entrepreneurs' businesses
   c. As a joke to see who can squeeze each other the hardest

4. How does the revelation of Rohr's "fall from grace" relate to the situation of the ex-cons she teaches?
   a. It reveals that people from all walks of life have imperfections.
   b. It sets an example of someone overcoming adversity.
   c. Both *a* and *b*.

5. Study how the word *enunciates* is used in the reading, and then choose the most accurate definition of the word.
   Enunciates (paragraph 10)
   a. Speak clearly
   b. Speak loudly
   c. Speak quickly

6. Study how the word *reform* is used in the reading, and then choose the most accurate definition of the word.
   Reform (paragraph 20)
   a. Make money
   b. Declare innocence
   c. Change positively

Summarizing

Write a summary of "Ex-Cons Relaunching Lives as Entrepreneurs."

Critical Thinking

- React to this comment by Rohr: "The qualities that made these men good at being bad guys are the same qualities that make effective entrepreneurs." What types of qualities is she talking about? Is she correct?

- How could this essay be characterized as a story within a story? Think about what two stories are going on at the same time in the essay.

- Consider the names of the two programs Rohr started: PEP (Prisoner Entrepreneurship Program) and Defy Ventures. Why do you think she chose those names? What expectations do the names create for the participants? For potential investors? For Rohr and her staff?

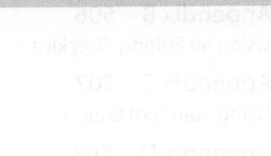

Part 9:

Appendices and Index

Appendix A

A Guide to Strong Writing

Figure A.1 serves as a guide to strong writing. Your writing will be clear and effective when it can check off each point. This checklist is especially helpful during revising, when you are deciding how to improve your writing.

Figure A.1 A Guide to Strong Writing

Ideas

☐ Does an interesting and relevant topic serve as a starting point for the writing?

☐ Is the writing focused, addressing a specific feeling about or a specific part of the topic? (Check the thesis statement.)

☐ Are there enough specific ideas, details, and examples to support the thesis?

☐ Overall, is the writing interesting and informative?

Organization

☐ Does the writing form a meaningful whole—with opening, middle, and closing parts?

☐ Does the writing follow a logical pattern of organization?

☐ Do transitions connect ideas and help the writing flow?

Voice

☐ Does the writer sound informed about and interested in the topic?

☐ Does the writer sound sincere and genuine?

Word Choice

☐ Does the word choice clearly fit the purpose and the audience?

☐ Does the writing include specific nouns and verbs?

Sentence Fluency

☐ Are the sentences clear, and do they flow smoothly?

☐ Are the sentences varied in their beginnings and length?

Conventions

☐ Does your writing follow the rules of the language?

Appendix B

Using an Editing Checklist

Figure B.1 serves as a guide to editing writing. This checklist is helpful for checking your writing for style, grammar, punctuation, and spelling errors.

Figure B.1 Editing Checklist

Words

☐ Have I used specific nouns and verbs?

☐ Have I used more action verbs than "be" verbs (*is, are, was, were*)?

Sentences

☐ Have I avoided improper shifts in sentences?

☐ Have I avoided fragments, run-ons, and rambling sentences?

Conventions

☐ Do I use correct verb forms (*he saw*, not *he seen*)?

☐ Do my subjects and verbs agree (*she speaks*, not *she speak*)?

☐ Have I used the right words (*their, there, they're*)?

☐ Have I capitalized first words and proper nouns and adjectives?

☐ Have I used commas after long introductory word groups and to separate items in a series?

☐ Have I used commas correctly in compound sentences?

☐ Have I used apostrophes correctly in contractions and to show possession?

Appendix C

Using Standard English

Standard English (SE) is English that is considered appropriate for school, business, and government. You have been learning SE throughout your years in school. Table C.1 shows the basic differences between non-Standard English (NS) and SE.

Table C.1 Using Standard English

Differences in . . .	NS	SE
1. Expressing plurals after numbers	10 mile	10 miles
2. Expressing habitual action	He always be early.	He always is early.
3. Expressing ownership	My friend car . . .	My friend's car . . .
4. Expressing the third-person singular verb	The customer ask . . .	The customer asks . . .
5. Expressing negatives	She doesn't never . . .	She doesn't ever . . .
6. Using reflexive pronouns	He sees hisself . . .	He sees himself . . .
7. Using demonstrative adjectives	Them reports are . . .	Those reports are . . .
8. Using forms of *do*	He done it.	He did it.
9. Avoiding double subjects	My manager he . . .	My manager . . .
10. Using *a* or *an*	I need new laptop. She had angry caller.	I need a new laptop. She had an angry caller.
11. Using the past tense of verbs	Carl finish his . . .	Carl finished his . . .
12. Using *isn't* or *aren't* versus *ain't*	The company ain't . . .	The company isn't . . .

Appendix D

Qualities of Voice

The following glossaries define terms that contribute to an author's writing voice.

Diction Glossary

Diction is an author's choice of words based on their correctness, clearness, or effectiveness.

- **Colloquialisms** are expressions usually accepted in informal or casual texts or speaking situations, but not in a formal situations.

  > "*Anyway*, the baby calf was standing underneath its mother, *just kind of* walking around, and the mother cow *took a 'dump'* on the baby calf's head."
  >
  > —Stephen Chbosky, *The Perks of Being a Wallflower*

- **Jargon** (technical diction) is a specialized language used by a specific group.

  > **Computer jargon:** *hypertext* (meaning "a system of web-like links among pages on the Internet or within a program")
  >
  > **Medical jargon:** *agonal* (meaning "a major, negative change in a patient's condition")
  >
  > **Political jargon:** *left wing* (meaning a "liberal, progressive approach")

- **Idioms** are words used in special ways that may be different from their literal meanings.

  > *brain drain* (meaning "the best graduates moving elsewhere")
  > *save face* (meaning "fix an embarrassing situation")

- **Slang** is the nonstandard language used by a particular group of people among themselves; it is also language used in fiction and special writing situations to lend color and feeling. Slang may have a brief lifespan and should be avoided in most academic writing.

  > *emo* (meaning "to be depressed, moody, and emotional ")
  > *iceman* (meaning "someone with nerves of steel")

- **Trite** language lacks depth or original, fresh thinking.

  > After the close call, the manager *leaped* from the dugout and *roared like a lion*.
  > Larisa is a *deep thinker*.

- **Vulgarity** is abusive, vulgar, or disrespectful language and should be avoided in acaemic writing.

  > *bastard* (used as a crude insult)
  > *prick* (an insulting reference for a person considered unpleasant)

Figures of Speech Glossary

Figures of speech are words or comparisons used in a non-literal sense to create meaning. These literary devices may contribute to a personal or satiric voice.

- **Metaphor** is a comparison of two unlike things in which no word of comparison (*as* or *like*) is used.

  "When you write, you lay out a line of words. The line of words is a miner's pick, a woodcarver's gouge, a surgeon's probe."   —Annie Dillard, *The Writing Life*

- **Simile** is a comparison of two unlike things in which a word of comparison (*as* or *like*) is used.

  "She stood in front of the altar, shaking like a freshly caught trout."
  —Maya Angelou, *I Know Why the Caged Bird Sings*

- **Personification** is when an animal, object, or idea takes on a human characteristic.

  "And what I remember next is how the moon, the pale moon with its one yellow eye . . . stared through the pink plastic curtains."   —Sandra Cisneros

- **Hyperbole** is an extreme exaggeration or overstatement.

  "I have seen this river so wide it had only one bank."   —Mark Twain

- **Understatement** is stating an idea with restraint, often for humorous effect.

  "He [our new dog] turned out to be a good traveler, and except for an interruption caused by my wife's falling out of the car, the journey went very well."   —E. B. White, *A Report in Spring*

Types of Irony

Irony is a twist or surprise in the story line, explanation, or set of circumstances that is designed to make a point. Irony may contribute to the creation of a satiric voice.

- **Verbal irony** occurs when a writer says one thing but really means another.

  A chef critical of a greengrocer's produce might say, "The carrots were so fresh they bent easily to my touch."

- **Dramatic irony** occurs when the reader or viewer observes or knows a critical piece of information that the subject of a text (a character, or person) can't see him- or herself. In *Lincoln*, viewers know that the president will be shot soon after he settles in at Ford's Theatre. He, obviously, has no idea that this is about to happen.

- **Irony of situation** occurs when there is a great difference between the purpose of an action and the result. In *Romeo and Juliet*, Juliet takes a drug to fake her death, while Romeo poisons himself because he thinks Juliet is dead. Juliet awakes and discovers her lover is dead, so she kills herself.

Appendix E
Understanding Word Parts

The information that follows shows common prefixes, suffixes, and roots. Many of our words are made up of combinations of these word parts.

Prefixes

Prefixes are word parts that come *before* the root words (*pre* = before). Depending upon its meaning, a prefix changes the intent, or sense, of the base word. As a skilled reader, you will want to know the meanings of the most common prefixes, including numerical prefixes (see Table E.1), and then watch for them when you read.

a, an [not, without] amoral (without a sense of moral responsibility), atypical, atom (not cuttable), apathy (without feeling), anesthesia (without sensation)

ab, abs, a [from, away] abnormal, abduct, absent, avert (turn away)

acro [high] acropolis (high city), acrobat, acronym, acrophobia (fear of height)

ambi, amb [both, around] ambidextrous (skilled with both hands), ambiguous, amble

amphi [both] amphibious (living on both land and water), amphitheater

ante [before] antedate, anteroom, antebellum, antecedent (happening before)

anti, ant [against] anticommunist, antidote, anticlimax, antacid

be [on, away] bedeck, belabor, bequest, bestow, beloved

bene, bon [well] benefit, benefactor, benevolent, benediction, bonanza, bonus

bi, bis, bin [both, double, twice] bicycle, biweekly, bilateral, biscuit, binoculars

by [side, close, near] bypass, bystander, by-product, bylaw, byline

cata [down, against] catalog, catapult, catastrophe, cataclysm

cerebro [brain] cerebral, cerebrum, cerebellum

circum, circ [around] circumference, circumnavigate, circumspect, circular

co, con, col, com [together, with] copilot, conspire, collect, compose

coni [dust] coniosis (disease that comes from inhaling dust)

contra, counter [against] controversy, contradict, counterpart

de [from, down] demote, depress, degrade, deject, deprive

deca [ten] decade, decathlon, decapod (10 feet)

di [two, twice] divide, dilemma, dilute, dioxide, dipole, ditto

dia [through, between] diameter, diagonal, diagram, dialogue (speech between people)

dis, dif [apart, away, reverse] dismiss, distort, distinguish, diffuse

dys [badly, ill] dyspepsia (digesting badly), dystrophy, dysentery

em, en [in, into] embrace, enslave

epi [upon] epidermis (upon the skin, outer layer of skin), epitaph, epithet

eu [well] eulogize (speak well of, praise), euphony, euphemism, euphoria

ex, e, ec, ef [out] expel (drive out), ex-mayor, exorcism, eject, eccentric (out of the center position), efflux, effluent

extra, extro [beyond, outside] extraordinary (beyond the ordinary), extrovert, extracurricular

for [away or off] forswear (to renounce an oath)

fore [before in time] forecast, foretell (to tell beforehand), foreshadow

hemi, demi, semi [half] hemisphere, demitasse, semicircle (half of a circle)

hex [six] hexameter, hexagon

homo [man] Homo sapiens, homicide (killing man)

hyper [over, above] hypersensitive (overly sensitive), hyperactive

hypo [under] hypodermic (under the skin), hypothesis

il, ir, in, im [not] illegal, irregular, incorrect, immoral

in, il, im [into] inject, inside, illuminate, illustrate, impose, implant, imprison

infra [beneath] infrared, infrasonic

inter [between] intercollegiate, interfere, intervene, interrupt (break between)

intra [within] intramural, intravenous (within the veins)

intro [into, inward] introduce, introvert (turn inward)

macro [large, excessive] macrodent (having large teeth), macrocosm

mal [badly, poorly] maladjusted, malady, malnutrition, malfunction

meta [beyond, after, with] metaphor, metamorphosis, metaphysical

mis [incorrect, bad] misuse, misprint

miso [hate] misanthrope, misogynist

mono [one] monoplane, monotone, monochrome, monocle

multi [many] multiply, multiform

neo [new] neopaganism, neoclassic, neophyte, neonatal

non [not] nontaxable (not taxed), nontoxic, nonexistent, nonsense

ob, of, op, oc [toward, against] obstruct, offend, oppose, occur

oct [eight] octagon, octameter, octave, octopus

paleo [ancient] paleoanthropology (pertaining to ancient humans), paleontology (study of ancient life-forms)

para [beside, almost] parasite (one who eats beside or at the table of another), paraphrase, paramedic, parallel, paradox

penta [five] pentagon (figure or building having five angles or sides), pentameter, pentathlon

per [throughout, completely] pervert (completely turn wrong, corrupt), perfect, perceive, permanent, persuade

peri [around] perimeter (measurement around an area), periphery, periscope, pericardium, period

poly [many] polygon (figure having many angles or sides), polygamy, polyglot, polychrome

post [after] postpone, postwar, postscript, posterity

pre [before] prewar, preview, precede, prevent, premonition

pro [forward, in favor of] project (throw forward), progress, promote, prohibition

pseudo [false] pseudonym (false or assumed name), pseudopodia

quad [four] quadruple (four times as much), quadriplegic, quadratic, quadrant

quint [five] quintuplet, quintuple, quintet, quintile

re [back, again] reclaim, revive, revoke, rejuvenate, retard, reject, return

retro [backward] retrospective (looking backward), retroactive, retrorocket

se [aside] seduce (lead aside), secede, secrete, segregate

self [by oneself] self-determination, self-employed, self-service, selfish

sesqui [one and a half] sesquicentennial (one and one-half centuries)

sex, sest [six] sexagenarian (sixty years old), sexennial, sextant, sextuplet, sestet

sub [under] submerge (put under), submarine, substitute, subsoil

suf, sug, sup, sus [from under] sufficient, suffer, suggest, support, suspend

super, supr [above, over, more] supervise, superman, supernatural, supreme

syn, sym, sys, syl [with, together] system, synthesis, synchronize (time together), synonym, sympathy, symphony, syllable

trans, tra [across, beyond] transoceanic, transmit (send across), transfusion, tradition

tri [three] tricycle, triangle, tripod, tristate

ultra [beyond, exceedingly] ultramodern, ultraviolet, ultraconservative

un [not, release] unfair, unnatural, unknown

under [beneath] underground, underlying

uni [one] unicycle, uniform, unify, universe, unique (one of a kind)

vice [in place of] vice president, viceroy, vice admiral

Table E.1 Numerical Prefixes

Numerical Prefixes

Prefix	Symbol	Multiples and Submultiples	Equivalent	Prefix	Symbol	Multiples and Submultiples	Equivalent
tera	T	10^{12}	trillionfold	centi	c	10^{-2}	hundredth part
giga	G	10^{9}	billionfold	milli	m	10^{-3}	thousandth part
mega	M	10^{6}	millionfold	micro	u	10^{-6}	millionth part
kilo	k	10^{3}	thousandfold	nano	n	10^{-9}	billionth part
hecto	h	10^{2}	hundredfold	pico	p	10^{-12}	trillionth part
deka	da	10	tenfold	femto	f	10^{-15}	quadrillionth part
deci	d	10^{-1}	tenth part	atto	a	10^{-18}	quintillionth part

Suffixes

Suffixes come at the end of a word. Very often a suffix will tell you what kind of word it is part of (noun, adverb, adjective). For example, words ending in -*ly* are usually adverbs.

able, ible [able, can do] capable, agreeable, edible, visible (can be seen)

ade [result of action] blockade (the result of a blocking action), lemonade

age [act of, state of, collection of] salvage (act of saving), storage, forage

al [relating to] sensual, gradual, manual, natural (relating to nature)

algia [pain] neuralgia (nerve pain)

an, ian [native of, relating to] African, Canadian, Floridian

ance, ancy [action, process, state] assistance, allowance, defiance, truancy

ant [performing, agent] assistant, servant

ary, ery, ory [relating to, quality, place where] dictionary, bravery, dormitory

ate [cause, make] liquidate, segregate (cause a group to be set aside)

cian [having a certain skill or art] musician, beautician, magician, physician

cule, ling [very small] molecule, ridicule, duckling (very small duck), sapling

cy [action, function] hesitancy, prophecy, normalcy (function in a normal way)

dom [quality, realm, office] freedom, kingdom, wisdom (quality of being wise)

ee [one who receives the action] employee, nominee (one who is nominated), refugee

en [made of, make] silken, frozen, oaken (made of oak), wooden, lighten

ence, ency [action, state of, quality] difference, conference, urgency

er, or [one who, that which] baker, miller, teacher, racer, amplifier, doctor

escent [in the process of] adolescent (in the process of becoming an adult), obsolescent, convalescent

ese [a native of, the language of] Japanese, Vietnamese, Portuguese

esis, osis [action, process, condition] genesis, hypnosis, neurosis, osmosis

ess [female] actress, goddess, lioness

et, ette [a small one, group] midget, octet, baronet, majorette

fic [making, causing] scientific, specific

ful [full of] frightful, careful, helpful

fy [make] fortify (make strong), simplify, amplify

hood [order, condition, quality] manhood, womanhood, brotherhood

ic [nature of, like] metallic (of the nature of metal), heroic, poetic, acidic

ice [condition, state, quality] justice, malice

id, ide [a thing connected with or belonging to] fluid, fluoride

ile [relating to, suited for, capable of] missile, juvenile, senile (related to being old)

ine [nature of] feminine, genuine, medicine

ion, sion, tion [act of, state of, result of] contagion, aversion, infection (state of being infected)

ish [origin, nature, resembling] foolish, Irish, clownish (resembling a clown)

ism [system, manner, condition, characteristic] heroism, alcoholism, Communism

ist [one who, that which] artist, dentist

ite [nature of, quality of, mineral product] Israelite, dynamite, graphite, sulfite

ity, ty [state of, quality] captivity, clarity

ive [causing, making] abusive (causing abuse), exhaustive

ize [make] emphasize, publicize, idolize

less [without] baseless, careless (without care), artless, fearless, helpless

ly [like, manner of] carelessly, quickly, forcefully, lovingly

ment [act of, state of, result] contentment, amendment (state of amending)

ness [state of] carelessness, kindness

oid [resembling] asteroid, spheroid, tabloid, anthropoid

ology [study, science, theory] biology, anthropology, geology, neurology

ous [full of, having] gracious, nervous, spacious, vivacious (full of life)

ship [office, state, quality, skill] friendship, authorship, dictatorship

some [like, apt, tending to] lonesome, threesome, gruesome

tude [state of, condition of] gratitude, multitude (condition of being many), aptitude

ure [state of, act, process, rank] culture, literature, rupture (state of being broken)

ward [in the direction of] eastward, forward, backward

y [inclined to, tend to] cheery, crafty, faulty

Roots

A *root* is a base upon which other words are built (see Table E.2). Knowing the root of a difficult word can go a long way toward helping you figure out its meaning. For that reason, learning the following roots will be very valuable in all your classes.

acer, acid, acri [bitter, sour, sharp] acrid, acerbic, acidity (sourness), acrimony

acu [sharp] acute, acupuncture

ag, agi, ig, act [do, move, go] agent (doer), agenda (things to do), agitate, navigate (move by sea), ambiguous (going both ways), action

ali, allo, alter [other] alias (a person's other name), alibi, alien (from another place), alloy, alter (change to another form)

alt [high, deep] altimeter (a device for measuring heights), altitude

am, amor [love, liking] amiable, amorous, enamored

anni, annu, enni [year] anniversary, annually (yearly), centennial (occurring once in 100 years)

anthrop [man] anthropology (study of mankind), philanthropy (love of mankind), misanthrope (hater of mankind)

anti [old] antique, antiquated, antiquity

arch [chief, first, rule] archangel (chief angel), architect (chief worker), archaic (first, very early), monarchy (rule by one person), matriarchy (rule by the mother)

aster, astr [star] aster (star flower), asterisk, asteroid, astronomy (star law), astronaut (star traveler, space traveler)

aud, aus [hear, listen] audible (can be heard), auditorium, audio, audition, auditory, audience, ausculate

aug, auc [increase] augur, augment (add to; increase), auction

auto, aut [self] autograph (self-writing), automobile (self-moving vehicle), author, automatic (self-acting), autobiography

belli [war] rebellion, belligerent (warlike or hostile)

bibl [book] Bible, bibliography (list of books), bibliomania (craze for books), bibliophile (book lover)

bio [life] biology (study of life), biography, biopsy (cut living tissue for examination)

brev [short] abbreviate, brevity, brief

cad, cas [to fall] cadaver, cadence, caducous (falling off), cascade

calor [heat] calorie (a unit of heat), calorify (to make hot), caloric

cap, cip, cept [take] capable, capacity, capture, reciprocate, accept, except, concept

capit, capt [head] decapitate (to remove the head from), capital, captain, caption

carn [flesh] carnivorous (flesh eating), incarnate, reincarnation

caus, caut [burn, heat] caustic, cauterize (to make hot, to burn)

cause, cuse, cus [cause, motive] because (to attempt to remove the blame or cause), excuse, accusation

ced, ceed, cede, cess [move, yield, go, surrender] procedure, secede (move aside from), proceed (move forward), cede (yield), concede, intercede, precede, recede, success

centri [center] concentric, centrifugal, centripetal, eccentric (out of center)

chrom [color] chrome, chromosome (color body in genetics), chromosphere, monochrome (one color), polychrome

chron [time] chronological (in order of time), chronometer (time measured), chronicle (record of events in time), synchronize (make time with, set time together)

cide, cise [cut down, kill] suicide (killing of self), homicide (human killer), pesticide (pest killer), germicide (germ killer), insecticide, precise (cut exactly right), incision, scissors

cit [to call, start] incite, citation, cite

civ [citizen] civic (relating to a citizen), civil, civilian, civilization

clam, claim [cry out] exclamation, clamor, proclamation, reclamation, acclaim

clud, clus, claus [shut] include (to take in), conclude, claustrophobia (abnormal fear of being shut up, confined), recluse (one who shuts himself away from others)

cognosc, gnosi [know] recognize (to know again), incognito (not known), prognosis (forward knowing), diagnosis

cord, cor, cardi [heart] cordial (hearty, heartfelt), concord, discord, courage, encourage (put heart into), discourage (take heart out of), core, coronary, cardiac

corp [body] corporation (a legal body), corpse, corpulent

cosm [universe, world] cosmic, cosmos (the universe), cosmopolitan (world citizen), cosmonaut, microcosm, macrocosm

crat, cracy [rule, strength] democratic, autocracy

crea [create] creature (anything created), recreation, creation, creator

cred [believe] creed (statement of beliefs), credo (a creed), credence (belief), credit (belief, trust), credulous (believing too readily, easily deceived), incredible

cresc, cret, crease, cru [rise, grow] crescendo (growing in loudness or intensity), concrete (grown together, solidified), increase, decrease, accrue (to grow) crit [separate, choose] critical, criterion (that which is used in choosing), hypocrite

cur, curs [run] concurrent, current (running or flowing), concur (run together, agree), incur (run into), recur, occur, precursor (forerunner), cursive

cura [care] curator, curative, manicure (caring for the hands)

cycl, cyclo [wheel, circular] Cyclops (a mythical giant with one eye in the middle of his forehead), unicycle, bicycle, cyclone (a wind blowing circularly, a tornado)

deca [ten] decade, decalogue, decathlon

dem [people] democracy (people-rule), demography (vital statistics of the people: deaths, births, and so on), epidemic (on or among the people)

dent, dont [tooth] dental (relating to teeth), denture, dentifrice, orthodontist

derm [skin] hypodermic (injected under the skin), dermatology (skin study), epidermis (outer layer of skin), taxidermy (arranging skin; mounting animals)

dict [say, speak] diction (how one speaks, what one says), dictionary, dictate, dictator, dictaphone, dictatorial, edict, predict, verdict, contradict, benediction

doc [teach] indoctrinate, document, doctrine

domin [master] dominate, dominion, predominant, domain

don [give] donate, condone

dorm [sleep] dormant, dormitory

dox [opinion, praise] doxy (belief, creed, or opinion), orthodox (having the correct, commonly accepted opinion), heterodox (differing opinion), paradox (contradictory)

drome [run, step] syndrome (run-together symptoms), hippodrome (a place where horses run)

duc, duct [lead] produce, induce (lead into, persuade), seduce (lead aside), reduce, aqueduct (water leader or channel), viaduct, conduct

dura [hard, lasting] durable, duration, endurance

dynam [power] dynamo (power producer), dynamic, dynamite, hydrodynamics

endo [within] endoral (within the mouth), endocardial (within the heart), endoskeletal

equi [equal] equinox, equilibrium

erg [work] energy, erg (unit of work), allergy, ergophobia (morbid fear of work), ergometer, ergonomic

fac, fact, fic, fect [do, make] factory (place where workers make goods of various kinds), fact (a thing done), manufacture, amplification, confection

fall, fals [deceive] fallacy, falsify

fer [bear, carry] ferry (carry by water), coniferous (bearing cones, as a pine tree), fertile (bearing richly), defer, infer, refer

fid, fide, feder [faith, trust] confidant, Fido, fidelity, confident, infidelity, infidel, federal, confederacy

fila, fili [thread] filament (a single thread or threadlike object), filibuster, filigree

fin [end, ended, finished] final, finite, finish, confine, fine, refine, define, finale

fix [attach] fix, fixation (the state of being attached), fixture, affix, prefix, suffix

flex, flect [bend] flex, reflex (bending back), flexible, flexor (muscle for bending), inflexibility, reflect, deflect

flu, fluc, fluv [flowing] influence (to flow in), fluid, flue, flush, fluently, fluctuate (to wave in an unsteady motion)

form [form, shape] form, uniform, conform, deform, reform, perform, formative, formation, formal, formula

fort, forc [strong] fort, fortress (a strong place), fortify (make strong), forte (one's strong point), fortitude, enforce

fract, frag [break] fracture (a break), infraction, fragile (easy to break), fraction (result of breaking a whole into equal parts), refract (to break or bend)

gam [marriage] bigamy (two marriages), monogamy, polygamy (many spouses or marriages)

gastr(o) [stomach] gastric, gastronomic, gastritis (inflammation of the stomach)

gen [birth, race, produce] genesis (birth, beginning), genetics (study of heredity), eugenics (well born), genealogy (lineage by race, stock), generate, genetic

geo [earth] geometry (earth measurement), geography (earth writing), geocentric (earth centered), geology

germ [vital part] germination (to grow), germ (seed; living substance, as the germ of an idea), germane

gest [carry, bear] congest (bear together, clog), congestive (causing clogging), gestation

gloss, glot [tongue] glossary, polyglot (many tongues), epiglottis

glu, glo [lump, bond, glue] glue, agglutinate (make to hold in a bond), conglomerate (bond together)

grad, gress [step, go] grade (step, degree), gradual (step-by-step), graduate (make all the steps, finish a course), graduated (in steps or degrees), progress

graph, gram [write, written] graph, graphic (written, vivid), autograph (self-writing, signature), graphite (carbon used for writing), photography (light writing), phonograph (sound writing), diagram, bibliography, telegram

grat [pleasing] gratuity (mark of favor, a tip), congratulate (express pleasure over success), grateful, ingrate (not thankful)

grav [heavy, weighty] grave, gravity, aggravate, gravitate

greg [herd, group, crowd] gregarian (belonging to a herd), congregation (a group functioning together), segregate (tending to group aside or apart)

helio [sun] heliograph (an instrument for using the sun's rays to send signals), heliotrope (a plant that turns to the sun)

hema, hemo [blood] hemorrhage (an outpouring or flowing of blood), hemoglobin, hemophilia

here, hes [stick] adhere, cohere, cohesion

hetero [different] heterogeneous (different in birth), heterosexual (with interest in the opposite sex)

homo [same] homogeneous (of same birth or kind), homonym (word with same pronunciation as another), homogenize

hum, human [earth, ground, man] humus, exhume (to take out of the ground), humane (compassion for other humans)

hydr, hydra, hydro [water] dehydrate, hydrant, hydraulic, hydraulics, hydrogen, hydrophobia (fear of water)

hypn [sleep] hypnosis, Hypnos (god of sleep), hypnotherapy (treatment of disease by hypnosis)

ignis [fire] ignite, igneous, ignition

ject [throw] deject, inject, project (throw forward), eject, object

join, junct [join] adjoining, enjoin (to lay an order upon, to command), juncture, conjunction, injunction

juven [young] juvenile, rejuvenate (to make young again)

lau, lav, lot, lut [wash] launder, lavatory, lotion, ablution (a washing away), dilute (to make a liquid thinner and weaker)

leg [law] legal (lawful; according to law), legislate (to enact a law), legislature, legitimize (make legal)

levi [light] alleviate (lighten a load), levitate, levity (light conversation; humor)

liber, liver [free] liberty (freedom), liberal, liberalize (to make more free), deliverance

liter [letters] literary (concerned with books and writing), literature, literal, alliteration, obliterate

loc, loco [place] locality, locale, location, allocate (to assign, to place), relocate (to put back into place), locomotion (act of moving from place to place)

log, logo, ogue, ology [word, study, speech] catalog, prologue, dialogue, logogram (a symbol representing a word), zoology (animal study), psychology (mind study)

loqu, locut [talk, speak] eloquent (speaking well and forcefully), soliloquy, locution, loquacious (talkative), colloquial (talking together; conversational or informal)

luc, lum, lus, lun [light] translucent (letting light come through), lumen (a unit of light), luminary (a heavenly body; people that shines in their profession), luster (sparkle, shine), Luna (the moon goddess)

magn [great] magnify (make great, enlarge), magnificent, magnanimous (great of mind or spirit), magnate, magnitude, magnum

man [hand] manual, manage, manufacture, manacle, manicure, manifest, maneuver, emancipate

mand [command] mandatory (commanded), remand (order back), mandate

mania [madness] mania (insanity, craze), monomania (mania on one idea), kleptomania, pyromania (insane tendency to set fires), maniac

mar, mari, mer [sea, pool] marine (a soldier serving on a ship), marsh (wetland, swamp), maritime (relating to the sea and navigation), mermaid (fabled sea creature: half fish, half woman)

matri [mother] maternal (relating to the mother), matrimony, matriarchate (rulership of women), matron

medi [half, middle, between, halfway] mediate (come between, intervene), medieval (pertaining to the Middle Ages), Mediterranean (lying between lands), mediocre, medium

mega [great, million] megaphone (great sound), megalopolis (great city; an extensive urban area including a number of cities), megacycle (a million cycles), megaton

mem [remember] memo (a reminder), commemoration (the act of remembering by a memorial or ceremony), memento, memoir, memorable

meter [measure] meter (a metric measure), voltameter (instrument to measure volts), barometer, thermometer

micro [small] microscope, microfilm, microcard, microwave, micrometer (device for measuring small distances), omicron, micron (a millionth of a meter), microbe (small living thing)

migra [wander] migrate (to wander), emigrate (one who leaves a country), immigrate (to come into the land)

mit, miss [send] emit (send out, give off), remit (send back, as money due), submit, admit, commit, permit, transmit (send across), omit, intermittent (sending between, at intervals), mission, missile

mob, mot, mov [move] mobile (capable of moving), motionless (without motion), motor, emotional (moved strongly by feelings), motivate, promotion, demote, movement

mon [warn, remind] monument (a reminder or memorial of a person or an event), admonish (warn), monitor, premonition (forewarning)

mor, mort [mortal, death] mortal (causing death or destined for death), immortal (not subject to death), mortality (rate of death), mortician (one who prepares the dead for burial), mortuary (place for the dead, a morgue)

morph [form] amorphous (with no form, shapeless), metamorphosis (a change of form, as a caterpillar into a butterfly), morphology

multi [many, much] multifold (folded many times), multilinguist (one who speaks many languages), multiped (an organism with many feet), multiply nat, nasc [to be born, to spring forth] innate (inborn), natal, native, nativity, renascence (a rebirth, a revival)

neur [nerve] neuritis (inflammation of a nerve), neurology (study of nervous systems), neurologist (one who practices neurology), neural, neurosis, neurotic

nom [law, order] autonomy (self-law, self-government), astronomy, gastronomy (art or science of good eating), economy

nomen, nomin [name] nomenclature, nominate (name someone for an office)

nov [new] novel (new, strange, not formerly known), renovate (to make like new again), novice, nova, innovate

nox, noc [night] nocturnal, equinox (equal nights), noctilucent (shining by night)

numer [number] numeral (a figure expressing a number), numeration (act of counting), enumerate (count out, one by one), innumerable

omni [all, every] omnipotent (all-powerful), omniscient (all-knowing), omnipresent (present everywhere), omnivorous

onym [name] anonymous (without name), synonym, pseudonym (false name), antonym (name of opposite meaning)

oper [work] operate (to labor, function), cooperate (work together)

ortho [straight, correct] orthodox (of the correct or accepted opinion), orthodontist (tooth straightener), orthopedic (originally pertaining to straightening a child), unorthodox

pac [peace] pacifist (one for peace only; opposed to war), pacify (make peace, quiet), Pacific Ocean (peaceful ocean)

pan [all] panacea (cure-all), pandemonium (place of all the demons, wild disorder), pantheon (place of all the gods in mythology)

pater, patr [father] paternity (fatherhood, responsibility), patriarch (head of the tribe, family), patriot, patron (a wealthy person who supports as would a father)

path, pathy [feeling, suffering] pathos (feeling of pity, sorrow), sympathy, antipathy (feeling against), apathy (without feeling), empathy (feeling or identifying with another), telepathy (far feeling; thought transference)

ped, pod [foot] pedal (lever for a foot), impede (get the feet in a trap, hinder), pedestal (foot or base of a statue), pedestrian (foot traveler), centipede, tripod (three-footed support), podiatry (care of the feet), antipodes (opposite feet)

pedo [child] orthopedic, pedagogue (child leader; teacher), pediatrics (medical care of children)

pel, puls [drive, urge] compel, dispel, expel, repel, propel, pulse, impulse, pulsate, compulsory, expulsion, repulsive

pend, pens, pond [hang, weigh] pendant pendulum, suspend, appendage, pensive (weighing thought), ponderous

phil [love] philosophy (love of wisdom), philanthropy, philharmonic, bibliophile, Philadelphia (city of brotherly love)

phobia [fear] claustrophobia (fear of closed spaces), acrophobia (fear of high places), hydrophobia (fear of water)

phon [sound] phonograph, phonetic (pertaining to sound), symphony (sounds with or together)

photo [light] photograph (light-writing), photoelectric, photogenic (artistically suitable for being photographed), photosynthesis (action of light on chlorophyll to make carbohydrates)

plac [please] placid (calm, peaceful), placebo, placate, complacent

plu, plur, plus [more] plural (more than one), pluralist (a person who holds more than one office), plus (indicating that something more is to be added)

pneuma, pneumon [breath] pneumatic (pertaining to air, wind, or other gases), pneumonia (disease of the lungs)

pod (see ped)

poli [city] metropolis (mother city), police, politics, Indianapolis, Acropolis (high city, upper part of Athens), megalopolis

pon, pos, pound [place, put] postpone (put afterward), component, opponent (one put against), proponent, expose, impose, deposit, posture (how one places oneself), position, expound, impound

pop [people] population, populous (full of people), popular

port [carry] porter (one who carries), portable, transport (carry across), report, export, import, support, transportation

portion [part, share] portion (a part; a share, as a portion of pie), proportion (the relation of one share to others)

prehend [seize] comprehend (seize with the mind), apprehend (seize a criminal), comprehensive (seizing much, extensive)

prim, prime [first] primacy (state of being first in rank), prima donna (the first lady of opera), primitive (from the earliest or first time), primary, primal, primeval

proto [first] prototype (the first model made), protocol, protagonist, protozoan

psych [mind, soul] psyche (soul, mind), psychiatry (healing of the mind), psychology, psychosis (serious mental disorder), psychotherapy (mind treatment), psychic

punct [point, dot] punctual (being exactly on time), punctuation, puncture, acupuncture

reg, recti [straighten] regiment, regular, regulate, rectify (make straight), correct, direction ri, ridi, risi [laughter] deride (mock, jeer at), ridicule (laughter at the expense of another, mockery), ridiculous, derision

rog, roga [ask] prerogative (privilege; asking before), interrogation (questioning; the act of questioning), derogatory

rupt [break] rupture (break), interrupt (break into), abrupt (broken off), disrupt (break apart), erupt (break out), incorruptible (unable to be broken down)

sacr, sanc, secr [sacred] sacred, sanction, sacrosanct, consecrate, desecrate

salv, salu [safe, healthy] salvation (act of being saved), salvage, salutation

sat, satis [enough] saturate, satisfy (to give as much as is needed)

sci [know] science (knowledge), conscious (knowing, aware), omniscient (knowing everything)

scope [see, watch] telescope, microscope, kaleidoscope (instrument for seeing beautiful forms), periscope, stethoscope

scrib, script [write] scribe (a writer), scribble, manuscript (written by hand), inscribe, describe, subscribe, prescribe

sed, sess, sid [sit] sediment (that which sits or settles out of a liquid), session (a sitting), obsession (an idea that sits stubbornly in the mind), possess, preside (sit before), president, reside, subside

sen [old] senior, senator, senile (old; showing the weakness of old age)

sent, sens [feel] sentiment (feeling), consent, resent, dissent, sentimental (having strong feeling or emotion), sense, sensation, sensitive, sensory, dissension

sequ, secu, sue [follow] sequence (following of one thing after another), sequel, consequence, subsequent, prosecute, consecutive (following in order), second (following "first"), ensue, pursue

serv [save, serve] servant, service, preserve, subservient, servitude, conserve, reservation, deserve, conservation

sign, signi [sign, mark, seal] signal (a gesture or sign to call attention), signature (the mark of a person written in their own handwriting), design, insignia (distinguishing marks)

simil, simul [like, resembling] similar (resembling in many respects), assimilate (to make similar to), simile, simulate (pretend; put on an act to make a certain impression)

sist, sta, stit [stand] persist (stand firmly; unyielding; continue), assist (to stand by with help), circumstance, stamina (power to withstand, to endure), status (standing), state, static, stable, stationary, substitute (to stand in for another)

solus [alone] soliloquy, solitaire, solitude, solo

solv, solu [loosen] solvent (a loosener, a dissolver), solve, absolve (loosen from, free from), resolve, soluble, solution, resolution, resolute, dissolute (loosened morally)

somnus [sleep] insomnia (not being able to sleep), somnambulist (a sleepwalker)

soph [wise] sophomore (wise fool), philosophy (love of wisdom), sophisticated

spec, spect, spic [look] specimen (an example to look at, study), specific, aspect, spectator (one who looks), spectacle, speculate, inspect, respect, prospect, retrospective (looking backward), introspective, expect, conspicuous

sphere [ball, sphere] stratosphere (the upper portion of the atmosphere), hemisphere (half of the earth), spheroid

spir [breath] spirit (breath), conspire (breathe together; plot), inspire (breathe into), aspire (breathe toward), expire (breathe out; die), perspire, respiration

string, strict [draw tight] stringent (drawn tight; rigid), strict, restrict, constrict (draw tightly together), boa constrictor (snake that constricts its prey)

stru, struct [build] construe (build in the mind, interpret), structure, construct, instruct, obstruct, destruction, destroy

sume, sump [take, use, waste] consume (to use up), assume (to take; to use), sump pump (a pump that takes up water), presumption (to take or use before knowing all the facts)

tact, tang, tag, tig, ting [touch] contact, tactile, intangible (not able to be touched), intact (untouched, uninjured), tangible, contingency, contagious (able to transmit disease by touching), contiguous

tele [far] telephone (far sound), telegraph (far writing), television (far seeing), telephoto (far photography), telecast

tempo [time] tempo (rate of speed), temporary, extemporaneously, contemporary (those who live at the same time), pro tem (for the time being)

ten, tin, tain [hold] tenacious (holding fast), tenant, tenure, untenable, detention, content, pertinent, continent, obstinate, abstain, pertain, detain

tend, tent, tens [stretch, strain] tendency (a stretching; leaning), extend, intend, contend, pretend, superintend, tender, extent, tension (a stretching, strain), pretense

terra [earth] terrain, terrarium, territory, terrestrial

test [to bear witness] testament (a will; bearing witness to someone's wishes), detest, attest (bear witness to), testimony

the, theo [God, a god] monotheism (belief in one god), polytheism (belief in many gods), atheism, theology

therm [heat] thermometer, therm (heat unit), thermal, thermostat, thermos, hypothermia (subnormal temperature)

thesis, thet [place, put] antithesis (place against), hypothesis (place under), synthesis (put together), epithet tom [cut] atom (not cuttable; smallest particle of matter), appendectomy (cutting out an appendix), tonsillectomy, dichotomy (cutting in two; a division), anatomy (cutting, dissecting to study structure)

tort, tors [twist] torture (twisting to inflict pain), retort (twist back, reply sharply), extort (twist out), distort (twist out of shape), contort, torsion (act of twisting, as a torsion bar)

tox [poison] toxic (poisonous), intoxicate, antitoxin

tract, tra [draw, pull] tractor, attract, subtract, tractable (can be handled), abstract (to draw away), subtrahend (the number to be drawn away from another)

trib [pay, bestow] tribute (to pay honor to), contribute (to give money to a cause), attribute, retribution, tributary

turbo [disturb] turbulent, disturb, turbid, turmoil

typ [print] type, prototype (first print; model), typical, typography, typewriter, typology (study of types, symbols), typify

ultima [last] ultimate, ultimatum (the final or last offer that can be made)

uni [one] unicorn (a legendary creature with one horn), unify (make into one), university, unanimous, universal

vac [empty] vacate (to make empty), vacuum (a space entirely devoid of matter), evacuate (to remove troops or people), vacation, vacant

vale, vali, valu [strength, worth] valiant, equivalent (of equal worth), validity (truth; legal strength), evaluate (find out the value), value, valor (value; worth)

ven, vent [come] convene (come together, assemble), intervene (come between), venue, convenient, avenue, circumvent (come or go around), invent, prevent

ver, veri [true] very, aver (say to be true, affirm), verdict, verity (truth), verify (show to be true), verisimilitude

vert, vers [turn] avert (turn away), divert (turn aside, amuse), invert (turn over), introvert (turn inward), convertible, reverse (turn back), controversy (a turning against; a dispute), versatile (turning easily from one skill to another)

vic, vicis [change, substitute] vicarious, vicar, vicissitude

vict, vinc [conquer] victor (conqueror, winner), evict (conquer out, expel), convict (prove guilty), convince (conquer mentally, persuade), invincible (not conquerable)

vid, vis [see] video, television, evident, provide, providence, visible, revise, supervise (oversee), vista, visit, vision

viv, vita, vivi [alive, life] revive (make live again), survive (live beyond, outlive), vivid, vivacious (full of life), vitality

voc [call] vocation (a calling), avocation (occupation not one's calling), convocation (a calling together), invocation, vocal

vol [will] malevolent, benevolent (one of goodwill), volunteer, volition

volcan, vulcan [fire] volcano (a mountain erupting fiery lava), volcanize (to undergo volcanic heat), Vulcan (Roman god of fire)

volvo [turn about, roll] revolve, voluminous (winding), voluble (easily turned about or around), convolution (a twisting)

vor [eat greedily] voracious, carnivorous (flesh eating), herbivorous (plant eating), omnivorous (eating everything), devour

zo [animal] zoo (short for zoological garden), zoology (study of animal life), zodiac (circle of animal constellations), zoomorphism (being in the form of an animal), protozoa (one-celled animals)

Table E.2 The Human Body

The Human Body

capit	head	gastro	stomach	osteo	bone
card	heart	glos	tongue	ped	foot
corp	body	hema	blood	pneuma	breathe
dent	tooth	man	hand	psych	mind
derm	skin	neur	nerve	spir	breath